T0227460

Security Strategy

From Requirements to Reality

Security Strategy

From Requirements to Reality

Bill Stackpole and Eric Oksendahl

 CRC Press
Taylor & Francis Group
Boca Raton London New York

CRC Press is an imprint of the
Taylor & Francis Group, an **informa** business

AN AUERBACH BOOK

CRC Press
Taylor & Francis Group
6000 Broken Sound Parkway NW, Suite 300
Boca Raton, FL 33487-2742

First issued in hardback 2017

© 2011 by Taylor and Francis Group, LLC
CRC Press is an imprint of Taylor & Francis Group, an Informa business

No claim to original U.S. Government works

ISBN-13: 978-1-4398-2733-8 (pbk)
ISBN-13: 978-1-138-44046-3 (hbk)

Library of Congress Cataloging-in-Publication Data

Stackpole, Bill.
    Security strategy : from requirements to reality / Bill Stackpole and Eric Oksendahl.
        p. cm.
    Includes bibliographical references and index.
    ISBN 978-1-4398-2733-8 (alk. paper)
    1. Computer security. 2. Information technology--Security measures. 3. Data protection. 4. Business--Data processing--Security measures. I. Oksendahl, Eric. II. Title.

QA76.9.A25S684 2011
005.8--dc22
                                                                    2010025968

Visit the Taylor & Francis Web site at
http://www.taylorandfrancis.com

and the CRC Press Web site at
http://www.crcpress.com

To my father who always pushed us to be the best we could be.

William "Bill" Stackpole

To my wife Elaine who has always stood beside me and encouraged and supported my efforts. I am truly a blessed man.

Eric Oksendahl

Contents

Acknowledgments

The authors wish to thank the following people for their hours of reviews, suggestions, and encouragement throughout the process of putting this book together.

Greg Gwash
Elaine Oksendahl
Dave Komendat
Carl Davis
Tim McQuiggan
Lt. Col. Thomas Stackpole, U.S. Army
Dave Cook
Butch Moody
Verdonn Simmons
Peter Oksendahl
Patrick Hanrion

A special thank you to Jennifer Reed who taught Bill's science class for six weeks so he could finish the book, and to Tim Lorenz who graciously gave him the time off.

Introduction

I need you to find a way to keep compliance from putting us out of business!

Ron Markezich
Corporate Vice President, Microsoft Online

Security as a business—what a concept! And to many security professionals it's a concept that few have had time to consider or have needed to consider. Compliance changed all that; it pushed information security into the executive suite where it's not only a jail sentence but a huge drag on the bottom line. Combine that with a major economic downturn and one has a lot of incentive to make security a value proposition. Both of us have watched this requirement develop in corporations and have witnessed security professionals struggle to get a handle on what it means to be a valued business partner.

We see two recurring themes: first is the lack of good business processes on the security side and second, a diminished understanding of the value of security on the executive side. It is these two issues that have inspired us to write *Security Strategy: From Requirements to Reality.* Our primary goal in writing this book is to teach security leadership and security practitioners how to select, develop, and deploy a security strategy appropriate to their organization. Our secondary goal is to support the implementation of strategic planning initiatives, goals, and objectives with a solid set of security tactics. It is also our hope that executive managers, marketing, and other business units will use this book to better understand the value security brings to the organization in the compliance-centric 21st century.

Businesses cannot survive in today's marketplace without information technology (IT), and IT cannot survive in today's computing environments without security. Today's leading companies are those that have solved the security conundrum and learned to leverage security to promote innovation, grab market share, and enhance brand. When Microsoft was being flogged by the industry for poor security, Bill Gates created a trustworthy computing initiative that united the company behind a single strategic goal: "to focus our [Microsoft's] efforts on building trust into every one of our products and services." In less than 10 years Microsoft propelled itself from whipping boy to market leader through innovation, commitment, and solid strategic planning. One of Microsoft's key initiatives was to consolidate security services into a single-customer-facing entity (the Microsoft Security Response Center). This is a strategy that we see as critical to the future success of security management. There should be one person to contact, one number to call, one website to visit, and one operations group to receive and respond to security events. It should never be the customer's responsibility to figure out who to call while dealing with a difficult or emergency situation.

We also believe in building a culture of security. Employees are your first line of defense; none of them leave their houses in the morning without locking the door, and none of them should leave their worksites at night without locking their computer and sensitive documents away. If you really want your employees to be your first line of defense, you need to teach them how, and you must be readily available, helpful, and responsive when they call. When the quality of Ford products began to diminish, the company moved Quality Assurance from a business unit to a business culture. Quality became "job one" for everyone working at the company from Bill Ford's Quality Council to the autoworker at the St. Paul assembly plant. This is our view of security; it is job one for every employee, and it needs to be promoted as such.

The challenges are substantial but not insurmountable. It will require a lot of effort on the part of the security group to build the strategic planning skills required, and it will take a fair amount of forbearance on the executive management side as things stumble forward. But the end results in cost reductions, brand enhancement, and operational efficiency are well worth the effort. Let's get started!

Approach

This book presents business strategy for security groups and tactics for implementing that strategy. It is unique in its approach because it focuses entirely on security strategy planning and execution. The book is about finding the strategy that works in your organization, building it, and implementing it to see real results. You won't find any point solutions here, no silver bullets, no magic formulas. What you will find is a comprehensive look at the structures and tools required to build a security program that really does enable and enhance business processes in your organization. The book is based on our experiences in working with large security groups to build and implement strategic plans and tactical solutions, but the book is equally applicable to smaller organizations looking for long-term security solutions.

We have divided the book into two parts. The first part is about business strategy. Although it is security-centric, executive managers reading this portion of the book will totally understand it. The second portion of the book is about tactics—the means needed to implement strategy. Security professionals will completely understand this portion of the book. The real value for both groups of readers will be reading the portions of the book that are not familiar to them. It is our hope that in so doing a viable synergy will develop between the two groups—one that allows security to take its place as a valued partner and contributor to the success of the enterprise.

Much of the security conundrum organizations find themselves in didn't develop overnight; it has been a long time in the making. While corporate (facilities) security is a long-standing discipline, information security, especially in the network arena, is a relatively new discipline, one that has been in an almost nonstop fight against an onslaught of attacks and a continuously changing landscape. It has taken time to develop the tools, processes, and skills needed to build effective security solutions. Although much remains to be done, the security industry has finally found itself in a place where it can begin to be proactive. A major part of that proactive effort is learning how to become a full-fledged partner in the business.

Security must become part of an organization's standard business processes and a partner in the promotion and profitability of the business. For years security professionals have been talking about how security enables the business; well, now it's time to step up and prove it. So roll up your sleeves, bolt on your armor, and get ready for some giant-killing ideas. Welcome to the business of security.

1. Decide, before you start, that you're going to change three things about what you do all day at work. Then, as you're reading, find the three things and do it. The goal of the reading, then, isn't to persuade you to change, it's to help you choose what to change.
2. If you're going to invest a valuable asset (like time), go ahead and make it productive. Use a postit or two, or some index cards or a highlighter. Not to write down stuff so you can forget it later, but to create marching orders. It's simple: if three weeks go by and you haven't taken action on what you've written down, you wasted your time.
3. It's not about you, it's about the next person. The single best use of a business book is to help someone else. Sharing what you read, handing the book to a person who needs it…pushing those around you to get in sync and to take action—that's the main reason it's a book, not a video or a seminar. A book is a souvenir and a container and a motivator and an easily leveraged tool. Hoarding books makes them worth less, not more.

Seth Godin

Terms Used in This Book

Business unit—To eliminate confusion between the organization as a whole and the business suborganizations such as departments and divisions, the term *business unit* has been chosen to refer to these suborganizations.

Consumer/Customer—The terms *consumer* and *customer* are used in a general sense. These terms include those external entities that purchase products or use services from the organization as a whole, as well as those external or internal entities that use the services of a business unit within the organization—for example, business units that use security services and/or products and are subject to security governance.

Core Competencies—*Core competencies* are the specific strengths of an organization that provide value in a market space.

Core Values—*Core values* are the operating principles that guide an organization's conduct and relationships.

Corporate security—The terms *corporate, physical,* and *facilities security* refer to the group that manages the security of physical assets such as facilities, equipment, and inventory. Corporate security is typically responsible for surveillance, building access controls, security officers, loss prevention, and associated events.

IT security—*IT security* refers to the group that manages the security of information assets stored, processed, and transferred on computer-based technologies. IT security is typically responsible for the confidentiality, integrity, and availability of digital information, compliance with statutory, regulatory, and industry requirements, and business continuity/disaster recovery planning for IT services.

Organization—This term, used in a generic sense, refers to *for-profit* and *nonprofit* businesses (companies, corporations, and enterprises) and *government entities/agencies.*

Security—This book takes a holistic approach to security, so the terms *security* and *security group* encompass both *corporate* and *IT security functions.*

Security group—To eliminate confusion between the organization as a whole and the security suborganization, the terms *security group* or *security function* have been chosen to refer to the security suborganization.

Stakeholder—A *stakeholder* is a party who is or may be affected by an action or actions taken by an organization, for example, employees, managers, board members, shareholders, customers, contractors, vendors, and partners.

Preface

The CEO looked up from his desk and said, "I'm sure you are all aware of our plans to form a joint venture with Coral Reef; this is a great opportunity for us but to be honest I have some real concerns about it. If you will pardon the pun, these guys are some real sharks. If we give them access to our network, they could steal us blind. I need you guys to tell me what the risks are." The CIO looked over his shoulder, "Matt?" With a slight grin, Matt, the CSO, replied, "There's no additional risk sir; we'll set up a SharePoint site for the project and that's the only thing they'll have access to." The CEO was about to express his delight when the CFO interrupted, "Well that might be true for remote access, but what about when they're here on campus?" "It's not any different," Matt replied, "Their laptops aren't part of our domain so they can't connect to any of our systems except e-mail, Instant Messenger, Web conferencing, and the project SharePoint." "But won't they look like one of our employees if they have e-mail and IM accounts?" asked the CFO. Matt replied, "Nope, all external parties have identities that start with F dash and their badges have a different color so our employees know they are 'foreigners.'" The CFO continued, "But they will have access to our offices and workspaces; isn't that a risk?" "There's always a risk that someone might go snooping around, but our identity and building access control systems are tied together. They will only have access to the buildings they will be working in, and we can track all other access attempts. We run a weekly report of all F dash building and computer accesses just to make sure they are behaving. If we suspect they aren't, we can always review the video surveillance to see what they were up to," Matt replied. "But they could still steal stuff!" the CFO exclaimed. Matt replied, "Yes they could, but not for long! They'd be violating the security policy they agreed to uphold and that's reason enough to send them packing." "Thank you gentleman, I believe we're good to go," said the CEO as he dismissed the meeting with a smile and a hint of disbelief. Was his security really that good?

The answer is yes. In three short years, Matt had managed to build a security program that not only protected the company's assets but also anticipated the company's future business requirements and security needs. And he did it with a modest capital investment and no increases in operational costs. Impossible, you say! Not at all. Matt was able to save a substantial amount of money by converging the facilities and information security groups into a single team and converting older expensive video and building access controls technologies to IP network-based devices. He used these savings and the reductions in operating costs to train and cross-train his staff to improve effectiveness and coverage. He also got capital monies to make improvements to the identity management system and to implement some new control technologies.

Successes like this are rare in the security community, so how did all this come about? Security strategy. Matt took the time to analyze the company's vision, goals, and business strategies, and then he sat down with the key stakeholders to identify existing issues, understand their goals, and learn what their expectations were for security. Next, Matt (with the help of his team and these stakeholders) created a three-year Security Strategic Plan aligned with and supporting the overall business strategy. Finally, he went out and sold that plan, implemented it, and demonstrated security's value to the business.

Security strategy is the missing gem in many security programs. It's not a common skill set among security practitioners and there isn't a lot of guidance on how to do strategic planning for security management. It was the authors' goal to remedy that situation by providing you with a practical set of tools and guidance to get you started down the planning path (Section I) and to help you build the processes and controls for implementing that plan (Section II).

There are a large number of strategic planning methodologies; trying to cover them all would be unrealistic. Fortunately, they all follow a similar pattern so we have addressed those components and compiled an exhaustive set of references you can use to further study the method you settled on for your company.

It is our sincere hope that this book will contribute to your success and make the practice of security strategic planning a common discipline in the industry. Welcome to security as a business!

Bill Stackpole
Eric Oksendahl

Authors

William "Bill" Stackpole, CISSP/ISSAP, CISM, former Principal Security Architect for Microsoft Online Services, has more than 25 years of IT experience in security and project management. In his past position, Bill provided thought leadership and guidance for Microsoft's Secure Online Services Delivery architecture. Before coming to Microsoft, Bill was a principal consultant for Predictive System, an international network consultancy where he was the architect and promoted the application security business. Bill holds a B.S. degree in Management Information Systems, a CISSP with an Architecture Professional endorsement. He is coauthor of *Software Deployment, Updating, and Patching* (Auerbach, 2007) and a contributing editor to Auerbach's *Handbook on Information Security Management* (Krause and Tipton). Bill is a former chair for the CISSP Test Development Committee and a current member of the (ISC)[2] Common Body of Knowledge committees for the CISSP and ISSAP certifications.

Eric Oksendahl, former Security Strategist for Boeing, has more than 25 years of experience as a business management consultant, senior facilitator, teacher, and program manager. At Boeing, Eric facilitated strategy development and implementation for the Security and Fire Protection division, including physical and information security. He designed and coordinated the use of strategy development and initiative deployment to integrate security practices into key business processes (e.g., international sales campaigns). Prior to that, Eric was a program manager at the Boeing Leadership Center where he conducted leadership development courses around the world that included Boeing management, supplier management, and customer management. Eric holds a B.A. from Montana State University and an M.A. in Communications from the University of Washington.

STRATEGY

This section of the book is about the selection, creation, and implementation of security strategy. Strategy is planning in any field: a carefully devised plan of action to achieve a goal, or the art of developing or carrying out such a plan long term (a year or more). In other words, a strategy is a plan for what work will be done and by whom.

Strategic planning is a discipline designed to encourage long-term thinking about an organization. Strategy is a creative act that combines both analysis and creative choices in future actions; it utilizes a structured process to create a formal, integrated enterprise plan. A strategic plan is NOT a tactical roadmap. However, strategic planning is both strategy development and implementation. Strategy realization requires leadership throughout all phases of the strategic planning process, which includes performance, monitoring, evaluation, and adjustment.

Although strategic planning tries to anticipate possible future environments in which the organization will be functioning, it does not attempt to make day-to-day operational decisions. Without well-executed implementation plans, strategy efforts remain, at best, wishes. Security managers must still manage and make decisions on a daily basis using good judgment, while retaining a sense of future direction. Some of these day-to-day decisions will cause a rethinking of strategic direction. This is normal and does not negate the need for a robust strategic planning process. There will be multiple planning iterations, and strategic plans may need to be adjusted to accommodate emergent strategic objectives. The roller-coaster ride of life's exigencies does not, however, cancel the need for good strategic planning.

Chapter 1

Strategy: An Introduction

If you can't describe your strategy in twenty minutes, simply and in plain language, you haven't got a plan. "But," people may say, "I've got a complex strategy. It can't be reduced to a page." That's nonsense. That's not a complex strategy. It's a complex thought about the strategy.

Larry Bossidy
Chairman, Honeywell International

Strategic Planning Essentials

Can you describe your current strategy in a clear, compelling manner in less than 20 minutes? Behind every compelling description of strategy that a CEO, CFO, CIO, CSO, or any other corporate executive might present is a strategic planning process. There are several basic elements and core principles in a strategic plan. The following is a brief overview of the basic elements; each of these elements and their subelements will be discussed in greater detail in the subsequent chapters.

1. **Preparation to Plan**—This element includes allocation of essential resources, coordination of personnel, and clear RAA (responsibilities, accountability, and authority) for the planning process. Herein lies the crucial first step of strategic planning requiring discipline, focus, and a willingness to ask tough questions while organizations prepare to face uncertainties, consider new possibilities, and decide on fundamental change. First efforts in strategy aren't perfect, but one should prepare to plan anyway. This is the first step of many little steps to follow in planning. You may want to engage an outside facilitator at the very beginning if you haven't done much strategic planning as a group.
2. **Big Picture Renewal/Creating a Strategic Foundation**—Here the cornerstones of any strategic plan are set, vision and mission are clarified, and reviews and analysis are conducted on data from environmental scans or other sources. Internal and external examinations are completed as an organization seeks to understand and prioritize influences and opportunities.

Here also is where the hard questions you have prepared in planning get asked—questions such as "Where do we want to play?" "What do we do best?" "What is our business?" "What are critical success factors?" "How will we communicate our plan and to whom?"

3. **Strategies and Actions or Focusing the Plan**—This is where the steps for how an organization will reach its vision are created. This may include elements like strategic objectives, goals, initiatives, actions, and/or critical success factors for getting there. Here is often where strategy maps or other tools help refine plans, prioritize requirements into specific goals, and link them to measures and initiatives. The goal of this stage is to map elements of strategy into daily operations. This is where the operational business plans are linked to overall strategic direction. This is where business goals, operational objectives, action plans, and performance measures are linked together. If an organization is not successful here, many groups may not understand how strategy impacts their organization, and, in fact, they may work at cross purposes. At this stage, it is imperative to tie together strategic goals, improvement objectives, action plans, and key performance measures. These will work together to guide an organization during the implementation of strategic plans. This element, too, is where a security group must relate overall business strategy to operations strategy and tactical objectives to tactical action plans.

4. **Implementation Schedule**—Typically, the implementation schedule is prioritized with specific RAA as the steps for implementation are determined. A schedule is documented with start, milestone, and completion dates for each major strategy. Strategic actions are linked to individuals with time frames and budget allocations.

5. **Metrics for the Plan**—The measures are created that will ensure the organization is headed in the right direction and determine whether it is successfully implementing the strategic plan. Metrics are integrated into a foundation for the business plan. The business plan should be linked to key performance metrics and compensation and, finally, integrated into a balanced scorecard or some other tracking document for regularly scheduled reviews.

   Metrics are acknowledged to be an important requirement for success, both strategically and operationally, but are often ignored. Several levels of good metrics are usually required for effective strategic planning. The top-level metrics that executive leadership consider are the roll-up enterprise dashboard or ***balanced scorecard*** metrics that usually entail key compliance and risk indicators, as well as key performance ***indicators*** such as return on investment (ROI), resource management, value delivery, and response times. As strategic plans move into initiatives, goals, specific objectives, and the like, obviously the metrics grow more specific and detailed to the organization and objectives ***as objectives become organizational tactics.*** Typically, security metrics are fashioned from two main sources, strategic initiatives and external standards required by audit results. Often, as a security group moves from a reactive posture to more of a planned posture, metrics from external standards will become a subset of strategic security metrics. Security metrics will become defined by strategic goals and not just audit results. (Eric watched a security group get hammered by audit results for two years. It was a lot better when the group came up with a successful strategic plan!)

   Defining metrics that work to move a strategic initiative forward are not easily attained. Take, for example, the discussion on cloud-based security metrics in a recent article in *CSO* magazine, "Clear Metrics for Cloud Security? Yes, Seriously," by Ariel Silverstone, CISSP. In her article she discusses the difficulty of developing metrics for the storage availability and integrity of Cloud utilization-type initiatives. Her conclusion is that only time will tell whether data from/in the Cloud will be deemed trustworthy by such metrics.

   Typically, as processes improve and organizations learn from each round of planning, metrics will become more specific, useful, and relative as success indicators. Metrics are a difficult issue to manage in the strategic planning process. These difficulties include linking strategic objectives with the key metrics and establishing the feedback loops required to effectively monitor the progress (success or failure of those objectives). The Information Security and Control Association (ISACA) recommends performance measurement monitoring and reporting on information security processes to ensure strategic objectives are achieved.

The performance metrics that ISACA recommends for IT security typically concern measures like number of incidents, number of systems where security requirements are not met, response times, violations, types of malicious codes, security incidents, unauthorized IP addresses, port and traffic types denied, access rights authorized, revoked, reset, or changed, and so on. You will find a number of examples of these types of metrics in the chapters of this book on tactics.

Captured metrics should also include the less quantifiable, but equally important, people aspects of security such as badging, social engineering, and workplace violence. IT metrics must also capture the harder-to-capture people aspects of computing such as sabotage, data theft, and misuse of computing resources. These statistics can be much harder to gather, quantify, and assess, but they are key issues IT security must face. This is made even more difficult in organizations where corporate and IT security are managed by different stove-piped functions in the organization and data are not rolled up into a common knowledge base. Good performance metric determination, monitoring, and assessment help inform and lay the foundation for the next cycle of strategic planning.

6. **Communication Plan Enacted**—A communication plan is put into effect, including clear communication strategies and dissemination plans for each predetermined target audience. Key messages, executive summary, and strategy documents are created, and the implementation plan is scheduled, with clear benchmarks established for evaluating success. Tactical objectives are employed throughout the organization and measured for success.

7. **Completion**—Results of the strategic planning cycle implementation are analyzed, and the lessons learned are incorporated into following planning cycles. Here is where unanticipated consequences, as well as unrealized and emergent strategies, should be reviewed, and key performance indicators and metrics refined. Often, while one strategic planning cycle is in completion, another planning cycle is being implemented, and perhaps plans are made for a following one.

Strategic Planning Process Evaluation

EXERCISE 1.1

If you are reading this book, it is likely that you are already part of a security group. To help you better understand where strategic planning fits into the security management process, we have devised this short self-assessment quiz. Before you continue reading, take a few moments to reflect on your current organizational status quo by answering the following questions:

1. Where is your security group spending the majority of its time right now, working to create change or reacting to change?
2. In the past year have you spent more time chasing situations or implementing your strategic goals and objectives in a systematic manner?
3. Is security viewed as a separate functional business unit or as a partner who contributes to the success of the overall strategic plan for your organization?
4. Do other parts of your organization consider you to be an enabler of organizational business strategies or a roadblock?

5. Do you have plans in place for possible changes in the marketplace so that you will be able to quickly course-correct?
6. Can your security leadership articulate a clear business purpose and function that the leadership of your organization understands and accepts?
7. What opportunities does the security group have now that it didn't have a year ago?
8. What problems or unintended consequences has your security group created for itself?
9. Are your corporate and IT security functions integrated around your organization's business needs or functioning as related organizational stovepipes?
10. How's your security group skill set depth (bench-strength) in strategic planning and implementation?
11. Is your security group better prepared to do analysis, planning, and implementation of your strategic plan than it was last year?
12. Are you quicker at all three functions?
13. What information and knowledge did you uncover last year that you didn't know you needed to know?
14. How good have you been at implementing your strategic plan this year? By what measures?
15. Are your metrics for implementation of your strategic plan better than they were the year before?
16. Are your metrics clearly linked to strategic goals?
17. Is your security group in regular conversation with the other functions of the organization to improve relationships and better understand business objectives?

Answering these questions may help you focus in on the concepts in this book that will be most useful in your security group. As you answered these questions, a number of organizational challenges undoubtedly came to mind. Here is a partial list of ongoing challenges for security groups:

■ Economic uncertainties and limited security funding
■ Stricter statutory and regulatory compliance requirements
■ Increased audits and audit requirements
■ Outsourcing and cloud-based service risks
■ A growing number of application breaches
■ A need for better tracking of incident responsiveness and resolution
■ Increased needs for third-party risk assessments and penetration testing
■ Stricter privacy requirements in every aspect of business (including increasingly complex customer relations management systems that now reach throughout an extended enterprise)

If that isn't enough pressure, at the same time strategic planning cycles need to be shorter in order to be responsive in much of organizational life. Cycles are shifting from years to months, months to weeks, weeks to days, and days to hours. Shorter cycle times for strategic thinking create a demand for leadership that understands not only the basics of strategic planning, but also the art of working within the organizational culture.

Now is the time to be preparing your organization's strategic plan and response or to adjust the plan you already have in place. Security is a function that requires good strategic leadership capable of setting strategy, communicating vision, and leading passionately. With strong strategic planning and execution skills, security will more likely be seen as a key enabler of business.

Security Leadership Challenges

Today, security leadership has to face new challenges every day in an environment that seems to present increasing unpredictability in economics, technology, and global threat trends. Absorbing new information that is produced at ever-increasing speeds, while coordinating the protection of people, property, and information on a day-to-day basis, is at the very least challenging, at the worst overwhelming. How enterprise leaders learn to cope, adapt, and process information is helped to some degree by new software and technology applications, but even that produces more data that have to be understood and acted upon.

Today's business environment demands security executives with keen business savvy, solid risk management fundamentals, and a whole systems understanding of the organization within which they focus. The current business reality is that security groups must balance the security needs of an extended enterprise that includes all elements in a value stream they support (from customer requirements to company processes and supplier inputs), while also meeting the requirements of an ever-increasing number of governance and regulatory agencies.

The role of security governance, ever-increasing compliance requirements, and the demands of effective integration of sound security practices into business processes and risk management efforts, requires strong leadership and the ability to communicate well beyond traditional business stovepipes. A holistic security management approach is required to create a comprehensive security strategy that aligns security goals with corporate/organizational goals. In addition, it is imperative for organizations that want to resolve ongoing security issues to engage multiple stakeholders in an effort to create a security-conscious culture.

The business case for enterprise security architecture has already been well made. Organizations need to develop and implement a security strategy that is integrated with the enterprise strategic plan. Good security strategy requires:

- Having the time and perseverance to plan
- Continual alignment of the plan with emerging business requirements
- An ability to design and implement an architecture supporting the plan (along with processes and policies required to implement and enforce the plan)
- Reporting and measurement methodology to track the plan
- Specific metric indicators of the plan's success or failure

Despite their importance, these key elements remain hard won and elusive for many organizations. Strategic planning is becoming increasingly important in a hypervelocity world. Thinking, planning, and moving quickly while controlling risk are essential skills. Today's security leadership must be able to continuously demonstrate the business acumen needed to move from concept to endgame for new business initiatives.

Getting Started

Strategic planning is essentially a process of gathering and analyzing information, and envisions ways to act on that information to better the business. It begins by understanding where the security group is—how it functions—within your organization. The fundamental question concerning security that must be asked is as follows: "Is security simply a servant of a corporate, organizational, or business strategy, or does it serve a greater purpose?"

In many organizations, people inside and outside of security would answer this question with a resounding "Yes, it is simply a servant!" Their primary rationale: "Security is a service provider within the organization, and services are not a source of strategic guidance for an organization." That being said, there are certainly many people inside security groups who are not only willing but more than capable of providing organizational strategic input, even if they are not a formal part of the organizational strategic process.

EXERCISE 1.2

If you haven't already read every organizational strategic plan you can get your hands on, get started now! If you are going to build a successful security strategy, you need to get a sense of the big picture in which your organization functions.

Value Proposition

From a systemic perspective, a secure workforce, secure facilities, and well-protected information resources are *actually part of the organizational brand, both product and service.* The security of products and services is now part of the organization's promise to the marketplace, enterprise stakeholders, and shareholders. It is imperative that organizations deliver on that promise, or they will soon become irrelevant. Organizational strategic planning can readily benefit from the security practitioner's viewpoint. Whether security is part of the organizational brand or has developed its own brand, it must be part and partner in the organization's strategic discussions. Brand is critical to security because the process of building a brand helps to convey important fundamentals that link security explicitly to the intent and promise an organization makes to its internal and external customers.

In the authors' experience, often other organizational functions view security as a roadblock to efficient business practices. However, leaving the security group out of the strategic planning process can result in a number of unintended consequences. One example of these unintended consequences is, perhaps, the decision to outsource back-office types of transactions to sourced companies in another country without including security in a strategic conversation. While economically that may be the right strategy, several important elements may be overlooked such as creating vulnerabilities to Personally Identifiable Information (PII) data or providing industrial espionage opportunities for data mining. There may be easy solutions, at a lesser cost, if security is included in the original planning, than managing these risks after the fact.

Conversely, if security wants a place at the strategic planning table, it will need to examine the strengths of its own leadership and answer these two fundamental questions:

1. "How can security help the organization achieve strategic goals?" In other words, "What will it take from security to enable the business/organization to get where it wants to go?"
2. "How can the security strategic plan be a living document updated periodically to reflect changes in organizational priorities based on industry trends, marketplace, or emerging technologies?"

The advantages of including security in organizational strategic planning and the Enterprise Risk Management (ERM) components of strategic planning are:

- Better understanding of potential risks in any strategic direction
- More accurate planning for budget allocations to manage those risks
- Quicker movement in strategic objectives for security integration into product, infrastructure, desktop, and business continuity processes

Other Challenges for Security and Strategic Planning

Another crucial issue for the security group in any organization is: *"How is the strategic plan (or portions of an organizational strategic plan) to be developed, updated, and what groups will participate?"* After the strategic plan is drafted, the fundamental questions of how to communicate, integrate, align, and update the strategic plan come into play. The bottom line for any security strategic plan is that other parts of the organization must understand it, or it will be difficult to achieve effective results protecting the organization's assets (people, material, and information) at an acceptable cost.

While a business/organization strategy is aimed at organizational **vision**, **purpose**, **mission**, **strategies**, **execution**, and **measurement of success**, an IT security strategy often focuses mainly on **information security architecture.** It is shaped by the organizational **goals**, **environment,** and **technical capabilities** the business requires in order to achieve its vision. Corporate (physical/facilities) security strategy focuses on **policies and procedures** for loss prevention and the protection of people and property. Corporate security is also guided by organizational goals, environment, and technology advances.

Often, issues arise in this natural tension between the organizational business philosophy (and business architecture) and the more pragmatic aspects of IT architecture. Ralph Whittle and Conrad Myric, in a white paper titled "Enterprise Business Architecture: The Formal Link between Strategy and Results," outline the formal link between architecture and strategy. In their words, "These bold new enterprises are not building some static, rigid new architecture, with a moat around the castle. Quite the opposite, they are building fluid, dynamic, integrated architectures capable of evolving with and supporting the corporate strategy. A fundamental requirement of the integrated architecture is that it must have the capability to evolve, change, and adapt in a predictive way." The problem for IT architecture achieving this goal, as Whittle and Myric define it, is that when it comes to organizational strategic planning and IT strategic planning, most IT architecture has not been funded or developed to the needed levels. This results in tensions for IT architecture including, but not limited to:

1. Unclear understanding of business/organizational requirements
2. Inflexible architecture that is unable to respond to environmental challenges
3. Piecemeal local approaches to architecture and security practices rather than integrated efforts, including lack of corporate and IT security integration
4. Unclear linkage to organizational strategy and metrics for successful implementation, scalability, and usability of security services
5. Piecemeal tactical efforts rather than a systemic architectural approach
6. Unmanaged costs or insufficient funding
7. Ineffective risk management efforts
8. IT security that hobbles the business

Fixing the problems that arise from these tensions is not an effort for the faint of heart. One of the requirements of security leadership is a well-constructed security strategy that aligns the strategy, vision, and objectives of the enterprise and answers these questions:

■ What is the business reason for doing this?
■ What are we trying to achieve?
■ How do we enable and support the enterprise achieving its strategic objectives?

Explicit answers to these questions help everyone in the organization, including those involved in security architecture, to make reasoned decisions for their pieces of the strategic puzzle. Without clear answers to these questions, it is difficult to acquire the upper management support needed to advance security strategy. Without explicit upper management support, security efforts are seldom successful. Gaining this support for strategic efforts is not only a critical success factor, but is often one of the most difficult things a security leader will do.

When Strategic Planning Should Be Conducted

Strategic planning should be part of organizational planning in the following situations:

- When an organization is newly formed.
- When reenvisioning is required.
- Before and during mergers or acquisitions.
- In preparation for a new venture, product(s), or service(s).
- When exogenous or outside shocks to your organizational environment require adaptation or refinement of a potential strategic scenario. (Scenario planning creates more than one option for an organization to pursue based on future impacts and may require more exploration when an unexpected event drastically changes the environment.)

At the very least strategy should be conducted on an annual basis to fit within your organization's business planning cycle, before monies are allocated for a given year in order to fund organizational requirements for accomplishing strategic goals and objectives. Throughout the year there should be organizational reviews of the strategic planning inputs, adjustments, updated action plans, and metrics. Strategic planning should be a planned part of organizational life throughout the calendar year, not as a "once-a-year, put-a-plan-in-a-binder and put-it-on-a-shelf until next year" activity. Security leadership should formally conduct a quarterly review.

Regardless of when your organization is engaged in strategic planning, paying attention to the language that is used in strategic planning can often help planners understand the organization and by utilizing new language, transform the organization.

Metaphor Analysis and Strategic Planning

Metaphors reveal how organizations think of themselves and are a window into organizational culture, attitudes, and beliefs. Metaphors can also be an important tool in transforming organizations and will often appear in the communication strategies for strategic change. A whole literature has evolved around analyzing organizational culture by the metaphors found in the everyday conversation on how organizations conduct business; an example is Donald Schon's concept of a *generative metaphor*. A generative metaphor is an "implicit metaphor that can cast a kind of spell on a community." In an implicit metaphor, the full subject is not explained, but is implied from the context of the sentence. Much of our daily communication in organizational life contains implicit metaphoric language. A branch of this literature assumes that one's approach to strategy is best caught by the metaphors employed in strategic planning sessions.

David Sibbit, president and founder of Grove Consultants International, has worked on strategic planning with organizations for many years by utilizing "story maps" that he and his consultants generate from the conversations held among strategic planning groups. Sibbit, in an article titled "Strategizing with Visual Metaphors," made the following observations about the power of metaphors:

> I serendipitously picked up a 2005 article I'd clipped from the *Harvard Business Review* called "How Strategists Really Think: Tapping the Power of Analogy." (It's available for $6.50 through the HBR website.)

Gavetti and Rivkin argue that there is a middle ground between formal, deductive analysis, which works well in information-rich, more mature industries, and trial and error, almost a necessity in very dynamic, untested emergent industries. "Many, perhaps, most strategic problems are neither so novel and complex that they require trial and error nor so familiar and modular that they permit deduction. Much of the time, managers have only enough cues to see a resemblance to a past experience. They can see how an industry they're thinking about entering looks like one they already understand, for example. It is in this large middle ground that analogical reasoning has its greatest power.

The frame of "strategy by analogy" is different from "visual thinking." These labels are metaphors that *provide a framing context that directly affects what a viewer or listener pays attention to.* And within the visual work the choices of what to illustrate, and most critically, the organizing graphic metaphor and its emphasis, open and close opportunities for engagement, discussion and interpretation.

Over the years we have heard many such metaphors, similes, and strategy analogies in our work with strategy groups, consultants, and educators. Metaphors can help employees look at old issues with a new lens or become a compelling new image of how an organization sees itself. During our careers, we have heard the following metaphors for strategy:

- A battle (and other military metaphors)
- A revolution
- A chess match
- Sailing a ship
- Sports strategy
- A game metaphor
- The solving of a puzzle
- A city-state, kingdom, domain, or enclave
- An organic system
- Conducting a symphony
- Part of the value chain or system
- Sailing a blue ocean, red ocean, purple ocean
- BBQ sauce
- Pizza

Organizations themselves can also be described by metaphors such as running a tight ship, part of a family, a dynasty, or parts of the body (e.g., IT is described as the nervous system, management as the brain, etc.). Learning to examine anything through a variety of metaphors often helps bring new insight and clarity to participants. A strong use of metaphor can galvanize quick understanding and provide different mental models with which to examine a topic.

Security strategy lends itself particularly well to these metaphors, and we use several in our own approaches. Bill Stackpole will frame the tactics chapters of this book in the metaphors of military tactics and enclaves (a distinct political geography, territorial culture, or social unit) and will discuss the principles behind his use of them. Eric's own favorite metaphor for conducting strategy sessions remains a "strategy jam" (see Figure 1.1). In fact, a musical jam can get cooking as well when ideas are being generated and integrated. A consulting colleague at Boeing, Andrew Moskowitz, and Eric conducted several "strategy jam" sessions for a newly formed group

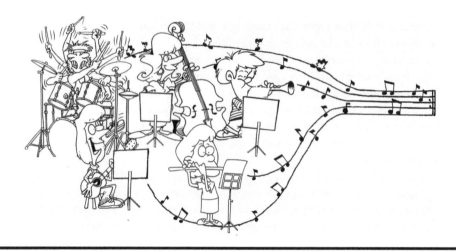

Figure 1.1 Strategy jam.

of support organizations. "Strategy jam" as a metaphor became very useful for conducting strategic planning for several reasons. Let's now examine three of the relevant principles behind the metaphor "strategy jam."

Need for Responsiveness—In today's environment, older methodologies for conducting strategy sessions are top heavy, have long lead times, and usually exclude inputs from the people who have the information and creativity needed for successful strategic planning. Consequently, these approaches may have little buy-in from employees and usually just end up as pieces of inert information bound in glossy folders or stored in a database somewhere. Employees have little knowledge of what's in the strategic plans and even less interest. Next year when the next round of planning begins, someone will blow the dust off the old plans, and the process will repeat itself.

Need for Collaboration—Our industries and organizations have been permanently impacted by Total Quality Management and Productivity-LEAN systems, Process Management rollouts, and Enterprise Risk Management integration, and we are currently trying to understand and assess the impact of Security Convergence on our industry. Never has there been a greater need to engage every ounce of creativity available in our organizations. And yet, for too many organizations, strategic planning remains the providence of executives or senior management. The problem is one of participation. When you try to tell or sell an organizational plan to employees who have had no opportunity to provide their thoughts and ideas, you get little buy-in, commitment, follow-through, or impact. A strategy jam, on the other hand, is an ongoing strategic conversation that is flexible, collaborative, and focused.

Need for Adaptive Skills—Creativity and intuition are the main focus when people and organizations need to adapt their organizational tactics to a "Big Picture Vision" and/or changing business model. Adapting and changing directions with continuous adjustments while executing are important aspects of jamming. This type of strategic jam session most often occurs in business in new product creation, new divisions, and start-ups. But even in more traditional strategic planning, there is still an ongoing requirement for these skills in a more orchestrated context. Ned Herrmann, author

> Life is like a band. We need not all play the same part, but we MUST all play in harmony.
>
> **Unknown author**

of *The Creative Brain,* puts it this way: "In the corporation of the future, new leaders will not be masters, but maestros. The leadership task will not be masters, but maestros. The leadership task will be to anticipate the signs of coming change, to inspire creativity." Lou Gertsner, former chairman of IBM, also referred to the need to be adaptive in strategic planning when he stated, "You have to be fast on your feet and adaptive or else a strategy is useless."

It is in that spirit that we approach strategic thinking. Every brain in an organization is part of the solution; yet, when asked, most managers estimate they were only tapping 20% of available creativity. (In some organizations that might be a little optimistic.) In a strategy jam session, each instrument has an input. Participants, like musicians in a musical jam session (blues, jazz, orchestra etc.), need to know the basics of strategic planning (i.e., the notes, chording, and frets of music), and, at the same time, they must be able to listen to the other musicians, pick up on what they are playing, and blend into a new creation, while responding to the audience (customers/stakeholders). So it is in a strategy jam: The players come with an understanding of the basic structures and components of strategic planning, listen to the other players, and create a new direction for the organization. Our goal for this book is to provide you with the scales and notes of strategic planning. The artistry and creativity with which those components are applied depend on you and on your approach to the art of strategy formation and execution and the requirements that match the organization in which you work. Whether your strategy jam is in the form of jazz, blues, or a more formal orchestra, it is our hope that you will be engaged, learning, curious, and optimistic.

> Somehow I can't believe that there are any heights that can't be scaled by a man who knows the secrets of making dreams come true. This special secret, it seems to me, can be summarized in four Cs. They are curiosity, confidence, courage, and constancy, and the greatest of all is confidence. When you believe in a thing, believe in it all the way, implicitly and unquestionably.
>
> **Walt Disney**

Strategic Planning as a Process

One of the key paradigms or mental models that should be established early in any strategic planning process is that strategic planning is NOT an event; rather, it is a process (ongoing, year round). Security managers have to know the strategic planning process, take it seriously, and be involved in integrating the plan into the day-to day activities of the security group. Remember, the process has to be linked to next year's budget as well. There are many processes for approaching strategic planning, and while they may have different steps, stages, or phases, the goal is still to produce a strategic plan that moves the organization forward in the right direction. For a basic understanding of strategic planning, perhaps the most widely known model of strategic planning is John Bryson and Farnum Alston's *Strategic Planning for Public and Nonprofit Organizations: A Guide to Strengthening and Sustaining Organizational Achievement* and the companion workbook *Creating and Implementing Your Strategic Plan.* In their workbook, the authors outline the following basic process:

1. Identify a strategic planning process that the organization will use.
2. Identify organizational mandates.
3. Clarify the organizational mission and values.
4. Assess the organization's external and internal environments to identify strengths, weaknesses, opportunities, and threats.

5. Identify the strategic issues facing the organization.
6. Formulate strategies to manage these issues.
7. Review and adopt the strategic plan or plans.
8. Establish an effective organizational vision.
9. Develop an effective implementation process.
10. Reassess strategies and the strategic planning process.

Bryson and Alston's description of the strategic process is different from and, at the same time, similar to the process we covered in the first part of this chapter. In the stages we discussed earlier, there are preparations to plan, big picture renewal, focusing the plan, implementation schedule, metrics, communication and completion. By considering different ways of approaching strategic planning, organizations define their own approach. What the process used in your organization will look like depends on the methodology you choose. In the next several chapters on strategic planning, we will discuss some of the methods currently available in the marketplace and consider how to integrate them into planning based on your organizational culture.

Requirements for Successful Strategic Plans

For any security strategic plan to be successful, several conditions are required.

- Organizational stakeholders (not just internal to security) are involved, and their support is garnered for the strategic plan. Inclusion of stakeholders in planning takes time and patience to gather.
- Prioritizing goals is essential for organizational focus and resource deployment.
- A clear plan should be developed with a limited number of strategic initiatives. Overly complex strategic plans with too many goals overwhelm every part of the strategic planning process from data collection to analysis, plan development, and implementation. Strategic plans should be succinct and easy to translate into tactical goals.
- Completed goals for conflicting mandates or goals should be reviewed, and one should watch for unintended consequences during implementation; this can be a real issue when business drivers for the enterprise are in conflict with business drivers for security.

Typical Example

Goal: Become a business enabler by meeting business expectations for security

- Measure security performance.
- Manage resources.
- Mitigate risk.
- Make sure that security understands and aligns activities with the strategic direction of the enterprise.

At a high enough level, this strategic goal makes perfect sense, but as the overall goal is put into organizational specifics, the specific drivers for the enterprise and security compliance requirements may come into direct conflict. If the sales and marketing components of the organization are competing in global economies, while ignoring or minimizing national or international security requirements, not only can organizational departments be at odds strategically, but audit findings may bring fines, government sanctions, and loss of business opportunities, as well as damaging the corporate brand and/or reputation. A more collaborative approach to strategic planning at the onset of planning can help reduce these conflicting pinch points in planning. This leads us to our next assertion about security and the organizations that security functions in.

Creating a Security Culture

We firmly believe that the only way organizations can achieve their security goals is to create a corporate security culture. Organizations cannot simply focus on technical solutions to security issues. The majority of these issues come from people and their interactions with technology. In order to move an organization forward, one can learn from the lessons of past major changes that affected the cultural identity of the organization and integrated themselves into the very fabric of daily work. Good examples are the quality movement, the productivity (LEAN, process management, etc.) movement, safety programs, and the more recent GREEN movement. Our belief is that organizations will ultimately benefit from creating an organizational security culture.

There are a couple of challenges to directing an organization toward a more holistic view regarding security. Most of the people inhabiting a security group are technical professionals. Moving an organization toward a culture shift requires both interpersonal and organizational skills. One solution to creating a plan for organizational change is to bring in outside consultants who specialize in change. Again, there are many examples of this from quality, Six Sigma, LEAN, and diversity programs that significantly changed organizational culture. While outside consultants can help craft a strategic plan for moving an organization forward, they should augment and NOT be the focus of any effort. Change should be led from the inside. Often many organizational resources are already present that can help security move in the direction of impacting organizational culture for the benefit of the enterprise. In the past, we have found help in the marketing, training, communications, and HR departments for planning and moving organizational change forward. Customer service-oriented people usually have good data regarding customer perceptions of an organization and can help build information security into an organizational brand. A security group can sometimes find internal consultants in the larger organization in which they function to help build both a strategic plan and strategic planning skills in the organization.

Security Continuum (Moving toward a Security Culture)

In a past project, Eric worked with outside consultants William Belgard and Steven Raymer (authors of *Shaping the Future: A Dynamic Process for Creating and Achieving Your Company's Strategic Vision*). A security continuum was developed between the security group and other business units to move organizational thinking from a compliance-based security framework (mental model) to a commitment-based security framework. The model utilized was from the American Center for Strategic Transformation. It depicts the transformation as a series of stages one might work through as security is integrated into a company. The process is similar to how the notion of quality and productivity were moved in the past decade from functional ownership (i.e., the Quality Assurance department) to an across-the-board organizational competency.

The transformational stages an organization goes through were labeled Functional Focus, Integration Focus, Communication Focus, Commitment Focus, and Systemic Focus. Within each stage, there are several components that demonstrate how the evolving notions of security will look in the arenas of technology, process, people, and organization.

The transformational stages basically track an organization as it moves from a compliance-based to a commitment-based security framework. In the compliance-based model, security is viewed as a necessary inconvenience (i.e., evil) and the security group as primarily an access control and emergency response-oriented function. The compliance model is technology driven and enforced by management. Security is seen as constantly restricting the flow of information necessary for organizational operation, while operating largely behind a curtain of secrecy.

The desired state of this continuum moves an organization toward a commitment-based security framework in which security is viewed as a competitive advantage. All employees now have a responsibility for security with adequate training and understanding of what constitutes security risk. The primary focus is systemic as the security system serves the extended enterprise, including partners, suppliers, and, in some cases, even customers. The core security principles in place are seen as a key competitive advantage that allows strategic partners to do business in a highly integrated way while protecting intellectual property and proprietary technologies and information.

Conclusion

Strategy is a long-term plan of action designed to achieve a goal that includes what work will be done and by whom. Strategic planning encourages long-term thinking and creative choices for future actions. It utilizes a structured process to create a formal, integrated enterprise plan. The security management program strategy must be directly linked to the organizational strategy or big picture. Producing an actionable strategy requires solid leadership throughout the development and implementation phases. Strategic planning is essentially gathering information, analyzing it, and deciding what you are going to do going forward. Metaphors provide an excellent way to gather data and analyze organizational cultures. The "strategy jam" metaphor is responsive, collaborative, creative, and intuitive, giving participants a sense of ownership in the plan and its success.

Strategic planning is an ongoing process; it is a journey. It demands leadership that understands not only the basics of strategic planning and the nuances of security, but also the art of working within the organizational culture. We believe that cultural change is the key to a successful security management program. Like the quality and productivity transformation of the past decade, security needs to take its place as an across-the-board organizational competency.

For any security strategic plan to be successful, organizational stakeholders must be involved and supportive, goals must be prioritized, scope must be limited and clear, and conflicting mandates must be resolved. Now is the time to prepare your security strategic plan. Build your vision and drive it forward with passion. Create an organization that truly is a key enabler of the business.

Chapter 2

Getting to the Big Picture

Many are so caught up in their own problems that they cannot see the big picture. Often, seeing the big picture can give one the perspective that makes illusive solutions suddenly easy to visualize. One form of hope can be accessed through stepping outside of yourself and seeing the bigger picture.

The Path

Real-life problems in business today require security managers to be able to see the big picture in order to solve them. Strategic planning is all about understanding the big picture in which you operate. Learning to see the big picture requires time and skill. By understanding the big picture, security managers can better lead their security function from a reactive posture to a more proactive posture in organizational life. In this chapter we discuss why strategic planning is essential for security groups; some of the strategic planning tools; models and methods that are available; and when to do strategic planning. We also examine keys, myths, and barriers to strategic planning.

Background (Why Should Security Bother with Strategic Planning?)

We have conducted and participated in many strategic planning sessions over the past 30 years. Like many other internal and external consultants or staffers, we have worked with groups to feverishly produce a strategic plan that inspired and invigorated the strategic planning group, only to see day-to-day operations overcome any sense of strategic direction and once dynamic and invigorative strategic plans become bookshelf relics to be dusted off and revisited when the next planning cycle came around.

Working within security, it is easy to dismiss strategic planning as something the upper echelon of an organization does, and security is simply positioned to react to the strategic plan and whatever unplanned exogenous shocks reality brings (e.g., newly passed regulations, security breaches, or unexpected organizational changes).

> Without a strategic plan your organization is just drifting on the tides of fortune with no real destination except extinction.
>
> **Eric Oksendahl**

There is also precious little out there in terms of resources to guide you through a thoughtful strategic planning process for security.

Without a strategic plan in place, a CSO comes to the enterprise leadership table lacking solid answers to the questions any good leader should be contemplating on a regular basis.

- Where is your organization going?
- What are you doing?
- How do you know how well you are doing?
- What are your priorities in the near term? The long term?
- Where would you suggest your dollar allocation go in case of an economic downturn or upturn?

A solid strategic plan helps provide thoughtful responses to those questions and brings credibility and direction to an organization. When other organizational leaders don't need to worry about security issues in their business because security leadership is able to understand and plan for those concerns, you are helping your organization achieve its business goals. A strong strategic plan will also move a security group out of a crisis model of operation into a more proactive model of operation.

Developing a solid strategic plan is applying basic business principles to the business of security. Security is part of the business, and if you want to be recognized as a business partner, you need to master this discipline. Creating a preferred future is not just for top managers in an organization. Organizations have to integrate quality, productivity, and customer service into every aspect of their business. Perhaps the next wave of integration will be creating a security culture in which security is everyone's business, not just the intimidating or mysterious work of a chosen few in the security group.

The menu of strategic planning methods to choose from grows each year. The strategic planning methodologies employed in an organization will depend on the organizational leadership, size of the organization, type of organization, culture and complexity of the organization, and expertise of its planners. A formal strategic planning process helps get the organization's leaders on the same page and moving forward in the same direction. Next are discussed just a few approaches and tools you have available to help you with your strategic planning process.

Menu of Strategic Planning Methods and Models

Let's be honest. If you bought this book to find a perfect method to make a perfect strategic plan, you won't find one. There is no perfect method for strategic planning. However, by examining various methods, models, and tools, you can glean what works in your organization. Table 2.1 presents some of the approaches, philosophies, tools, and techniques that have proven useful in strategic planning.

You'll have to admit this is quite the laundry list and it's only partial! Time does not permit us the luxury of expounding on the methods and merits in each of these models; at best, all we can do is provide guidance on how to pick the model or models that best fit your organizational needs. A basic guideline for any method chosen is that strategic plans are meant to be guides for the general direction in which an organization moves, NOT detailed roadmaps or blueprints for managerial daily work. Strategic planning is more about creating an informed and a shared frame of reference for daily decision makers, and is NOT a specific set of steps for each manager. Strategy

Table 2.1   Planning Methods and Models

Strategic Planning Methods, Models, and Tools	Strategic Planning Methods, Models, and Tools
Values-Based Strategic Planning (Center for Strategic Planning)	Force Field Analysis (Porter's Five Force Analysis Model)
Situation-Target-Proposal (STP Model)	Draw-See-Think Model
See-Think-Draw Model	Systems Thinking Disciplines (Peter Senge's Shared Values Model)
Environmental Analysis	SWOT Analysis (Strengths, Weaknesses, Opportunities, and Threats)
PEST Analysis (Political, Economic, Social, and Technological)	Balanced Scorecard
Process-Based Strategic Planning	Team-Based Strategic Planning
Rapid Strategic Planning	The Viable System Model of Strategic Planning
Dialogue/Storytelling/Making	Storyboarding
Gap Analysis	Game Theory
PDCA (Plan-Do-Check-Act)	Scenario Planning
Stakeholder Analysis	Strategic Options
Story Maps	Chaos Theory
Shaping the Future	Visualizing the Future
Blue Ocean Strategy	Change Management (creating a wave of change via strategic planning)
Basic Model of Strategic Planning	Issues-Based or Goal Model
Alignment Model	Self-Organizing Model
Risk Management Model	Process Management Model
SABSA (Sherwood Applied Business Security Architecture) Model	Strategy Activation
Simplified Strategic Planning Model	Preferred Future

is about corporate interpretation and reinterpretation of how best to proceed forward based on emerging possibilities.

Strategy cannot be a linear progression of steps, as the problems faced in organizational life are much too complex to ever be totally understood. Constant learning is required for organizational survival. There remains uncertainty and vagueness in any strategic plan. Strategic planning is a collaboration determining the best path to get us from where we are now to where we want to go.

Which Strategic Planning Tools?

Which models and tools, you ask, should you use? The answer is, "It depends." It depends on where you work, the organizational culture in which you work, the planning skills and capabilities of your organization, the speed (time lines) at which you are required to plan, and the current strategic capacity your organization has developed. It has been our experience from over 50 years of combined consulting, education, and facilitation that organizations employ any number of these tools and approaches at the same time in different parts of the organization, including within the security group itself. This is true in business, government, nonprofit, church, and educational realms.

Perhaps the ideal state is a single approach, uniformly utilized and applied. This should give an organization a competitive advantage, and in some instances that is true. Dutch/Shell is a well-known example of a scenario-planning effort in the late 1960s and early 1970s that prepared them well to deal with the oil crisis in the early 1970s. Despite past success, the scenario planning model may not match an organization's culture or organizational planning needs; even if it does, it will still require strong organizational sponsorship and leadership, or it may not be uniformly adopted. The same can be said for Senge's Fifth Discipline approach to creating a learning organization, Belgard and Rayner's Visualizing the Future approach to creating the future you want to live in now, or the layered matrix Sherwood's SABSA Model approach for creating a structured framework for security planning that works to design an enterprisewide security architecture and service management.

All models, methods, and philosophies require sponsorship, training, organizational adoption, and mastery to ever have a chance of working consistently. Regardless of whether your organization has one approach or several to strategic planning, elements of strategic planning are the basic building blocks of any approach. In the next section we will look at the essentials.

What Are Security Plan Essentials? (Analysis, Planning, and Implementation)

If you boil strategic planning down to its basics, you'll find that the elements more or less fall into three distinct buckets or phases:

1. Analysis—Painting the internal and external "big picture" for strategic planning
2. Strategic planning—Setting the desired direction for an organization
3. Implementation plan—Creating the roadmap to realization

Typically in organizations, part of the analysis includes an overall evaluation of the business environment security must manage its business in. The goal is a thorough understanding of the greater organizations' strategic plan. Although the greater organizational strategic planners have already done an external and internal analysis, the security group must perform its own analysis as the inputs for the security strategic plan include a number of different or more detailed elements. That being said, it is important to begin with a clear understanding of the organizational strategic plan. In organizations that have more than one business unit, security needs to garner an understanding of each business unit's strategic plan in which their own plan will reside (much like the Russian "matryoshka" dolls that nest one inside the other). As a group proceeds through these three phases of strategic planning (analysis, planning, and implementation), there are several important things to remember.

Learn the Big Picture of the Extended Enterprise

If you are not already part of the overall strategic planning process (or the organization you are part of isn't), then get your hands on your enterprise organizational strategic plan and study it carefully. As you start to develop your own strategic plans, be sure other parts of your organization's leadership (outside your organization) have a chance for input and review of those portions of your security strategic plan that are applicable to their organizations.

Many organizations try to shortcut the analysis phase and end up failing to include business drivers, business unit direction, environmental scans, or big-picture input into their planning cycles. When not enough time has been spent gathering big-picture probabilities, the likelihood increases that the organization will be more reactive to the environment than proactively helping shape the environment. In marketing jargon, this would be called market-shaping activities instead of market-reacting activities. Market-shaping activities involve the identification of the drivers shaping demand, a survey of what existing products and services might be supplied to meet that demand, which in turn helps identify gaps in the market and the development of a strategy for market-shaping activities. A similar approach can be used to plan a proactive security strategy. First gather the information needed to identify the issues affecting organizational security (now and into the future), then compare existing and future requirements to your current capabilities to identify gaps in security functionality. Next build a strategic plan to fill those gaps. Figure 2.1 charts some of the basic domains within an enterprise that a security group must consider as it develops strategy.

Include a High-Level Risk Assessment as Input

Your part of the business is security; risk assessments are a common part of security management. Get your hands on the best risk assessments you can find, including anything generated by the enterprise risk management group, and use them as part of the input for your own strategic plan. Risk assessments help quantify and thus prioritize where the organization may need to develop or refine strategies to manage risks affecting the organization's ability to accomplish its goals. We have found that as security groups grow and mature they also tend to create internal risk assessment measures (such as risk ratings for individual geographic sites) that are quite useful in strategic planning.

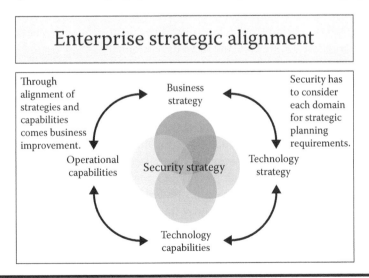

Figure 2.1   Enterprise strategic alignment.

Link Your Strategic Plan to the Organization Strategic Plan

Weaving the general framework of your strategic plan into the organization's overall strategic plan is an important part of the process. Make the links tangible and measurable as you go. In really large organizations, there may be several levels of links depending on how much organizational structure you report up through. The links may also change somewhat during reorganizations, mergers, and acquisitions. (See Figure 2.1.)

Building a solid measurable strategic plan will help you move an organization from a reactive "save the day" (often at a much greater cost) model to a well-planned and executed strategy that has carefully allocated security dollars to specific priorities based on well-defined links to the organization's strategic goals and vision. Finding the right metrics to assess the success of your strategy is not an easy step; it takes practice and refinement to master.

Business leaders are less prone to believe security hand-waving and the-sky-is-falling approaches to getting funding. They want to see the hard numbers and reasoning backed up with solid evidence (i.e., risk assessments) rather than emotional appeals. The key to success is a security strategic plan that is aligned with the overarching organizational strategic plan, including budget planning. Keep in mind, however, that good strategic plans are driven by strong strategic initiatives, not just budget. Don't sell your security efforts short for budgeting reasons; make a strong case for those initiatives, and the money will follow.

Develop Flexibility and Fluidity in Your Department

Your ability to adapt implementation plans to different cycles of strategic planning, business initiatives, emerging trends, new regulations, and the like is critical to success. A fortress mentality will not serve you well. Continual technology changes require a number of skill sets from an IT department: an eye for developing technologies, a penchant for applying and deploying those technologies, the heart of a teacher to help educate and persuade senior management to utilize those technologies, and the hands of a conductor to coordinate implementation of those technologies with other units. Rigidity sends customers looking for solutions and support elsewhere. Learn how to serve your customers; be flexible and fluid in strategy and execution.

> Don't try to tell the customer what he wants. If you want to be smart, be smart in the shower. Then get out, go to work and serve the customer!
>
> **Gene Buckley**
> *Sikorsky Aircraft*

There are a myriad of strategic planning methods, but they all incorporate three basic elements: analysis, strategic planning, and implementation. Before building your security strategy, it is critical to have a clear understanding of the organization's overall strategic plan. This may require analyzing multiple plans in organizations with multiple business units. Shortcutting the analysis phase leads to an organization driven by the environment instead of one proactively shaping it. Management is weary of the-sky-is-falling approach to security strategy planning; link your plan and initiatives to the corporation's. Build in solid metrics for measuring success and use inputs from the analysis phase and risk assessments to prepare your budget numbers and the evidence supporting those numbers. Finally, build a culture of customer service into your security group; being flexible and fluid while maintaining the security of your company's assets is a delicate balance. Doing it well makes you an enabler; doing it poorly makes you a target for outsourcing.

When Should Strategic Planning Be Done?

The short answer is "it depends" or maybe even "continuously." There are several considerations regarding timing for strategic planning. Matching the business planning cycle of the overarching organization is an important consideration but not the only one. Typically in larger businesses, a planning cycle may be annual, with various stops during the year to run metrics, tweak targets or goals, consider options, and the like. For some industries an annual cycle just doesn't work because the environment changes too fast. In that case, moving to a bi-annual cycle in strategic planning may be required. Product rollouts and major technology shifts are two other events likely to influence planning cycles. New product rollouts can have substantial impacts on IT infrastructure and security. New products and services may also precipitate major shifts in technology, for example, moving large portions of your transaction processing from internal to cloud-based applications.

We recommend at a minimum conducting one complete planning cycle each year, beginning whenever the organization business cycle starts. It is best to have your strategic plan coordinated with the organizational strategic plan and in concert with the other division planning (i.e., business plan, financial plan, marketing plan, operational plan, etc.). At a minimum, the plan should be reviewed quarterly, and action plans, tactics, and so on updated to reflect the review cycle. Consider adding more planning cycles in fast-paced environments and during major change events (especially those not in the original plan), such as a new venture, merger, new product/ service offering rollout, or major technology shift.

The key to successful planning is staying nimble; don't be stuck on calendar cycles, learn to apply strategic skills quickly, and change course as needed. In the competitive, quick-paced environments in which we work this ability is crucial. Remember, strategic plans can be based on various lengths of time; five years might be the goal, but time frames in months are often the reality. Most organizational managers spend more time doing and less time planning than they would like. In our experience working with many levels of managers, a typical manager spends between 40 and 80% of his time doing something (operations), 20 to 60% managing (people issues), and 0 to 5% planning (strategic thinking). Many recently promoted managers come from the ranks of doing and spend much time learning how to manage people as new managers. Often, as a manager proceeds in her career, less time is spent doing, and more time managing people issues and attending countless meetings. Once a manager moves to the executive level, it is difficult to push aside doing and managing activities to begin practicing planning. Yet, when managers are asked to rank which of these three categories have more impact on organizational outcomes and results, most managers will agree that the ranking should be planning, managing, and then doing.

Top leaders can better impact an organization by balancing their personal schedule to allow them to spend more time on strategy and planning, and less time on managing and people. In a reactive environment, the first thing that usually gets short-shrift is strategic planning, with the unintended consequence of relegating the organization to a perpetual focus on reactive operations and tactics, and management issues. There is a lesson to be learned here, regardless of the cycle organizations need to be dedicated to doing strategic planning and doing it well.

Doing strategic planning well requires that managers first of all make planning a priority in their schedule. Second, good planning requires organization and a robust planning process in place; otherwise planning efforts will often result in frustration and confusion among the planners and staff. Third, in order to create time for planning, managers must often delegate part of doing and managing to others in order to create the time for good planning. Delegation not only helps create time but it helps develop your staff as well.

Six Keys to Successful Strategic Planning

The following six elements of strategic planning are the keys to successful strategic planning:

1. Simplicity
2. Passion (emotional energy)/Speed of Planning and Adapting
3. Connection to Core Values
4. Core Competencies
5. Communication
6. Implementation

Simplicity

> Simplify, there is no value in complexity, it's too difficult to manage.
>
> **Bill Stackpole**

Regardless of the methodology and tools employed, a strategic direction must be simple enough to be understood by not only the strategic planning committee, but every stakeholder in an organiza-

The future belongs to those who believe in the beauty of their dreams.

Eleanor Roosevelt

tion. One good metric for assessing the clarity of your strategy is an "elevator speech." An elevator speech is a 60-second summary of your strategy that presents a compelling overview of strategic direction. The speech should be short, easily understood, and motivating. If you can't easily build an elevator speech, it's time to simplify. Organizational vision comes from understanding the current realities of the organization, possessing a keen sense of where the organization needs to go, as well as having a plan for bridging the gap between the present reality and the desired future.

> **Exercise 2.1**
>
> Preparing an elevator speech helps you give a consistent message about your strategic direction, helps build support, and strengthens your personal and organizational network. Keep it short, simple, direct, and real.
>
> An elevator speech that explains security strategy should include the following questions:
>
> 1. Who are we?
> 2. What do we offer the organization?
> 3. What problems are solved, and what opportunities are realized by our strategic direction?
> 4. Why is our strategy better than other solutions?
> 5. What is the value to the listener?
> 6. What should they do about your message?
>
> Now practice, and make your speech compelling, personal, and heartfelt.

We've watched corporate CEOs deliver a compelling version of company vision and strategic direction over and over again for years to different audiences. Each time it sounded new and fresh and always generated great questions from audiences ranging from Wall Street to employees to customers and shareholders. It was the questions from the audience that created the dialogue and forged a deeper understanding of the direction of the company as well as provided insight into what various elements of the extended enterprise thought about the direction. A CSO, CIO, and other security leaders should develop the same ability to speak with energy, conviction, and clarity about security and its role in enterprise success. They should also be ready to listen and respond to questions from employees, customers, suppliers, or other extended enterprise stakeholders.

Our approach utilizes a holistic view of security; this isn't the traditional view of security. Holistic security seeks to understand the impact of security issues on the entire enterprise. Holistic security functions as a fully integrated part of an organizational system. The assumption is that systems have to be understood as wholes rather than as a sum of their parts. This includes technology, processes, information, and, most importantly, people. A holistic approach takes into account the entire organization as it makes decisions. A holistic approach to security starts with bringing together different security silos into a single functional team that works collaboratively to support the organization's security needs. The benefits of using a holistic framework are a better understanding of the organization's security requirements, the impact of security issues on organizational performance, and the best way to optimize the dollars spent to mitigate those issues. A whole systems view of security seeks to understand:

- Who security stakeholders are and how they work together to produce value in an organization
- The future security impacts of current industry trends
- The real (accurate) security state of the organization as it exists today
- The competitiveness factors driving security changes
- The unique contributions security makes to the world around them

The goal is a complete understanding of the most important elements of the infrastructure and how we can make the future of our organization more secure. From understanding, the security group can begin to form a more cohesive organization with *one strategic mission* and one set of consistent goals designed to promote collaboration between the different security functions and the other service groups security works with. The second goal is to understand the security culture of the security group—not only how the people working in security treat and interact with each other and their customers, but also how the organizational culture perceives security as a whole.

By creating a "whole picture" understanding of organizational risk, security groups can better assist organizational leaders in understanding security issues, identifying strategies to mitigate risk, implementing policies to manage risk, and deciding which risks to simply accept. A "whole picture" understanding of organizational security issues also helps identify and eliminate redundancies within an organization. Eliminating wasteful repetitions such as the multiple-user identities and utilizing economies of scale by converging systems with common functionality across an enterprise can help reduce overall operating costs. Think we're dreaming? Many security leadership articles of late discuss "holistic security" as a fundamental requirement of staying relevant, whether you are working at IBM, BWX Technologies, the U.S. Department of Energy, Wells Fargo, or a U.S. Department of Defense contractor.

Strategic efforts based on simplicity facilitate organizational adoption, promote a holistic understanding of security, and produce cost-effective results. Simplicity must be part of all our security endeavors.

Passion (Emotional Energy) and Speed of Planning and Adapting

> We may affirm that nothing great in the world has been accomplished without passion.
>
> **George Friedrich Hegel**

If a strategic direction has no emotional connection for those who are charged with moving, implementing, selling, telling, living, breathing, and executing the strategy, the strategic direction is DOA (Dead on Arrival). Strategic planning is a marathon, not a sprint. It takes emotional stamina for an organization to move toward a vision. It takes speed and passion to win in today's environment: speed to get good data from the frontlines of an organization into the planning process; speed to analyze the data; speed to react to it; and speed to move in an altered direction when necessary. Once a year planning cycles for strategic planning are DEAD; they are too slow, too ponderous, and too removed from today's business cycles. Current practices spend too much time looking at the past to predict future trends or trying to explain what went wrong in previous planning cycles. Many tend to focus on year-long market research cycles, big glossy pictures, and graphs instead of considering inputs that will drive the organization into the future.

Recent research from Korean academic W. Chan Kim and from Renée Mauborgne has found that the key difference between companies that achieve high growth and those that don't is the way that they approach strategy. According to Kim and Mauborgne, value innovators challenge competitive thinking; they identify new market space and position themselves to exploit it, even if that means moving beyond the traditional boundaries of their business. Security can be part of an organizational "value proposition," but in order to accomplish that end security practitioners will have to challenge current thinking, identify new ways of providing organizational security, and position themselves to exploit it. Our experience with security professionals is that there is often a strong sense of core values in those who choose to work in the security field. Strategic planning efforts need to leverage that passion, make those values explicit, and link them clearly into strategic plans.

Connection to Core Values

Core values are the emotional engine that drives people and organizations forward. Being explicit about a strategic direction and how it links to the organization's core values and competencies helps everyone understand why the energy, focus, and costs are worth it. Values are the "how" an organization expects to conduct business. Values that are understood, communicated, and made part of an organization's vision help guide the daily activities of those who work within that organization. When people understand the values that are at the heart of an organization, they have a better understanding of how to move toward realization of that vision.

In light of the recent lapse of sound ethical strategic planning in many sectors of business and government, we would suggest centering any strategic planning process soundly around an examination and planning from the core values of your organization. A regular reexamination of strategic direction to assure it is holding true to the core values of an organization is as fundamental to organizational health as a regular medical exam is to physical health. One only has to examine recent headlines to discover strategic planning gone awry. They are prime examples of leadership abandoned once sound organizational values to further goals become more aligned with corporate avarice, greed, pride, recklessness and worse. When organizations fixate on a single arbiter of fiscal health such as stock price or competitive advantage, it often leads them down the path of compromise, causing them to shed core values in pursuit of wealth, status, power, and prestige. Abandoning an organization's core values can quickly end in the crippling or ultimate demise of a once thriving, successful organization.

The failure of Washington Mutual Savings and Loan (WaMu) is a great example. WaMu was a well-run Seattle-based bank that was ripe for acquisition by one of the larger banks. Instead of being acquired, however, WaMu executives decided that they would acquire and adopt a rapid growth strategy. First, WaMu acquired a number of small and midsize banks to strengthen its position in the Northwest. Then in the mid-1990s it expanded to California with the purchase of American Savings, but the acquisition forever changed the home-spun nature of the bank. WaMu used the mortgage business it acquired in the American Savings deal to fuel its unprecedented growth, but in the process it abandoned the core values on which it had been founded. WaMu entered into the Adjustable Rate Mortgage (ARM) business, adopting the "balloon" option that gave borrowers three to five years of low payments that ballooned into much larger payments that frequently resulted in defaults. WaMu had always held its own loans, but now it started to bundle and sell them off. Internal controls for measuring and managing risk were disabled, allowing increasingly riskier loans. Then in 1999 WaMu abandoned the last vestige of its core values when it acquired Long Beach Mortgage's subprime mortgage business. The "friend of the family" had become obsessed with the profits it needed to fuel its growth and escalate the value of its stock. In September 2008, WaMu paid the price for its folly, when federal regulators took over the bank, putting an end to a 119-year-old Seattle institution, one that had made it through the Great Depression and the 1980s Savings and Loan crisis.

> In the end the bank failed because its leaders abandoned its historical balance between growth and prudence.
>
> **Bill Longbrake**
> *WaMu CFO*

We have personally seen billions of dollars lost when an organization in which we worked had leaders who lost sight of the organization's core values. The cost to the organization and the personal cost to the employees were huge and took many years to overcome. It is important to build continual reminders into day-to-day management activities of what an organization's core values are and how they show up at work. It can be as simple as finishing a staff meeting with a closing story, an award, or an example that catches your staff "doing the right thing."

Core Competencies

Core competencies are the specific, extraordinary abilities that give your organization an edge in the marketplace, service sector, or the like, and cannot be easily imitated. They deliver value to customers in the form of technical expertise, customer and supplier relationship, product development, organizational culture and/or employee involvement. C. K. Prahad and G. Hamel developed the main ideas about core competencies in both their series of *Harvard Business Review* articles and their follow-on best-selling book *Competing for the Future*.

Analyzing a company's core competencies helps determine which strategies, activities, and practices need improvement. In addition, it is helpful to determine which competencies to develop in-house and which to outsource. This can be done at multiple levels in a company, including the security group. The key questions to use when conducting a core competencies analysis are as follows:

1. Does the activity provide unique or valued potential access to the market?
2. Does the activity add value?
3. Is it difficult for competition to imitate the activity?

The advantages of developing a short, refined list of core competencies is that it produces a realistic view of the skill sets, processes, and systems the company is uniquely good at performing.

It helps to generate focus on the value-adding activities. And finally, it helps in the decision process used to determine which activities are candidates for outsourcing.

In our experience, this can be a difficult activity within a specific organization like security. As an organization lists the key services and activities it engages in and then begins to sort through whether they are unique or common, the first tendency is to overstate uniqueness. Upon closer examination, many activities are not unique. This quality can be determined at an organizational level by asking, "Can this service be contracted out?" For example, guards who enforce physical security may be classified as a common service that could potentially be contracted out.

Changing business models can also impact the core competencies needed in an organization. If, for instance, an organization moves toward a systems integrator model of providing security services rather than a proprietary in-house security group, the core competencies will shift. Previously, service skills may have been core competencies; now, core competencies, such as contract management, may become crucial for career and organizational success.

Communication

> The best strategic plans in the world are not likely to be successful if they are not effectively communicated to those who must implement them: the employees.
>
> **Jake Laban and Jack Green**

A strategic plan must be communicated in multiple ways to multiple stakeholders. Secrecy about strategic plans hamstrings organizations through lack of understanding, absence of ownership, and insufficient input. Strategic plans have to be communicated, and a dialogue of rich information must be continued throughout the planning and implementation phases. No strategy remains static; daily events provide a constant flow of information to be reviewed.

Information sharing between the elements of the whole system or value chain is essential to good strategic planning. That requires forming a team with members from various departments and equipping them with the communication tools they require for cohesive collaborative planning.

Leadership in today's marketplace requires straight talk. By straight talk, we mean talk that is honest, clear, and sensitive to the moment. In addition, today's realities require an organizational environment in which straight talk is not only encouraged but valued. Ask yourself, "Do the employees in my organization feel that they can speak the truth concerning what they observe and feel to me or the leadership of this organization?" The key to creating an environment of open communication is respect—respect both for one another and for the opinions that are voiced.

Jake Laban and Jack Green argue that communication itself may be the strategic framework that helps make winning strategy. In an article titled "Communicating Your Strategy: The Forgotten Fundamental of Strategic Implementation," published in Pepperdine University's *Graziadio Business Report*, Laban and Green outline a strategy for communicating an organization's business strategy. In this approach they suggest the following as a winning communications strategy:

1. **Build the communications strategy as a STRATEGY.** Develop a big-picture communications strategic goal, clearly define communication objectives and change them as required over time, and identify critical tactics (which in turn can provide a good metric for feedback and evaluation of the program).
2. **Understand the communication channels chosen.** Recognize channel limitations (e-mail, SharePoint, video, etc.), match the channel to the desired level of interaction and

feedback needed, and remember that multiple channels are often necessary for strategy implementation.

3. **Apply the appropriate packaging technique.** Use the language of the consumer/end-user to aid understanding and execution, use well-constructed communication to disseminate and reinforce corporate culture, and avoid pandering to the lowest common denominator, instead challenging laggards to catch up with high performers.

Regardless of your approach to communication, having a communications plan is essential for getting the word out. In the past, we have found success working with a communications professional from the enterprise communications group. If available, tapping into communication professionals can greatly assist your own planning efforts.

Implementation

I saw that leaders placed too much emphasis on what some call high level strategy, on intellectualizing and philosophizing, and not enough on implementation.

Larry Bossidy and Ram Charan

A good strategic plan means nothing without implementation. Having a clear implementation plan is crucial to successful strategy. Integration is key to the successful implementation of strategic initiatives and objectives. Your implementation plan must be linked to those initiatives and objectives. Implementation is the enacting plan to integrate security into the organizational system and often extend it into the supply chain as well. Integration is sometime referred to as security convergence. *Security convergence* refers both to the threat side and the solutions side of security. It takes a sophisticated holistic (systems) model to understand and plan for integration.

Some examples of security convergence are Enterprise Security Risk Management models that help provide input into strategic planning. An Enterprise Security Risk assessment demands a rollup or convergence of subject matter expert recommendations of assessing and managing security threats throughout the entire system, both physical and IT security.

Security convergence is more than integration of security departments throughout an organization (although that is a start; see Chapter 6 of this book for additional information on this topic). Developing a holistic view for convergence issues requires a collaborative dialogue between multiple functions within an organization to better understand the common risk concerns, challenges, and possible solutions. This includes physical, personnel, and information security, import/export, business/competitive intelligence, intellectual property and brand protection, privacy, fraud prevention, ethics, supplier management, legal, investigation and background checks, business continuity, disaster recovery, disaster preparedness, emergency services, and safety/OSHA (Occupational Safety and Health Administration). The focus is on getting security solutions integrated throughout the company's business architecture from research and development (R&D), operations, and sales to product and service delivery. Security's job is to help build value throughout the value chain of the organization through cost-efficient risk mitigation.

It is also important to include integration at the tactical level of security planning. As an organization puts in place core security activities, the right tactics for the people, process, and technology aspect of security convergence need to be selected. Integration is not easy, nor is it made easier at the most tactical and concrete level—the processes and architecture put in place by the strategic plan.

Typically, an implementation plan will include action plans, budget plans, responsibilities, authority, and accountability guidelines as well as a schedule for implementation, monitoring, and a communication plan.

Myths about Strategic Planning

One of the major obstacles to implementation is the perceptions that people in the organization have about strategic planning. Myths about strategic planning can keep a security group in the dark ages lagging behind their business partners, misunderstood, and regarded as less than professional by enterprise leadership. Myths about strategic planning abound. Here are just a few of the most prevalent myths in organizational life.

1. **Strategy is just pie in the sky; strategy is different than real jobs.** Strategy is a leader's job and like any skill requires discipline, practice, and education to master. If you consider yourself a leader in a security group, strategic thinking is now part of your job description. Strategic planning is arguably the most important part of your job, as a good strategic plan will guide all of your organizational efforts. Without a strategic plan your organization is just drifting on the tides of fortune with no real destination except extinction.
2. **Strategy is a written plan sitting on a shelf or residing in a data file somewhere.** Long gone are the days in most organizations when strategic planning was a once-a-year exercise accomplished at an executive retreat somewhere and then dispensed to the masses. It's not the written plan that is the important aspect of planning; it is the mental framework it gives employees when making everyday tactical decisions in the organization. A strategic plan is really the way people think about the work they are doing now. A good strategic plan helps employees change the way they think about their jobs.
3. **Strategy belongs to the top of the organization.** Although the leaders of organizations are certainly responsible for strategic direction, other elements of organizational life need to take part in strategic planning for several reasons. First, these perspectives and inputs are invaluable to the internal analysis of the organization. Second, they also provide important information regarding external environmental trends that people's jobs bring them into contact with and insights into specific customer needs. Third, people are much more likely to commit themselves to a vision and strategic plan if they have a voice in helping to create it. The fourth and final reason, and perhaps the most important one, is that building the strategic planning capacity of your organization gives you a competitive advantage.
4. **Looking at past trends helps us plan for the future**. Power to drive an organization comes from a compelling vision for the future, not a retrospective view of the past. As strategic planners, our goal is to connect to the emotional energy of the people in an organization and move toward a future they want to inhabit. When people are emotionally connected to a potential future, many of the traditional problems in strategic planning are greatly diminished (i.e., lack of communication, information, and commitment). There are things to be learned from the past, but do not let the constraints and disappointments of yesterday be an arbiter of the future (i.e., the "We tried that already and it doesn't work!" syndrome). At the same time, strategic planning does not attempt to predict the future, although it helps you work toward a preferred future. Good planning will reduce organization risk but will not eliminate it. Good planning, through the exploration of alternative futures, helps build an organization that will be better able to respond as future changes take place.

5. **We are in control.** Although security leaders certainly have the mantle of leadership and all the responsibilities that go with that position, they are not in control of all the outcomes, nor do they have the power to do strategic planning alone. Good strategic planning is collaborative in nature and requires people's willing participation. People in positions of power routinely overestimate their ability to impact organizational changes. Whether we are talking about mergers and acquisitions or victory on the competitive battlefield, at best, leaders influence and help guide organizational action, not determine it. The actual execution of any strategic plan occurs only when employees choose to adopt it and change their behaviors to move toward its vision. Some corporate CEOs have discussed how once they thought that at the next level of management they would finally have enough power to really impact change. At each new level, however, they consistently found that they did not have sufficient power to be in control in the way they had expected.

6. **Change is a disruption.** Change, as we all know, is seemingly the only constant in organizational life. The pace of it seemingly increases with each passing decade whether in technology, occupation, or social environments. Security groups that are reluctant to move into wholesale change will soon find themselves looking for another job.

That being said, there is a balance that must be achieved. Failing to adapt to the modern realities of the business world moves organizations toward obsolescence; *too much* change breeds chaos. Anna Rowley, in her book *Leadership Therapy: Inside the Mind of Microsoft,* names change as one of the top 10 problems Microsoft managers face. According to Rowley, over the course of their employment, Microsoft employees experience 13 times the number of change events (e.g., reorganizations, new managers, position changes) that someone working in the banking industry will experience. Major changes are usually short-term disruptions. Continuous change is continuous disruption; it is unsettling to employees, stressful to work environments, and costly to companies.

Managing a security group requires both the flexibility and stability of leadership and the security group, especially in a compliance and governance function. Learning to move quickly, while keeping an organization cool, calm, and collected, takes skillful leadership at every level.

Barriers to Strategic Planning

A good deal of strategic planning…is like a ritual rain dance, it has no effect on the weather that follows, but those who engage in it think it does.

Brian Quinn
quoted in Tom Peters's article "Strategic Planning, R.I.P."

Pushing through to the Next Level of Strategic Breakthrough (Inside/Outside Organizational Input/Output)

Security by its very nature seeks to create a more secure environment for an organization, its assets, people, and information. Keeping an organization competitive in the marketplace demands new ways of doing business with increased risk. Not every aspect of a strategic planning is a "safe bet." Sometimes thinking requires trying something new that creates organizational disturbance of the old order or "safe way" of doing things.

Strategy is like sex. When all is said and done, more is said than done.

Bill Tregoe

Learning and perfecting strategic thinking practices individually and as a group are important leadership skills for any organization. Taking those skills to the next level of breakthrough is crucial to survival in the increasingly competitive and ever faster moving business world. Security has traditionally been a reactive field across the board. While tactical plans may abound, historically speaking security has been incident driven. This situation has to change: If they are to be taken seriously, security groups must get out of the hair-on-fire, the-sky-is-falling reactive mind-set and grow adept at strategic thinking and at planning and communicating those plans in the language of business.

Going Slow to Go Faster, or Don't Just Do Something, Sit There (Honing Organizational Strategic Planning Skills)

Like any skill set, the ability to conduct strategic planning seldom just happens. Developing strategic planning skills takes time, practice, and continuous learning. The more leadership responsibility one has, the more these skills should be developed. It is our belief that strategic thinking skills are developed as part of organizational relationships, not just as an individual skill set. According to Peter Senge and his colleagues in *The Fifth Discipline Fieldbook,* strategic, creative, and conceptual thinking is developed through a practice of inquiry that engages the learner. That means that periods of action require periods of reflection to assimilate the lessons learned at both the individual and the collective levels. Yet, how many of us as individuals, much less as organizations, have actually built individual or organizational capacity for reflection into our daily activity? In most organizations, taking time to reflect is seen as a huge luxury at best and as a sign of incompetence or nonproductivity at worst. Other then the obligatory end-of-the-year summary of accomplishments and congratulations, little organizational time is spent collectively reflecting on and inquiring about how we go about our work together and what have we learned in the process. Create space for learning!

Think Ahead, Act Now

What you cannot do is simply react to conditions, continue to do the same thing the competition is doing, remain static, or stay tactically focused. Leadership requires laser focus on execution in the present, while guiding today's activities with a continual eye toward the future and remembering the lessons of yesterday. As a leader, you model the ability to act responsibly today, while focused on the future. The moment you have in front of you right now lays the foundation for tomorrow's change.

Strategic Business Principles and Workplace Politics

As anyone who has worked for any length of time in any human enterprise knows, one aspect that makes strategic planning interesting is the trump card of office politics. When an organization is engaged in office politics, often the results can be artifice, gaming, resistance, counterproductive activities, insecurity, blame, rebellion, and more, resulting in a toxic organization that fails to get the participation, information, and creativity that strategic planning requires to be successful. The truth remains that office politics are part of all work environments. The question is how to navigate them as an organization practices the fine art of strategic planning, forming vision, mission, strategic initiatives, plans, measures, and the like.

As Damian D. "Skipper" Pitts, former U.S. Marine, now business professional and university instructor, discusses in his excellent book, *Building Great Teams: Charting the Path of Organizational Politics,* politically savvy leaders understand the "why" and "how" of shaping great teams. They make decisions for the benefit of the future. They understand the "culture" in the system which the team must influence. They also know how to use the Six Political Signs of Business Leadership:

1. A clear "vision" of issues
2. An understanding of the "value" drivers within the team
3. "Behavioral" influence of leadership on the future picture
4. "Strategy" modeling (enterprise decision making)
5. Strategic "execution" (governance)
6. "Duplication of protocol" (learnable-teachable methods for future engagements)

Pitts's background gives him keen insights into building great teams. He underlines one of the problems we have seen repeatedly in our organizational consulting work. Organizational leaders fail to achieve their goals not because they lack organizational talent but because they are naïve as to the basic complexities of team dynamics. In his very readable book, Pitts outlines the strategy execution smart leaders use, what type of team they need to function in their specific organizational environment, the key skills to look for and those to avoid, and how to coax top performances from team members. His metaphor of choice is "great teams know how to successfully engage the battlefield."

Office politics has many faces and tactics, and is a real part of work life. Patience, honesty, and authentic behavior go a long way toward managing office politics. Staying flexible, listening well, identifying issues and problems rather than attacking people are methods that also help work through office politics. The key is to minimize the effect of office politics on your own behavior and maximize your own influence.

Looking for Niches, Voids, Under-Your-Nose Advantages

A prime example of finding a niche (this one was right under security's nose) is being aware of the enabling function security can play in the ever-changing requirements of the global marketplace. Current business drivers demand cross-functional, cooperative, integrated, collaborative design and delivery of products and services in the marketplace. Security strategy resides at the nexus of potential organizational moves into the marketplace because of the increasing use of information technologies. With the right strategies in place, a security group can be strategic for the entire enterprise in avoiding risks from mounting regulations and increasing threats to information. As design groups move into new market spaces, including security in the strategic planning sessions can help innovation advance more quickly and with less risk.

Overcoming Negative Perceptions of Security

Let's face it: Other groups in the organization have perceptions about security that inhibit your working relationship and strategic planning efforts. Sometimes those perceptions may be well earned by past behavior; other times it may be because much of what security does is not fully understood. Here are just a few of the negative perceptions that you may have to work to overcome:

- Security is not a business enabler; it is a business hobbler or disabler.
- Security has black and white solutions to everything.
- Security personnel are arrogant and bossy.
- Security doesn't understand business.
- Security is a roadblock and/or a stop sign.
- Security is guns, gates, and guards.
- IT security is rude and hard to understand.
- Security personnel are reluctant to embrace change.
- Security is inflexible.

The key to building successful relationships for a security organization is to avoid getting defensive and learn to manage negative perceptions in a way that is productive for the organization. If these are regular comments about your security group, what are you doing to change those perceptions? Is your security group moving toward professional excellence while providing services and governance with grace and humility? Do you work to develop relationships with your organizational counterparts and to understand how you can provide better security solutions, not more problems? Have you learned the language of your consumer/customer groups and how to communicate security concerns in terms they can understand?

Averse to Outsourcing

Outsourcing is a business requirement. Sometimes strategically outsourcing certain functions may be risky, but often, after an initial resistance from the security group, not only is outsourcing a commodity security service possible, it often allows better security. Outsourcing is part of the landscape in the service industry. You must be able to analyze your organization's value-creating activities and unique contributions to the enterprise with meaningful metrics. When you do, sometimes the best answer is still outsourcing. Remember to factor in contract management; your group will still be responsible for contract management as well as Service Level Agreement (SLA) compliance (i.e., ensuring the quality of the delivery of services from the subcontractor). If you can't provide security services for better value than your consumers demand, you will have a difficult time answering the outsourcing question.

Reluctant to Change Quickly

According to Peter Gregory, a consultant with the Hart Gregory Group, the primary job of an organizational chief security officer (CSO) is to be a change agent in the way people work, both in terms of policies and procedures and culture. Gregory states, "That person needs to be savvy enough to enact effective change that improves security, without alienating end users or management. It won't work if people don't respect the CSO." The primary focus of the emerging role of CSOs is to create organizational change that enables secure business processes in a dynamic technological environment. The best security is a culture of security; to achieve it, the CSO's focus has to be one of change agent.

Stovepiped Organization Out of Touch with Business Realities

Organizations that operate without the benefit of other parts of the organization's perspective are at a distinct disadvantage. There is much to be gained by putting business leaders, legal counsel, and security leadership in the same room to work through a strategic approach to their organization. Clearly understanding each other's perspectives will help an organization move forward.

Much of the strategic integration software available in the various methodologies discussed in later chapters is about getting information to where it is needed to make better business decisions and to move it out of the organizational stovepipes where it now resides. While software and Web applications are part of the answer, so are the human connections we need to develop and maintain the key organizational relationships. Without these connections it's nearly impossible to assure the security of the modern extended enterprises we work in today.

Always Looking for the Next Magic Technology Bullet

While it is important to have a segment of security constantly scanning technology for new possible applications, too often the promises of the new technology turn into premature or ill-fated implementations. People will always remain the most vulnerable aspect of security, despite the next best technology coming down the pike. While IT security can be particularly vulnerable to negative organizational perceptions of technology, physical security is not immune. We have both personally witnessed overexuberance by security personnel over technologies ranging from software analytics packages to forensic techniques, information technology systems, video analytics, new badge technology, weapons (e.g., taser technology), and more. Although understanding new technology and being trained in new security systems is part of the job, no new technology solves all problems. Often, managing perceptions about how the new technologies will be used is as important as the proposed benefits of technology adoption; if the public, employees, or executive leadership perceives the solution as encroaching on people's safety, privacy, or freedom, the best return on investment (ROI) in the world won't justify its adoption.

Promises, Promises You Can't Keep

> It is an immutable law in business that words are words, explanations are explanations, promises are promises but only performance is reality.
>
> **Harold Geneen**

When promises are made and not kept, trust is eroded. Unfortunately, corporate troubles and scandals around the globe have damaged the public's trust. Trust levels are at record lows for government, clergy, management, corporations, banks and more. Lack of trust hurts brands and business. Consistency and credibility are required to set and maintain others' expectations of security. Security, of all service functions, requires credibility in order to be an effective enterprise partner. Integrity is an integral part of security services both for the data it is responsible for and the people who deliver security services. Make it your business to walk with integrity in all relationships, internal and external. Demand it of yourself and the people who work for you.

Developing Strategic Thinking Skills

> Begin challenging your own assumptions. Your assumptions are your windows on the world. Scrub them off every once in awhile, or the light won't come in.
>
> **Alan Alda**

Developing strategic thinking skills helps security managers better meet challenges in an unpredictable future. Learning to think strategically often requires managers to think in new ways, especially those managers who have recently been promoted from frontline leadership ranks, where operational tactics and handling of the crisis of the day have become second nature. Strategic thinking requires something different. By taking the time and effort to learn strategic thinking skills, you can better serve your customers, employees, organization, community, and family as you think not only about what to do today, but what to do in the future to better serve their needs.

Strategic planning skills are more than just learning about the tools and methods of strategic planning such as SWOT (Strengths, Weaknesses, Opportunities, and Threats) analysis, environmental scans, value chains, and other available tools. Strategic planning also requires leaders who have strong business acumen, industry awareness, and broad business knowledge, a sense of best practices in the field, emerging trends, customer expertise, and more. In short, a security leader now needs an MBA-style skill set to survive and thrive. Our own observations on recent CSO promotions bear this out.

So how does one begin to develop strategic thinking skills as an individual? Many of us have lived in a world where our lives and careers have been formed by reactions to other events, and often they are events that just happen, not something planned. Strategic thinking is not the province of an ivory tower, the educated, or the highest tier of an organization. Strategic thinking skills are critical for everyone. They can be developed in a variety of ways; following are a few simple methods you can use.

Create Time for Thinking

This may sound trivial, but in our experience, lack of time for thinking is often a major obstacle for leaders, especially those who have come from tactical, action-oriented environments. Learning to set aside time both individually and corporately to think and plan is critical for developing strategic thinking skills. You can begin in small ways, by learning to include time for strategic thinking and planning as one of the resources required in other types of planning you already do. For instance, career planning, vacation planning, and home building or remodeling are all personal examples of strategic planning in action. Many managers already serve in community organizations—ranging from churches to Scouts to Little League—that need planning. Helping plan yearly schedules, personnel, and facilities requirements are all part of strategic planning.

As mentioned earlier in this chapter, delegation is an important method for freeing up time in your work environment for strategic thinking and planning. In our work with organizational leadership, time to think can be the single hardest piece to carve out of a demanding work schedule, and yet it can also be the most productive. Some choose an early morning workout as the time for their thinking; others use transit time in cars, planes, and the like. Make time as important a resource as money when it comes to developing your strategic thinking.

Scan

Strategic planning requires strategic data from multiple sources, including, industrial, governmental, occupational, global, and technological sources. It's important to build in multiple sources of big-picture information and new ideas to stimulate your own thinking about the work and world you inhabit. You will be doing the same job five years from now except for the books you read and the people you meet. Becoming and staying a continuous learner is a requirement for strategic planners of any stripe. Scanning and reading books, magazines, and online resources, and attending conferences all help develop critical thinking and critical reading. It is also important to read materials that are outside of your discipline so that you can develop wide-angle views and thinking.

Inquire

> Appreciative Inquiry was the catalyst for a positive step change in customer service at British Airways in North America. The use of Appreciative Inquiry transformed the entire organization in ways that we could not have imagined.
>
> **Dave Erich**
> *Executive Vice President, British Airways*

Curiosity about people, why they think the way they do, how things work, and what perspectives others bring can be most helpful in identifying your personal blind spots and learning new information to help in your planning. Peter Senge has well outlined how to develop inquiry skills in his seminal work, *Fifth Discipline: The Art and Practice of the Learning Organization*. Learning to use inquiry skills promotes your own personal development as well as facilitates your understanding of your own and others' mental models, which in turn help examine both the assumptions stemming from those mental models and the unintended consequences of those assumptions. Inquiry is a great skill to develop for precision questioning, for getting to the "5 Whys" of cause and effect for a given problem. The "5 Whys" are a basic problem-solving technique that was developed by the Toyota Production system in the 1970s. The strategy looks at any problem and asks "Why?" and "What caused the problem?" The first "why" often promotes a second "why," the second "why" a third, and so on, hence the technique's name. The focus of the technique is determining the root cause of a problem.

Another technique is Appreciative Inquiry, which has been defined by Cooperrider and Whitney as the cooperative search for the best in people, their organizations, and the world around them. It involves systematic discovery of what gives a system "life" when it is most effective and capable in economic, ecological, and human terms. Appreciative Inquiry involves the art and practice of asking questions that strengthen a system's capacity to heighten positive potential. It mobilizes inquiry through crafting an "unconditional positive question" often involving hundreds or sometimes thousands of people. Appeciative Inquiry is a way to find out what works in your organization. It is both a process and a philosophy. It's part of how leaders think in a "learning organization." Entire organizations like British Airways have used Appreciative Inquiry to transform the customer service aspects of their organization. It can be a great tool to stimulate change, galvanize employees, and discover "sacred organizational cows" that are impeding progress. Inquiry used well helps build communication throughout an organization.

Focus Long Distance/Practice Short Distance

> Perception is strong and sight weak. In strategy it is important to see distant things as if they were close and to take a distanced view of close things.
>
> **Miyamoto Musashi**
> *legendary Japanese swordsman*

Learn to see the future and imagine the changes required now to get there. A security leader needs the ability to look long and at the same time focus close. Typically, an organization's "global"

You see things; and you say "Why?" But I dream things that never were; and I say "Why not?"

George Bernard Shaw

strategic plan demands a security leader who can translate that global plan into implementation plans for the short term. Long-term strategic planning now has to turn into short-term strategic objectives that fit in budget categories; require disciplined execution, sound fiscal decision making, customer-focused solutions, a superior corporate culture; and maximize employee contributions, consistent service and product quality, and accurate talent acquisition and growth to support a long-term strategic direction. We will consider several different resources that help develop these skills as we review scenario planning and discuss futurist experts and others who help organizations bring future thinking into today's planning.

Anticipate

Only those who can see the invisible can accomplish the impossible!

Patrick Snow

In a customer-facing organization, it is important that all learn to anticipate customer needs. By doing that better than the competition, companies win contracts; by doing that with employees, leaders win productivity. If you want to grow a business, much less stay in business, you have to create a culture that learns to anticipate customer needs. Whether you call those customers clients, end users, consumers, internal customers, or something else, the bottom line is that security has customers. Determine who uses your products and services and learn to provide them better than anyone else by anticipating what your customers want from your organization. Then supply products and services with humility. It's easy to lose sight of the customer side of organizational life when part of what you supply is an enforcement function regarding security issues.

Communicate

The first key of communication is to practice open communication. Strategy requires collaboration. In turn, collaboration requires strong communication skills, listening skills, inquiry skills, and expressive skills. To have good strategy, every level of an organization must have the ability to be heard. Security leadership must model that behavior daily if you wish to get the best from your organization. Practice daily honest and open communication with employees. As in inquiry, the key is engaging employees at every level of your organization. Excellence can be happening anywhere in your organization; communication helps you find it, develop it, and keep it.

Security leadership must also be good at communicating with other business leaders in order to convey security priorities. Understanding and using the language of business is as important as understanding the business of security or the emerging technologies that impact the realm of security.

Evaluate

For every complex problem, there is a simple solution that is wrong.

George Bernard Shaw

Strategic planning requires continuous evaluation from cross-functional decisions, organizational performance to plan, to the overall effectiveness of a strategic plan. The Johnson and Sholes mode for evaluation is one method of performing evaluation. In this model, strategic options are measured against three criteria:

■ *Suitability (Would it work?)* Does this strategy make sense economically, organizationally, and environmentally? Can we leverage economies of scale, our experience, our capabilities, and our core competencies?

> You can have the best technology in the world, but without education, policy and ongoing testing, you haven't even started.
>
> **Dave Juitt**
> *CTO Bluesocket, Inc.*

■ *Feasibility (Can it be made to work?)* What resources will we need to get or develop?
■ *Acceptability (Will organizational members work it?)* What are the expectations of our stakeholders (employees, customers, suppliers, shareholders, etc.)? What is the potential risk involved? What are the consequences if we fail? What is the potential return? What will stakeholders gain? What will customers get? What will employees get? What will shareholders get? What is the possible range or reaction from stakeholders? What will customers think? What will employees think? What will shareholders think?

Each of the three criteria has a number of analysis tools that can be helpful in evaluating strategic options. Table 2.2 presents a sampling of possible evaluation tools.

Evaluation is a critical thinking skill for strategy. Creative thinking and critical thinking are both part of strategic planning. Often, leaders are predisposed to many types of critical thinking and are less familiar with creative thinking, but in order to play to win you must use them both.

Practice Flexibility

> Do not repeat the tactics which have gained you one victory, but let your methods be regulated by the infinite variety of circumstances.
>
> **Sun Tsu**

Strategic thinking about the future is not a straight line of planning from now until some point in the future. Learning to anticipate large shifts in future environments and potential responses will help keep you agile when the unexpected arises. Many formalized strategic models build multiple possibilities into strategic thinking such as scenario planning.

Table 2.2 Analysis Tool Criteria

Suitability	Feasibility	Acceptability
Prioritization or ranking of strategic options	Cash flow analysis	What-if analysis
Decision-trees	Forecasting	Stakeholder mapping
What-if analysis	Breakeven analysis	
	Resource deployment analysis	

Learning to discover and recognize your own mental models and explore them will also help you develop mental flexibility. Mind-sets can be like blinders that prevent you from seeing opportunities. A signal that you have just found an inflexible mental model occurs when something that is said stirs a strong emotional reaction in you. Learn to breathe deeply, and then examine the assumptions you are making about what was just said, the inferences you are making about the person who said it, and your usual reactions. When you listen well to what others think, feel, and observe—when you stretch past your own comfort zones—you begin to learn something new. Security can sometimes be about the inflexibility of requirements, strategic thinking, and imagination, and great communication requires the flexibility in ways of learning about yourself and others.

Conclusion

In this chapter we examined why strategic planning is essential for security groups, what strategic planning tools, models, and methods are available, when to do strategic planning, and what keys, myths, and barriers to strategic planning exist. In the following chapters we will examine more specifically what strategic elements should be considered in detail. When a strategic plan has been completed, the plan documentation typically contains the following elements:

- Definition of security (taking into consideration current and expected legal, regulatory, and business information security requirements)
- Explanation of why security is important and how security enables the business/organizational objectives (business strategy)
- Specific and clear benefits of an effective security management system
- Security objectives (goals) that are linked to primary business objectives
- A clear (or vivid) description of the desired security framework for integrating security into the organization in the future (one to five years)
- A description of how security objectives will be accomplished, who has the RAA (responsibilities, authority, and accountability) for each objective and how progress will be tracked and measured
- A brief description of overall information security risk posture and a brief overview of risk assessment results (and the major risks)
- Risk management strategy (risk tolerance)
- A description of known problems and issues regarding security management (and the current obstacles to effective security management)
- A description of trends in security and how they will impact the organization (and how the organization should adjust itself)
- Security outsourcing strategy (what should be kept in, what should be outsourced based on analysis of commodity versus unique current in-house processes)
- Implementation plan
- Communication plan
- Security awareness and training strategy for the organization
- Measures (metrics) or key performance indicators for monitoring the strategic plan
- Strategic plan review schedule
- A documented process for maintaining and updating strategic plans

In the next chapter we will look at methods for including the consumer voice in your strategic plans.

Chapter 3

Testing the Consumer

> If you want to be creative in your company, your career, your life, all it takes is one easy step...the extra one. When you encounter a familiar plan, you just ask one question, What ELSE could we do?
>
> **Dale Dauten**

Introduction

Security strategic plans impact every aspect of an organization because every business process and every person in the organization is subject to the security policies and practices (standards) adopted by the business. This includes employees, contracted

> A satisfied customer is the best business strategy of all.
>
> **Michael Leboeuf**

staff, partners, and suppliers, and extends to customers and shareholders as well. Understanding how security applies to each of these entities is essential to the formulation of an effective security strategy. Without the input and support of these consumers, the plan is doomed to failure before the first page is written.

Getting a handle on who are consumers of security services and products can be a bit daunting, especially when sorting through huge organizations that may have multiple sectors or business units spread around the globe. At the same time, new business realities require a more systemic look at the extended enterprise, the associated value systems, and the services and information being accessed. As business processes are streamlined, new security requirements emerge from internal customers, as well as external suppliers within the value system.

Other interesting challenges arise for security as both enterprise employees and customers accept more responsibility for security. An article published by Javelin Strategy and Research titled "Consumer Willingness to Share Responsibility for Security Allows Financial Institutions to Cut Losses and Increase Profitability" discusses a 2009 report titled "Understanding Consumer Willingness to Fight Fraud." The report states that consumers are not only willing to be involved in security, but also are actually eager to partner with banks and credit unions to protect themselves from fraudulent transactions. Mary Monahan, managing partner and research director at

Javelin, states, "Eight in ten consumers view security as a shared responsibility, and since more than half of all consumers choose a payment company based on safety from fraud, banks and vendors can use this to determine how to market their products more effectively." As we have stated in earlier chapters, security is now part of many businesses' organizational brand and requires careful management. In this chapter we will discuss how security groups can clarify, define, and prioritize consumer segments to better understand how to satisfy the multitude within an extended enterprise that interacts with the governance and service functions provided by security.

Definition of Consumer. In this book, we use the terms *consumer* and *customer* in a general sense. The terms refer to those external entities that purchase products or use services from the organization as a whole, as well as those external or internal entities that use the services of a business unit within the organization. Examples are business units that use security services and/ or products and are subject to security governance.

In the context of this chapter, we regard any party directly impacted by security strategy as a consumer of the security strategic plan. Parties that are not within the organization's security management purview are not customers but may be indirectly impacted by strategic plan requirements. For example, a service provider may be required to have a certain certification.

Defining the Consumer Buckets

Defining and prioritizing the consumer groups you are serving will help define the initial framework for the customer input portion of the security group's strategic plan. Security leadership can improve overall strategic decision making by including key consumer data in the analysis portion of strategic planning. By clearly defining your customer base, collecting key customer information, and analyzing it, the security group can incorporate quality customer input into their strategic planning efforts. Evaluating the extended enterprise to identify who will consume what part of the security's services, products, and governance helps create a clear understanding of who your customers are. Security's planning for creating customer value and satisfaction depends on a clear understanding of how the operational reality of security will apply to each element of the extended enterprise entity (i.e., operations, procurement, IT, enterprise customers, and suppliers). In this chapter, we will look at several enterprisewide approaches to capturing and analyzing customer data and the role that security may play in those enterprise efforts. We will also look at more immediate techniques for gathering customer information specifically for security.

We will also review the philosophies and tools of customer data analysis, discuss the challenges in utilizing that data, and examine some of the processes and methods that can be used to incorporate quality customer information into your strategic planning. We will also consider some of the questions that arise for the security practitioner engaged in customer data creation.

What Historic Issues Are We Trying to Resolve or Avoid?

By better understanding the enterprise-level approach to customer data and how a security group can utilize it to better understand the requirements of its own customers internal and external to the enterprise, security can help itself and the enterprise move toward a more successful future.

Too often the security group makes assumptions about its compliance role in an organization without taking into consideration the impact of its actions. The result is often unintended consequences in other parts of the system that greatly affect efficiency, productivity, and satisfaction with the overall system. The compliance role of security can become exceedingly egregious to other organizations without good communication between security and internal as well as external customer groups.

What Are the Challenges?

One thing is certain: Customer groups want security to do a better job of making the security management function transparent to the business processes it supports and to better control operational costs. This wish poses some significant challenges for any security group trying to maintain the safety and security of the enterprise, especially in light of the massive supply chain integration taking place as a result of a true global economy.

There are many approaches to acquiring and analyzing customer data, as well as recently developing trends. We will review two recent enterprise trends for achieving a better understanding of customers: Customer Value Management (CVM) and Customer Relationship Management (CRM) practices. CRM is the broader of the two approaches and is used by many enterprises that are involved in business-to-business (B2B) types of tranactions. On the one hand, CRM helps organizations better target a message to broad groups of people. CVM, on the other hand, creates tools that attempt to model the psychology of value to help an organization better understand why their clients buy from them. Both of these approaches to consumers at an enterprise level will have an impact on security domains for several reasons; first, much of the information generated in any of these domains must be kept secure; second, security is often a consideration in the customer-facing aspects of relations management; and third, IT functions are at the heart of creating and maintaining these systems. While CRM and CVM are actually processes, they are driven by the technology and software applications that allow them to be integrated into many different types of companies. As companies employ these practices, they impose additional demands and requirements on IT functions for implementation, maintenance, and security. Protecting the customer data generated and the overall business is crucial to the success of these applications.

> Customer service is not a department, it's an attitude.
>
> **Unknown**

Customer Relationship Management (CRM)

Another buzzword, especially in the information technology industry, has been Customer Relationship Management or CRM. CRM is a form of or subset of Enterprise Relationship Management (ERM). In *TQM* magazine in an article titled "Success in the Relationship Age: Building Quality Relationship Assets for Market Value Creation," Jeremy Galbreath (2002) describes ERM as a process or approach designed to harmonize and synergize the different types of relationships that a firm engages in so that the firm may better realize significant targeted business benefits. Lots of companies have built quite sophisticated CRM systems in the last decade or so, ranging from Starbucks, IBM, American Airlines, Blue Cross Health Care, and others. In addition, start-up companies are quickly adopting, adapting, and integrating CRM into their strategies.

Companies are now looking at how CRM can help make them more successful by providing an extensive customer information database that Sales, Marketing, Service, and other departments can use in a variety of ways to better serve the customer. CRM starts with a basic business policy focused on the customer and then redefines company policies, processes, and procedures based on understanding its current customer base, what satisfies them, and what it will take to attract new customers.

The theory is that changing your business model to a customer-centric one will help your company become more profitable by gathering customer data that helps you satisfy their needs. The security function is an important aspect of an enterprise that is moving in this direction. For instance, as company processes become more customer-centric, security can help a company avoid costly mistakes by providing security policies, processes, and control measures designed to ensure the confidentiality of customer data, including document-shredding requirements, clean desk/ locked cabinet policy, and customer data accountability for terminated employees.

Although CRM originally started as a category of software tools, this discipline has grown to include a companywide business strategy approach, including all customer-facing sectors of the greater enterprise. Implementation of CRM can dramatically impact the revenues and success of a company. A CRM approach changes the way marketing, sales forces, and customer service sectors do business through analytical capabilities integrated throughout these organizational groups. Software vendors such as Oracle, Microsoft, SAP, Amdocs, and Salesforce.com are designing CRM software and systems for the marketplace. A most notable trend has been the recent growth of tools delivered via the Web, particularly the development of cloud computing, which drastically reduces the costs of utilizing a CRM approach in small and medium companies. Companies like Google, Signals, Zoho, Dropbox, and MailBigFile are rapidly developing cloud services that allow business to save time and money in CRM applications.

In companies that are utilizing CRM data, it is important to have security policies in place before CRM is made fully functional. It is also important to create security policies for the customer that are clear, respectful, and nontechnical and provide easy access to help information. In a holistic approach to CRM, security will want to work with the entire value chain from subcontractors to the customer to ensure secure processes and seamless policies throughout the value chain.

In a recent Enterprise Security Today article titled "Protecting CRM Customer Data Requires Vigilance," Sanjeet Mall, a CRM architect at SAP, is quoted as saying, "Companies should consider the issue of CRM and customer data security critically important, and this is true for companies of all sizes.... Considering the regulations around customer information plus the value of keeping it secure, companies really need to think about security as part of a holistic IT governance strategy.... CRM is just one application, but customer data lives in many parts of an organization, typically connecting to ERP or financial systems, supplier management systems, or even living outside the company if in a CRM on-demand solution, and so on."

The lessons learned so far in companies that have begun to implement CRM are the need for a clear strategy, risk assessments, benefits analysis, and cost quantifications in these areas: processes, people, and technology. Poor planning, adoption, implementation, integration, and lack of a solution focus can create disappointing results.

Customer Value Management (CVM)

Many groups have been looking at Customer Value Management (CVM) as the next strategic step in better utilizing customer data. Companies are looking at how CVM can help their organization make better use of their CRM strategies and programs. The premise of CVM is that a company must develop the right strategy for attracting and keeping the right customers by providing better value for them than competitors can. This requires the entire company to focus on how it contributes to the market's perception of the value it creates for the customer. Companies also determine *which customers* have the highest value for them so that they can better manage the value they receive. It is important to remember that an organization has to create value in order to take value. This requires an understanding of the "Value Proposition" your organization is making to its customers. A Value Proposition is a clear summary of why a customer should use a product or service you offer. It is a tangible description of the business results you offer. When companies adopt a CVM approach, customer service becomes a portfolio rather than a ubiquitous and standardized service or product approach. This helps companies better manage the assets they have at their disposal to bring the greatest value to the organization. Metrics regarding CVM typically come from three sources:

1. Short-term cash flow
2. Long-term growth options
3. Risk management

To be useful, customer value data must be segmented by customer group, especially if the organization supports very different types of customers. Customer value has become a primary input for strategic planning, and is tied to operational plans and performance measures. Some best-practice organizations have also begun to tie customer value data to employee satisfaction, market share, revenue growth, and profits.

Recently, customer data collection and analysis has trended away from customer satisfaction-based metrics to customer value metrics. Customer satisfaction metrics are now a subset of customer value. Customer value data point to what customers value about your organization's products and services such as price, responsiveness, ease of use, and customer service.

Regardless of the methodology currently utilized by your security group, it is important to systematically evaluate who are your consumers, stakeholders, or customer groups. What value do you provide for them? How do you know what they value about your organization? What information do you have about them? How are you integrating that information into your strategic planning? How do you plan to get better information?

You can see that a CVM approach makes data a strategic company resource that helps them make better and more informed decisions. As customer data is accurately identified and ranked around customer characteristics and behaviors that have the highest impact, a company can leverage that data across the entire enterprise to decrease risk and increase profitability and customer value received.

When Should You Collect Consumer Data?

There are several critical junctures in the strategic planning cycle when customer input needs to be gathered and integrated into the overall strategic planning processes for a security group. The first critical juncture includes the following data points:

1. An analysis of the industry and market forces
2. A risk analysis of current and emerging risks
3. An analysis of the organization (i.e., a SWOT—Strengths, Weaknesses, Opportunities, and Threats—analysis)
4. Integration of feedback from stakeholder groups and program evaluations (customer groups are key stakeholders)

How and when this feedback is gathered will vary from organization to organization depending on the business sector, size, and organizational culture. Some examples of typical customer data that can be used in SWOT analysis or in customer satisfaction and loyalty efforts are as follows:

- Internal stakeholder feedback ranging from
  - self-assessment data
  - internal audit information
  - enterprise governance reports
  - financial control reports
  - customer value/satisfaction data
- External stakeholder feedback ranging from
  - external government reports, evaluations, and audits
  - independent third-party audits, evaluations, reports

Regardless of whether your organization utilizes CRM, ERM, CVM, or similar methodologies and associated technologies to help manage consumer data, security groups will do well to include consumer, customer, and end-user data (however they may be defined) as important arbiters of both strategic direction and measures of the success of strategic initiative implementation. Consumer feedback should be included throughout the life cycle of any security service, product, or governance role. In the next section of this chapter, we will discuss some basic methods for collecting consumer data in day-to-day organizational life.

Quick Customer Assessment

Methods for testing ideas, services, and product lines on your customers to identify applicable strategy elements are numerous, ranging from electronic surveys, focus groups, in-depth interviews, hallway conversations, letters, phone calls, hosted conversations, dialogue sessions, and more. Although online surveys are the easiest and most economical method of getting data, they will not serve all security assessment needs.

When developing customer value surveys, it is important to capture data that goes beyond typical satisfaction levels and captures behavioral expectations. Feedback surveys should focus on behavior or product characteristics that create value in the eyes of your customers (either internal or external). Metrics should get at the specifics that help your organization create value, including flexibility of service provision, resolution speed, ability to solve the unexpected security issue, or other key factors that help your organization distinguish its services.

While getting consumers specific feedback is important in understanding what helps achieve customer satisfaction, today's competitive environments require even more. In most cases, consumer expectations increase, not decrease. It is important to be getting data that helps you move toward where customer satisfaction levels are moving. Continuing in ongoing conversation with internal and external customers is an important method of understanding where those expectations are and where they might be going next.

Managing Key Internal Relationships

In cases where there are long-held barriers between your security group and other parts of the organization, a facilitated dialogue session, in which you spend more time listening to their issues and working on ways to move forward together and coming to agreements that will impact your strategic plan, may be quite powerful in mending organizational fences. Often, these types of conversations may require the skills of an external consultant or facilitator. A meaningful conversation can go a long way toward helping the security group's brand and garnering missing cooperation from other groups. This effort can be especially difficult when security groups have become overly entrenched in their positions and stovepiped in their reporting structures. A good security leader will find a way to begin the dialogue and continue toward cooperative principles. Peter Senge and colleagues' *Fifth Discipline Fieldbook* outlines many good strategies and tools for working toward dialogue in the "team learning" section.

Conducting Face-to-Face Interviews

In some instances, taking a consulting approach is the best way to collect data and begin the process of co-creating a security strategy for a customer group either internal or external to the organization. We have both been participants in formal and informal interviews with selected customer group executive leadership. Sometimes these interviews have included subset groupings of the selected group to get a good cross section of data from multiple perspectives at once. This methodology can take considerable time, especially if the interviewees are strung across the globe and have typically tight executive schedules. Patience and lots of rescheduling will serve one well. The prize is getting to spend time listening directly to key customers give you very crucial information about how your security group is doing in their estimation and what more they would like to see. The information gathered in a face-to-face interview can be much more valuable than an e-mail or electronic survey (both of which can also be important data points.) One of the keys in learning to use customer feedback is thinking about it as a continual process, not an isolated series of events.

Guidelines for How to Solicit Feedback

There are many useful guidelines to consider while getting customer/consumer feedback.

1. **Don't waste the customer's time or inconvenience customers.** Some customer groups are constantly surveyed and/or audited electronically by multiple groups, asking similar questions, with no coordination and less follow-up. If you are part of a large organization, the chances of this occurring increase greatly. Sometimes getting multiple internal groups to begin coordinating electronic surveys and/or audits can be a strategic action item in itself that reduces cost, increases productivity, and improves data collected.

   Not wasting the customer's time holds especially true when scheduling personal interviews. Send your questions ahead of the interview, don't expect that customers will read them, and always take an extra copy of the questions to the interview itself for their use. Let your customer lead the conversation if needed, and stick to the time frame requested, unless the interviewee grants you more time because he or she has more to say. Always follow up with a thank you for the interviewee's time and information.

2. **Make sure you understand what the customer is trying to tell you.** Follow up on responses when you are unsure of what the customer meant. Sometimes customers have difficulty finding the words to describe their experience, and other times you just need more data to accurately understand what they are trying to tell you.

3. **Don't make promises you can't keep.** It is important to underpromise and overdeliver. If you tell customers that you will follow up with them, follow up with them in the agreed-upon time frame. It is important that you let your stakeholders know what data you are collecting, how you intend to collect them, what the results are, and what you plan to do with those results. Remember, a good brand is a promise kept.

4. **Give your customers enough time to understand what you are asking and time to reflect on their response.** Not all of us are able to deliver opinions instantaneously when asked. Some prefer a thoughtful approach and take time to think and craft a careful response. Whatever method you choose to gather feedback, give respondents ample time to reflect.

5. **Listen, listen, listen.** (This can be very difficult when you have an irate customer, especially one who has a head of steam.) Active listening is an act of respect. Good listening takes patience, focus, and practice. Inquiry and listening skills are crucial for getting beneath the surface of feedback, particularly in group formats.

6. **Follow up in a timely manner.** This is true in general when collecting customer information, but it is especially true with information gathered from employees (internal customers). One of the biggest complaints regarding employee surveys is that the employees seldom see any action from the feedback given, or the feedback loop is years later, long after they have forgotten what their input was. Worse yet is doing nothing with the feedback, in which case as the customers watch for action and see none, they lose any confidence that their input matters. It's better to not gather feedback at all than to gather it and do nothing with it.

Designing Customer Feedback Surveys

The steps in designing feedback surveys are fairly straightforward. However, there are three prerequisites you should satisfy before you move forward with another survey. First, determine what type of survey makes the most sense given the strategic requirements for the data. Second, determine whether you need external help with the survey design and implementation. Third, get buy-in from the organizational groups to be surveyed. Once you are satisfied you have met these conditions, proceed to the following steps:

1. **Determine goals for survey.** What customer groups should be included in the survey? Are there any noncustomers that should be part of the survey? Will you use a "War Room" approach, online conference, focus group, interview sessions, and the like, or a combination of these methods to gather, review, and communicate results? Who will determine the content of the survey?

2. **Choose the method and tools.** Determine what the best methods are to identify the key factors in your customer service that distinguish your organization from the competition. What method will help you understand the **customer rating** of that factor? What analytical tools and methodologies are most helpful in analyzing the data? How will major groups who use this data act on the results? How will the information be integrated into strategic planning and/or operational business plans? How will the results be translated into operational measures that help line personnel drive improvements? What method will you use to link customer data to business results? What best practices and organizational standards already exist for making a survey?

3. **Write survey questions.** Once you have decided on the objectives of the survey or interview, decide what question types will best measure the customer data you have decided to collect. Typically, a survey will contain a variety of open and closed questions or response questions with a Likert-type rating included. Keep questions easy to answer. In an increasingly global environment, consider those respondents with English as a second or third language. Will you need to have translated versions of the survey? Layout, scale, length, and open-ended questions are important details to consider when implementing a customer or employee survey. Watch out for leading or biased questions:

> *Leading Question:* "Do you like the convenience of our online security clearance application system?"
> *Less Leading Question:* "Has our online security clearance application system met your needs?"

4. **Test the survey on a beta customer group.** Engage a group with whom you already have a good relationship, preferably a local one so that it's easy to follow up on the results. Writing questions is an art; it's very difficult to get a single set of questions that can be used universally. Different customer groups and job roles often require asking different questions. Look for gaps in the information you collect and adjust the survey accordingly.

Online Survey Guidelines

Using an online survey tool can save a lot of time. It not only tracks who has participated but also captures and compiles the answers for easy analysis. However, there are some caveats you need to consider. First, there's the **technology aspect**: Does everything work properly? Can you access the survey from multiple browsers? Do all the links work? Getting someone to take a survey is a victory that will quickly turn to defeat if the site doesn't function correctly. Second is the **question of usability**: Is the website easy to use? Are the survey instructions clear? Is everything in the right place and easy to navigate? Participants are likely to quit before completing the survey if the site is difficult, confusing, or frustrating to use. The final question is **content**: Have you proofed all the materials well? Not only is it embarrassing to have participants correct your spelling and grammar errors, but it's even worse if those errors skew the results.

Focus Group Guidelines

Focus groups can improve the richness of your results because they provide an opportunity not only to capture the answers you seek but also to understand the passions, experiences, and skepticisms behind those answers. When conducting focus group meetings (either online or face to face), you will need to consider the following: Who should attend? It's important to get a broad set of perspectives. Inviting people from a diverse mixture of job functions across the customer group is one way to accomplish this but be cognizant of manager-managed relationships. People are less likely to share openly in the presence of their management. Second, how will the meeting be orchestrated? Will a moderator script be required, or will the meeting use a facilitated dialog? Finally, how will session content be captured? Will the session be recorded or will notes be taken? Good notes are critical to understanding the results and are also useful for facilitating further discussion among participants.

Surveys are a viable way to collect customer inputs, but they follow the 80–20 rule: Do a good job designing, constructing, and testing your survey before you deploy. Get external help if you need it. Find some friendly local groups to help with the beta testing. After you have conducted one or more sessions, evaluate your results, tweak your methodology, incorporate all the lessons learned, and deploy. Remember, you only get one shot, so make it a victory!

Deploying a Survey

A survey may be deployed online, by paper, in person, on the telephone, through cyber technologies, or a combination of methods. They may be conducted by an external group or through in-house means. A key consideration is the cycle time required for deployment, data collection, analysis, and feedback to surveyed groups. The longer the cycle time, the less meaningful will be the results. Another consideration is how you kick off the survey: You can be low key, or you can create a large organizational kickoff.

Measuring Customer Satisfaction Results

Results should be compiled into a final report that includes the method, results, and recommendations from the survey. Carefully preplanning your reporting strategy will help you get the most out of your survey. Typically, there are several levels of reporting, ranging from an executive summary to a general report to customized reports for specific groups. The target of any survey is getting and reporting recommendations out of the data that helps leadership change the organization.

Although the results of one survey can be helpful, it is even more important to develop and conduct ongoing tracking of customer satisfaction to monitor improvements and manage overall satisfaction. Let's face it: Customer satisfaction is an economic imperative in today's intensely competitive, rapidly changing, highly complex business environment. Becoming customer-centric is more important now than at any time in the past. Customer satisfaction is an important aspect of quality measurement and requires daily management of your service with a focus on "learning from customers." In order to do this effectively, an organization needs to establish a baseline set of data on customer satisfaction, identify specific areas of poor performance and sources of customer dissatisfaction, as well as sources of customer value. Lack of customer satisfaction equals risk, and risk equals possible loss in customer loyalty and (ultimately) profit. Security groups must retain and use valuable information about their consumer to enhance their business strategies and product and service offerings. Those organizations that actively manage customer value and satisfaction are leading their security group forward toward success.

Integration of Consumer Data

> Do you mind if I list people, assets and maybe reputation before all the zeros and ones? It's a damn shame that [security] professionals with their heads screwed on straight failed to include the whole landscape of security metrics in their leadership model from the get-go.
>
> **Anonymous**

In today's information economy, with its rapid changes and continuous technological innovations and evolutions, the speed with which a group can analyze and integrate meaningful consumer metrics is part of the competitive landscape. There are many challenges as companies must integrate customer data across multiple sales channels, like brick and mortar, e-commerce, catalogs, and telephones into one unified view of the customer. Another function that has developed is the use of "customer hubs." Customer hubs allow companies to combine data cleansing, matching, and management with integrated stewardship and administration. Further exacerbating these challenges is the constant restructuring and strategic mergers of companies, which combine and recombine different service groups with multiple information systems and datasets, while creating constant changes in operational processes. One of our colleagues was recently talking with someone involved in the early days of Starbucks' CRM implementation about the challenges he had to overcome in order to produce usable data from multiple sources and databases; data that eventually made its way into executive reports and that ultimately impacted Starbucks' stock price.

Despite these challenges, the demand for better use of consumer data is increasing. Good consumer data-management practices require a strong infrastructure of support, including network, storage, data backup, communications linkages, and high-speed connectivity. As the technology shifts toward better collection of data, so do the staff technology skill requirements and abilities to manage the data. It's important to adhere to the information management basics, notably:

■ Identify existing and potential issues in managing consumer information.
■ Define the method of consumer information flow.
■ Develop and retain people with skills in information technology.
■ Integrate legacy enterprise applications with the front end of the information management system.
■ Evaluate and redesign functional activities on value added to consumer.
■ Align performance metrics to redesigned processes.
■ Align metrics with specific individual RAA (responsibilities, authority, and accountability) for monitoring.

The goal of designing strong infrastructure, training staff, and aligning metrics is, of course, to enable, align, and motivate internal customers and to create a customer-centric approach in all organizational processes. As with any strategic initiative that requires major change, it is the employee frontline that will put the strategy into effective action. It is management's job to provide the leadership, infrastructure, and training required to move the organization toward success.

Although IT leaders seem to be the ones leading the metrics charge in the definition of security metrics databases, we contend that this should be an interdisciplinary effort between both IT and physical security elements. Metrics should be developed for all aspects of security from IT security to the various physical security elements such as investigations, workplace violence, emergency notification, emergency response, disaster preparedness, business continuity, supply chain security, and incident reporting of various types; metrics that reflect the needs of local and global security constituencies and their various stakeholders.

A discussion in "The Metrics Quest," an article written in the November 2004 *CSO Security Leader* newsletter by an anonymous security executive, cited the following lessons learned:

■ Engage your internal business unit clients in identifying one or two metrics vital to their success. Consider loss reduction (be specific), cost reductions, shorter cycle times, use of technology versus use of people, elimination of vulnerabilities that impact uptime, reliability, and so on.

■ Recognize that risk analysis is a must. If you aren't doing risk analysis, we assume you are looking for a job. These projects offer a potential wealth of metrics and bolster your recommendations to corporate leaders.

■ Identify incident trends important to key senior managers. Track changes monthly or quarterly. Focus on what's important in your business. Consider safety violations, workplace violence, public safety, emergency medical technician response times, issues that invite regulatory sanctions, losses as a percentage of sales, number of employees who are subjects of business-conduct investigations.

■ Develop a few value indicators that you can track with a high degree of reliability. Candidates: security's cost per employee, cost as a percentage of sales or revenue, property protection cost per square foot of occupied space, case cost versus recovery cost, and case cost over time. Also, do some services cost benchmarking with your peers. These metrics tend to be more comparative in nature, so make sure you are comparing apples to apples.

■ Set up a security council to develop metrics goals if security functions are spread among various departments.

■ Develop a couple of confidence indicators, such as annual customer satisfaction surveys posted on your corporate intranet. Or track business process improvement recommendations, made in incident postmortems, to see which are accepted and which are rejected.

■ Build your annual business plan around two or three "reach objectives" that have at their heart a specific measurement such as "in the next fiscal year, reduce background investigation cycle time by 15% and case cost by 5%."

■ Lastly, keep it simple and check your numbers.

The bottom line for developing metrics is that you must develop metrics that matter to your customers. Obviously, the top tier of customers you must satisfy are the C-Suite executives, and knowledge of what matters most to them should figure strongly in creating security metrics that are meaningful to everyone in your company.

Conclusion

Gone are the days when service and governance groups could settle for little or no measures of consumer or customer satisfaction. Today's business and economic realities demand that groups go beyond measuring a baseline of "customer satisfaction" made of ill-defined, poorly administered, and limited evaluations of customer data. In the Internet Age of "click-the-button" expectations, security must also collect consumer data in an effective and a timely manner. Quick response and satisfaction of consumer needs are now basic. Today, a drop in customer satisfaction indicates a loss of confidence by the customer in the organization and leads to a subsequent gain for your competitor. Anticipating and understanding consumer needs and designing your security services to "delight the customer" are now part of your job. Keeping your customer in mind in everything you do is now "job one." As enterprises move toward increasing customer-centric business models, it becomes increasingly imperative for security that all groups in the security group be involved and aligned in customer-centric strategies.

Chapter 4

Strategic Framework (Inputs to Strategic Planning)

There is a slightly odd notion in business today that things are moving so fast that strategy becomes an obsolete idea. That all you need is to be flexible or adaptable. Or as the current vocabulary puts it "agile." This is a mistake. You cannot substitute agility for strategy. If you do not develop a strategy of your own, you become a part of someone else's strategy. You, in fact, become reactive to external circumstances. The absence of strategy is fine, if you don't care where you're going.

Alvin Toffler

Introduction

In Chapter 3 we discussed the tools and methods used for gathering, analyzing, and reporting data from security consumers or customers. In this chapter we consider how the information gathered from our consumers should be integrated into a commonly understood framework for strategic planners. Often that framework is created by conducting an overall environmental scan.

This chapter is about identifying and understanding the basic inputs that are critical to creating the mental framework for strategic planning. The inputs we discuss help ensure that your future security program will meet the needs and expectations of the organization you support. These inputs are the elements of organizational planning and the principal inputs for all strategic activity. A typical security strategy is a plan to mitigate risks while complying with legal, statutory, contractual, and internally developed requirements. But a security strategy resides inside an organizational strategy that may have very different drivers than a security strategic plan. In order for the two strategic plans to align and work well together, there must be a clear understanding of both plans and clear links between them that are well understood throughout the greater enterprise.

Learning to conduct external and internal environmental analysis helps prepare a security group for strategic planning. From our perspective, security is an organizational problem that must be framed and solved in the context of the enterprise's strategic drivers, which are derived from a thorough environmental scan. From the combination of internal and external analysis, the *prioritized data* can be filtered through a SWOT matrix to further refine the potential strategic direction.

In this chapter, we will review the environmental scan (see Figure 4.1) and the following inputs:

- Regulatory and legal influences
- Industry standards
- Marketplace and customer base
- Organizational culture
- National and international requirements (political and economic)
- Competitive intelligence
- Business intelligence
- Technology environment and culture
- Determination of business drivers

As the environmental scan considers each arena, prioritized business drivers will emerge that help determine an organization's future direction. We will also discuss the need to be future oriented in day-to-day security operations.

Environmental Scan

What business strategy is all about (what distinguishes it from all other kinds of business planning) is, in a word, competitive advantage. Without competitors there would be no need for strategy, for the sole purpose of strategic planning is to enable the company to gain, as efficiently as possible, a sustainable edge over its competitors.

Kenichi Ohmae

An environmental scan is basically collecting information about environmental characteristics. Organizational scanning is crucial to organizational survival. Good environmental scanning

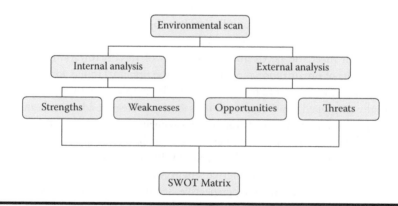

Figure 4.1   Environmental scan.

practices help an organization adapt to its environment. In terms of organizations and strategic planning, an environmental scan involves considering the factors that will influence the direction and goals of the organization. An environmental scan includes consideration of both present and future factors that might affect the organization since strategic planning is for the future, not just the present. Environmental scanning often refers just to the macro environment, but we will consider it from its broader perspective and include industry, competitor analysis, marketing research (consumer analysis), technology trends including new product development (product innovations), and the company's internal environment.

The importance of environmental information depends on the degree to which the success of the organization is dependent on its environment. In the business literature, the organization's dependency on its environment is referred to as perceived environmental uncertainty (PEU). Gordon and Narayanan (1984) identified factors that determine PEU. These factors include the

> Look for what's missing. Many advisors can tell a president how to improve what is proposed or what's going amiss. Few are able to see what isn't there.
>
> **Donald Rumsfeld**

nature of the society, economic stability, legal stability, political constraints, and the nature of the industry, the customer base, and the organization. We will consider several elements of PEU later in this chapter.

An environmental scan is the gathering and analysis of factors impacting the strategic direction and goals of the organization in which you work. This includes both the current as-is conditions and the possible future states of the environment. The environmental scan should include **external** factors such as markets (both current and potential), demographics, technology trends, market trends and predictions, government regulations, or pending legislation likely to impact your organization, as well as elements from the **internal** environment such as current architecture, infrastructure, personnel, organizational structure, and assets. The scan should include what, if anything, is needed to accomplish proposed strategic plans and objectives (see the Technical Environment and Culture section of this chapter). Business drivers can be determined and prioritized after conducting a thorough environmental scan.

Environmental scans should be conducted by groups or individuals over a specified period of time prior to strategic planning work. Scans can take many different forms ranging from Bill Gates's ensconcing himself in a secluded hideaway to review white papers written throughout the year by Microsoft employees to a dedicated team that performs a thorough environmental scan, generates a market trend report, creates future (vision) white papers, does scenarios planning, and so on.

An element or subset of an environmental scan may be a **competitive analysis** that looks at your organization's strengths and weaknesses in relation to those of the competitors in that market space. The ultimate goal is to leverage your strengths and minimize your weaknesses to more effectively compete in your selected market space. This information should be included in a typical SWOT analysis for the organization. Although an environmental scan helps gather the information needed, a SWOT analysis sorts the information and prioritizes it for inclusion in strategic planning. In the following segments of this chapter, we examine the major arenas security groups should include when conducting an environmental scan.

Regulations and Legal Environment

> In some ways, with the security challenges this country has faced, we have had to put in rules and regulations for business to be able to sustain their growth and create jobs.
>
> **Wayne Allard**

Obviously, this arena is tremendously important for anyone working in the security sector. The legal and regulatory arena is usually one of the primary business drivers for security groups engaged in strategic planning, as exemplified by Microsoft's troubles early on in this arena in both the United States and Europe or Google's more recent issues within China. The hand of regulation has grown heavier each year as lawmakers continue to underscore the importance of security by enacting new laws and regulations. A security group is bound to uphold and abide by the policies, laws, and regulations found in this arena. In many organizations, tracking this constantly changing set of compliance requirements is a full-time job for the legal department, IT security, physical security, and organizational leadership.

In the past decade, worldwide governmental changes in data security, privacy, and information management statutes and regulations have been continuous. Enforcement has become a major challenge for compliance and security operations. Many security groups are subject to an increasing number of audits from numerous external agencies without any additional budget to support those efforts. Outsourcing is also impacting compliance requirements. Keeping current with proposed legislation that will impact your industry and having strategic plans in place to absorb those impacts are critical to the responsiveness and flexibility of a security group.

A close examination of your organization's internal audit process can also help provide needed corrections in internal processes and procedures that regulate compliance. In order to leverage internal audit processes for needed corrections to security controls and processes, it is necessary to be able to define for the internal audit team what constitutes an effective security control or process, and to determine which controls and processes are under security's governance. Too often, we have seen audit findings relayed to security for correction where the control or process in question is outside the purview of the security group (i.e., rightly belonging in another organization). To fully understand the drivers for internal audit, be sure to analyze the statutory, regulatory, industry, business partner, and external audit requirements as well. These will give you additional insight into the components of your organization that are shaped or influenced by compliance. A thorough understanding of the regulatory and legal environment will provide better data for analysis and the determination of the business drivers for security. Another important arena for consideration in an environmental scan is that of industry standards.

Industry Standards

Any time you sincerely want to make a change, the first thing you must do is to raise your standards.

Anthony Robbins

Customer demands create standards in every industry. There seems to be a perpetual flow of changing industry standards. One of the fields where standards are changing rapidly is, of course, the IT industry. We now have higher standards for bandwidth, power, performance, reliability, flexibility, integration, connectivity, real-time solutions, energy efficiency, and security. Standards in industry after industry are changing at increasing speeds driven largely by the development of new technology. Even so, standards typically lag technology developments by at least a generation.

Hold yourself responsible for a higher standard than anybody else expects of you.

Henry Ward Beecher

We need to include industry or business partner regulations as potential inputs to environmental scans as well. Many organizations are subject to industry-specific regulations, for example, health care and Health Insurance Portability and Accountability Act (HIPAA) or financials and 12 CFR 208.61 (Code of Federal Regulations for banks in the U.S. Federal Reserve System). Some business partnerships may also be subject to specific regulations; for example, if you supply components to a partner that manufactures military equipment, your organization may be subject to International Traffic in Arms Regulations (ITAR). If you are a global supplier, perhaps ISO 27001 is a required standard. The International Standards Organization's (ISO) 27001 is an example of a widely recognized security standard that sets the international standards in business continuity planning, system access control, system development and maintenance, physical and environmental security, compliance, personnel, security group, computer and network management, asset classification, and control and security policy. The American National Standards Institute (ANSI) is an example of a national nonprofit organization that oversees the creation, promulgation, and use of thousands of norms and guidelines that directly impact businesses in nearly every sector.

There are similar standards groups that shape, create, and enforce standards for each type of security discipline from IT to every aspect of physical security. As in government regulation, all of these elements must be considered in order to build an effective security strategy. Most industries have external associations and other support organizations you can use (e.g., the American Bankers Association) to identify existing standards and the minimum requirements for the industry.

There are also benchmarking standards that may drive strategic security initiatives for competitive reasons. It is important to determine the business-sensitive processes in the industry value chain in order to better understand which industry standards are most relevant for the enterprise. Business-sensitive processes are where the organization you support generates revenue and value to your customers. By understanding these processes, the security group will be able to better identify the security requirements and vulnerabilities associated with each business process. If you don't understand your industry's value chain, or even know what a value chain is, then you definitely need to get a handle on the value chain concept because it is a major part of the business environment you are supporting.

A *value chain* is a basic analysis of an industry or business to identify the activities the organization engages in to develop competitive advantage and create value for the organization. Those value-generating activities are what are defined as a value chain. Michael Porter in his seminal work, *Competitive Advantage: Creating and Sustaining Superior Performance*, introduced a generic value chain model (Figure 4.2) that captures a sequence of activities that are common across a broad range of firms.

The value chain model is used as an analysis tool to determine the core competencies that enable an organization to achieve a competitive advantage. A competitive advantage can be achieved through efficiency, differentiation, and/or market focus. Organizations use this tool to analyze business unit interrelationships and find opportunities for synergy, process improvements, and cost reduction. Once core competencies are determined, many firms will source other activities in the value chain and focus on the core competencies that provide a competitive advantage. As firms streamline their own value chain, they often begin to look at additional opportunities in

Figure 4.2   Value chain.

coordinating upstream and downstream value chains with suppliers, partners, distribution channels, and customers into what Porter called a *value system*. Many retailers, automakers, petrochemical companies, and others have become masters at managing large value chains and systems.

Value chain analysis has been used to create dynamic systemic change in industry after industry over the past few decades. This analysis is typically part of an organizational strategic plan that can affect many organizational strategic initiatives that the security group must subsequently support. It is essential for security professionals to understand the value chains and systems that their organizations support. You must be able to recognize and plan for the security challenges that may arise as your organization moves into or expands its extended enterprise or value system. Understanding external agency industry standards (such as auditing functions) and how they impact the organizational value chain is equally important. Often, industry benchmarks have already been established and these often become metric targets for the success of one or more strategic security initiatives.

An industry benchmark, for instance, may be the average length of time that it takes a security clearance to make it through a government clearance process. If the industry standard is 18 months between clearance application and the granting of a clearance, and a competitor has found a consistent methodology that moves that average cycle time to 6 to 8 months, a security group must well consider making a 6- to 8-month cycle time their new benchmark for a strategic initiative. The obvious reasoning behind moving beyond the industry standard in this case is the productivity efficiency goals of the business unit the clearance process is serving. The reduction of cycle time for a clearance by almost by two-thirds is a significant increase in productivity.

Another example of industry standards that impact a security group are changes to statutory and regulatory requirements for suppliers. Security procedures may have to become more integrated throughout the industry global value chain as various legislative bodies change requirements in certain industries. An example is the requirements regarding controlled technical data for any supplier that provides services for the U.S. (or any other country's) defense industry. Staying abreast of the regulations and finding creative solutions to conduct business across multiple cultures, legal systems, and businesses grows ever more challenging. As firms continually move into global systems, the challenges for security to think globally and systemically also increase. Many industry groups, alliances, and vendors help craft solutions for increasingly complex requirements.

Industry standards often lag behind what is occurring in the marketplace, as we have often seen in the past with e-commerce standards, cloud computing, and social networking site, to name just a few. When this occurs, security groups must use their own resourcefulness to find answers to emerging technology questions such as, "What do I need to make my system sufficiently reliable and secure?" "Who can I trust to tell me what standards are required?" "What are the minimum security requirements?" "Where are the current best-practice benchmarks?" As time passes, industry standard security metrics become more available as various groups and agencies begin to provide increasingly specific requirements.

In any security group's strategic plan, industry standards are an important arena for consideration. The tensions between enterprise business drivers and security business drivers will become more explicit as they are examined in light of regulations and legal environments, industry standards, and the expectations of the marketplace. For instance, there have been "brutal standardization" requirements for cloud-based IT infrastructure and management for companies that either work in the government sector or supply information to it. The tension is driven by user expectations of governmental organizations to provide timely service and information, while enterprise architecture and conflicting governmental standards and requirements lag behind consumer demand. Thorough investigation will help you better form your strategic plan to support the enterprise environment in which your security group operates. Next, we will examine an important part of the overall value chain system, the marketplace–customer base of an organization.

Marketplace–Customer Base

The most beneficial type of partnering you can engage in is partnering with your customers. The benefits are compelling. You use it to gain customers, protect them from predation by competitors, and to protect your profit margins.

Curtis E. Sahakian
Managing Director, Corporate Partnering Institute

Security services have both internal and external customers. In the past, security often was regarded as a compliance or governance organization, and its organizational life took place behind closed doors. The demands of organizational life in the 21st century have pretty much ended that role except for some still very cloistered domains such as investigations and executive protection.

Today security groups face the same financial targets as other members of the organization: pressure to reduce costs, outsource functions, and do a better job managing their business. Internal customers are starting to ask the hard questions, "What have you done for me lately?" "Are you managing your service like a well-run business function?" "Do the benefits you provide compel me into partnership?"

The question facing security is the same one facing many other organizational functions. "Are we a prime deliverer of security services, or are we moving toward a security services-integrator business model for the delivery of security services and products?" Organizations have answered this question in three different ways.

1. In-house security model
2. Security services-integrator
3. All security services outsourced

You retain the responsibility for all security services if you operate in the in-house model for security services. This, of course includes maintaining customer satisfaction. As a security services-integrator, an organization provides some security services and manages all contracted security services for the enterprise. A security services-integrator has responsibility for establishing contract terms and conditions, as well as establishing and tracking all the performance metrics required to monitor and supervise contractors. Finally, all security services may be outsourced to obtain greater expertise and a greater range of services, or to decrease cost. Should security services be outsourced, the institution retains the same responsibilities for security as if those services were performed in-house.

The outsourcing of some or all security services can be a very painful change for a security group, involving a number of major paradigm shifts, process reengineering, risk reassessments, loss of in-house expertise, and so on. Once internal security functions are outsourced, security leadership must carefully manage the transition with good communication about the reasons for the change, the future skills sets that will be needed (and those that won't), changes to policies and standards, and any new processes (e.g., a new security help desk).

By reviewing customer data and determining who your customers are, what they value, and what their needs are, you can better position your group to meet or exceed those customer needs. This helps you focus on business drivers and strategic objectives that matter.

> We only have two sources of competitive advantage:
> 1. The ability to learn more about our customers than our competition.
> 2. The ability to turn learning into action faster than our competition.
>
> **Jack Welch**
> *former CEO, General Electric*

Organizational Culture

> The greatest change in corporate culture—and the way business is being conducted— may be the accelerated growth of relationships based...on partnership.
>
> **Peter F. Drucker**

Determining the organizational culture in a security group, the business units it serves, and the greater organization as a whole can be quite helpful in every phase of strategic planning. Carefully analyzing cultural norms can help provide clues to successful deployment of strategic planning. Cultures can vary widely from group to group in an organization. For instance, a security group may serve one group that has a very structured, process-driven, inflexible, hierarchical risk-averse organization, while another group is loose knit, entrepreneurial, globally savvy, flexible, informal, and cutting edge. Moving forward with successful security implementation is going to require different strategies in each culture, as a one-size-fits-all approach will seldom be successful. By analyzing and understanding the ways the constituents of the organization interact and how they engage each other, the security program can be tapered to gain acceptance in an organization and thereby function more effectively.

This particular input to strategic planning is especially crucial for newly arrived security leaders to an organization, even more so if they come from an entirely different sector, for example, from the federal government to commercial business. Learning to understand an organizational culture that is in place is absolutely essential in providing strategic direction and leadership, especially if that direction is going to be new and different. We have personally witnessed newly hired executives quickly lose traction in a new organization because they did not take the time to understand the new culture, and it was never long before they moved on or retired.

Another organizational nexus important for learning about a group's culture is in mergers, acquisitions, and/or reorganizations that now include the resulting mix of different organizations as part of the same group. Even with seasoned leadership in place, many missteps can occur when a strategic plan is put into action without the leaders first garnering a keen cultural understanding.

Another pivot point for understanding cultural differences may involve plumbing or delving into an existing organization for employee descriptors of their current culture. Security leadership can also benefit from soliciting from employees descriptors of the organizational culture that the employees would like to be part of. The organizational values held, behaviors exhibited, and shared mental models and beliefs are key to understanding a group's culture. We have found individual and group surveys and interviews to be helpful in gathering this kind of information. To get an idea about corporate culture, listen to what people both inside and outside say about the culture. Corporate culture is created by the way people speak to each other and treat each other and their customers.

Of course, we would be remiss if we did not mention knowing the culture of potential competitors and other significant organizational threats such as the forces of industrial espionage, cyber criminals, and hackers in general. Understanding the culture and ways of potential threats is imperative for good strategy. The reader will find many examples of utilizing cultural knowledge of potential threats in the tactical chapters of this book.

> We cannot enter into informed alliances until we are acquainted with the designs of our neighbors and the plans of our adversaries. When entering enemy territory, in order to lead your army, you must know the face of the country—its mountains and forests, its pitfalls and precipices, its marshes and swamps. Without local guides, you are unable to turn to your account the natural advantages to be obtained from the land. Without local guides, your enemy employs the land as a weapon against you.
>
> **Sun Tzu**

National and International Requirements (Political and Economic)

> Indeed, to some extent it has always been necessary and proper for man, in his thinking, to divide things up; if we tried to deal with the whole of reality at once, we would be swamped. However when this mode of thought is applied more broadly to man's notion of himself and the whole world in which he lives (i.e., in his world-view) then man ceases to regard the resultant divisions as merely useful or convenient and begins to see and experience himself and this world as actually constituted of separately existing fragments. What is needed is a relativistic theory, to give up altogether the notion that the world is constituted of basic objects or building blocks. Rather one has to view the world in terms of universal flux of events and processes.
>
> **David Bohm**

Many business drivers for security are the product of national and international requirements. It is critical to identify and understand the inputs relevant to your industry in order to build a strategy and security program properly balanced between risk reduction and efficient operations. Much of the external regulatory environment, external audit environment, and political climate of your organization must be factored into your determinations in this arena.

The security requirements that arise from national and international requirements are tremendously varied and in various states of flux depending on the industry and global regions in which you function. Some industry groups like aerospace have long-standing organizations in both national and international segments that provide guidelines, requirements, and regulations that will be input into security strategic plans.

Some international standards have been evolving in place for some time and have created well-recognized standards for organizations such as ISO, which was discussed in the Industry Standards portion of this chapter as well. Other arenas have emerging voices such as a new forum for multi-stakeholder new policy dialogue, the Internet Governance Forum (IGF), or the World Wide Web Consortium (W3W), which is the international standards organization for the World Wide Web, or the nonprofit public benefit corporation, the Internet Corporation for Assigned Names and Numbers (ICANN). ICANN is a not-for-profit public-benefit corporation with participants from all over the world dedicated to keeping the Internet secure, stable, and interoperable.

Often, the key to newly emerging standards groups that may impact an organization is early participation to affect informed change within that standards organization.

Another nexus point for strategic planning is taking into account changing international security standards as a national organization moves into additional international domains for distribution of their products and/or services. Depending on the scope of the service or product that will become internationally distributed and supported, the international requirements complexity factor can be exponentially increased to the point of taking years to decipher all the additional requirements.

In each of these instances, keeping abreast of potential changing national and international policy dynamics, participating in the policy dialogue where possible, and including potential and emerging requirements in the input for strategic planning are important considerations for any strategic effort.

Competitive Intelligence

> It is now absolutely possible to decide to abandon traditional sources of information like subscriptions, journals, closed databases and the like, and focus entirely on getting *all* of your information for free from the Internet, *all* of the time from the Internet.
>
> **Marydee Ojala**
> *Social Media for Competitive Intelligence Seminar*

Another rich arena for data that may be included in an environmental scan is **competitive intelligence (CI).** The Society of Competitive Intelligence Professionals (SCIP) defines competitive intelligence as

> a systematic and ethical program for gathering, analyzing, and managing external information that can affect your company's plans, decisions, and operations.
>
> Put another way, CI is the process of enhancing marketplace competitiveness through a greater—yet unequivocally ethical—understanding of a firm's competitors and the competitive environment.
>
> Specifically, it is the legal collection and analysis of information regarding the capabilities, vulnerabilities, and intentions of business competitors, conducted by using information databases and other "open sources" and through ethical inquiry. SCIP's members conduct CI for large and small companies, providing management with early warning of changes in the competitive landscape. CI enables senior managers in companies of all sizes to make informed decisions about everything from marketing, R&D, and investing tactics, to long-term business strategies. Effective CI is a continuous process involving the legal and ethical collection of information, analysis that doesn't avoid unwelcome conclusions, and controlled dissemination of actionable intelligence to decision makers.

In essence, CI is the disciplined process of gathering and analyzing data in order to help business leaders make more informed business decisions. CI is gathered to determine the risks and opportunities within a marketplace before they are obvious to the average observer.

Many multinational and global companies have been engaged in CI gathering now for decades. Petrochemical companies, pharmaceutical companies, and manufacturing groups have long created their own CI units to protect against threats and market changes, as well as look for opportunities. The question for an organization that engages in this type of intelligence gathering is, "Do we perform this in-house, hire consultants, or do a combination?"

Both large and small businesses engage in regular and ongoing CI in order to make the right market decisions, have viewer surprises, and help put competitive data in context. Small business that can't afford to hire outside consultants or don't have full-time staff devoted to CI analysis will often collect data informally from media such as newspapers, television, and the Internet, other businesspeople, competitors' staff, and competitors' customers or clients.

Security groups are often required to focus protection efforts on thwarting illegal attempts at CI like industrial espionage or theft of intellectual property. However, *legal* CI gathering and analysis have become a cornerstone of strategic planning.

Business Intelligence

> Collecting information about customers is relatively easy. Analyzing customer information for potential cross-sells, increased revenue streams, and improved service is more challenging. But getting the information to the front line in a timely manner and thus providing further competitive edge is proving increasingly difficult for many corporations.
>
> **Gerry Davis**

Business intelligence (BI) is another term used for a similar type of information gathering from a field of industry, and it may even be considered a core competency in some companies. BI is the systemic analysis of historical, present, and predictive trends of business operations of your own organization, whereas competitive intelligence focuses more on external data from other companies and doesn't necessarily rely on the same type of rigorous technology-based analytical processes used in BI. BI helps organizations obtain a better view and understanding of potential business trends to determine whether they are opportunities or threats. A good BI system helps an organization to take action from a systemic data context. Many consulting companies, Microsoft, SAS, IBM, Business Intelligence.com, and others, have existing products and services that can assist organizations who wish to apply business intelligence analytics.

Technical Environment and Culture

> If you think technology can solve your security problems, then you don't understand the problems and you don't understand the technology.
>
> **Bruce Schneier**

Increasingly, security is seen as a technology-driven function in many organizations. Technology solutions are one of the "silver bullets" from which many security promises are made. Many security groups have a natural affinity for technology and have spent their careers mastering the ability to ride the next wave of

> Technology is dominated by two types of people: those who understand what they do not manage and those who manage what they do not understand.
>
> **Archibald Putt**

technological solutions. Yet, security professionals are well aware that organizational security does not result from technical infrastructure alone. The security of an organization's assets requires that all organizational employees work together to ensure a secure organization. Security issues are business issues, not just technology issues, and should be framed as such. Moving an organization from a compliance-based security model to a holistic model requires changes not only in technology, but also in the processes, people, and organization itself.

That being said, it is still important to review the technology arena for input into an environmental scan. The key is to not overemphasize the importance of technology in how the rest of the organization perceives security problems. There are two major areas to consider in looking at the technology arena: the technical environment (present and future) and the technical culture(s) of an organization. The **technical environment** of the present is a survey of the infrastructure of deployed technologies in place organizationally. A survey helps identify what systems are in place, the level of sophistication of those systems, legacy systems that will need to be updated or replaced, and so on. In a large and complex organization, this task can be a daunting one, for hundreds of thousands of assets may need to be identified. This type of survey will often require security to coordinate multiple departments to get an accurate assessment. There is also the question of "right" technology. Does what we are doing now make any sense? Are we really providing value for the enterprise? Careful analysis of customer requirements and the benefits provided will help inform future technology decisions.

A future survey helps identify what technologies are likely to be employed, should be employed, have convergence implications for security, and/or what potential cost/savings implications will accompany those technologies. The **technical culture(s)** input is more a look at specific organizational subcultures that have developed as a result of supporting various technologies. This can be extremely important later in strategic planning as communication and solutions are devised for determining how best to accommodate those subgroups.

As increasing numbers of organizations begin to move toward more systemic approaches to security, the technology drivers also began to shift. In a purely compliance environment, technology reviews tend to remain a functional security responsibility. The focus may be on increasing surveillance equipment and the like for security personnel to better monitor control access points and information systems and to observe the behaviors of individuals on or adjacent to company sites.

As an organization moves toward a "commitment focus" for security, the technology requirements begin to shift as well. Technology is now evaluated for alignment with strategic objectives around likely reduced impact or disruption to organizational work flow, cost effectiveness, reliability, and consistency. When technology changes are made, they are widely communicated through the workforce in order to create a greater willingness to accept and use new technology. Consideration is given to how security technology will impact the entire value chain system of the extended enterprise. This requires designing technology systems and processes that create secure but easy access to relevant information by all partners, suppliers, and customers.

An environmental scan typically includes all of the arenas we have considered so far in its internal and external analysis. From the arenas of regulatory and legal influences, industry standards, marketplace and customer data, organizational culture influences, national and international inputs, and technology infrastructure come the determination of business drivers. The forces that are primary business drivers for an enterprise versus the security group may differ somewhat, but it is important to understand both sets in order to effectively determine a strategic plan for moving your organization forward.

Business Drivers

> [Strategy is] a mental tapestry of changing intentions for harmonizing and focusing our efforts as a basis for realizing some aim or purpose in an unfolding and often unforeseen world of many bewildering events and many contending interests. [Its aim was] to improve our ability to shape and adapt to unfolding circumstances, so that we (as individuals or as groups or as a culture or as a nation-state) can survive on our own terms.
>
> **John R. Boyd**

Business drivers are external or internal influences (such as market forces) that significantly impact and/or set direction for programs, business, or organizations. They are typically the forces that "drive" your business forward.

Business drivers help frame the validation of organizational mission and confirmation of business objectives (augmented by stakeholder analysis); hot issues are identified, and key performance indicators and critical success factors are identified. These in turn help define specific business objectives, provide a sense of urgency and motivation, and create guiding principles and expectations of employees for successful implementation of the changes required.

The identification and understanding of business drivers is crucial to adapting a security function to the organization it supports. In any organization a key set of factors will drive it forward. Different organizations will have different drivers depending on the market or customer space they serve. In business the questions asked are, "What makes us money?" "Where does the profit come from?" "What are the key 'drivers' that make us money?" "What business are we really in?" The Sherwood Applied Business Architecture (SABSA) model is one of the strategic planning frameworks that can greatly assist a security group in determining a security view of the world. The SABSA methodology is most helpful in strategic planning.

Successful management of security requires understanding the enterprise's strategic drivers for two reasons. Strategic drivers can provide **advantages** or **conflicts** with a security group's strategic plan. As you link and align your own plan to the enterprise strategic plan, some of the enterprise strategic drivers will inevitably conflict with those of security. An enterprise is looking for ways to ensure profitability and productivity, while a security group is inevitably concerned about managing organizational risk. Because of the ever-increasing use of technology, global market factors, and the changing dynamics of the extended enterprise, it is even more difficult to keep security activities and strategic drivers aligned with those of an enterprise. The natural tension between quick response to an ever more demanding marketplace and the careful planning required to manage enterprise risk presents security leadership significant challenges. Today's security leaders must be up to the challenge and able to overcome barriers.

Business drivers may be prioritized by importance, impact, or requirements that will influence the organization in question. A high-priority business driver will typically require a strategic response from an organization in its planning, which in turn may foster one or more strategic initiatives. There is not a one-for-one correlation between business drivers and strategic responses, or between strategic responses and strategic initiatives. A strategic response may address more than one driver. For example, business drivers might be globalization and further penetration of electronic trading in a sector of business. This driver requires a strategic response such as bolstering market data and analysis. The response in turn drives multiple strategic initiatives such as enhancing electronic trading tools and improving data capacity and transaction costs (but you don't improve costs; rather, you lower, control, accept them, etc.).

The Tower Group chose IT security as one of the top 10 business drivers in 2009 for the banking industry. The other nine drivers in the Tower Report were the current economic environment, regulatory change and compliance, competitive threats, changing customer preferences, revenue growth, operational efficiency, business growth and competition, customer loss/dissatisfaction, and fraud and financial crime. According to Tower analysts, the examples of potential strategic technology initiatives arising from the IT security driver in 2009 included:

■ Upgrade of loan processing modification collections/foreclosure processing
■ Modification of systems to deploy new processes for compliance
■ Improvement of analytics and performance management
■ Automation and streamlining of processes and employment of Software as a Service (SaaS)
■ Outsourcing and consolidation of systems
■ Support for improved fraud detection and risk analysis
■ Improvement of data access controls and data tracking; expanded use of encryption

In addition, the Tower Report pointed out the need for banking institutions to develop a more sophisticated understanding of enterprise performance metrics and drivers to better comply with current regulations as well as new regulatory requirements.

Business drivers are an important input for any strategic plans developed by a security group. The challenge for a security professional is to try to find the right balance between protecting enterprise assets and processes while, at the same time, enabling the enterprise to do business.

After the organization has reviewed and prioritized its business drivers, it is important for the security group to gain a clear understanding of the primary business drivers because these provide the impetus for strategic security program initiatives. By clearly understanding the business drivers, the security group gains additional insights into the motivations and expectations of its stakeholders, which in turn help tune the security program's short-term objectives. In today's litigious environment, here are some possible current business drivers at an extended enterprise level.

Business Drivers for the Enterprise

1. Legal liability (today so much is driven by who can sue you)
2. Emerging regulations from multiple sectors (e.g., international, national, industry)
3. Fear (of the public, enterprise stakeholders, economic uncertainties, etc.)
4. Brand value
5. IT (certainly a business driver as cited by the Tower Report)
6. IT, a partner with innovation
7. Increases in risk while companies transit to new technology

It's not difficult to see that security business drivers and initiatives must be clearly articulated and linked to enterprise drivers. As security's role in business continues to evolve and change, becoming a risk manager and trusted adviser to the executive suite of an enterprise is crucial to maintaining security leadership longevity. Security's strategy must map clearly and logically to the extended enterprise.

The most important thing I've learned since becoming CEO is context. It's how your company fits in with the world and how you respond to it.

Jeffrey Immelt

So far in this chapter we have reviewed how an environmental analysis (which reviews regulatory and legal influences, industry standards, marketplace and customer data, organizational culture influences, national and international inputs, and technology infrastructure) helps inform the internal and external analysis process required for good strategic planning. From this analysis an organization can determine its best sense of business drivers.

These tools can also be helpful to nonprofit organizations. While nonprofits may not compete for market space, they do compete for everything from volunteers' time, dollars, and work that similar charitable organizations are doing. We have found environmental scans to be quite useful in planning for churches, missions, and various nonprofit organizations.

Additional Environmental Scan Resources

In addition to conducting your own environmental scan analysis, you may find additional help from outside services in formulating your overall data gathering and analysis required for strategic planning. Many outside agencies and consultant groups will gladly assist you in your work. The following section presents a few examples of such services that may prove beneficial.

Benchmarking is very popular today—but companies benchmark the wrong thing. They benchmark what other companies do, when they should be benchmarking how those companies think.

Unknown

Benchmarking is a way to evaluate the efficiency and effectiveness of your organization by comparing your services to those of similar organizations in your business sector. Executive management utilizes benchmarking data to identify opportunities for operational cost reduction. Security services may already be included in those benchmarking reports. Benchmarking IT and corporate security services can be beneficial for improving internal security processes, finding ways to reduce cost, and improving efficiency in internally provided services, including guard services, reception, parking management, alarm services and CCTV, monitoring, personnel badging, search dog handlers, and so on.

A number of groups can help you with this process. For example, Shared Services Benchmarking Association (SSBA) conducts benchmarking studies to identify practices that improve the overall operations of their members. SSBA™ offers free membership for the employees of any group that manages shared services for a corporation. The SSBA is part of the Benchmarking Network, Inc., which is an international resource for business process research and metrics. Groups like this provide many kinds of benchmarking resources from industry standards to studies, reports, interest group roundtables, benchmark training, and more. You will find benchmarking associations in nearly every industry that will also be beneficial in building business expertise. Professional benchmarking associations present many opportunities for networking, educational opportunities, and as industry support.

Benchmarking yourself against other security services helps determine how efficiently you are providing security services and identifies places where you might gain efficiency by adopting industry "best practices." Benchmarking provides the data to answer questions such as: "Are we above or below average in our costs, our cycle time, quality of services, and customer satisfaction metrics?" "Can I explain to management why our security position is right or needs to be changed?" "Do we have a strategy in place to move us where we need to be?" Remember: Your competition for security services is also getting smarter, faster, and better connected globally. They aim to change the way the security industry does business. Are you leading or following?

Scenario Planning

Thinking through [scenario] stories, and talking in depth about their implications, brings each person's unspoken assumptions about the future to the surface. Scenarios are thus the most powerful vehicles I know for challenging our 'mental models' about the world and lifting the 'blinders' that limit our creativity and resourcefulness.

Peter Schwartz

Scenario planning is an approach to strategic planning that considers frameworks from multiple perspectives, with a focus toward building multiple paths toward the future. This approach formulates plans or prepares appropriate responses to probable future trends and events. The plans produced usually cover a range from best-case to worst-case probabilities. Many organizations use it to make flexible long-term plans. Scenario strategic planning has been in the toolbox of strategic thinkers for five decades now. Through determining key driving forces, prioritizing those forces by potential organizational impact, selecting possible scenarios, analyzing selected scenario environments, and constantly monitoring key environmental factors, scenario planning helps strategic planners determine which scenarios are the most adaptive to emerging realities.

When an organization utilizes scenario planning, an environmental scan is done, and several key external forces are selected. Planners imagine changes in the environment as those forces move along a continuum and adapt strategic issues and goals that might arise as the environment changes around an organization—for example, changes in regulatory environments and technology development. For each significant change in force along those selected key issues, a planning group develops organizational scenarios for best case, okay/neutral case, and worst case. Planners then look at alternative strategies for the organization over the next three to five years to adapt to each of the scenarios chosen.

Scenario planning takes each strategy within the scope framed by key issues selected, defines the key stakeholder, gathers information, analyzes trends, and looks at possible forces and critical uncertainties in each of the selected scenarios. From these a "framework" is created for each of the possible scenarios chosen. Typically, a scenario is continuously tested by modeling and/or analysis, as the actual path of unfolding events is monitored for key indicators to adjust scenario plans.

Scenario planning helps organizations to better handle sudden shifts in reality whether technological, regulatory, cultural, economic, or otherwise, through the development of multiple strategies. Scenario planning can give organizational stakeholders a better understanding of potential risks and improve organizational responsiveness to future development. By considering a wider range of strategic options, an organization can be more nimble and flexible in responding to unfolding events. Testing potential scenarios also helps the robustness of strategic plans. In the converging world of security, scenario planning provides a combination of creative and critical thinking skills, as well as convergent and divergent possibilities, while considering the advantages and disadvantages of both.

The difficulty, or hard work, of scenario planning is determining the critical factors or driving forces. As scenario planning has evolved, the move has been from the selection of two key forces (i.e., a two-dimensional framework, for example, one based on regulatory environment and openness to markets) to models that now utilize multidimensional frameworks. Regardless of which method you might choose in scenario planning, many of the same challenges remain in utilizing scenarios, notably:

1. Developing strong senior management support for utilizing scenario planning. (Organizational cultures can be extremely resistant to new forms of strategic planning. Scenario planning, if conducted correctly, should challenge and change organizational assumptions about the future, which often creates organizational discomfort and resistance.)
2. Adapting scenario planning to the decreasing planning cycle times required in organizational environment. (You will find benchmarking associations in nearly every industry that will also be beneficial in building business expertise. Professional benchmarking associations present many opportunities for networking, educational opportunities, and industry support.)
3. Keeping consideration broad in determining the probability of scenario in initial discussions.
4. Determining key driving force factors, major forces/minor forces.
5. Crafting detailed and compelling stories for each scenario.
6. Linking scenarios to tactical actions. (Each scenario requires specific strategies associated with organizational action.)

Scenario planning helps determine potential frameworks for differing versions of the future. Scenario planning can help an organization move more quickly and nimbly in rapidly changing environments.

> There is nothing more difficult...than to take the lead in the introduction of a new order of things.
>
> **Niccolo Machiavelli**

Futurist Consultant Services

The role of a futurist (and anyone can be one)—is to honor the past, inhabit the present (notice what's going on now) and engage the future—to be involved in a process of stimulating our friends and our loved ones and even strangers to getting the grips with the fact that the future itself is a race between self-discovery and self-destruction.

Richard Neville

Another method of envisioning future developments that will potentially impact your organization is hiring futurist consultant services. We aren't talking about crystal balls, psychic hotlines, or other types of star gazing, but thoughtful consultant services that help an organization imagine and move toward a desired future. These types of services are quite useful for developing think tank sessions to identify important areas of exploration for an enterprise and then providing methodologies for

> (Futurists focus) in any of three areas:
>
> 1. Forecasting the future, using quantitative and qualitative means,
> 2. Imagining the future, using primarily intuition and writing skills, and
> 3. Creating the future, using techniques of planning and consulting.
>
> **Glen Hiemstra**
> *Futurist*

in-depth exploration of future events, trends, and developments. From this focused exploration and analysis, the organization can then develop strategic priorities, initiatives, and strategic plans. Futurist consultant services can greatly assist an organization in scenario planning as well.

Regardless of whose services you employ in your efforts or whether you choose to create your strategic plans from largely internal resources, the key to good strategic planning is to remain forward looking in day-to-day activities as a security leader.

Blue Ocean Strategy versus Red Ocean Strategy

Why join the navy if you can be a pirate?

Steve Jobs

Blue Ocean strategy, developed by W. Chan Kim and Renée Mauborgne of INSEAD, an international business school, is an approach to strategic planning through the metaphors of Blue and Red Ocean strategies. These strategies are approaches to the marketing universe. Red Ocean strategy refers to a competitive model of approaching the market, which has specific and defined boundaries in which groups compete. As the market grows smaller with increasing competition, eventually competitors battle it out, turning the oceans red. In contrast, Blue Ocean strategy approaches strategy from a more exploratory set of assumptions in which market space is shaped or created and is therefore "uncontested." Competition is much less relevant, as the game of marketing has not yet been shaped in Blue Ocean strategies. The course that must be set in Blue Ocean strategy is that of "value innovation." Strategies must create value for both the consumer and the enterprise through innovation. The Blue Ocean approach is critical of Michael Porter's approach, which produces low-cost providers or niche players in the market. Blue Ocean's creators maintain that by using their approach you can create both value and low cost across market segments.

A whole set of tools have been created for companies utilizing this approach to strategy, such as Strategy Canvas, the Tipping-Point Leadership approach, and the Four Actions framework (Table 4.1). Many of these tools existed in previous strategic planning methods and are employed by those who use Six Sigma Practitioners and other strategic management approaches.

Table 4.1 Strategic Planning Tools

Basic Tools of Blue Ocean Strategy	*Frameworks/Methodologies Applicable to Strategy Execution*
The Strategy Canvas	Tipping-Point Leadership approach
The Four Actions framework	Four Organizational Hurdles framework
Eliminate-Reduce-Raise-Create	Kingpins approach, Fishbowl management, atomization
Grid	Hot spots, cold spots, and consigliere approach
The initial litmus test for Blue Ocean Strategy: focus, divergence, compelling tagline	3 E Principles of Fair Process

Source: Vector Study.

Additional tools/methodologies/frameworks for strategy formulation are as follows:

- The Six Paths framework
- The sequence of the Blue Ocean strategy
- The buyer utility map
- The buyer experience cycle
- The profit model of the Blue Ocean strategy
- The price corridor of the mass model
- Four-Step Visualizing Strategy Process
- Pioneer-Migratory Settler Map
- Three Tiers of Noncustomers framework

Companies that have used Blue Ocean strategy frameworks include Southwest Airlines, Netjets, Cirque du Soleil, Home Depot, Nintendo's Wii, and China Mobile. The critics of this approach to strategy (and there are many) maintain that even a Blue Ocean approach to strategy is overly simplistic and will eventually turn red. The challenge remains to be the first to sail into a new Blue Ocean strategy, which is basically a get-there-first with the most creativity approach.

Future (the Need to Be Forward Looking)

> Neither a wise man nor a brave man lies down on the tracks of history to wait for the train of the future to run over him.
>
> **Dwight D. Eisenhower**

Clearly, strategic planning has to be forward looking in design, even though many of the inputs into strategic planning are datasets from the past (i.e., risk management metrics, forecast budgets, already determined infrastructure requirements, enacted policies, customer requirements). And yet, strategic planning requires a visionary mind-set that anticipates and prepares for possible futures. This synthesis of past data and insight into the political, economic, technological, regulatory, and human resource realms that are driving change require a continual kind of conjecturing or reframing of possibilities.

A future-oriented security group may seem like a bit of a conundrum to normal organizational perception of security. It has been our collective experience that occasionally security leadership has underdeveloped strategic planning skills. Even

> I skate to where the puck is going to be not where it has been.
>
> **Wayne Gretzky**

where this might be true, security leadership may still be making informal strategic decisions that are not always clearly understood or communicated to the rest of the organization. When this occurs, often the organizational leadership's resulting actions toward security are less than desirable. Conversely, when security leadership has a clear sense of the future and their strategic plan is well integrated to organizational strategic goals and objectives, and they meet organizational expectations and fiscal targets, then security leadership is well regarded as an important member of the leadership team.

Many of the latest discussions about the role of security leadership in magazines like *CSO* refer to the changes required for CSO, CIO, and CISO roles in many companies. The days are past when a technical expertise regarding security is enough to successfully lead a security group. As the security field has matured, organizational expectations for leadership skills in security now include increased focus on risk management, expanded knowledge of ever-expanding policy and regulatory requirements, and increasing business savvy regarding the organization.

Conclusion

Strategic planning is hard work and requires time, knowledge, practice, and skill to master. The challenges it presents are many. When security groups engage regularly in strategic planning, they can create robust plans by considering the frameworks we have just reviewed. In the distillation process of determining key business drivers, conducting a vital environmental scan, reviewing internal and external business requirements, and gaining a firm understanding of these arenas, a strategic planning group can provide a basis for detailed planning as well as better explain the business to others to help inform, motivate, and involve them in a well-developed security strategic plan. Security can become more than a business problem to be solved. Security can become a business core competency that helps enable the business and creates organizational resiliency to market vicissitudes.

Understanding the framework inputs to strategic planning forms the cornerstone of strategy. The critical success factors for framework implementation are:

- Using a business-driven strategic planning methodology
- Showing clear vision and planning
- Having committed management support and sponsorship
- Possessing strong data management skills
- Using quality sources of data
- Mapping the solutions to the organizational requirements
- Creating a robust framework
- Determining and prioritizing key business drivers both at the enterprise level and for a security group itself (they may be in conflict)

Some things cannot be spoken or discovered until we have been stuck, incapacitated, or blown off course for awhile. Plain sailing is pleasant, but you are not going to explore many unknown realms that way.

David Whyte

Chapter 5

Developing a Strategic Planning Process

Strategic Planning is a process by which we can envision the future and develop the necessary procedures and operations to influence and achieve that future.

Clark Crouch

How fast can you plan? Strategic planning as a process isn't that complex. However, in a ready-aim-fire, culture it's not easy to do. One person's template is another person's track over the edge. Just read the reviews of any strategic planning book and try to find consistent agreement about its efficacy and usefulness. We've watched a strategic planning process that makes perfect sense to an IT security professional absolutely lose every single other security leader in the room. The IT professional had worked for a year with the entire security group and, yet they abandoned the planning process wholesale because it was too IT and technical. The strategic planning process didn't make sense to the heads of the other departments, and most of them hadn't had much experience in strategic planning. As the security group continued on without much strategic direction and even less fiduciary accountability, soon strategic direction was imposed by the new vice president of the division. After a long and difficult year, the department as a whole began to master the art of strategic planning. Within a couple of years, strategic planning grew easier for the entire security department even as targets got more difficult to achieve. Practice, focus, and a basic strategic planning model go a long way toward garnering enterprise support for a security group.

In this chapter we will review the basics of most strategic planning processes from getting ready to plan to planning itself and the implementation of a strategic plan. In a larger enterprise, a security group's strategic plan will be informed by a number of other strategic processes going on in the extended enterprise. Often a security group's strategic plan must be integrated with:

1. Enterprise strategic plans
2. Business units' strategic plans
3. Functional strategic plans (as in the case of security being part of a shared services group)

4. Operational strategic plans (including LEAN, Six Sigma, and Quality programs)
5. Technology strategic plans (including IT, physical security, and cloud services)
6. Other types of strategic plans such as business

A security group must be mindful of what other strategic processes going on around them are likely to influence the framework of their own planning. They may also manage at least two of their own strategic plans simultaneously. Typically, an organization will manage at least two strategic planning cycles at the same time. For example, as one planning cycle is completed, another has typically begun, so elements of a security group may be engaged in the final tracking of the implementation phase of one strategic plan while simultaneously preparing for the beginning of another strategic planning cycle. No one said strategic planning is easy! However, the strategic planning process becomes simpler with practice and more seamless between strategy formulation and implementation.

Before you get started on strategic planning and engage a planning group, you should consider several important questions:

1. Who are the appropriate people who need to engage in the planning effort?
2. Are the right stakeholders from both the internal organization and external enterprise involved in the strategic planning process?
3. Are the executives who need to be involved in this strategic process informed and knowledgeable about the process and the organization?
4. Who has the RAA (responsibilities, accountability, and authority) for the strategic plan? (The RAA should include the final completion of the plan, the process for completing the plan, and the plan itself.)
5. Who will get the plan when it is complete?
6. Who are our enterprise champions, sponsors, and the like?
7. What constraints do we have around the planning process? (Time, personnel, resources, information, etc.)
8. What other bigger picture (extended enterprise strategic plans) do we need to align to or be aware of?
9. Is our present strategic plan relevant?
10. What are the roadblocks and barriers for strategic planning?
11. What are key success factors for us in planning?
12. What collaboration tools and/or technology do we have access to that can facilitate planning efforts?

Once you have developed clear answers to these questions, your team is ready to begin. Before we begin our discussion of the overall strategic planning process, let's review some of the basic responsibilities that should be assigned prior to beginning a strategic planning process.

Roles and Responsibilities

There are many levels of roles and responsibilities to consider in strategic planning. The first is who is responsible for the plan to plan, facilitating the plan, participating in the plan, stakeholders, and so on. Typically, the RAA for that level should be detailed in one of the planning documents for strategic planning. That document typically presents the steps or stages of the planning process itself and states who has responsibility for it. Those responsible vary from facilitator to the board of directors, various executives, and internal planning staff. Several committees and subcommittees may also be part of the RAA documents. Often there may be an executive sponsor for various segments of the strategic planning as well. The typical stages included in a document that outlines the RAA are as follows:

1. Preparation to plan
2. Review and revision of vision/mission/values, and so on
3. Data gathering for input to planning
4. Development of the plan's framework
5. Creation of a strategic plan
6. Refinement of the strategic plan (possible "catch-ball" process)
7. Reviews of the strategic plan
8. Approval of the strategic plan
9. Communication of the strategic plan
10. Predetermined reviews against the plan
11. End-of-the-year performance to plan

During the strategic planning process outside facilitators, coaches, outside stakeholder reviews, independent third parties, various internal stakeholders, and outside experts of various kinds may deliver both input or specific RAAs. A roles and responsibilities document will help you track who is responsible for which elements as you proceed through a planning cycle.

Several industry groups like Toyota, Hewlett-Packard, and Bank of America include another step in their systemic approach to strategic planning. Planning methods such as Hoshin Planning developed by Dr. Yoji Akao will also use a "catch-ball" phase of the planning process that allows the middle management groups to actively interact with senior management in order to create a much more robust and practical strategic plan by further capturing and cementing strategic goals into organizational reality. This additional stage of the process will create more revision cycles as a strategic plan is integrated further down into the actual implementation segments of the organization. The Hoshin Planning process can work quite well with the balanced scorecard approach and is a method that further focuses an entire organization on a single goal.

Process and Procedures

The process and procedures may vary depending on the method of planning you choose, the size and type of your organization, and the culture of the organization in which you work. However, there remain some consistent guidelines in any planning process, notably:

- Before you start, be clear about the process, methods, and materials you will need and produce.
- Have full and active executive support.
- Have strong employee involvement.
- Be consistent and thorough in your planning, analysis, and implementation.
- Communicate your plan well to all stakeholder groups.

Organizations are like people in regards to strategic planning. Both individuals and organizations who engage in regular strategic planning are more successful in achieving their goals and success. If you want a frame for your organization's short-term budgets and financial goals, if you want employees to have a stronger sense of security regarding the organization's future direction and goals, if you want needed change and growth, if you want better control of operational problems, and better communications and relationships within and without your organization—then develop strong strategic planning skills and use them.

Get Ready to Plan for a Plan

Over our careers we have found wide variations in groups' experiences with strategic planning, their ability to plan, and the results of that planning. Our experience ranges from groups that had given up on strategic planning (because of bad experiences using complicated strategic planning models) to groups working in well-trained teams that were quite comfortable with strategic planning (and had developed detailed processes that delivered quantifiable results and a strong reputation within the organization).

> If you ask managers what they do, they will most likely tell you that they plan, organize, coordinate and control. Then watch what they do. Don't be surprised if you can't relate what you see to those four words.
>
> **Henry Mintzberg**

Henry Mintzberg in his book *The Rise and Fall of Strategic Planning* wrote that leaders, managers, and companies have adopted methods of deciding what to do and how to implement them without considering the fundamental assumptions and experiences with those methods. He cites three fallacies that have arisen about strategic planning:

1. Discontinuities can be predicted.
2. Strategists can be detached from the operations of the organization.
3. The process of strategy-making itself can be formalized.

Mintzberg goes on to argue that strategic thinking should be encouraged in general throughout the organization and that without involvement in the strategic process it is difficult to be connected with a strategic direction. His point is that in many formal strategic processes there is an inability to react quickly to sudden exogenous shocks. When strategists are too detached from operations, they create plans that are not linked into the important processes of an organization, which will have limited impact. When a strategic planning group is too formal, it is removed from the organization, increasing the chance of office politics, detachment from employees, and lack of potential insights that reside in other parts of the organization. Like much of the quality movement, Mintzberg argues that strategic planning cannot be done well without the involvement of line management.

Another important element of Mintzberg's discussion is the type of strategic intents created in planning. Typically, the strategic literature refers to two types of strategies: deliberate and unrealized. Deliberate strategies have to do with the strategic intents that have been realized by an organization, whereas unrealized strategies are those that were planned but not realized. A third type of strategy that Mintzberg encourages organizations to develop is called emergent strategies. These strategies usually happen outside of a published plan, but they are not necessarily bad strategies. The question is how can strategic planning better incorporate the learning from emergent strategies instead of ignoring them or trying to cover them up because they don't fall inside the scope of deliberate planning?

Regardless of the formality or informality of the method your organization employs in strategic planning, the important questions are, "How are you involving the people in your organization in planning?" and "How are you incorporating emergent strategies and the lessons learned that are happening every day in your organization?"

We have the following conventional assumptions about strategic planning. First, planning is part of the overall strategic management process and is strongly associated with organizational processes and fiscal performance. Second, it is more than probable that the competitive elements of your environment engage in strategic planning; if you don't, you are more likely to be at a distinct disadvantage. Third, we believe that developing and documenting your strategic process helps you get better results and learning throughout your organization. Fourth, we believe that with all elements of your organization engaged in the strategic planning process, you will increase organizational teamwork, responsiveness, flexibility, creativity, and effectiveness. Remember to keep the strategic process moving and engaging. We will consider the strategic planning process in terms of four basic stages: planning, preparation, facilitation, and completion.

Planning, Preparation, and Facilitation

Some basic keys for setting the tone within your organization are the following:

1. **Study**—Take time to learn about planning methods and the culture you are working in, what planning method best suits the culture you work in, and the time frame that you will have for planning.
2. **Make time**—Make the time to plan; investing time in planning is crucial for strong execution, and it requires top management support and engagement. Be clear about the time and resources that it takes to conduct strategic planning and get them in place through negotiation and buy in from executive management. Time and resources will be required in every stage of strategic planning including implementation and metrics.
3. **Choose participants, facilitator, and results wanted**—Determine who will be involved in strategic planning, assign a core planning team, and determine whether you will be an internal or external facilitator, or both, and for which planning sessions. There are advantages and disadvantage to each. Table 5.1 examines a number of the advantages and disadvantages of using an internal or external facilitator.
4. **Develop a clear statement of what you wish to accomplish (for both the entire process and each individual session)**—Use the facilitator to help you if needed, and then communicate to the planning group and your organization.
5. **Define the outputs and outcomes expected from the strategic planning process**—What you will have when you are finished are, among other things, vision and mission creation or assessment, strategic initiatives, perspectives, objectives, performance measures and targets, strategy maps, documentation, reports, white papers, balanced scorecard draft.

    The **inputs** your process will require include environmental scan information and reports, business drivers, SWOT analysis, market reports, benchmarking data, audits, customer/stakeholder feedback, and emerging strategies that came about during the last implementation cycle.
6. **Choose a strategic planning process**—Explore the variety of formats or variations of processes available to conduct strategic planning and choose the one that best fits your organizational culture, resource, and time constraints. There are advantages and disadvantages to each format, and every organization not only has its own culture, but how it performs strategic planning varies tremendously. Many well-tested models are readily available in the marketplace.

Table 5.1 Types of Strategic Planning Facilitation

External	Internal
All can participate	Understands culture
Brings outside resources	Knows how things are done
Has third-person perspective	May know where resistance is
Is not entrenched in cultures	Carries less cost
Can talk about "elephants" in room	
Is easier to navigate internal politics	
Disadvantages	
Additional cost	Finds it harder to negotiate corporate politics
May not be there for entire cycle	Can't be a participant if facilitating
Takes time to learn culture	Has difficulty expressing insights
	Is harder to get respect of the group

7. **Manage your planning environment**—Face-to-face planning sessions are very different in dynamics than virtually facilitated sessions; make sure the methodology and facilitator skills are appropriate. One key to good strategic planning is creating an environment that is not being constantly assailed by the demands of the work environment from e-mail, cell phone, BlackBerry, instant messaging, and other technology. Getting an environment and giving a group time to focus are critical for success. How long will your sessions be—several sessions long or just one long session, face-to-face or virtual, or a bit of both? How will you conduct presession activities to get participants up to speed? What kinds of follow-up will you plan?

   Last, but not least, how does the facilitator's style work with the elements of the planning process chosen? Develop specific agendas for each meeting which complement the facilitator's style of working.

8. **Execute**—Conduct, implement and review, reevaluate, and revise your strategic plan based on data you gather.

9. **Completion**—Once you have completed a strategic plan, run through the necessary review cycles, and completed the formal documents and reports, the strategy must be communicated in multiple formats, including presentations, releases, staff reviews, and written reports. Working with a communication focal will help design a communication plan for getting the strategic plan out and keeping it there.

In the next section of this chapter we will discuss the fundamentals of creating a strategic plan once the plan for planning is in place. Those elements will include the following:

1. Building of a strategic foundation that includes the questions "What is this organization about?" and "Where do we want to play?" or vision/values/mission/strategic initiatives
2. Analysis stage of strategic planning

3. Strategy formulation or planning stage (which will include goals, objectives, and targets)
4. Implementation and/or a reality check focusing on "How are we doing?"

Building a Foundation for Strategy (High, Wide, and Deep)

Planning strategy follows a process regardless of the various models and tools employed in developing, deploying, and tracking strategic intent. First you build your foundation for security strategy by answering these questions:

1. What business are we really in?
2. Where are we?
3. Where do we want to go?
4. What do we have to work with?
5. What's happening that can help or hurt us?

Although the terminology may differ from model to model, some basic building blocks are at the heart of all strategic processes. The differences in model choice for organizations is often based on stability of industry, cycle time requirements for strategic planning in that environment, strategic planning skills of leadership, and the degree of accuracy required in modeling possible courses.

A number of questions should be answered in any security group regarding the strategic planning process:

1. Is our strategic planning process documented?
2. Does our organization understand and know the process?
3. Is the process followed as documented?
4. Is the process changing and evolving? (It should be as you learn from each planning cycle.)

If your organization is involved in any kind of quality movement, such as ISO standards, this shouldn't be new news. Documenting basic operational processes is part and parcel of being a support organization in a quality environment and helps everyone in the organization understand and improve the strategic planning process from year to year.

> Without a vision, the people perish.
>
> **Proverb**

Here are the basic steps taken in a relatively stable planning environment.

1. Vision/mission/corporate values/strategic objectives
2. Analysis (environmental scanning, SWOT, etc.)
3. Strategy formulation (goals, measurable objectives)
4. Strategy implementation (assigned action steps)
5. Evaluation, control metrics

In the Beginning

Strategic planning is worthless—unless there is first a strategic vision.

John Naisbitt

Vision, Mission, and Strategic Initiatives

> Teamwork is the ability to work toward [a] common vision: the ability to direct individual accomplishments toward organizational objectives. It is the fuel that allows common people to attain uncommon results.
>
> **Andrew Carnegie**

Vision Statement

All strategic planning processes begin with intent. Intent is nothing more than choosing a potential course of action or forward movement. The organizational culture and strategic planning method chosen will determine how careful, considered, comprehensive, and important a vision is for an organization. Intent typically will be driven by the engine of organizational vision. Depending on the planning philosophy and methods deployed, this strategic activity may be called strategic visioning, creating a shared vision, creating a vision/mission statement, creating a vivid description, or determining an organization's reason for being or sense of purpose.

From vision come passion, direction, mission, and the first level of strategic initiatives. Often the highest level vision encompasses mission and initiative, which remain in place for some period of time as they are focused on a time many years away. Crafting a strong, inclusive, far-sighted vision statement and/or mission statement is not an especially easy task and often takes a facilitator to move a strategic planning body through the phases of crafting them. Numerous methods can be used to develop vision statements. Choosing one or another again depends on the type of organizational culture in which one works. Even creating a "shared vision" (i.e., the Fifth Discipline) that builds from people's personal vision toward a co-created organizational vision has elements of telling, selling, testing, and consulting. A strong vision statement serves an organization well for many years as it navigates the vicissitudes of organizational challenges. A vision statement typically encompasses an organization's beliefs and values and reflects back on who we are and where we want to go. It is the framework and engine for all strategic planning. In essence, a strong vision creates the future destiny of an organization. A vision statement should be clear, simple, and specific. Every member of the enterprise should be able to understand and speak it and, ideally, feel strongly about it.

> Vision without action is a dream. Action without vision is simply passing the time. Action with vision is making a positive difference.
>
> **Joel Barker**

The process of creating a vision may vary somewhat depending on how you choose to create a vision. Creating a shared vision or a preferred vision is different from creating a vision statement. Creating a vision is both a product and a process. Here is an example of how companies or organizations may choose to create a vision. Often a facilitator or team of facilitators may be used in this process:

1. Conduct a thorough environmental scan (including stakeholders, customers, employees, and other members of the extended enterprise).
2. Seek specific answers to questions posed to representatives of the various stakeholder groups.

   ■ With regard to security, what kind of company do we want to be?
   ■ What are our core values? (How do we want to do business together?)
   ■ What do we want our reputation to be?

- How will we add value in our market?
- What products or services do we want to continue to offer, begin to offer, stop offering, or outsource?
- On what customer segments do we want to focus?
- How would you describe what you see in the future?

3. Hold discussions throughout your organization to find the answers to these questions and provide information to the strategic planning team.
4. Create a preferred future from the compiled data that includes a clear vision and mission statement. Other products may be produced as well, including a description of what the future looks like based on the input from enterprise stakeholders.
5. Disseminate the visioning and strategic planning results back to all stakeholders.

If your organization already has a vision and mission statement, this may be a shorter process of review. As organizations grow, often their vision and mission may shift; you will want to reflect that fact in the vision and mission statements.

> The leader's job today, in 21st-century terms, is not about gaining followership. Followership is an outmoded notion. Leadership starts with gaining alignment with the mission and values of the organization: What are we about? What do we believe as a group? Goldman Sachs, where I serve on the board, has achieved solid alignment around its mission: "The clients' interests always come first." At Medtronic, we aligned around the idea of "alleviating pain, restoring health, and extending life." It was clear that anyone who didn't buy into that could work somewhere else.
>
> **Bill George**

Mission Statement

An organizational mission statement is a written, easy-to-remember and easy-to-understand sentence, a short list of bullet points, or a paragraph illustrating a business's goals and purpose. Ideally, a mission statement is no more than 25 words. A mission statement defines the organization's purpose and defines what it is that we do. The purpose of a mission statement is to help guide organizational employees in making critical decisions in day-to-day operational decisions. A mission statement should clearly answer the question "What business are we in?"

A mission statement should focus on one theme of an organization. Internal and/or external facilitators or consultants can help facilitate crafting strong vision and mission statements. There are also software tools available on the Internet that will help you build, refine, and focus a mission's statement. Whatever approach is used, the creative process takes time. Brainstorming is the first part of the process of creating a mission's statement; second is focusing the statement on a key attribute of an organization's service or product that distinguishes its brand or approach. Getting input from various parts of the organization and crafting a strong mission statement that is motivating to an organization both take time, not rubber stamping. Remember, you are the one who must consider the particular needs and wants that determine whether your mission statement stands as it is or will need to be changed. Your mission statement will help you determine whether or not your plans are really strategic.

Strategic Initiatives

After the creation of organization vision and mission comes the priority of focus, which is determined by the overall environmental scan and responses from extended enterprise stakeholders. That prioritized focus is usually framed as a strategic initiative. A strategic initiative focuses on an issue that will have significant impact on organizational results. Cross-functional organizational support is required for a strategic initiative to succeed. Strategic initiatives often have their own team working through similar stages to strategic planning itself: initiating, launching, implementing, gaining momentum, and making metrics reviews of progress. Generally, strategic initiatives will focus on the organization's market position, reputation, sales, market share, earnings growth, or high-level organizational positioning in the marketplace. Strategic initiatives are limited in number and help guide an organization in making foundational changes for a long-term focus that help invigorate, transform, and focus an organization. Strategic initiatives will also generally come out of the next phase of strategic planning analysis. Strategic goals and objectives will in turn help the organization accomplish strategic initiatives. For a security group, many of these initiatives will often be framed by the larger enterprise, business unit, or functional initiatives. Many of them will include operational strategic initiatives, such as productivity, impact, and customer-focused initiatives, that will directly impact security. If your enterprise is focused on a LEAN Six Sigma initiative, you can bet part of your strategic plan will need to consider that initiative as well.

> If you are planning for one year, grow rice. If you are planning for 20 years, grow trees. If you are planning for centuries, grow men.
>
> **Chinese Proverb**

Analysis

Data collected for the strategic planning process are gathered, reviewed, and analyzed at each stage of the the strategic planning process. It is at this point that many of the tools cited in earlier chapters prove themselves useful for methods of sorting through the data gathered to identify trends and potential direction. Strategic planners take a hard look at an internal analysis of the organization's **strengths** and **weaknesses,** juxtaposed with external probabilities in the near term that will create **opportunities** or **threats**.

> You shouldn't have a long term strategy anymore, because you won't be able to move fast enough.
>
> **Orit Gadish**

Some tools that are useful for the analysis stage are as follows:

- **Environmental scans** are a useful wide outside look for strategic planners for providing external data regarding the opportunities and threats portion of a SWOT. Many types of environmental scans are useful from market surveys, trend data, or tools like **Porter's five force analysis,** which evaluates barriers, suppliers, customers, substitute products, and industry rivalry. **PEST analysis** is another external analysis sorting tool that considers political, economic, social, and technology factors in the overall environment.
- **SWOT analysis** is useful for determining organizational **strengths** and **weaknesses**, prioritizing **opportunities** and **threats,** and planning a course forward. An internal analysis of a security group's strengths and weaknesses should consider the main elements of the security group such as its current culture, organizational structure, future staffing requirements versus the current employee base, current employee skill sets versus future demand, operational capacity, and efficiency, infrastructure, and financial resources. While an internal analysis can generate a lot of data, utilizing a SWOT analysis can help simplify and prioritize the information that will be relevant to strategy formation.
- The **SABSA** (Sherwood Applied Business Security Architecture) **Model** for security strategic planning tackles the analysis portion of strategic planning by requiring an analysis of all business requirements for security, especially those in which security has an enabling function through which new business opportunities can be developed and exploited.

■ **Scenario planning** is a strategic planning method used by some organizations to make flexible long-range plans. Scenario planning may be used in conjunction with other planning models such as System Thinking or Computer Based Modeling programs to produce new insights into the future, unprecedented cultural shifts, regulation environments, impending technology horizons, and so on.

These are just a few of the many available approaches that will help an organization advance through the analysis and planning phases of strategic planning. Many other strategic analysis methods, tools, and philosophies are discussed in other chapters in this book. Once you have articulated a direction in which you intend to take the organization and have created an analysis of current state, then you will deal with a strategy formation to move you in the direction you wish to go.

Strategy Formation (Goals, Measurable Objectives)

All men can see these tactics whereby I conquer, but what none can see is the strategy about which victory is evolved.

Sun Tsu

Strategy formation answers the question: "Now that we know where we want to go, how will we get there?" Once a strategic planning group has created a clear picture of the organization and its challenges, the next step is to produce a strategic plan with goals, objectives, scenarios, or strategic alternatives. This stage of the plan is still typically high level and abstract, and can even be somewhat generic if one uses basic industry strategies like one of Porter's strategies (e.g., cost leadership).

A typical strategy will include strategic goals, which are usually set for a one- to three-year period. These goals are set in place following an analysis of what is going on inside and outside the organization. Once the strategic goals have been determined, the next task is to determine how those goals will be reached through initiatives, objectives, and targets with time lines and RAA assigned to each. Goals are formed using SMART (**S**pecific, **M**easurable, **A**cceptable to those trying to achieve those goals, **R**ealistic, and **T**imely) or SMARTER (which adds **E**xtending the capabilities of those trying to achieve the goals and **R**ewarding them) guidelines.

In addition to SMART goals or SMARTER goals, strategic planners may also opt for the occasional stretch goal. A stretch goal is usually aimed at a longer period than a year and is a significantly challenging goal that causes an organization to find a way to achieve outside the current norms. Innovation and creativity are required to achieve stretch goals. The purpose of employing stretch goals in an organization is to inspire efforts that exceed what is currently possible. Stretch goals can only be achieved through creativity, invention, and innovation.

Once strategic goals, objectives, and targets have been created from the planning function, the equally important implementation phase of strategic planning begins. Good strategic plans are nothing without great implementation. Effective security leaders have to do both regardless of their predilection. Security by its very nature tends to attract those who are quite good at implementation. The key to good implementation is also the ability to move quickly from a strategic implementation plan to emergent or adaptive strategies when either unexpected regulatory or competitive moves require it. What often gets missed is the integration of those new strategic adaptations at an organizational level back into the strategic planning cycle.

Implementation (a Bias toward Action and Learning)

A good plan, violently executed now, is better than a perfect plan next week.

General George S. Patton Jr.

The implementation phase answers the following questions:

1. Now that we think we know the direction we want to take, what are the next steps, who will take them, and how will we track how well we are doing with our plan?
2. What do we do with information that tells us this might be the wrong direction?

Strategy? Keep moving, anywhere, somewhere, but keep moving.

Ulysses S. Grant

Some important questions for consideration in the implementation phase of planning are:

1. Who has oversight and review authority for plan content?
2. What measurements of performance will we use?
3. How often will we review progress (e.g., monthly, quarterly, biannually, annually)?
4. Who is responsible for measuring progress?

Chi Wen Tzu always thought three times before taking action. Twice would have been quite enough.

Confucius

In our experience, the implementation stage of strategic planning is one of the most difficult parts of strategic planning. Strategy without effective implementation is just organizational wishing. Implementation is difficult for several reasons. First, in larger organizations (like most organizations in which we have worked), the people responsible for implementations are often different from the high-level strategic planners. This creates the need for good communication, understanding, and buy-in. Conversely, this creates the risk of miscommunication, misunderstanding, and resistance. Implementation of a strategic plan is similar to any change management effort and requires clear sponsorship, structure, measures, and reward and recognition systems. This section of the strategic plan should document a set of specific steps, phases, and activities required to get to the end-state. This is the strategy for moving forward.

Do not repeat the tactics which have gained you one victory, but let your methods be regulated by the infinite variety of circumstances.

Sun Tsu

Keys to Success for the Implementation Stage of Strategic Planning

1. A well-defined strategic planning process.
2. Clear and visible executive support, sponsorship, and involvement.
3. An empowered strategic planning team.
4. Involvement of all levels of the organization (inclusive not exclusive approach).
5. Thorough analysis of internal and external competitive data (while some information is the same at the top level of strategic planning, additional data are required as you go though the varying levels of an organization, particularly when it comes to organizational strengths and weaknesses).

6. Clear priorities and a strategic plan with both strategic and tactical objectives.
7. Implementation plan (spelling out the cost, duration, priority order, and accountability for each strategy and tactic). This phase of strategic planning is part of the tactical playbook for day-to-day activities telling employees the priorities and presenting the logic for actions they need to take in their daily work.
8. Review, reevaluation, and revision of the strategic plan, yearly at a minimum, quarterly more optimally, and even more often in fast-moving environments.
9. An organizational understanding of how to do strategic planning with the adjacent understanding of the need for strategic planning.
10. A commitment to change.

Feedback, Tracking, and Control

> However beautiful the strategy, you should occasionally look at the results.
>
> **Winston Churchill**

The feedback, tracking, and control phase answers the following questions:

1. How will we know we are getting where we'd like to go?
2. How are we doing in achieving the results we want?
3. Is there any new information we need to know?

There are several questions to consider in this element of strategic planning:

1. What are the key success factors that will tell our stakeholders that we are on the path to success?
2. What performance metrics should we use?
3. How often should we schedule a regular review of strategic goals and their relevant metrics?
4. What cost avoidance can be expected, and how can this be ascertained?
5. How do we capture cost-benefit data and determine return on investment (ROI), both quantitatively and qualitatively?
6. How often should we assess progress to determine whether recalibration is needed?

Creating effective feedback, tracking, and control elements presents many challenges, not the least of which is understanding multiple levels of tracking data. Tracking data is more detailed the farther into the implementation plans that you go. At the same time, there is a need for information and/or data that is meaning-

> Setting a goal is not the main thing. It is deciding how you will go about achieving it and staying with that plan.
>
> **Tom Landry**

ful and that flows up to executive-level tracking in tracking tools such as a Balanced Scorecard Strategy Map. The Balanced Scorecard Strategy Map came out of the Harvard Business School from Drs. Robert Kaplan and David Norton as a performance measurement framework. A balanced scorecard helps any industry, government, educational, or nonprofit group to align strategic initiatives, goals, and objectives with the organizational vision, mission, and strategy while monitoring organization performance. Executives usually want to see data that tells them whether or not the strategy plan is on track. Top-level executives will review data clusters around topics like operations management, customer management, innovation, and regulatory and social processes that may impact strategy. Only high-level security metrics are likely at the top levels of the company (such as number of incidents and response time). But at each level of review (the next levels of review are operations as a whole, followed by security as a whole, then security departments or programs as a whole), you will need to determine what data elements are required and relevant to the specific group reviewing them. There is often a new or an emerging set of metrics.

Determining what gets reported at the executive level from IT versus what gets reported by physical security is seldom a well-defined metric. Metrics may fall into qualitative or quantitative categories. The difficulty is determining which security metrics are most relevant to the organization you find yourself in. Different organizations measure different aspects of security, depending on whether you work in government, business, educational, or nonprofit sectors. Security metrics are very much an emerging discipline compared with more mature fields like finance or operational productivity metrics. However, organizations continue to press on in the refining of meaningful security metrics. The National Institute of Standards and Technology of the U.S. Department of Commerce is a significant force in helping determine effective metrics for security.

As shown in Figure 5.1, metrics are developed, collected, and analyzed for four basic perspectives: Learning and Growth, Business Processes, Customer, and Financial. The Learning and Growth perspective will typically include metrics regarding employee training and corporate cultural attitudes toward ongoing learning. The Business Processes perspective includes metrics

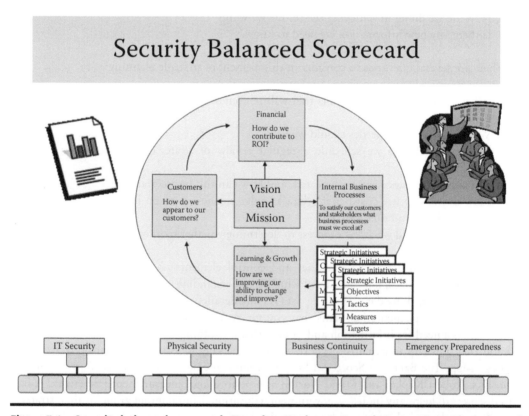

Figure 5.1 Security balanced scorecard. (Based on Kaplan, R. S., and Norton, D. P. *The balanced scorecard: Translating strategy into action.* Harvard Business School Press, Boston, 1996.)

related to the health of core business processes in the organization and how well they meet customer requirements. The Customer perspective will utilize customer satisfaction and value metrics to determine overall company performance. The Financial and Business Processes perspective will focus on finance metrics, risk metrics, and cost-benefit metrics.

As strategy is developed, metrics are collected and analyzed. A strategy map is created to logically show the specific linkage between each strategic objective and the cause-and-effect chain. Many software packages are available to create basic balanced scorecards, but it is the organizational skill and mastery of this approach that can make this a very valuable tool. This tool can provide a framework for strategic planners to help identify what must be measured and done. Increasingly, organizations that began with basic scorecards have continued to refine their use of this methodology to help guide the day-to-day decisions of their organization. Many success stories and illustrations of the effectiveness of the approach are available on the Web.

Completion

The completion phase of strategic planning is as important as the first phases. The completion of a strategic planning cycle should inform the first phases of the next strategic planning cycle with the metrics, measures, and results of the completion phase of the last planning cycle. Here is the opportunity to celebrate the successful completion or milestones toward success of deliberate strategies with all employees. It is also in this cycle that the unrealized and emergent strategies can be analyzed and reviewed to move forward.

Best Strategies (Strategies That Work)

> Faith in yourself, in your friends, in your colleagues and most of all, faith in your ability to impact our future is the best strategy I know.
>
> **Seth Godin**

Updated strategies have the best chance of continuing to work. Here are a few questions to jump-start the review of your current strategy:

1. Does your security strategy work as well as it used to? (Yesterday's strategy rarely keeps working.)
2. Have current issues rendered your old strategies inadequate? What needs to change in the face of emerging threats: increasingly smarter mobile devices, cloud technologies, drive-by attacks, and so on?
3. Are you tracking emergent strategies in your organization to better analyze how you are coping with new threats?
4. Are you tracking unrealized strategies to learn from your failures?
5. Are your security policies, processes, and procedures documented?
6. Can you quickly update them as your organization learns?
7. Has your strategy created a culture of security in the organization you serve?
8. Are the tools and metrics you employ helping you implement and refine your strategy? (These include operational metrics, technology metrics, business metrics, compliance metrics, and risk metrics.)

9. Is your security strategy usefully linked to enterprise strategy, functional strategy, business strategy, and the like?
10. Have you created a security culture that thinks strategically? (What are the security objectives for mission-critical business functions? To what risks is the organization vulnerable? Will your security architecture defend your vital systems, networks, and applications? Do you have the required security policies and procedures in place? What requirements do you have for the next cycle of security awareness and training?)

Regardless of the methodology you are currently employing for strategic planning, the need to create, refine, link, and track strategy will continue. The elements of a successful security strategy process—preparing to plan, facilitating, planning, implementing, tracking and integrating results into the next planning cycle—will all remain. Aside from the mechanics of planning, there are also all the relationship and communication issues around strategic planning that are essential for success, such as top organizational support, cross-functional links to other support organizations, and well-developed communication plans. Strategic planning requires both creative and analytical thinking skills, which often reside in different segments of the organization. Traditionally, security has focused on their roles in compliance and audit and in their roles in protecting people, property, and information. That remains an important part of strategic planning. However, security practitioners must focus on more than regulatory issues; they must now also zero in on business problems. In our increasingly global environment, security groups must move from being seen as a slow-moving, necessary evil to an enabler of innovation and business. You can't fly blind into the storm of global environments, new technology convergence, and fast-changing roles, or you'll inevitably be seen as a costly overhead. Learning to get security issues and concerns into organizational planning efforts earlier in the value stream of creation and innovation will produce benefits across the organization in terms of reduced complexity, cost, and cycle time. In order for security to work in innovative parts of organizational life, you must be able to demonstrate the ability to partner with the organization. Security cannot afford to remain just risk averse; it must also learn to see strategic opportunities. You must learn to make time for strategic thinking, to know the business, to speak the business, and to work with the business you support. Build relationships and look for win-win scenarios, not "I'm right and you're wrong, wronger, and wrongest." Security today requires a new mind-set that looks beyond saying "No." Instead, it says: "Tell me what you want to do and where you want to go and I will do my best to help you get there in the best, quickest way, while protecting the brand, reputation, people and assets of this organization."

Conclusion

Strategic planning as a process isn't that complex, but that doesn't make it easy to carry out. However, the strategic planning process does become simpler with practice. While the ideal would be to have the entire enterprise using the same methodology, this is seldom the case. In this chapter we reviewed the basic components common to all the methodologies. The most important part of constructing a strategic plan is to make sure it aligns/integrates with the enterprise strategic plan and related business units strategic plans.

Before getting started, take some time to determine who should be involved in the strategic planning process. Make sure to get the right stakeholders involved; that will make implementation much easier. Once you have established the RAA for the strategic plan, pick the tools you will use and get started! There are some consistent guidelines you can follow; for example, know ahead of time what process and methods you will use and what the deliverables are. Get executive support and have strong employee involvement. Be consistent and thorough in your planning, analysis, and implementation and do a good job communicating with all your stakeholders.

We have the following conventional assumptions about strategic planning:

1. Planning is part of the overall strategic management process.
2. The competitive elements of your environment engage in strategic planning.
3. Developing and documenting your strategic process helps get better results and learning throughout your organization.
4. All elements of your organization should be engaged in the strategic planning process.

As difficult as it may be, you must make time to plan, and once you get started you need to carefully manage the process so that it continues moving forward to completion. Strategic planning has five basic components: (1) vision/mission/corporate values/strategic objectives, (2) analysis, (3) strategy formulation, (4) strategy implementation, and (5) evaluation, control metrics.

Vision creates passion, direction, mission, and the first level of strategic initiatives. Mission defines the organization's purpose and guides the staff's critical day-to-day operational decisions. Data gathering and analysis take place throughout the strategic planning process. Data is gathered through environmental scans and analyzed using SWOT, SMART, or a similar analysis tool.

Strategy formation involves the definition of initiatives, objectives, targets, and time lines for bringing the plan to fruition. Once strategic goals, objectives, and targets have been created, the implementation phase begins. This section of the strategic plan documents the specific steps, phases, and activities required to get to the end-state. The final element in strategy formation is feedback—tracking the success of your plan and initiatives. The completion of a strategic planning cycle should provide the metrics, measures, and results needed for the first phase of the next strategic planning cycle. It is also an opportunity to celebrate with everyone the fulfillment of your strategic goals and the positive impacts they have had on the business. It is also the time to analyze and review unrealized and emergent strategies for the next planning cycle. The next chapter examines security convergence, a security strategic objective that the authors believe is essential to successful enterprise security management.

Chapter 6

Gates, Geeks, and Guards
(Security Convergence)

Convergence brings the opportunity for greater operational efficiency and the potential for contributions toward the organization's profitability.

Robert Messemer
CSO, The Nielsen Company

Introduction

A comprehensive security strategy must encompass both logical and physical security. Call it convergence, consolidation, cooperation, or anything else for that matter, but the bottom line is that achieving a consistent view of enterprise security risk requires the integration of both logical and physical security. A simple example is account control; there is one and only one user for each account. If Roger is in the office, he shouldn't be logging in on a remote access system and vice versa. No one can be in two places at the same time: Either Roger gave his credentials to someone else to use or the account has been compromised. Enforcing this level of account control is impossible without integrating facility access and computer access information. Security convergence has been a common topic of discussion in the physical and information security communities for the past several years, but the conversation is quickly moving into the executive suite where C series officers looking for ways to reduce overhead costs find security convergence an attractive opportunity. And why not? The organizations have overlapping goals and common budget requirements, and they have been converging at the technology level for some time. Technology advancements on both sides of the fence have fostered dependences between the two functions. The introduction of physical devices such as smartcard identity badges and access tokens brought physical security into the information security realm, and the introduction of digital CCTV (Closed Circuit TV), PC network-based controllers, and other IP-based devices brought logical security into the physical security realm. For the IT security group, the primary driver was risk reduction: a way to overcome the inherent

91

weaknesses of passwords. For the corporate security group, the drivers were cost reduction and loss prevention; replacing expensive proprietary systems and outsourced monitoring with low-cost PC-based systems was a huge cost savings, especially on the maintenance side. For example, getting a high-capacity VCR repaired costs in the neighborhood of $2,000; replacing a disk on a DVR with 10 times the recording capacity costs only around $200. Improved capabilities and lower costs allowed the corporate security team to expand its loss prevention efforts with increased video surveillance. Networked technologies helped centralized monitoring to further reduce costs by eliminating the need for security officers in branch offices and other remote locations. The use of these technologies also required the involvement of IT. Devices needed to be attached to the IT network, software ran on business systems (PCs), and maintaining the system required an SQL DBA (whatever that is!). Technology skills are not the strength of corporate security and safety professionals. Conversely, identity vetting, access control, incident response, and investigations are not information security personnel's strong suit. Both parties benefited from the increased cooperation, but it wasn't convergence; both groups continued to operate separately.

Realizing the full benefits of security convergence requires a lot more than occasional collaboration; it requires the decisive strategic integration of IT and corporate security resources to produce an organization capable of delivering increased value to the enterprise. One of the major drivers for this integration is the fundamental change in the way business is conducted in the information age. Enterprises are no longer self-contained business entities; they build global value chains, outsource, partner, collaborate, and engage in joint ventures with other organizations, even with direct competitors! Modern business uses these cooperative models to design and deliver products and services to the marketplace. Security is at the nexus of these organizational moves from two perspectives. First is the need to secure our innovations against attack. No matter how innovative your idea, if it gets hacked, it may be impossible to recover from the bad publicity and reputational damage. Second is securing the collaborative channels to protect company information resources from unnecessary exposure. This is more than IT security; in many instances it involves physical access controls and surveillance. For security to be part of an organization's "value proposition," it must begin to function as a whole and leverage the strengths of both security disciplines to identify new ways to provide organizational security (and position itself to exploit it). Convergence is often pitched as cost saving through efficiency or organizational simplification. There is some economy to be gained from reduction in management overhead, but for the rank and file the organizations remain fairly static; security officers still report to corporate security and IT people to IT security. The real gains are in efficiency.

Compliance is another driver from two perspectives. The first is the need to comply with specific IT and physical security requirements; the second is to prove compliance with those requirements. Another common driver is security awareness. This is not employee security awareness; this is security "security awareness." Corporate security and IT security personnel have very different views of security. When you merge those views together, you get a much greater awareness and appreciation for the challenges and the solutions of each discipline. Global operations is another big driver. Corporate security is accustomed to dealing with government and law enforcement entities, so they are better equipped to handle subpoenas, court orders, discovery requests, international investigations, and so on, although IT will likely be the organization that actually supplies the data. The final driver is insider threat. Insider risks cross the traditional line of separation between corporate and IT security. Attacks may involve sabotage, fraud, theft or embezzlement, misuse of computer equipment, or misappropriation of privileged information.

Terms and Definitions

Security Convergence—Convergence by definition is the occurrence of two or more things coming together. In its simplest form, *security convergence* is using IT technologies to facilitate physical security functionality—for example, attaching video cameras and DVRs to an IP network. Two other common technology integrations in recent years are One Badge (smartcard and facility access card integration) and One Identity (logical and physical identity management integration). Though beneficial, these efforts are a long way from the enterprisewide risk management strategy we are proposing. That level of convergence implies "the integration, in a formal, collaborative and strategic manner, of the cumulative security resources of an organization in order to deliver enterprisewide benefits through enhanced risk mitigation, increased operational effectiveness and efficiency, and cost savings" (Tyson 2007). This definition makes security convergence part of an overall business security strategy. It doesn't take technology out of the equation; rather, it puts technology in its proper place as the facilitator of the logical and physical security objectives in convergence.

Physical Security—*Corporate security* is the common term used to describe the organization that manages the security of facilities and personnel. Corporate security is often part of a larger facilities management group that includes fire, safety, and building automation.

Logical Security—*IT security* is the term most commonly used to describe the group that is responsible for protecting computer-based (digital) information. Most IT security groups are part of an overall IT group responsible for the implementation, operation, and support (and sometimes the development) of IT systems.

One Badge—*One Badge* is the consolidation of identity, facility access, and logical access onto a single device. An example is a smartcard that acts as a picture badge, a proximity device for garage and building entry, and a means of computer access.

Benefits of Security Convergence

The technology benefits are only a small part of the advantages to be realized by a true strategic alignment of these two security functions. Other advantages include:

- Cost savings
- Improved security/risk management
- More effective event/incident management
- Better user experience
- Improved compliance and compliance reporting
- Cohesive business continuity planning

Cost Savings

Although organizations may experience some reduction in costs from the elimination of management overhead, the real cost benefits of convergence are in efficiency. Common management means the strengths of each discipline can be leveraged to improve performance and effectiveness. IT handles the technology aspect of physical security controls, corporate security handles the customer aspect of smart badge issuance, and data from IT and physical security controls are merged to eliminate wasteful redundancy. The consolidation of badging and identity management is a great example. Instead of multiple cards and management groups, a single group handles both functions. Instead of duplicate data entry for user identities, a single identity is established to service both physical and logical access controls. This has the added advantage of lower maintenance costs, and the reduction in complexity provides measurable performance advantages.

Another advantage of the new organization is that both sides of the house gain a better perspective on security. By working with each other and learning from each other's strengths, the team becomes more effective than its previous two parts. This doesn't happen overnight; training plays a major role in making it successful. Cross training the staff makes personnel more versatile, eliminating costly overlaps. Investigations are a good example; they often require an IT and a corporate security officer to complete, but cross training eliminates the need for two people and the associated expense.

Moving physical access controls to IP network-based devices provides a greater ROI for the IT infrastructure while reducing cabling and installation expenses for surveillance and physical security controls. However, the real value of this integration is the ability to replace expensive resources with much lower cost solutions. For example, network-attached video cameras can be used to monitor remote locations via the company's wide area network (WAN), thereby eliminating the need for security officers in some of those locations. Network-based controls make it possible to monitor the security and safety system throughout the enterprise, eliminating the need for expensive third-party monitoring services. It also enables the engagement of much lower cost Internet-based monitoring services. Finally, the elimination of expensive proprietary solutions substantially reduces yearly maintenance and support costs.

Improved Security and Risk Management

Creating one complete and unified model for security increases the effectiveness and efficiency of security processes and controls in both realms. For example, a combined identity management solution reduces the time required to provision a new user and to revoke access upon termination. A combined access control solution improves authentication by adding the factor of physical presence (location) to logical access. Hospitals are a great example. HIPAA restricts healthcare worker access to the medical records of the patients *they are providing care to.* It's not unusual for a healthcare worker to provide services in multiple wards in any given workweek (sometimes any given workday), so access to medical records becomes a function of their physical location. If they log on to a workstation in surgery, they can access surgery patient records; if maternity, they have access to maternity patient records; and so on. When this control is tied to the worker's schedule, it supports full accountability for compliance purposes. The ability to quickly provision and revoke access also facilitates business processes involving external partners, vendors, and contractors. Facility and computer network access can be granted quickly, configured for a specific duration, and revoked at a moment's notice.

The alignment of physical and logical security policies improves the organization's ability to deal with risky devices such as USB drives, camera phones and portable wireless devices. One company Bill visited had a very strict policy regarding cameras; cameras had to be left at the guard station when he entered certain areas of the plant. Being a good citizen, he placed all the prohibited items into the tray, wrote his name on the tag, and handed it to the guard, who promptly reached in, extracted his USB camera pen, and returned it to him with the comment, "Pens are okay"!

The combined staff is more versatile than the two individual unit staffs. The skills, mind-sets, even the terminology between corporate and IT security personnel are very different. Corporate security personnel are predominately former law enforcement types, whereas IT security people are predominately technology types (i.e., geeks). Each discipline has strengths that can be leveraged to provide improved security functionality on both sides of the house. In separate stovepiped organizations there is little onus for this is to happen. Lowes provides a great example of how valuable this integration can be; their IT and loss prevention staff worked together to create a point-of-sale (POS) reporting system that highlighted suspicious activities. IT knew how to build and deliver the report, but they didn't know what to look for. Loss prevention provided those answers. The following story illustrates the opposite side of the coin.

SIDEBAR: DOLPHIN SPOKEN HERE

The meeting began with one of the leads from corporate security explaining their plans to replace their aging video surveillance equipment with higher resolution cameras and digital video recorders (DVRs) that would permit them to increase surveillance, centralize monitoring, reduce video search time, and so on. The speaker had done a thorough job of investigating and selecting the solution; the demo was impressive. Only one detail remained: The new devices didn't use dedicated coaxial or fiber-optic cables; they attached to the IP network, and that's why this meeting with IT was called. The IT director was the first to respond with assurances that this was certainly a doable thing and that they had his full support for this important collaborative effort. At this point he left the meeting, leaving his technical team to work out the details. The next person to speak was the network manager, who asked how much bandwidth the application required; he followed this with questions about virtual private networks (VPNs), QoS (quality of service) settings, ports, and protocols. Then the systems guy began asking about how much power, rack space, and network connectivity the DVR servers required, and he was followed by the operations lead. They might as well have been dolphins: The corporate security people had no idea what these people were talking about and after saying, "I don't know" a few dozen times, they switched to taking notes and "Can we get back to you on that?" The project got done, but the experience left a very bad taste for the corporate security people who made every attempt to avoid involving IT in future projects. On the IT side, the reaction wasn't much better; not only were the corporate security people short on answers, but they hadn't budgeted any money for network connectivity either, which didn't go over well with the IT folks. While the story does illustrate how very different these two disciplines are, it also demonstrates how much benefit can be derived from getting this diversity of skills working together to meet business objectives.

More Effective Event/Incident Management

Combining corporate and IT security produces a staff that is better able to deal holistically with enterprise security risks. Instead of having two teams dealing with the same incident, you have a single cohesive team discovering facts, sharing information, and making informed decisions. Besides reducing the number of respondents, security convergence enhances a number of other elements of incident response and incident management, including better coordination of resources in critical and emergency responses. Having both disciplines working in a common operations center means information from physical controls and IT controls can be more easily collated for more effective responses and better management of ongoing incidents. Consolidated physical and IT controls provide better detection of malicious activity. When physical and logical systems are separate, acquiring and collating logs becomes time consuming, often resulting in discovering malicious activities well after the fact.

Consolidated access and identity information also facilitates investigations and forensics by providing a sequential log of events tied to specific identities. This is particularly valuable for countering insider threats (the threat of malicious activities by internal staff). Insider threats are some of the most harmful security breaches. Incidents of insider malfeasance typically cause three times the damage an external attacker causes. Insider risks cross the traditional line of separation between corporate and IT security; attacks may involve the sabotage of equipment, fraud, embezzlement, or theft of privileged information. These activities are often reported to corporate security first, but investigations inevitably involve IT personnel. Combining security resources not only streamlines the investigative process but provides a much broader understanding of the situation as a whole. It also provides a response that assures the evidence required to discipline or prosecute the individual or individuals involved is properly collected and preserved.

User Experience

One of the biggest wins for security convergence is the improvements it makes to the end-user experience. A positive user experience is critical to the health of a corporate security culture. Security convergence helps this effort because it provides a single view of security, a single point of contact, a common information portal, and a consolidated response. In addition, initiatives like One Badge simplify the end-user access experience, enhancing the image and value of security services.

Regulatory Compliance

Convergence improves compliance from two perspectives. The first is the need to comply with specific IT and physical security requirements; the second is to prove compliance with those requirements. Having both disciplines working together on compliance solutions results in more comprehensive and cost-effective solutions. Physical controls can be incorporated to compensate for software weakness; conversely, IT systems can be used to enhance or overcome physical security weaknesses. Proof of compliance is aided by the ability to combine information from physical and logical security sources. Suppose, for example, that someone was accused of unauthorized access to a patient's record from a particular location. The combination of video surveillance information, security officer observations, facility access logs, and IT access logs makes it possible to positively refute or confirm the claim. In many organizations today, this kind of evidence gathering would take days; in a converged environment, it can be done in a few hours at the most.

Another key value is the ability to prove regulatory compliance. A number of regulatory restrictions (like the earlier HIPAA example) are in place regarding access to specific types of information (e.g., the Sarbanes-Oxley Act, Gramm-Leach-Bliley Act, International Traffic in Arms Regulations). Consolidated access and identity management greatly simplifies the compliance reporting process and in some instances may reduce the scope of some compliance audits.

Legal compliance is another win. Corporate security is accustomed to dealing with government and law enforcement entities, so they are better equipped to handle subpoenas, court orders, discovery requests, international investigations, and so on. In contrast, IT organizations are ill prepared to handle these types of queries, although they are most likely the ones to supply the required information. Convergence improves both the timeliness and quality of the response.

Improved Business Continuity Planning

When business continuity planning (BCP), physical security, and IT security are completely separate functions, trying to determine which assets are critical and require the best protection is an effort in futility. Each group provides a different answer, but in the converged model everyone has a view of the entire risk spectrum, so they can better position their assets in the overall recovery plan. In BCP and DRP (disaster recovery planning), security is the first logical function that has to be restored. No one can gain access to network or host resources without security services being operational. Physical security can provide important logistical and security support for these efforts; they become the "eyes and ears" of the organization as equipment, personnel, and/or media are moved to alternative computing facilities.

Other Improvements

Not all the benefits of security convergence are related to security. Several other business processes benefit from these convergence technologies, including operations and telecommunications. Video surveillance cameras can be used for teleconferencing; they can also be used to monitor production and shipping operations. For example, a shipping manager could monitor a critical shipment to make sure it got out on time or intervene if it didn't look like it would. For some industries the ability to include video images into a transaction record is also valuable.

The benefits of converging physical and logical security are compelling, especially for larger organizations. In tough economic times, the cost savings alone are worth the effort; combined with the improvements to security and long-term gains in business productivity, it's easy to understand why a majority of medium and large businesses have active security convergence projects of one type or another—projects that are not without their own challenges.

Convergence Challenges

> The ability of smart card systems to address both physical and logical (information systems) security means that unprecedented levels of cooperation may be required.... Nearly all federal officials we interviewed noted that (changing) existing security practices and procedures within their agencies…to integrate them across the agency was a formidable challenge.
>
> **Joel C. Willemssen**
> *Director, U.S. General Accounting Office*

Although the benefits of converging are substantial, some industry pundits believe that converging these two similar but parallel universes is simply not practical. Some say the focus should be on collaborative processes, while others advocate organizational change. The authors are in the latter camp: There needs to be a single vision, a common strategy, and a single command structure.

Security convergence has a number of similarities to the numeric controls (NC) machinery integration. When numeric controls were first introduced into machine shops, there were two very distinct camps: On one side were the union machinists working hard to protect their jobs, and on the other side there were the "college boys"—the NC programmers, engineers, and computer-aided engineering (CAE) operators trying to replace those jobs with automation. Cooperation was the equivalent of committing treason. Amidst all the turf wars and politics, the business objectives somehow got overlooked. Eventually, NC technology became the standard and the business goals for increased productivity and efficiency were realized, but the transition would have been much smoother for everyone involved if the focus had been on the business. At the shop where Bill worked, some machinists found new roles in the integrated environment, others remained in their existing roles, and still others found opportunities elsewhere. Those who took the opportunity to acquire new skills were the ones who fared the best. The corporate security realm is undergoing the same type transition: PC- and network-based technologies are going to become the standard. The question that arises is, "Can we do a better job on the transition?"

Focusing on the business and its objectives for convergence is the best way to deal with turf issues; the effort must include any new stakeholders too. Their objectives may not be security related, but they are still business related and so deserve consideration. Culture clash is another major challenge. Corporate security personnel have law enforcement backgrounds, whereas IT security personnel have technical backgrounds. The skill sets, mind-sets, processes, and even the terminology are very different for the two groups. While IT people love to experiment with new technologies, corporate security prefers to stick with what is proven and reliable, which makes sense when you think about it. If your facility access system fails, all movement within the facility ceases. Think about what that would mean in an airport.

Processes are also different; corporate security focuses on loss prevention and safety, IT on data loss. The IT people come to the table with threat models and risk analysis, whereas corporate security personnel come armed with hardware, site plans, and building blueprints. Although the new technologies are producing intersection points in these processes, a concerted training effort and a smart command structure are needed for successful integration. The integration will produce new roles requiring new skills. Not only is a common management structure needed, but that management needs to have the skills required to effectively handle both disciplines. One of the issues that will need to be dealt with is compensation. The pay disparity between corporate security positions and IT security is substantial. Melding and upgrading skill sets is going to require rethinking some compensation models, but career and compensation advancement can also be a major selling point for convergence. These are not the only challenges companies will face, but they are the most common ones. Companies would do well to include strategies for dealing with them when planning for security convergence.

Success Factors

A successful security convergence project consists of some pretty standard factors including executive sponsorship, buy-in from the management of the organizations being converged, thorough planning, good communications, and ongoing training. Executive sponsorship cuts down on the politics and turf war aspects of things and makes it much easier to get buy-in from the managers involved. Memos are nice, but getting a face-to-face meeting with the executive sponsor and the group manager is more effective. A successful convergence project is going to take a lot of planning; most managers who have gone through the process recommend small incremental steps starting with the "big wins." That is, things that can be accomplished in relatively short time frames and demonstrate real business value should be tackled first—for example, establishing a common help desk function for both groups and creating a single portal for security information, request forms, and so forth. Planning must include defining personnel roles for the new organization and the skill sets expected. This exercise will help solidify the training curriculum and training plans. One of those roles will be the chief security executive, the person ultimately responsible for enterprise security in all its forms. Organizations that perform similar functions but have separate reporting structures create unnecessary business risk, and some of those risks are substantial. A few years ago Bill performed a security assessment for a large communications company that had a development division and a production operations group with a separate reporting structure. All the company's applications were designed, developed, staged, tested, and secured by the development division. Once the application was approved for release, it was handed off to the operations group for production implementation. Critical to the success of this process and its applicable security functionality was keeping these two environments (staging and production) in sync with each other, which everyone assumed was absolutely the case—except that wasn't the case: In the process of implementing new systems, the production group made all sorts of configuration changes, many of which affected security. When the final report was issued, the development group screamed "bloody murder," but it mostly fell on deaf ears. The production group had a flawless uptime record, and they had no intention of risking it by implementing the development configurations. What's interesting is that the two groups had a record of exemplary cooperation, but getting this issue resolved required the involvement of two senior managers, two vice presidents, two senior vice presidents, and the chief operating officer. Where security is involved, you simply can't tolerate this level of stovepiped operations; too much is at risk.

An alignment of policies and procedures will also need to take place in order to establish a unified operations model. Organization should consider establishing a security operations center (SOC) consisting of facility and data security professionals. This ensures a single response to an incident and the application of the best resources to process and resolve it. The other big benefit comes from the sharing of expertise between team members, which produces a better rounded and more effective staff.

There are a number of things to look out for during your convergence effort. First is the increase in security risks when physical security systems are attached to the business network. Cisco learned the lesson the hard way when a virus on the network took all their Windows-based video servers offline. The company had no video surveillance for a day and only partial coverage for another two days. Fortunately, the outage didn't result in any major losses, but it did result in a project to ensure it didn't happen again. Another issue is bandwidth utilization, which is actually a twofold issue. First there's the risk of impacting business systems with video and access control traffic. Second is the risk of insufficient bandwidth to adequately manage responses in an emergency situation. Coordinating a response to a major incident can generate hundreds of pages, text, instant messages, and e-mail messages, as well as a very large amount of voice/radio traffic. Business networks are not typically designed to handle this type of spike in network traffic, nor are they designed to give this traffic preference over other activities. Which brings us to the final lesson learned: the importance of involving IT network and systems engineering in the planning, design, and purchase decisions for facility security systems. Future planning is critical. Everyone involved needs to understand what the requirements, costs, and impacts are going to be, or risk losing some critical security functionality down the road.

Conclusion

The most successful security convergence efforts depend on good preparation, sponsorship, and planning. Training is key to bridging the cultural and procedural differences between the groups. The goal should be to cross train staff to improve incident coverage, reduce operating overhead, and increase staff versatility. The new organization should make every effort to improve the end-user experience through unified leadership, operations, information, and support. The best approach is an incremental integration that focuses on "big wins" and projects such as One Badge that simplify user access. The long-term goal is to achieve a consistent view of enterprise security risk through the integration of logical and physical security into a single unified entity.

You have to understand that security isn't just physical security or logical security, it includes the human element and all three elements must be addressed. This must be understood outside the security and IT departments in order for an organization to be effectively proactive about security, which is the only way success in security will be achieved.

Stan Gatewood
Chief Information Assurance Officer,
University of Southern California

SIDEBAR: BOOZE ALLEN HAMILTON MODEL OF SECURITY TRANSFORMATION

A 2005 Alliance for Enterprise Security Risk Management report titled "Security Convergence: Current Corporate Practices and Future Trends" traces the convergence of security functions at multiple levels in Enterprise Risk Management in people, process, and strategy. Included in this driving shift are a change in thinking and operating from a functional, technical orientation toward an adaptive approach to risk management. In this model as well, there is a shift from

- A stovepiped security functional view to an enterprise view
- Behind-the-curtains governance to active governance board involvement
- Techno-speak to a creation of common language with peers
- Techno-speak to a common language executives can understand
- Functionally defined roles and responsibilities to multiple competencies
- Command-and-control leadership to empowering and enabling leadership
- Functional knowledge to a broad business understanding

In other words, security, just like quality and productivity, is now everyone's business.

Companies that are moving in this direction are already taking steps to place security at the core of their business. Creating an enterprisewide corporate risk management council to help integrate security governance structure is one such example. Once you begin to take a long view of enterprisewide security and accountability for managing enterprise risks, your organization is well on its way to moving from risk being security's problem to risk being a legitimate business concern.

TACTICS

Strategy without tactics is the slowest route to victory. Tactics without strategy is the noise before defeat.

Sun Tzu

Part One of this book defined strategy; the broad plan of action for reaching our information security goals. This section of the book covers the means for carrying out that strategy. The tendency of readers at this point is to jump directly to the tactics they have the most interest in, but we believe readers would be best served by reading Chapter 7 (Tactics: An Introduction) first. It contains the basic framework the authors used to drive their selection and use of the tactics in this portion of the book.

Chapter 7

Tactics: An Introduction

Tactics are procedures or sets of actions used to achieve a specific objective. In military operations, tactics define a number of maneuvers designed to give the attacking or the defending force an advantage. For example, a flanking maneuver is used to confuse and demoralize an enemy force by attacking its position from multiple directions. Confusion causes people to hesitate, and hesitation in war can be fatal. The military objective is to defeat the enemy; flanking is one means to accomplish that objective. Frontal assault and Blitzkrieg are two other examples of offensive tactics. There are also a number of defensive tactics, including camouflage, reconnaissance, and the use of specialized weapons such as surface-to-air missiles, to deal with specific attacks. Each of these tactics has a parallel in the enterprise security realm. This portion of the book covers a number of physical and information security tactics; the focus is primarily on defensive tactics because offensive measures have liabilities associated with them that most nongovernment organizations do not want to deal with. Nonetheless, there are a couple of offensive measures that certainly have merit and are worth studying.

Tactical Framework

A target can be attacked in only so many ways. All tactics, offensive or defensive, are based on this limitation. In medieval days there were two basic ways to defeat a castle: assault or attrition (siege). Castles had a number of tactical features designed to give the defenders a decided advantage, including observation towers, high walls, moats, drawbridges, and fortified gates. Assaulting a castle was a costly proposition, especially in human lives, and there was no guarantee of success, so many commanders chose siege instead. Castles were designed for that contingency too; they had water wells and storehouses of food. Unfortunately, if the castle noble couldn't rally anyone to help break the siege, supplies would eventually run out and the defenders would be forced to surrender.

Castles provide a good metaphor for today's IT environments because the attacks used against IT systems mirror those used against castles—Trojan horses, malicious insiders, spies, impersonation, and so on. What has changed, however, is the configuration of the castle and the alliances of the king. Medieval castles had two or three possible entries; today's computer networks have dozens of entry points (i.e., attack paths or vectors). Castles were self-contained defensive structures with well-guarded entrances; today's computing environments can have a number of alliances that grant access to any number of unknown (or at least unverified) entities. These changes (just like changes in modern warfare) require subsequent changes in defensive tactics. The German Blitzkrieg during World War II is a defining example. The German assault against the highly regarded French Maginot line demonstrated how a small force using advanced technology with skill and daring could overcome even the most robust defenses. The good news is—despite Hollywood's firewall-busting depictions—that there are no tanks (or for that matter any cannons) on the Internet. This does not, however, eliminate the need for us to adjust our defensive tactics as the tactics of our attackers change. Modern warfare offers some interesting advances. For example:

- Spreading out defenses to negate the effects of artillery and aerial bombardment.
- Using defenses laid out in depth to absorb the initial assault of mobile armored forces.
- Keeping a strong mobile reserve for employment against the main assault.
- Replacing a static defense with armored mobile defenses that would absorb the initial assault just long enough to set the conditions for a counterattack. (This was the premise for the defenses in Europe against the massive armored formation of the Soviet Union during the Cold War.)

Warfare in the 21st century has become even more complicated with the introduction of irregular threats (e.g., terrorism) where attackers use modern technology electively to inflict damages and promote their interests. Irregular threats more closely resemble what IT professionals deal with, and like our military counterparts, we use many of the same tactics including "hardening" the facilities and systems that would be the target of such an attack, employing quick incident response forces to rapidly deal with any contingency, and gathering the intelligence needed to detect potential attacks so that we can be prepared for them. Modern armies detect potential attacks through reconnaissance in the air with spy planes and unmanned aerial vehicles, reconnaissance on the ground through patrolling and sensors, and collection of information from electronic and human networks. The parallels in physical and logical security in the corporate environment are not hard to realize, although CCTV surveillance is substituted for aerial reconnaissance. More attack options are available today than ever before (irregular threats are increasing), which makes the tactical framework larger, but it still has a fixed boundary. Whether you are talking about physical or logical targets, tactics are still based on the attack limitations of the opposing force.

Facilities—Physical Attack Scenarios

Theft of assets (data or equipment) is the primary goal of physical attacks against computing facilities. The second most common goal is disruption of service (the loss of data and processing availability). Revenge is yet another common motivation. Seven basic attack scenarios can be used to achieve these goals. Most physical attacks require physical access or proximity except those that can be conducted through a commercial (or other) transport mechanism (e.g., a mail bomb). The seven basic physical attack scenarios are as follows:

1. **Assault**—people-based attacks usually conducted in stealth and frequently involving small arms or other weaponry. Assaults are used to overcome or overwhelm physical protections; steal, damage, or destroy assets; and disrupt operations. Robbery is the most common form of assault. Workplace violence, riots, and terrorism are other examples.

The important thing to remember about assault is that it is the only scenario that can result in the theft of assets. Theft requires a conscious (human) decision. The other attack scenarios may facilitate the thief's access to an asset, but they cannot result in the attacker taking possession of that asset.

2. **Bash**—mechanized assaults; the use of vehicles, heavy equipment, aircraft, and the like, to overcome physical protections (e.g., 9/11 airliner crashes). This scenario is frequently used in combination with a people-based assault to quickly defeat physical protections, but it may also be used to disrupt operations by destroying critical resources or threatening the safety of facility personnel. The best example of this technique is the video of the thief who backs his truck through the front window of a convenience store to bash an ATM off its base, which he then throws into the back of his truck and drives off!

3. **Blast**—the use of explosives, compressed gas, or other blast agents to overcome physical protections, destroy equipment and facilities, or disrupt operations. This scenario is sometimes used in conjunction with an assault to quickly defeat physical protections.

4. **Burn**—the use of fire, acid, or other deterioration agents to overcome physical protections, destroy equipment and facilities, or disrupt operations. This scenario is sometimes used as a diversion in assaults but is more often employed for sabotage or revenge attacks because it is simple to execute.

5. **Flood**—the use of water or other liquids to destroy equipment and facilities or disrupt operations. While water is particularly effective against electronics and computer equipment, it is not a common attack scenario. Most computing facilities carefully monitor and control the use and availability of water within the facility.

6. **Poison**—the use of air, liquid, or food-borne agents to overcome personnel and disrupt operations; examples include gas, smoke, and stink agents. This scenario is sometimes used as a diversion in assaults but is more often used for sabotage or revenge attacks because materials are readily available and the attack is simple to execute.

7. **Siege**—cutoff of access; power; communications; heating, ventilating, and air conditioning; water, or other necessities in an effort to damage or destroy equipment and disrupt operations. This is a very effective scenario, but it can be very difficult to execute and sustain it for an extended period of time. Most computing facilities are designed to withstand these types of failures, and help is readily available in most cases.

The remaining techniques might be classified as annoyance attacks, including false alarms, bomb scares, and light and noise annoyances, which are aimed primarily at disrupting operations. There are any number of possible ways to carry out these attacks. Understanding the attack methods is less important than understanding the limitations (scope) of each scenario. Focusing on attack methods results in point solutions, whereas focusing on attack scenarios results in comprehensive (or multipoint) solutions—solutions that counter multiple attack methods in overlapping scenarios. For example, if we understand that all physical attacks (with the exception of assault) at worst will result in a loss of data availability, we can focus our tactics and control objectives on measures that counter that loss across the entire spectrum of attacks. Let's call this *tactic business continuity planning*. The best tactics are those that use tactical principles to efficiently and effectively counterattack scenarios—something we must never lose sight of in our strategic and tactical endeavors.

IT Systems—Logical Attack Scenarios

There are six basic attack scenarios against computer systems if the attacker does not have physical access or proximity:

1. **System flaws**—Exploit weakness in the operating system, services, hardware, firmware, or software, including coding errors (e.g., buffer overflows) or architecture flaws (e.g., Remote Procedure Call [RPC]).
2. **Configuration flaws**—Exploit errors in the system configuration, including blank or default passwords; enable anonymous or guest accounts and incorrect share of file permissions (e.g., EVERYONE Read/Write).
3. **Unsecured trusts**—Exploit trusts with other systems by poisoning domain naming services (DNS), routing and address resolution entries, or using existing database or Distributed Component Object Model (DCOM) connections to compromise data.
4. **Malware infection**—Implant a piece of malicious code on the system using an e-mail attachment, a malicious download, or a drive-by-attack website.
5. **User impersonation**—Compromise a legitimate user's credentials by guessing or cracking their password, getting them to disclose it (e.g., phishing), or by capturing it with a man-in-the-middle system or a sniffer.
6. **Process flaws**—Become a user on the system by gaming the provisioning process, or convincing (or coercing) someone to create an account for you (i.e., social engineering).

In addition to these scenarios there are seven basic attack scenarios against a system's network connections:

1. **System flaws**
   a. Data access—Exploit weaknesses in the operating system, hardware, firmware, protocol, or services to access data (e.g., cracking wireless encryption) or to access other networks (e.g., virtual local area network [VLAN] hopping).
   b. Denial of Service—Exploit a weakness in a transit node to cause it to fail (e.g., Ping of Death), slowdown (e.g., starvation attack), or malfunction sending data into a black hole.
2. **Passive wiretapping**—Capture data or credentials in transit on a link using a sniffer or a man-in-the-middle system.
3. **Data insertion**—Write data to the link such as a cookie or a packet with credentials to gain access to a resource.
4. **Node impersonation**—Become or compromise a transit node on the link to capture the data or credentials passing through it or to redirect traffic to another system.
5. **Configuration flaw**—Exploit the configuration of a transit node to gain access and redirect traffic to another system (e.g., ARP, routing or DNS poisoning).
6. **End-point impersonation**—Appear to be the legitimate end point of the link by cloning the real system or by DNS poisoning.
7. **Process flaws**—Become a permitted node on the link by convincing or coercing someone to add your transit node to the network. Once attached it can be used to capture data and credential.

These descriptions contain just a small number of possible methods used to carry out these attacks, but it isn't the methods that are important. Understanding the scope (boundaries) of the attack scenarios is what's important. When we begin to break our strategy down into specific tactical objectives, we must keep the big picture in mind. We need to focus on the attack scenarios, not the attack methods. Here's a quick example. Implanting a piece of malicious code on the system is a common attack scenario. What is our objective? Preventing the code from getting there or preventing it from doing any damage when it does? Most would say both, but in truth only the latter really matters. Preventing unauthorized code from executing on the system is a more effective and efficient control than using a control that compares every piece of data coming into or going out of the system to 2 million virus signatures! The best tactics are those that use tactical principles to efficiently and effectively counterattack scenarios. Another advantage of this approach is the ability to clearly see what attack scenarios you have control over and which you do not; this information is particularly valuable when you are assessing outsourced services.

Objectives Identification

As stated earlier, tactics are used to achieve a particular outcome, so it stands to reason that those outcomes (objectives) must first be identified before an appropriate tactic or tactics can be selected.

The process involves breaking down the strategic plan into smaller point solutions. For example, the strategy may call for the proper management of privacy-related information. Under that strategy heading, we can identify a number of specific objectives at the people, process, and technology levels, including training, operational procedures, access controls, and identity assurance.

The broad category may be "excellence in operations," with the specific objectives being ironclad identity management, least privilege access controls, and so on. In Figure 7.1 the security objective is listed under each tactic. The description provides additional tactical details. Once these objectives have been identified, the resources, time, and effort needed to achieve them can

Security tactics	Description
Defense in depth Manage risk across all layers of the computing environment	Securing the perimeter and network Secure hosts and applications Secure data security and privacy Secure operations and personnel Physical security
Excellence in identity management User authentication, user privacy, data access, and facilities access	Practice the principle of least privilege Enforce accountability Enforce privacy and privacy rights Audit identity assurance processes
Excellence in security engineering Engineer software, hardware, and facilities to be secure.	Secure by design Secure in development Secure in deployment Redundant and fault tolerant
Excellence in operations People, processes, and technology to maintain and operate secure systems	Practice good supervision Maintain and monitor system security Audit and monitor for compliance Practice incident response Awareness and staff skills training

Figure 7.1   Security objectives and tactics.

be determined. It is vitally important to fix these objectives before moving on to the tactics for achieving them. If your objectives are not fixed, they will shift, and the results will be a tremendous waste of time and money.

First Principles

> In disquisitions of every kind there are certain primary truths, or first principles, upon which all subsequent reasoning must depend.
>
> **Alexander Hamilton**

In the early 1300s while King Edward was busy putting down the Scottish Rebellion led by William Wallace, the Welsh launched their own rebellion. King Edward had left the castles in Wales sparsely defended: A mere 13 soldiers were stationed at Carmarthen, yet they were able to ward off an attack by more than 300 Welsh rebels. This was possible because castles incorporated a number of important tactical principles that gave the defenders a decided advantage. The following sections detail the military and security "first principles" we used to guide our reasoning and tactical recommendations for the remainder of this book.

> Now there are five matters to which a general must pay strict heed. The first of these is administration; the second, preparedness; the third, determination; the fourth, prudence; and the fifth, economy.
>
> **Wu Ch'i**

Observation Principle

Observation is the central principle of security. It acts as both a deterrent and a detector—a deterrent because people are less likely to intentionally do something wrong if they think someone will see them doing it and a detector because observation is how we determine something is wrong (or at least has the appearance of being wrong). Virtually every security measure is based on one or both of these observation elements. We tend to think of observation in terms of vision, but this is only partially correct. Physical security uses personnel and video cameras (CCTV) to monitor sensitive areas, but it also relies on devices to expand or aid that vision—devices that detect (observe) other activities such as a door opening, glass breaking, or something moving across a room.

Observation provides early warning of potential danger so that we can prepare defenses; presents evidence of an existing attack so we can respond; and gives us the information we need to use our forces effectively against the key points of attack. You could think of these three functions as reconnaissance, sentry, and command, respectively.

Offensive units use reconnaissance to locate and engage the enemy; defensive units use reconnaissance for early-warning purposes. By observing and assessing an enemy's strength, readiness, and attack plans, reconnaissance gives the defending force time to prepare and deploy appropriate countermeasures. Modern military units use spies, recon teams, satellite imaging, and unmanned drone aircraft for reconnaissance purposes. Similar techniques are used in the information security realm. Reconnaissance information is gathered by organizations like AT&T, Microsoft, and Symantec. These groups track abnormal and malicious activity on the Internet to help organizations prepare for and respond to attacks. The Microsoft Malicious Software Removal tool is a good example. Whenever the tool removes a malicious piece of software, it reports the IP address of the host and the name of the malicious software to Microsoft so that outbreaks can be tracked by location and intensity. Several organizations compile reconnaissance information on emerging or potential threats, and post this information on the Internet for others to use. The SANS Internet Storm Center is one such site; most of the major antivirus vendors provide this type of information as well. In addition, a number of subscription services provide timely threat and attack information, for example, the Websense and SurfControl Internet Threat Databases. Some Managed Security Service Providers (MSSPs) furnish this information as part of their management service. These services will proactively send warnings and alerts to their customer base if an attack is imminent.

Sentries are deployed along the perimeter of an encampment in order to provide attack notification and to try and slow down the attacking force while defense forces rally. Sentry positions were often enhanced with noisemakers or other devices designed to alert sentries to movement along the perimeter. In IT we employ intrusion detection and other logical and physical perimeter controls to protect our key data repositories and processing installations.

The command function will be discussed in the next section; here let it suffice to say that the commander's ability to make effective decisions when responding to an attack is based wholly on what he or she or others can observe.

Observation is central to security. If we want to have a successful security management program, we need observant people. We need to train people to be observant. This is more than awareness training. Most awareness training is focused on process: "do this, don't do that." We want people who can assess a situation and say, "What's wrong with this picture?" Those people won't open an attachment on an unsolicited e-mail. Those are the people who will pick up the handouts left behind in the conference room. And those are the people who will call the security desk when they suspect something "just isn't right."

Whether defensive or offensive, observation is one of the most important principles in tactics. All our tactics should include an observation element that can alert us when an attack is imminent or manifest. The tactics we employ must also be able to provide sufficient information to direct responses to the key points of attack.

Response Principle

Effective security is based on the ability to respond to wrongdoing; the quicker the response, the less the damage. Response relies heavily on observation, but it is also tightly linked to the timeliness principle. Whether primary or reserve forces, the ability to rapidly concentrate troops to repel an attack is critical. At Carmarthen Castle wide corridors in the walls and wide walkways atop the walls made it easy for troops to move from one attack point to another. Today attacks against IT systems are highly automated, making it possible to compromise a large number of systems and proliferate further attacks very rapidly. Consequently, our people, processes, and technology must be equally efficient at repelling these attacks through timely automated responses, reliable communications, and near real-time alerting. The tactics we employ must also provide specific enough information to facilitate quick and effective responses to the key points of attack.

Timeliness Principle

Timeliness refers to the appropriateness of the time interval between two events. The cell phone is a great example; one of the things that is absolutely unacceptable is getting missed call or voice mail notifications two or three days after the fact. There is an appropriate time frame for delivering this information and two days isn't it! It's really a matter of the value or usefulness of the information that tends to decline over time. People call you because they want to talk to you now, not because they want to wait two days for a return call. Timeliness ensures that information is available and acted upon when it is most valuable. In the security realm timeliness means:

■ Information about control failures and security violations is reported in real time to someone (or some process) that can take action on them.

■ Information about suspicious activities is logged and reported in real time to someone (or some process) that can take action when the activity exceeds established thresholds.

■ Information about security-related activities is logged in real time, preserved, and reviewed at reasonable intervals.

■ Information about threats or imminent attacks is delivered early enough for countermeasures to be devised and deployed.

In reality, there are many other security time frames to consider, including process intervals for antivirus signature updates, system patching, trouble ticket response and resolution, and disaster recovery. Finally, timeliness applies to our people. People receive timely supervision, timely training (not months before the training is needed or months afterward), and timely recognition. The effectiveness of our tactics depends on our ability to operate them in a timely manner. Timeliness must be an integral part of our tactics and tactical planning.

Preparedness Principle

Ben Franklin once said, "By failing to prepare you are preparing to fail." The authors couldn't agree more, and if we had to pick one thing that IT security is really bad at, this would be it. The potential for DDoS (Distributed Denial of Service) attacks was known years before the first one was manifest, but no one really prepared for them. After the attack on Amazon, eBay, and Yahoo, the threat became "real," and the experts were all over it. This is the equivalent of waiting until someone takes a shot at the president before you assign Secret Service agents to protect him.

Preparedness has three equally important elements: people, process, and technology. To manage security and security incidents effectively, you need skilled people, a proven process (i.e., Incident Response Plan, Disaster Recovery Plan, etc.), and the appropriate weapons (tools). Yet, very few organizations have an employee skills management process or a viable security training budget. Misconfiguration is the most common cause of security breaches involving firewalls, but half of the firewall administrators Bill has interviewed over the years have never had any formal training on the devices they are managing. The process side fares only slightly better; most companies have some kind of incident response or event management process, fewer have a formal (documented) plan, even fewer have a plan that has been tested, and very few have regular drills/practices. In one instance, Bill was sitting in the War Room at a customer site when the Incident Response Team was activated to deal with the Code Red worm. Team members were notified by e-mail and text message to call into the incident management conference bridge immediately. Two hours later they were still trying to get critical resources to join the call; people had changed jobs, left the company, changed cell phone numbers, and the plan had not been updated to reflect those changes (nor was there a process for maintaining notification information).

The final piece of preparedness is weaponry—the tools required to make the process work. The process will tell you what needs to be done; the question is, "How fast can you get it done?" A tale of two companies will serve to illustrate the point. The Network Intrusion Detection System (NIDS) at Company A notified IT security that a system infected with MSBlaster was attached to the internal network. Based on the NIDS information, the team was able to determine that the system was attached to one of six network concentrators. By accessing each concentrator and reviewing the ARP tables, they were able to narrow the system down to a particular port (elapsed time: 30 minutes), but before they could trace the wiring from the concentrator to a physical port in a conference room, the problem disappeared (meeting over!). Now, the investigation would need to move to: Who scheduled the room? Who attended the meeting? Who connected to the network? Instead, the investigation was terminated; better luck next time! Company B had the same event show up on their NIDS. The IT security team opened up the network trace tool, identified and disabled the concentrator port in question, and mapped the port to a connection in a conference room. Then they opened up the black listing tool and added the system's machine (MAC) address to prevent any further network access (elapsed time: 8 minutes). Next they sent an agent to the conference room to notify the user so that they could open a trouble ticket and get the worm removed (total elapsed time: 20 minutes). Not only was this a timely and effective response, but it was also quite the "wow" factor for all the meeting attendees—wow enough for everyone to want to learn more about these tools. Preparedness is about being proactive and having the tactical vision and understanding necessary to equip the security team with the skills, processes, and tools they need to be successful. Preparedness provides tactical advantage.

A man surprised is half beaten.

Thomas Fuller
Gnomologia

Economy Principle

IT security professionals think of the economy principle in terms of control costs. The cost of protecting data should be commensurate with value of the data. In other words you don't spend $100,000 on security to protect something worth $50,000. However, there is a military perspective for this principle that is far more valuable: economy of forces.

Observation and preparedness make it possible to economize on the forces required to repel an attack. The story of the rebel attack on Carmarthen Castle in Wales is a perfect example of this principle. Thirteen well-trained and disciplined soldiers, a large cache of weaponry, and excellent observation and command processes defeated 300 rebels without a single casualty. You can also see how this principle has played out in modern warfare; as warfare has progressed, fewer and fewer troops are required to accomplish the mission. Some of this reduction is due to better training, some to better weaponry (increased firepower), but mostly it is due to observation. Laser targeting is a great example. From great distances a soldier can "paint" an enemy position with a laser that directs bombs to that position. Streaming video from drones helps direct artillery, mortars, and other ordinance to specific targets, allowing a small force to rapidly advance on and overcome an enemy position. On the defensive side this is equally true. A small force properly positioned and supplied can repel a much greater force.

Economy of force is of great interest to CFOs and other executive managers looking for ways to cut overhead expense, but this isn't a common motivation for security departments. This is, in our opinion, another big failure of our profession. Instead of focusing on high-value solutions like expert observation and quick response, the industry has focused on layered technology. Please don't get us wrong; the authors are not against defense in depth; it is a very valid tactic. In fact, we have dedicated an entire chapter to the topic (see Chapter 8). What we are saying is that it is possible to achieve an adequate level of protection without overdoing it.

Let's take Network Intrusion Detection (NID), Host Intrusion Detection (HID), Application Intrusion Detection (AID), and Data Intrusion Detection (DID) as examples. Security professionals understand that the closer the control is to the target, the more effective it will be; yet, enterprises insist on investing huge amounts of money in Network and Host Intrusion Detection systems (NIDS and HIDS). Why? We all understand that the primary target of an attacker is data. We have also seen a major shift of attacks from operating system (OS) and network to applications. Why aren't we focusing on data and application intrusion detection systems (DIDS and AIDS)? These are much more valuable, especially in cloud-based scenarios where an attacker with a stolen credit card can bypass all the network and host security controls and directly attack the application and its data sources. NIDS and HIDS have very limited value in this scenario; however, AID and DID systems would not only work, but would be far more accurate (have fewer false positives) than their host and network counterparts. If we apply the principle of economy of force, we can eliminate NID and HID systems, rid ourselves of tons of near worthless data, and substantially reduce the time and/or computing power it takes to identify and respond to an attack. Is this what the industry is emphasizing? No! Instead, the industry is saying that the way to economize is to outsource the monitoring and analysis of all this worthless data to a managed security service provider (MSSP). That may be cost reduction, but it's not economy of force.

If you're a security professional reading this, you're probably thinking the authors are heretics, and if you're an executive manager you're probably thinking we're saviors. Actually, neither label is correct. All we are trying to say is that our tactics need to focus on what really matters and on what produces the best results. If you are sure your systems are well configured and are resistant to attack, why do you care if there are malformed or attack packets on your network (provided they aren't impacting system performance)? Again, please don't misinterpret what we're saying: We are not saying these packets should be ignored (the source should be tracked down and eliminated if possible), but as long as they are not a threat to your data, they do not warrant an immediate response. If our force is sufficiently equipped to defend our prize possession (i.e., data), expending resources on these other forms of intrusion detection is a complete waste.

Intrusion prevention has similar issues: It is looking for specific abnormal behaviors, but the kinds of behaviors that put data at risk such as query return size aren't within the scope of network or host intrusion prevention systems. A good AIDS or DIDS would recognize and limit the response or salt the response with bogus records (which could be used to detect and repel further attacks). The obvious question is, "Where do you get AIDS and DIDS systems?" That's a good question: At this writing, a small number of companies offer Web application intrusion detection solutions, and no one offers DIDS solutions. That's bad news for people looking for off-the-shelf solutions. If you build software in-house, there is a decent body of research to help you add these features to your software and data management solutions (see Chapter 11).

The economy principle focuses resources on the most effective and efficient tactics and control objectives. The principle balances technological costs with process and force economy to simplify data protection tasks and reduce operational overhead.

Maintenance of Reserves (Coverage) Principle

Maintaining an adequate reserve force allows the respondent to react quickly to attacks and unexpected developments. In the military it is customary to keep about a quarter of the forces in reserve. In a corporate context it's easier to think of this principle as the coverage principle—having sufficient resources to effectively manage security operations, respond to attacks, and deal with other unexpected events. Coverage begins with people. Nothing trumps a well-trained staff in day-to-day operations, especially in attack or breach situations. The goal of coverage is to have skilled people always available to manage security operations and responses. This includes a staff that has been cross trained to cover periods of illness, vacation, training, and other absences. Skills management has already been mentioned in a previous section, and it is not our intent to beat the point to death, but ensuring proper coverage for security functions requires a good understanding of what critical skills are required and of managing training and staffing to make sure you have a sufficient number of people with those skills. This includes in-house expertise from IT and other departments or divisions, as well as external expertise such as penetration testers, forensics consultants, and law enforcement. If you have high-value or high-sensitivity data, you may want to consider keeping some of these external resources on retainer or contract. Effective tactics require a sufficiently skilled staff. Tactical planning must include a thorough assessment of the knowledge, skills, and abilities (KSAs) required for each control objective.

The coverage principle also extends to security management processes. Processes are essentially a command framework, in the sense that they identify key resources and direct how those resources will be used. Good processes ensure that the information required to make decisions is collected and available when it is needed, and good processes provide the order and guidance needed to make those decisions efficient and effective. Process is the commander at Carmarthen Castle going to the top of the observation tower to gather information about the enemy's attack points and his troop positions, and then quickly repositioning troops to counter those attacks. Coverage means our processes are capable of effectively dealing with all the aspects of a situation. From his corner tower, the commander at Carmarthen Castle could only observe attacks against two of the castle walls. Fortunately, these were the only two walls the rebels could attack; otherwise, the process would have required a soldier with signaling capabilities in the opposite tower. When planning and selecting tactics, it's not going to be possible to foresee every conceivable situation, but it is possible to build a framework capable of covering the normal and the unexpected. This must be what we strive for in our tactical planning endeavors.

Technology is the final aspect of coverage. Computing environments are so complex that it's nearly impossible to find a single solution that covers everything. Conversely, "securing almost everything" is an oxymoron. Security is only as good as the weakest link; leaving some things unprotected is like locking all but one window in your house. Guess which one the thief came through? Each of our tactics and associated control objectives must apply to all our systems and must encompass all of the associated attack scenarios. A tactic that protects your systems from outside attacks and leaves them wide open to insiders is a poor solution. Coverage says our controls apply equally across our entire environment.

SIDEBAR: MAY DAY! MAY DAY!

After the 2000 May Day riots in London, Scotland Yard employed a number of these tactical principles to deal with future May Day protests and violence. First, they increased their observation capabilities with some 2,000 video feeds, including teams of roving police "spotters" armed with cameras. Second, they used this surveillance to rapidly direct officers (with the appropriate equipment/weaponry) to any emerging trouble spot. This rapid response capability gave the respondents the edge; they were able to break up crowds before they gained any malicious momentum. Scotland Yard kept a large force in reserve as well. In addition to the "all hands" deployment of central London police officers, more than 1,000 officers from surrounding boroughs were kept in active reserve.

Redundancy Principle

Security failures are some of the most impactful events an organization can experience. These failures involve not only security breaches but also system/equipment failures. For example, losing a building or computer access control system will keep people from getting to their workspaces or accessing the applications they need to do their jobs. They also include failures in security processes that create vulnerabilities, allow vulnerable systems in the production environment, or hamper incident responses and disaster recovery. The redundancy principle states that security functions should have no single point of failure.

Technology redundancy is a fairly well-understood discipline. Most vendor solutions have some level of redundancy or high-availability functionality built in, and we encourage the use of these technologies in all primary solutions. However, our tactics must include redundancy in supporting technologies as well. Communications for incident management is a great example. When the Red Code worm hit Dallas, Texas, it infected a large number of companies, including the company where Bill was working. The IT security manager requested his assistance, so Bill followed him to the War Room where the manager promptly dialed in to the conference bridge only to receive a busy signal! Apparently, hundreds of companies were using this bridge to manage the crisis, and there were no more circuits available. The alternative was to use the conference-calling capability of the company's PBX, but it was limited to 8 connections, actually 16, because the room had two phone circuits. Now the fun began. First everyone had to be notified to abandon the bridge and get into the office as soon as possible. Conference rooms were taken over at each business location and became part of the conference call on one phone. The other phone was used to call "critical" personnel, including the CIO, the manager of IT operations, and the network engineering lead. Two hours later almost everyone was on board, but little had gotten accomplished in the interim unless you consider having another thousand or so systems infected with the worm an accomplishment! One other interesting resource issue came to light when the security manager attempted to share his desktop with people in the other conference rooms. The traffic generated by the worm had clogged the wide area network connections, making it nearly impossible to maintain a reliable Netmeeting connection. Even getting e-mails delivered was a challenge. The loss of the conference bridge and network-based communications greatly impaired the organization's ability to rapidly respond to a critical situation, and they had no viable alternatives.

The story stands to illustrate both a technological issue and a process issue. The Incident Response Plan had no built-in contingencies to deal with a conference bridge failure. The conference bridge was a single point of failure. If no one activated the conference, people just waited and nothing got accomplished. Incident response is only one example of the importance of this principle; our tactics should include redundancy for all security processes. When Bill worked at Predictive Systems, this was known as the "four eyes" rule. According to this rule, one person does the work and another person verifies it was done correctly. This is the standard process for commercial aircraft maintenance; all repairs require an inspection and signoff before the aircraft is permitted to fly. Unfortunately, this practice is not standard in many security-related functions. Perhaps the best demonstration of this is the number of security failures attributed to misconfiguration. The possibility of misconfiguring a device is substantially reduced if someone is verifying the changes to a security control. The goal of the redundancy principle is to avoid these issues and ensure that security functions continue to operate effectively even in times of duress.

Least Privilege Principle

The principle of least privilege—only granting users or processes access to the resources they require to accomplish their assigned tasks—has been around since the inception of IT security. However, the application of least privilege in business IT systems is practically nonexistent. Part of the problem is application related—poor security designs that require applications to be run with elevated privileges or grant excess permissions to application resources and data. The other major problem is the lack of management tools. There are no Top Secret or RACF management facilities for workstations and servers. PCs may have the computing power of a mainframe, but they have the management capabilities of a moron. Equating users with access to specific resources is an arduous task even if you are using a common platform. Throw in a couple of different platforms, and it becomes near impossible.

That having been said, it still doesn't change our need to protect data and computing assets. The business process mapping component of security strategy helps address this issue by identifying the key business functions and the resources that support them. Combined with an organizational chart, it makes it fairly easy to determine who needs access to what. Unfortunately, it will not tell you what permissions they require; this is where security process comes into play. The provisioning process must capture required permissions, and the revocation process must capture what permissions to remove. Furthermore, our change processes must include an evaluation of the impact of a change on access privileges. Technology solutions in this area are likely to remain sparse mostly because of the complexity of the environment. However, cloud computing does offer an opportunity for better management tools because the model mirrors a mainframe.

Today least privilege is really a trade-off between functionality and protection, and too often protection is on the losing side. Our tactics should endeavor to enforce the principle of least privilege in some meaningful manner. At the very least, access should be divided into three distinct categories:

1. Viewer—someone with privileges to read information
2. Contributor—someone with privileges to read and write information
3. Administrator—someone with all privileges

Commonality Principle

Complexity is the antithesis of security; the more complex an environment becomes, the more difficult it is to secure. The goal of the commonality principle is to minimize complexity through standardization. The ideal environment from a security standpoint has all the same systems with the same set of security controls configured the same way. The reality is far from the ideal; multiple systems, configured differently, running different applications, and using different security controls is the norm. To make matters worse, the data formats are different too. When security information resides in multiple places in different formats, the consolidation and processing of that information become difficult, time consuming, and often labor intensive. In addition, the processes do not scale, and they cannot be easily automated. This is where commonality comes into play.

Commonality establishes consistent repeatable processes that facilitate information collection, processing, and reporting. Any process that is consistent and repeatable can be automated. Automation increases process efficiency and accuracy, expands the scope of observation, and reduces response time. This is accomplished by standardizing on a specific set of technologies for the storage and transfer of information, for example, using technologies with SQL Server data stores. Having a common database technology means information can be easily transferred between systems using built-in SQL server data connectors and database joins. Transfers can be done continuously in near real time instead of being reformatted and processed in a periodic batch job. SQL Server also supports another important commonality factor: scripting (customization). The ability to customize data transfers and data manipulation means controls can be easily modified to support new requirements or emergency situations.

Table 7.1   Primary Components Supporting Commonality

Factor	Description
Storage	Scalable data storage with the following capabilities: 1. Real-time data transfer 2. Search and/or indexing 3. Customizable data transfer and data manipulation
Transfer	Scalable multipath (redundant) transfer mechanism for security data and alerts
Format	Common formats for security data and alerts including a common naming convention for each data field
Alert	A scalable alert processing facility (e.g., System Center, OpenView) with fully customizable alert processing and multiple notification channels (e.g., pager, text messaging, e-mail, voice, etc.)
Report	A scalable reporting engine having native data access and a robust set of reporting features such as: • Tabular data display • Sorting, filtering, and grouping • Chart and graph generation • Dashboarding • Multiple export formats (e.g., Excel, PDF, HTML)

Commonality focuses on standards rather than functionality. Standard protocols may not be the most robust or the most secure options, but they will be the most interoperable and have the largest selection of well-supported products in the marketplace. For example, use of a standard alerting protocol such as the Simple Network Management Protocol (SNMP) Trap means that the data generated on any platform (i.e., Windows, UNIX, Cisco, Nortel) can easily be forwarded, received, and processed by most network management consoles, including Microsoft System Center, HP OpenView, and Tivoli NetView (all of which have fully customizable alert processing capabilities). The commonality of components and customization facilitates the collection, processing, and reporting of security data, functions that are critical to the success of security management and the enterprise. For the primary components supporting commonality, see Table 7.1.

The commonality principle is a major contributor to the interoperability and efficiency of our security solutions and must be one of the factors considered when you are formulating your tactics and control objectives.

Conclusion

Tactics are procedures or sets of actions used to achieve a specific objective. Before tactics can be selected, it is necessary to break down the strategic plan into smaller point solutions to identify objectives. Once the objectives are known, it is possible to apply tactical principles in the selection and deployment of controls. It is important to realize that in any given strategic planning cycle you will have realized objectives, unrealized objectives, and emerging objectives. In other words, depending on the resources, budget, and so on that you have available, you will reach some objectives, others will not happen or will only be partially realized, and new objectives will crop up that were not anticipated. A wise commander keeps an appropriate amount of resources in reserve to deal with changes in the tactical requirements. There are only so many ways a system can be attacked; all tactics, offensive or defensive, are based on this limitation. Understanding the limitations of attack scenarios allows us to focus on the tactical principles that most efficiently deal with the threat. Tactics share a set of primary truths or "first principles" that guide their development, selection, and deployment. These principles are an integral part of the tactical framework the authors used to drive their selection and recommended uses of security tactics.

As we shall show, defense is a stronger form of fighting than attack.

Carl von Clausewitz
On War

Chapter 8

Layer upon Layer (Defense in Depth)

The best defense…is a lot of defense.

Frank Hayes Sr.
Columnist for *Computerworld*

Introduction

This chapter is about defense in depth, a multilayer, multidimensional protection scheme designed to absorb and progressively weaken an attack. The term *defense in depth* has for many years been a catch-all phrase for the information security industry, so it is probably worthwhile to spend some time explaining exactly what this tactic is.

Let's start with what defense in depth is not. Defense in depth is not just technology. The traditional understanding of defense in depth has been based on a five-layer model that begins with perimeter defenses and progresses through network, host, application, and data protections. Companies that have implemented protections at two or more of these layers have "defense in depth." Vendor products that provide these protections are "defense-in-depth" technologies. The primary problem with this model is that it is technology-centric; it doesn't properly address the people and process (operations) side of the equation. Furthermore, advances in technology and services have greatly eroded the usefulness of this model. For example, wireless technologies and "any data, any time, on any device" initiatives have completely redefined the term *perimeter*. Online and cloud computing services connect users directly to applications, bypassing perimeter, network, and host controls. These advances require us to think of defense in depth in an entirely different manner. Figure 8.1 shows how cloud computing has turned the old defense-in-depth model on its head.

What is defense in depth? Defense in depth is a multilayer and multidimensional protection scheme; multilayered in the sense that an attacker must overcome more than one defensive measure to achieve their objective. It is multidimensional because those defenses address different

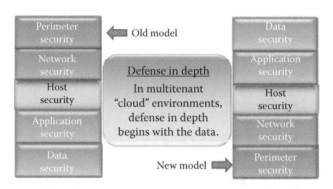

Figure 8.1 Old and new five-layer model.

aspects of an attack; some protect, some detect, and others respond. Remember, the primary objective behind defense in depth is *time*. A good defense-in-depth implementation is designed to absorb and progressively weaken an attack, thus providing the responder with sufficient time to organize the resources and weaponry required to repel the attack. This requires the application of multiple overlapping protections at the people, technology, and operational process levels.

Thirteenth-century castles are classic examples of defense in depth. They not only provided multiple barriers (layers) that the attacker had to overcome, but they also addressed the essential dimensions of a good defense—observation, rapid response, and weaponry. Castles contained a core (inner ward) where the most valued assets were kept; surrounding the core was an inner wall, with one or two entry points (gates) and multiple fortifications, including archery slits, kill holes, and stockpiles of weaponry (see Figure 8.2).

The inner wall provided a fallback position for the king's soldiers should the outer wall be breached. This seldom happened. The outer walls were massive, surrounded by moats or ditches and supplied with ample watchtowers for observing the attackers and directing responses. Wide passageways in and atop the wall allowed troops to rapidly deploy to points of attacks. An ample cache of weapons at each defensive position gave the defenders a decided advantage. The outer gates were equally fortified, reinforced with iron, barred with massive beams, and protected by drawbridges. So daunting were castle defenses that prior to the invention of the cannon, most commanders chose to besiege rather than attack a castle. The good news: There are no cannons on the Internet and laying siege to a site (i.e., denial of service) is a short-lived attack.

Castles didn't start out as defense-in-depth structures; 11th-century castles were primarily wooden-fenced mounds easily defeated with a good fire. In the 12th century the wooden fence was replaced with a stone wall and a tall stone tower or "keep." The keep was like a castle within the castle and was generally considered to be the final defensive structure. Keeps were also used as living quarters and for storing armory. The battering ram was the primary nemesis of these structures because keeps were not designed to allow defenders to actively fight back. Later in the 12th century, keeps were constructed on the outer walls to provide observation and the means to fight back. The inner court of the castle became known as the "ward." Overhangs were added to the walls, providing a platform on the top of the wall from which defenders could shoot arrows, drop stones, pour hot liquids, and so on. Beginning in the 13th century, a second wall around the structure was added creating a second or "outer" ward. Ditches and moats were constructed around the outer wall and strong gatehouses with metal-reinforced

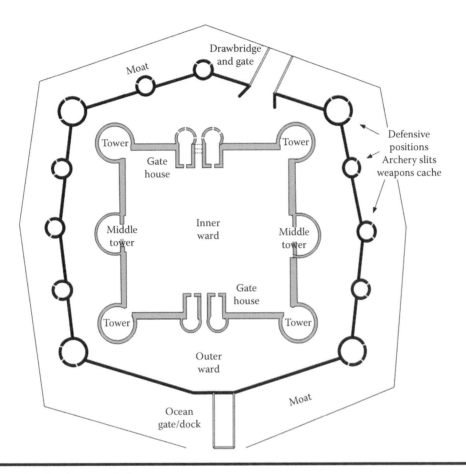

Figure 8.2   Castle ground plan.

doors and drawbridges were added. The wall walkways were broadened, and slotted stones were added to the top to provide cover for the defenders. Finally, archery slits and kill holes were added to provide the defenders with good cover and a wide field of fire. These improvements in castle fortifications made it possible for a relatively small force to hold out against a much larger adversary. The evolution of castle defenses offers a good analogy for information security; just as castles changed in response to changing threats, so also must our information security defenses.

Defense-in-Depth Objectives Identification

Other chapters in this book provide specific tactical information for implementing defense-in-depth controls; this chapter only addresses objectives identification for defense in depth. It is important to understand that the primary objective behind defense in depth is *time.* This has two aspects: first, require the attacker to expend lots of time and resources attacking, and second, have near real-time attack detection and rapid response capabilities. This is much easier said than done in a world of zero day exploits, worms, and distributed (BOT) attacks, not to mention disparate security controls that are scattered across multiple governing authorities.

Today defense in depth really becomes a question of what you have direct control over (your enclave), how that environment relates to other enclaves and the supporting infrastructure, coupled, of course, with the threats that are present in each instance. Today's computer environments require more than technological controls. People and operational processes are critical to overall security and must always be taken into consideration. In the past we were concerned primarily with what was coming into our environment; today, we must be equally concerned with what is going out.

Information Environments

Today we find three common information environments: in-house, hybrid, and hosted. In-house is a localized computing environment (enclave) consisting of people, technology (i.e., end-user systems, servers, communications systems, etc.), and operational practices that are under the control of a single authority governed by organizational policy. On the other side of the spectrum is the hosted environment consisting of people, technology, and operations that are under the control of an external authority governed by contract. This is not to say that hosting environments are not governed by internal organizational policies; they undoubtedly are, but the customer's security requirements are seldom the same as the provider's, and these differences are usually specified in the service contract. It is also important to note that the hosting environment is also an enclave; to the provider it is a localized computing environment under the control of a single authority. The hybrid environment combines in-house and hosted services to form an environment with multiple control authorities and multiple governing vehicles (policies and contractual agreements).

Attached to these environments are two other elements that must be considered for objectives identification: networks and supporting infrastructure. Networks provide data transport between enclaves. Network service providers also consist of people, technology, and operational practices (which may or may not be under a single authority) governed by contractual agreement(s). The supporting infrastructure includes all the organizational capabilities that provide support for the information processing environment, including human resources, training, and purchasing. Each of these elements has different information security requirements and very different security objectives.

Threats

Each environment is also subject to a number of different threats including natural disasters, physical hazards, and human malfeasance. Natural disasters include floods, earthquakes, lightning, solar flares, fires, and other naturally induced hazards. Physical hazards are human-induced threats, including structural failures (e.g., building collapse), machinery, and equipment failures (e.g., ventilation systems), water damage from plumbing or fire suppression systems, explosions, hazardous material spills, and so on. Human malfeasance includes acts of sabotage, terrorism, spying, hacking, riots and looting, criminal enterprises, corrupt officials, and disgruntled employees, as well as damages from careless or accidental actions.

Natural disasters are typically addressed by business continuity planning (BCP) and/or disaster recovery planning (DRP) objectives. These objectives may include some physical hazards, but the majority of physical hazards are addressed by physical security and facility operational security objectives. Human malfeasance poses the greatest danger to information security and is by far the biggest driver of defense-in-depth objectives. Human malfeasance can be grouped into four basic types of activities:

1. Passive attacks—traffic analysis, data capture (sniffing attacks), and other types of eavesdropping
2. Active attacks—session stealing, data tampering, vulnerability exploits, malicious code introduction, and other types of attacks that generate traffic or unnecessarily consume resources
3. Insider attacks—passive or active attacks generated by someone with authorized physical or logical access
4. Distribution attacks—malicious modifications to hardware or software at the source (manufacturer) or during distribution

Objectives identification must include measures to address these attacks, as well as the threats posed by incidental human error.

Environmental Objectives

Now let's take a look at the defense-in-depth objectives for the various information environments we have identified.

In-House Objectives

The emphasis for in-house enclaves is usually the perimeter/enclave boundary, with additional defenses at the network and host levels. Objectives are focused on well-defined and controlled gateways between the enclave and external entities. Objectives within this environment will vary depending on business type, data value, and applicable regulations, but the following list is fairly common.

1. Operational excellence for security controls
2. High assurance identity management
3. Timely incident response and resolution
4. Limited and controlled boundary access points
5. Effective logging, detection, and alerting capabilities
6. Superior personal supervision, training, and skills management

Note that these objectives provide coverage for people (6), technology (4–5), and operational (1–3) security while promoting the principles of observation (5) and rapid response (3). What these objectives do not fully address are insider attacks and attacks against applications and data. This, however, is not uncommon for in-house environments; a surprising number of companies simply do not address insider threats.

Limited and Controlled Boundary Access Points

As stated earlier, this is a main security focus for in-house environments. Castles divided defenses into zones that progressively limited access, and when you think about it, access is the basis of all security. Confidentiality is about limiting read access to information, integrity is about limiting write access, and availability is about ensuring access (the CIA model). Authentication and authorization control access to systems and data, whereas audit controls record access to these elements (AAA model). The Trusted System Evaluation Criteria (TSEC) model is designed to prevent unauthorized access, modification (write access), destruction (write/delete access), or denial of access to systems and data. Therefore, the same principles used to defend castles can be applied to in-house enclaves by leveraging advances in network bandwidth, firewall, and proxy technologies. The following discussion presents one possible scenario for implementing limited and controlled access points in a local (in-house) computing environment.

The local computing enclave, the other enclaves it connects to, and the associated infrastructure are areas that have a well-defined set of member entities and a set of access rules to define what entities (people or processes) can reside in the enclave, what entities have access into the enclave, what entities have access out of the enclave, and what accesses within the enclave are permitted. A simple example is the Internet (although it is hard to imagine it as an enclave) where any IP entity can be placed in the enclave, any entity can gain access into the enclave, any entity in the enclave can gain access out, and connections within the enclave are generally not restricted. The Internet is like the countryside surrounding the castle: Anyone can move into the area, and they are free to move about as they please, visiting people and villages to conduct their business. By contrast, the castle keep was a highly restricted area where a limited number of nobles resided and access to and from the keep was limited to a handful of trusted individuals (members of the court).

IT resources are placed into enclaves based on their value to the corporation. Although there can be any number of enclaves within the local computing environment, four are fairly common: core, internal, extranet, and external. Each enclave has a specific set of security rules that govern internal operations and accesses from other enclaves. As in the castle, the most valuable assets are placed in the core enclave, which is protected by a well-defined security boundary, limited access points (gateways), continuous monitoring, and highly restricted access. Resources in the core enclave would include critical network and corporate services such as directory, time and name services, messaging, network management, and backup systems, as well as major corporate databases and other valuable data stores.

Enclaves are governed by a set of security rules that define five specific things:

1. What entities can be located in the enclave
2. How entities interact within the enclave (internal operations)
3. What external entities are allowed access into the enclave
4. What internal entities are allowed access outside the enclave
5. How these activities will be monitored

These rules limit and control the enclave's boundary access points. For example, in the core enclave the only entities allowed are critical systems, maintenance and support processes, and system administrators. Interactions are limited to:

- Authentication/authorization traffic between systems and the credential authorities (domain controller, directory services, certificate services, etc.)
- Domain naming (DNS), Network Time (NTP), traffic between systems and infrastructure servers
- Monitoring traffic between systems and the system management stations (Microsoft operations manager, IBM Tivoli, HP Openview, etc.)
- Backup traffic between systems and backup services

■ Audit traffic between systems and audit collection services (Syslog, Audit Collection Service, etc.)
■ Operations and maintenance traffic between systems and their administrators

External entity access is limited to point-to-point proxy connections. All connections into the core must originate on an authenticated system and connect to a specific core system using specific protocols. For example, the PeopleSoft front end is allowed to create an open database connection (ODBC) to the backend SQL server located in the core. This connection must go through an application firewall that only permits this point-to-point connection using ODBC protocols. Or, as an alternative, the front end must use IPSec to connect to the backend through a firewall that limits this point-to-point connection to the IPSec protocol.

All core system connections to external entities are denied unless explicitly permitted, and these are limited to point-to-point proxy connections using specific protocols. For example, internal DNS servers forward name resolution requests to specific ISP or Internet-based servers through an application firewall that implements split DNS to hide internal addresses. System administrators are allowed read access to external websites for support and informational purposes; these connections must go through an HTTP proxy that authenticates the user, logs all accesses, and prohibits any type of file or script transfer.

The final piece is the monitoring requirements. For the core, all systems are equipped with integrity checkers (such as Tripwire) and host-based intrusion detection/prevention systems (IDS/IPS) configured to automatically alert security/support personnel when security violations are detected.

The internal network enclave would have less stringent rules. For example, within this enclave, connections are not limited to predefined point-to-point restrictions, but peer-to-peer connections between desktop machines are prohibited and all server connections require IPSec authentication. External connections into the enclave are restricted to point-to-point connections from known entities (employees, partners, vendors, etc.) on specific protocols but do not require application firewalls. Outbound connections to the Internet permit read and download access to websites through a proxy equipped with virus and malicious script scanning and detection. Monitoring with automated alert generation is applied to external enclave connections, and centralized logging is configured for all servers and hosts in the enclave.

This scenario provides a model that organizations can use to define defense-in-depth objectives for their particular computing requirements. This kind of limited and controlled access would have been difficult in the past because of bandwidth restrictions, but increases in network bandwidth and appliance processing capabilities make this scenario plausible today.

Effective Logging, Detection, and Alerting Capabilities

Monitoring is one of the five rules essential to good enclave governance; it is also a critical tactical principle. You can't keep someone from attacking your systems anymore than King Edward could keep people from attacking his castles. All you can do is limit the effectiveness of those attacks with early detection and targeted responses. Monitoring is the equivalent of the castle's high tower. Effective monitoring makes it possible to detect and react to dangerous activities and attacks before they cause any significant damage.

What Constitutes Effective Monitoring?

Effective monitoring has three primary characteristics. First, it provides near real-time detection and alerting; second, it is continuous; and third, it provides information with a high degree of integrity. A monitoring system that tells you "you have been attacked" is worthless. It's like the guard in the movie *Rob Roy* who runs to the shoreline and shouts threats at the attackers as they row away across the lake. The damage is already done. After-the-fact information may help you understand what went wrong and make corrections to ensure it doesn't happen again, but that is little consolation to the business or the customers that suffered a data breach.

Castle towers provided continuous observation; soldiers were posted in them 24 hours a day. Monitoring systems need to do the same. Hackers attack systems at night, on weekends, and holidays because those are the times when no one is actively monitoring those systems. A monitoring system that does not provide continuous observation and detection is worthless. An attacker will find and exploit the times when the "guards" are not on duty.

Quality of information is probably the biggest challenge to effective monitoring. There are three aspects to consider: accuracy, reliability, and relevance. Inaccurate information is probably more damaging than no information at all because it sends people off on "wild-goose chases" rather than directing resources to the real problem. Not only must monitoring system accuracy record and convey information, but that information must not be alterable. Information that can be tampered with is unreliable and requires the expenditure of resources for validation.

Information relevance is a challenge because monitoring systems can collect huge amounts of information, much of which is of little value. Much like the tower guard hollering, "The villagers are dancing in the dell!", it is interesting but hardly threatening. Enclave security rules regarding monitoring must address relevance at two levels. First, what should be logged? For example, core enclave monitors would include all failed and successful authentications, authorizations, and accesses as well as all privileged activities. Second, what event or series of events will generate alerts to security personnel? In other words, what activities constitute abuse, such as someone logging in using a generic account (i.e., guest, administrator, root, etc.)? In the core enclave, both local system event logging and centralized logging are used to maintain the integrity of the information. These audit records are processed and reviewed daily. The internal network enclave would have similar alerting requirements, but less stringent logging and log review requirements because the criticality of these systems and the value of the data stored on them is substantially lower than that of core systems.

Operational Excellence for Security Controls

Alert processing and consistent periodic log reviews are part of operational excellence. Operational excellence is a crucial component of defense in depth. More than enough good technology is available to secure our systems, but it is only as effective as our ability to properly configure, operate, monitor, and maintain it. In fact, the more capable (i.e., complex) a piece of technology is, the more likely it will fail if not managed properly. A great example is the firewall access control list (ACL). A company Bill worked with was trying to resolve a bottleneck issue with their firewalls. When first installed, the firewalls worked great, but as time went on data flows increased and performance decreased. The problem—14,000+ filter entries! It seems that the company had a reasonable process for adding ACL entries but no process for periodically validating or removing them. Consequently, the ACLs had grown until evaluating them took so much processing that it was impacting network performance. However, that's only half the story; there were no permanent records of who requested the filter entries so you couldn't ask if it was still needed. Bill's task was simply to optimize the list so that it could be processed faster!

Apparently, the thousands of security holes the list created weren't of concern. Poor operational practices result in poor information security; excellent operations increase observation, attack detection, and responsiveness.

Superior Personal Supervision, Training, and Skills Management

Coupled tightly with operational excellence are personnel supervision, training, and skills management. You MUST have proficient personnel configuring and operating your security controls. You MUST have sufficient personnel to respond to failures and attacks 24/7, and you MUST have a command structure that can effectively monitor and direct those resources. In recent years, the industry has seen an interesting shift in proficiency. The old "hackers" are retiring and are being replaced by a new generation of system and application operators. The difference between the two is significant; the hackers knew how to troubleshoot and resolve system and application problems, whereas their replacements (with few exceptions) only know how to operate and maintain systems. When something goes terribly wrong, external expertise is required to resolve the issue. While this scenario may be acceptable for routine issues, it is completely unacceptable when the enclave is under a sustained attack. You need people with the training and expertise to respond in a measured, proficient, and effective way. Having a well-managed training and skills tracking program is the only way to ensure this level of expertise.

Supervision is another area that is seriously lacking in most IT organizations. Supervising highly privileged IT personnel is more than giving directions; it is involvement in people's lives and the monitoring of their activities. That's incredibly difficult to do when you have 40 people to supervise and half of them are on the other side of the country; which incidentally is a fairly common scenario in today's business environments. While distributed management might be a sensible approach for sales and service personnel, it is utter insanity when you are talking about highly privileged IT administrators. Supervisors need to be aware of how their administrators are conducting themselves on the job and cognizant of circumstances that might adversely impact job performance. Dr. Mike Gelles in his paper "Exploring the Mind of the Spy" talks about a combination of behaviors exhibited by people who eventually go rogue. It's a surprisingly accurate description of some of the rogue IT people we've encountered over the years. Unfortunately, it's rare in today's IT world to find any significant level of behavior monitoring, and there are plenty of horror stories attesting to this lack. San Francisco network administrator Terry Childs is a great example. He basically held the city's data network hostage for over a week by refusing to divulge the administrator passwords to his supervisors. Who was watching this guy? How on earth did he get this much control over these resources without anyone noticing? Yes, his conduct was completely unacceptable, but it was a lack of proper supervision and monitoring that made it possible.

High Assurance Identity Management

An excellent operational capability must include high assurance identity management, especially for remote/external connections. Data compromise begins with access, and access begins with identity. The most effective attack against a system is to become a legitimate user of the system, the second most effective is to pose as a legitimate user, and the third is to exploit a system trust. All of these attacks give the attacker direct access to system data and resources. This is what makes phishing and other social engineering attacks so popular, and this is why high assurance identity management is so important.

What Is High Assurance Identity Management?

High assurance identity begins with the vetting process for identity requests—that is, obtaining assurance that the requestors are who they claim to be and have been properly authorized to receive an identity. The second aspect is identity authentication; the process of validating a presented identity. High assurance identity uses multiple factors such as third-party validations (e.g., Kerberos, Radius, PKI, etc.), tokens, and biometrics. The third aspect is the assignment of permissions to data and computing resources (i.e., authorization). High assurance identity management will enforce the principle of least privilege. An entity (person, system, or program) can only get access to the data and resources required for the proper execution of its duties.

Timely Incident Response and Resolution

Defense in depth is designed to absorb and progressively weaken an attack, providing the responder with *time*—time to assemble and deploy the resources needed to repel an attack. Castles were designed to facilitate rapid response to attacks. The tops of the walls and the passageways inside the walls were wide to facilitate the quick movement of troops and equipment, and a cache of weapons was kept at each defensive position. Because the observation towers overhung the corners of the wall, commanders could easily observe what the attackers were doing (e.g., they could see where attackers were placing ladders against the wall) and reposition troops to counter those efforts. Enclaves need similar response capabilities.

The rate at which automated attacks can compromise systems and propagate themselves is amazing and disconcerting at the same time. The F variant of the Sobig worm spread worldwide in less than 24 hours. The Conficker worm compromised 1.1 million systems in a single day and more than 3.5 million in a week. As alarming as these propagation rates are, research shows that the same infections within a local (in-house) computing environment would propagate even faster. When you couple this with how quickly exploit code appears once a flaw is known, the rapid response capabilities become paramount. There are a number of excellent resources on incident response and response planning, so there is little reason to go through them here. The main items to focus on are the following:

- **Preparation**—Stockpile the required tools, build the required procedures, and train your people in how to use them. Conduct drills to increase proficiency and eliminate bottlenecks. There's no time for training when you're in the middle of an attack. Make like a Boy Scout, be prepared! This also means staying aware of the latest attacks and devising methods for countering them.
- **Short response times**—Get resources working on the problem as quickly as possible. An active worm like Conflicter can compromise 12 systems a second! You cannot afford to delay your response. An aerospace company Bill worked with held two days of talks, trying to decide how to recover from a breach without killing production. By the time they decided what to do, there wasn't a system in the company that didn't have exploit code on it!
- **Reliable communications**—Ensure that all responders can be reached and have multiple methods for information dissemination. For example, an attack that generates high levels of network traffic makes network-based communications nearly worthless, so it is wise to have a voice conferencing alternative.
- **Authority to act**—Empower the response team to make the hard decisions. In the case of the aerospace company, the security team had no authority to make decisions that might in

any way impact production; those decisions had to be thoroughly vetted with management. We doubt anyone really knows what information was lost by the breach, but we can tell you the cost of fixing the problem was more than doubled because the security team did not have the authority to isolate, update, or shut down systems. Yes, there is the potential they may make a few bad decisions from time to time, but they'll learn from them. It is always better to be safe than sorry.

Defense-in-depth objectives for local enclaves tend to focus on boundary access points. This is perfectly reasonable, but it shouldn't be the sole emphasis. Insider threats must also be taken into consideration. Objectives must encompass technical, people, and operational elements. This includes the processes required to achieve operational excellence, high assurance identity management, and timely incident response. These processes are supported by superior personnel supervision, and effective access, logging, and monitoring controls. Having an enclave under a single governing authority is a big advantage because it facilitates rapid directed responses and can be subject to direct supervision and monitoring. The hosted and hybrid environments split these functions among multiple authorities.

Shared-Risk Environments

Before moving on to hosted and hybrid environments, it is important to introduce the concept of shared risk. Systems that connect across enclave boundaries (e.g., an in-house laptop connecting to a hosted mail server) have a certain level of trust extended to them. This trust is usually extended by mutual agreement between the controlling security authorities of each enclave and is typically based on an audit of each party's security policies and practices. The problem with this arrangement is that audits are only a snapshot in time; the security state of systems is under continuous change as applications and updates are applied. The possibility exists that at some point in time, one or more of the systems involved in cross-enclave connections will develop a vulnerability that exposes the other interconnected systems to potential exploitation. When shared risk exists in an environment, defense-in-depth objectives must address this exposure to ensure that the protection level of one system is not compromised by vulnerabilities in one of the systems it interconnects with.

Hosted Objectives

There are two scenarios for hosted environments: consumer and provider.

Consumer Scenario

A fully hosted environment has no in-house enclave; all services are delivered to the consumer (end user) through a networked connection. Microsoft's Business Productivity Online Standard Suite (BPOS) is an example of this type of service. Small and medium-size businesses can receive e-mail, instant messaging, Web conferencing, and collaboration services via the Internet; no in-house systems (other than end-user laptops or PCs) are required. This simplifies but does not eliminate defense-in-depth objectives. Technological controls for host systems and applications, personnel training, and contract management processes are still required. Additional objectives may apply, depending on business type, data value, and applicable regulations, but the following list is common.

1. Limited and secured host access points
2. Limited and controlled application execution
3. Secure host operations
4. Excellence in service provider management

These objectives address the people, technology, and operational aspects of this scenario. The primary emphasis is on the security of the end-user system, which includes a competent and knowledgeable operator.

Limited/Controlled Host Access Points and Application Execution

The first two objectives are technology based, so they will be covered together.

For the most part, the standard technological controls and control settings installed with the operating system are sufficient to limit and secure host access. These include:

- Protocol-level protections against malformed packets, SYN, and fragmentation attacks
- Port-level protections such as selective response, packet filters, and stateful firewalls
- Socket-level protections such as IPSec and SSL
- Application-level protections like data execution prevention, sandboxing, code signing, user account control, file integrity checks, and file permissions

Some supplemental controls are warranted; antivirus and anti-spam controls are pretty standard. The inclusion of other controls depends primarily on the value or sensitivity of the data retained on the system. It is not unusual, for example, to include full-disk encryption on laptops to guard against data loss from laptop thefts.

Secure access to hosted services is pretty much a standard feature in online products. Secure Socket Layer with certificate authentication is typical. The real challenge in this scenario (or for that matter any of these scenarios) is the unlimited access systems have to other potentially dangerous content. These include the threat of system compromise from malware in downloaded files or message attachments, as well as code implanted by a hacker sponsored or compromised website. The latter are commonly called attack sites—sites that attempt to infect your system with malware when you visit. These attacks are difficult to detect, and in many cases the owner of the site may not be aware of the attack code. The Storm worm was one of the first pieces of malware to use this technique, but many have followed suit, including the Beladen attack code (implanted on 40,000 websites), hacks to Facebook applications that redirect the user to an attack site, and the Nine Ball attack code, which is also an attack site redirect.

Addressing the malicious content issue is a two-edged sword. If the goal of a fully hosted environment is to eliminate the need for in-house IT staff, adding site-filtering or health-monitoring applications like Cisco's NAC or Microsoft's NAP to your end-user systems is not going to be an acceptable solution. The alternative—code execution controls, malware detection, and user education—is somewhat less effective but doesn't require in-house staff either.

Many of the code execution controls are standard features of the operation system (OS); others come standard with the applications. For example, beginning with Windows XP SP2, Data Execution Prevention (DEP) became a standard feature of the OS. DEP uses a combination of hardware and software technologies that prevent code execution in memory areas designated for data storage. DEP primarily protects against buffer overflows and other types of attacks that attempt to subvert the exception-handling processes in the OS. Most modern browser applications include code execution protections as well. The best known protection is the Java sandbox, which limits what Java scripts downloaded to the browser are allowed to do. In Windows Vista, Microsoft introduced a similar mechanism—Mandatory Integrity Control (MIC)—which deals with ActiveX-based malware. MIC limits the execution privileges of code downloaded by the browser—any code! It accomplishes this by assigning a low integrity level to downloaded files. Low integrity files cannot modify files or settings with higher integrity; like the Java sandbox, MIC allows the code to run but prevents it from doing any damage. Unfortunately, these controls do not extend to other Internet-facing applications; malicious code downloaded via an e-mail attachment or in Instant Messenger executes with full user privilege, and if the user is logged in as administrator, it runs with full administrator privileges!

Secure Host Operations

This objective could just as easily be labeled "superior user training" because it is mostly about training your personnel to use their computing resources securely. Users must be able to recognize and deal appropriately with abnormal or suspicious behaviors. This includes social engineering (e.g., phishing) attacks, malware proliferation, viruses, root kits, and so on. We suspect the person who came up with the adage "You can't fix stupid" was a computer support professional. Computers are tools to most people; they need them to get their work done. When computers work well, the "if it ain't broke don't fix it" mentality usually prevails. When they don't work well, people start looking for ways to fix the problem, which usually includes altering or disabling system or application security features. Your best defense against this type of behavior is education. Smart users do not make dumb decisions. Teaching users how to securely operate their systems should be one of your key defense-in-depth objectives.

Excellence in Service Provider Management

The previous topics have dealt with the security of information within your direct control. This topic deals with data security and compliance issues for data that is outside your direct control (i.e., stored at the service provider). Assuring compliance with organizational, regulatory, and legal requirements for this data requires a well-defined and expertly administered service provider management program. However, it is rare to find such a program even among companies that have been using outsourced services for some time. It is also rare to find any security-related service levels in hosted service contracts.

There are a number of possible explanations for these issues. The most obvious one is lack of expertise or understanding. Computers, networks, services, and the like are complex; the tendency, especially among small and medium-size businesses, is to simply trust the expertise of the provider and to accept the audit reports the provider supplies as proof. Two other common causes are time and the lack of contract management skills. Ensuring the security of off-premise data and contracted services requires a consistent and thorough effort, but most companies do not have dedicated resources for the task. Instead, the task becomes an ancillary duty for someone (which usually means it gets attention only when it needs attention). From an information security standpoint, this is unacceptable. Regardless of the physical location of the data, it is still *your* data, and you bear the ultimate responsibility for its security and compliance.

It's not just a matter of resources and time either; it's also a matter of skills. Outsourced IT services have some unique aspects to them; the people managing them need to be properly trained to deal with these ambiguities. For example, how do you align and validate your security and compliance requirements with those of your providers?

Service providers achieve profitability by delivering commoditizing services to a large audience. The approach leaves little room for customization, especially when customer-specific security requirements are involved. Nonetheless, it is your responsibility to prove that the contracted service complies with your requirements. The simplest way to do this is to map your requirements to the practices and audit requirements of the provider. For example, if your security policy requires failed logons to be logged: (1) Does the provider log failed authentications? (2) Is this functionality regularly audited to prove it works properly? (3) Can you get a copy of the audit report? (4) Can you get a report of the logged events for compliance reporting purposes? Chances are the provider already does all four things: The terminology may not be the same, and the methodology may be a little different, but the net result is the same: What they do meets your compliance requirements. The only remaining caveat is whether or not you can get that information when you need it, and that requirement should be part of your service-level agreement with your provider.

Summary

Defense-in-depth objectives for consumers of hosted services are focused on two things: the end-user device and service provider contract management. Standard operating system and application security controls are usually sufficient to secure locally stored data, provided users are trained in secure computer operations. Ensuring the security and compliance of information processed, transferred, and stored by a service provider requires well-defined service-level requirements and a consistent, thorough service contract management program.

Provider Scenario

The provider's environment is an in-house enclave (it is an environment under the control of a single authority) with an interesting twist. In addition to the in-house objectives, the provider must include objectives for application, data transit, and data storage security. Application objectives are required because the consumer is authorized direct access to the application and for all practical purposes bypasses perimeter, network, and host protections. The provider must also guard against unauthorized data exchanges (leakage) between service consumers and deal with shared-risk threats from vulnerable (improperly secured) end-user systems. Finally, the providers must be able to prove they are meeting their security Service Level Agreement (SLA).

Before discussing specific service provider security objectives, it's important to differentiate between the various types of services. This section discusses two principal service environments: shared and dedicated. In a shared service environment, services are provided to customers through a common set of resources. Customer data is processed, transported, and stored on systems that are used by any number of other customers. Web conferencing is an example of a shared service. Customers may have an individually assigned conference center, but they are using the same application, network facilities, and storage all the other customers are using. By contrast, a dedicated service provides a mixture of applications, networking, and storage services for a single customer. Traditional hosting services are a good example; the systems at the service provider are primarily an extension of the customer's network that is operated and maintained by the service provider. In a fully dedicated environment, the applications, networking, and storage involved are dedicated to a single customer; they are not shared across multiple customers. The only thing that is shared are support services (trouble ticketing, monitoring, backup, etc.). Fully dedicated environments are not the norm; they are typically reserved for sensitive or high security applications, such as financial services and the military. Most dedicated services provide a dedicated application that

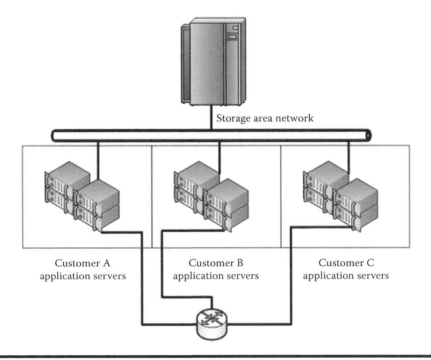

Figure 8.3 Shared storage scenario.

shares network and storage facilities with other customers—for example, a dedicated mail server that shares network and SAN storage with other dedicated customer servers. (See Figure 8.3.)

In the case of Web applications, the customer may share the Web service as well. The distinguishing attribute is addressing; dedicated services are extensions of the customer's network and therefore provide network addressing that is either on the customer's network or in the customer's name space. With these distinctions in mind, let's move on to the defense-in-depth objectives that are unique to service providers.

These additional defense-in-depth objectives might be expressed as

1. Uncompromising application security
2. Exceptional customer data isolation
3. Shared-risk mitigation
4. Superior accountability

These objectives address the technology and operations aspects that are unique to this scenario. The primary emphasis is on data security for shared services. There simply cannot be any data disclosure across customer boundaries, and the provider must be able to prove there wasn't in the event an accusation be raised.

Uncompromising Application Security

Becoming an authorized user on a system is one of the most productive ways to attack it. There's no need to overcome external network and host protections; your identity gives you direct access to many system resources. All you need to do is find a way to exploit a flaw in one of those resources to gain unauthorized access to the system. Compromised Internet sites are a great example of this. Anonymous is a valid user on the system with valid permissions granting read and execute privileges to system files and applications. In December 2009 attackers used these permissions to execute a SQL Injection attack that compromised over 130,000 websites. The same type of attacks can be executed against online services as well; it just requires a valid user identity for the service.

Depending on the type of service being provided, getting that identity can be a trivial pursuit or a major endeavor. For commoditized services like Windows Live, getting a user ID means you must provide a valid e-mail address. For shared services like Microsoft Online, a valid e-mail address and credit card are required. For dedicated services, a valid customer user ID is required. The latter can be a real challenge, but the other two are trivial. How an attacker obtains the identity really doesn't matter; the fact that an attacker can use that identity to directly attack and compromise service applications and systems is the real concern. Perhaps, even more disconcerting is the fact that a single service identity frequently provides access across multiple services. Once a system has been compromised, this shared trust can be exploited to propagate the attack across service boundaries. This is why application-level security is a critical security objective for service providers. In light of the privileges being granted to users, service providers must provide uncompromising application security. The slightest user exploitable flaw can easily result in a massive compromise.

Exceptional Customer Data Isolation

Service providers must also provide exceptional customer data isolation. Whenever a service processes, transfers, or stores data from multiple customers, there is the possibility for data leakage between customer entities. The threat is more prevalent in shared services because all customers use the same resources, but data leakage is also a threat in dedicated services because customer environments use a common set of service support applications. For example, information from multiple customers can be found in service desk, performance, backup, and monitoring systems. Although this information may be more difficult for an external attacker to compromise, it is still susceptible to disclosure from human or application error. For example, one of the service providers Bill worked with had a recurring problem with service ticket reporting. Operators would sometimes include cross customer information in service reports. The issue was as much a problem with the application as it was with the operators, but that didn't make the customer whose information was leaked feel any better, and it certainly was detrimental to the provider's reputation. The problem, to some extent, is systemic. Applications that have been designed for internal use, including monitoring and ticketing systems, typically do not have robust security features.

The threat of cross customer data leakage in shared environments is even greater. Data is present in shared memory during processing, intermingled during transport, stored in shared databases, and backed up to common media. The threat is further exacerbated because these data elements have different levels of sensitivity and are subject to different regulatory and legal requirements. Although there is no practical way for a service provider to know what these sensitivities and requirements are, nonetheless, customers have a reasonable expectation that the provider will provide appropriate protections. And if the customer is wise, they will make those expectations part of the service-level agreement. Exceptional customer data isolation must be a priority security objective for service providers.

Shared-Risk Mitigation

Another aspect of security that service providers have little control over is the security state of customer systems. Nonetheless, the provider must grant these systems access to their services and find a balanced way to mitigate the risks these systems pose. The term *balanced* is used here in the sense that the mitigation must reduce the risk to acceptable levels without adversely impacting the end user. Forcing a customer to use health certificates or to go through extended system scans before they can access your service isn't going to be a good solution.

Shared risk is somewhat easier to deal with in shared services environments because these services are usually limited to very specific ports and protocols. Consequently, there are far fewer exploits to deal with. In dedicated environments, especially those that provide direct connections to the customer's network, things are a little more challenging. Often these connections involve bidirectional communications that make port-based filtering difficult; for example, service systems may use customer-based services like DNS or Active Directory. Routing and other network protocols may also be involved.

Shared-risk mitigation is one of the most challenging objectives faced by most service providers, especially those that provide dedicated services. At one service provider Bill worked with, responding to customer-based attacks was a frequent occurrence. The attacks seldom presented any real threat, but they were a constant and unnecessary drain on security team resources. Shared risk is an issue that must be addressed. Failing to address it in your security objectives puts you at risk of compromise or even worse, in the untenable position of having to prove your service was not the source of a customer breach.

Superior Accountability

Compliance has had a huge impact on IT services. Before the onslaught of regulatory and legal requirements, the most valuable commodity in IT was knowledge. Knowledge gave you the ability to demonstrate competence, resolve problems, implement solutions, and the like. That same knowledge is still needed, but today the most valuable commodity is proof. Compliance isn't about what you know—it's about what you can prove. It's about liability: the penalties you will incur if you cannot prove compliance. Some of these penalties are contractual; others are imposed by regulators, and still others by the courts. So daunting are the possible liabilities that one of the priorities for security at Microsoft Online was "keeping compliance from putting us out of business."

Superior accountability is the best way to accomplish this objective. Accountability is the ability to provide irrefutable proof of what actions were taken and by whom they were taken. In today's regulatory and legal compliance climate, it is a critical security objective for every service provider.

Summary

Defense-in-depth objectives for providers of hosted services are focused on two things: data security in processing, transport, and storage; and the mitigation of risks associated with customer connections and compliance-imposed penalties. Uncompromising application, networking, and storage controls are the best overall goals for data security management. After all, data compromise is the end goal of the attacker. Mitigating shared risk is a balance between risk reduction and serviceability. Shared-risks are easier to deal with in shared services than they are in dedicated services, especially those directly connected to the customer's network. Superior accountability builds credibility with customers and provides the best defense against compliance and legal liabilities.

Hybrid Objectives

Hybrid environments are common in today's commuting environments. The lower cost of hosting and online services made the outsourcing of systems and services very attractive. Technically, a hybrid environment is an IT configuration that has some in-house services and some hosted services, but this definition is probably too generic for this discussion. There are hundreds of possible hybrid configuration scenarios ranging from simple website hosting to fully outsourced server farms. Consequently, there are a lot of variances to the security objectives for these scenarios. And, of course, the objectives of the consumer are going to be different from those of the provider.

This discussion of the services scenario has been divided into four levels:

1. **Uncoupled**—services where the consumer is always the initiator of the connection and is primarily pushing data to the provider. An example of this type of service scenario is a hosted website. The consumer makes a secure (SSL) connection to the website usually via a public network to update Web page content.
2. **Loosely coupled**—services delivered through a public network where consumer data transfers are bi-directional. The consumer is the party that initiates all the actions (i.e., connections, data transfers, etc.). Once the consumer is connected, the provider may request that the consumer take a specific action such as update their client software, but the provider cannot initiate that action. Web-based e-mail is a good example of this scenario.
3. **Fully coupled**—services delivered through a dedicated connection (e.g., a virtual private network [VPN]) that allows either party to initiate an action (i.e., a connection or transfer data). The connection is bi-directional; the consumer can push and pull information, and so can the provider. Applications that use federated identity are a good example; the end user (consumer) initiates a connection to the service, and the service validates the connection request by contacting the customer's in-house authentication service to verify the user's access permissions.
4. **Fully integrated**—services that are characterized by full-time dedicated connections and bi-directional data exchanges. These services can be initiated by either party. An example of this type of service would be a hosted backend database management service supporting an interactive end-user application. The consumer performs reads and writes against the database, and the service regularly queries the consumer's authentication server to validate user access. The service may also use other customer-based services such as DNS, Time, and WINS.

Consumer Objectives

Consumer objectives are based on the level of service being provided. Uncoupled services have very modest risks associated with them. The primary concern is the security of the content that is stored at the provider. In the case of website maintenance, there is the possibility of a "drive-by" attack when the consumer connects to the service if their website has been compromised. A "drive-by" attack uses a background process to install malicious code such as a keystroke logger on the connected system. This code can then be used to capture user credentials and other information to further the attack. The presence of attack code could be the fault of the provider (e.g., failing to apply patches for a known exploit), or it could be the consumer's fault (e.g., the Web application is vulnerable to SQL Injection). Having a website with attack code on it is also a downstream liability should that code cause damage to users of the site. Another possible issue is the compromise of credentials passed on a public network. The most likely scenario here is a redirection attack (e.g., DNS hijacking). However, these attacks are mitigated with SSL certificate-based site authentication.

Standard end-user system security configurations are usually sufficient to guard against code download in a drive-by attack. Assuming you have users knowledgeable enough to deal properly with website certificate warnings, the primary security objective in this scenario is provider management, ensuring through regular audits and reporting that the provider is properly safeguarding the data you have entrusted to their care.

Loosely Coupled Scenarios

This scenario is similar to the uncoupled scenario in that it is subject to the same types of drive-by and redirection attacks. However, there is an additional risk associated with the data being pulled from the site. In the case of a Web-based mail system, this data would include executables (scripts) and message content (text, html, attachments, etc.). Client side scripts are necessary to the robust functionality of many Web-based applications, but they can also be subverted to perform malicious acts via a distribution attack. The most common example of this type of attack is the replacement of script or other executable content on a Web server with malicious code. When a user calls this function, the malicious code downloads and executes on the user's system (also see drive-by attacks). It is also possible to get malicious code installed by modifying the source before it is installed. A developer could intentionally do this, or a system on which the code is stored could be compromised and the code tampered with. The bigger concern is the potential for malicious code in downloaded content. Message attachments are notorious for distributing attacks. The "I Love You" virus is probably the best known example, but malicious attachments are still in wide use.

Protecting against malicious code downloads must be a key security objective in hybrid environments. This includes protections against rogue scripts. The other key objective must be service provider management, ensuring the provider is properly protecting your data. The provider must be able to report on who accessed code, configurations, or data related to your service and what, if any, changes were made. For really critical data (e.g., backups), even this level of reporting may not be sufficient control, in which case data integrity objectives must also be considered. Data integrity ensures that data are not altered while they are stored at the provider; this is crucial to the proper restoration of failed systems, meeting record retention requirements, and so on.

Fully Coupled Scenarios

This scenario is a true enclave-to-enclave connection. It differs from the previous two scenarios because the connections take place over a dedicated circuit. The connection may traverse a public network, but the systems are not exposed to the public. This reduces the risks associated with external threats, but amplifies the need for shared-risk mitigation for two principal reasons: there is an established level of trust between the parties, and the circuit by default permits all types of traffic. Without restrictions these connections provide the perfect conduit for the spread of malicious code. The unrestricted access issue requires well-defined boundary protection objectives and the trust issue makes shared-risk objectives imperative.

Federated identity is a good example of a fully coupled system. Figure 8.4 depicts the following workflow: The consumer attempts to access a service, the service collects the user's

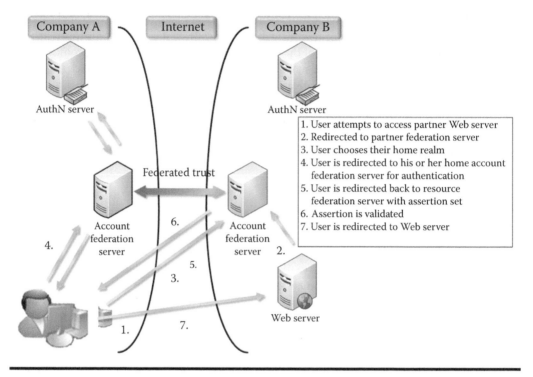

Figure 8.4 Federated identity scenario.

credentials, and then the service passes them to the provider's identity management system (IMS) for authentication. The provider's IMS uses the enclave-to-enclave circuit to forward the credentials to the customer's identity system and receive back the required authentication and authorization claims.

In some instances, this exchange may take place across a public network, but the connection is still a private connection because mutual authentication of each system involved in connection is required. Any other connection attempts are simply ignored. This scenario does require that access control objectives be defined.

Fully Integrated Scenarios

This scenario is similar to the fully coupled scenario; communications take place on dedicated circuits, but the integration between the systems is such that the provider's enclave functions like it is part of the consumer's enclave. For example, one of the consumer's identification management systems may be co-located at the provider. The range of services flowing between the enclaves can be extensive. One organization Bill worked with kept its business applications in-house, but farmed its e-mail, instant messaging, collaboration, network management, monitoring, backup, provisioning, and patch management to its service provider. The arrangement helped the company focus on its core business, but it also created an operating environment that was nearly impossible to secure. Every attempt to apply security measures to the enclave connection or services either caused an unacceptable degradation in performance or caused something to fail completely. In this scenario, there must be a primary emphasis on shared-risk and service provider management security objectives and a secondary emphasis on access control and boundary protection.

SIDEBAR: RISKS ASSOCIATED WITH OUTSOURCED SERVICES

Unfortunately, the required emphasis on shared-risk and service-provider management often isn't there. The tendency is for the consumer to trust the provider and the provider's protections, but this isn't prudent. Once, during an assessment of a provider's site Bill found a hole in a filter that allowed one consumer to create database connections to a server in a neighboring enclave. Fortunately, it was found before it could be exploited, but this was a collaborative application development site; just imagine how much damage could have been done! It is imperative that the consumer fully understand the risks associated with using outsourced services and resources. There is no such thing as a free lunch; every scenario has an associated set of risks. A decision to use outsourced services does not change your obligation to keep your data secure. You cannot transfer this responsibility to the provider, and it is guaranteed that the provider has no intention of taking on that responsibility either. The data belongs to you; make sure you understand what it will take to ensure its security.

Provider Objectives

Consistency is the best scenario for a service provider. It is far better to have one standard set of security objectives to work from than it is to provide customized security scenarios for individual customers. For example, if the service provider has fully hosted customers, it may be advantageous for the provider to treat every scenario as if it were fully hosted. While a "one size fits all" approach is the most cost effective, it can be difficult to reconcile it to the customer's particular requirements. This is especially true in hybrid scenarios where a high level of integration is present. The security objectives discussed in the fully hosted scenario (uncompromising application security, exceptional customer data isolation, shared-risk mitigation, and superior accountability) apply in the hybrid scenarios as well. This section covers objectives that are specific to the different hybrid environments.

Uncoupled Scenarios

Uncoupled services are based entirely on consumer-initiated actions. The connection is typically a secure socket layer (SSL) connection on a public network (i.e., the Internet). The connection is primarily used to configure or update content on the service. The primary concern on the provider side is boundary protection because these services are exposed on a public network. The concern is not with the security of the service per se, but with the utilities and tools. For example, if the consumer uses FTP to transfer content to their site, how does the provider support this functionality in a secure manner? To a lesser extent, distribution attacks are also of concern because it is possible for the consumer to knowingly or unknowingly upload malicious code to the site. Providers must address these risks in the security objectives for uncoupled services.

Loosely Coupled Scenarios

The concerns in this scenario are the same as those in the uncoupled scenario, but the shared risk and distribution issues are amplified because the connection is bi-directional and in most cases, code must be installed on the end-user system for the service to work properly. The code could be a browser add-on, script, or a custom application. Web-based conferencing is a typical example of this scenario. The service is exposed to the Internet and uses SSL connections for conference scheduling, configuration, and attendance. Presenters may upload content, and attendees may stream content in real time or download saved/stored records (i.e., video or audio records, stored presentations, etc.). The end user must download and install browser code to support the conferencing functionality, and in some cases (e.g., Netmeeting) the end user may install a stand-alone client application. The provider must establish security objectives to guard against the corruption or compromise of the code they are distributing and must establish objectives for securely delivering that code and subsequent updates.

Fully Coupled Scenarios

This scenario is characterized by dedicated connections and bi-directional data exchanges initiated by either party. These connections may be across a public network, but the services involved in the connection are not exposed on the public network. Nonetheless, the main concern here is still boundary protection. Each of these connections represents a potential attack vector; not from the Internet, but from the consumer, and the more services supported on the connection, the greater the potential risk.

King Edward built his castles on waterways for resupply and reinforcement purposes because his enemies had no real means of attacking water-based targets. Consequently, these activities could take place unharassed. This is also one of the advantages of dedicated connections between provider and consumer enclaves, but it does not dismiss the need for good access controls and boundary protections. The castle's water entry was a potential source of an attack; it had to be guarded and access carefully controlled. The depiction of the castle water entry in the movie *The Man in the Iron Mask* is a superb example; the steel gate completely sealed the water entry (it couldn't be climbed over and no one could swim under it), and the dock area had a single narrow passageway into the castle. Like the castle water entry, dedicated service connections must be protected against attacks. Security objectives for fully coupled scenarios must address the shared risks associated with dedicated service connections.

Fully Integrated Scenarios

The same attack vector issues noted earlier apply to the fully integrated scenario (see Figure 8.5) as well and may be somewhat amplified because of the increased integration of the systems. Scenarios that include co-located customer security management systems also increase the need for accountability; the provider must be able to account for all interactions they have with these systems should a security issue with these systems surface. Say, for example, someone enabled the guest account and it was used to compromise a system. The provider better be able to prove it wasn't one of their personnel that enabled the account; otherwise there is a high probability that the provider will be blamed for the breach and will therefore be liable for damages.

Fully integrated scenarios require a greater emphasis on shared-risk mitigation and accountability objectives, as well as well-defined access control objectives. Under no circumstances should the provider trust the expertise or capabilities of the consumer and, where possible, the provider should include shared-risk responsibility and cost recovery in the service contract. Another important consideration when defining the objectives of this scenario is the impact these objectives may have on service performance, as well as the impact (required changes) they may have on the customer's computing environment. Backup services are a great example; they almost always require an agent to be installed on the consumer's system, which could potentially conflict with other installed system software and applications. Backups may require that the system be offline for a period of time, or customer processes can be impacted by consuming excessive amounts of network bandwidth or system processor power. The provider must also consider shared support services (trouble ticketing, monitoring, backup, etc.) when establishing the security objective of this scenario.

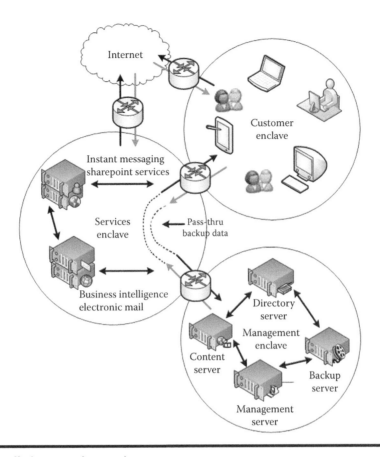

Figure 8.5 Fully integrated scenario.

Conclusion

Defense in depth is a multilayer and multidimensional protection scheme designed to absorb and progressively weaken an attack, thus providing the responder with sufficient time to organize the resources and weaponry required to repel the attack. Defense in depth applies multiple overlapping protections at the people, technology, and operational process levels. Some defenses protect, some detect, and others respond by alerting operations staff and activating additional controls. The primary objective behind defense in depth is *time*.

Thirteenth-century castles are classic examples of defense in depth. They not only provided multiple barriers (layers) that the attacker had to overcome, but they also addressed the essential dimensions of a good defense: observation, rapid response, and weaponry. Watchtowers provided early warning of attack, and moats, walls, and reinforced gates proved formidable obstacles to attackers. Wide passageways atop and inside the castle allowed troops to rapidly deploy to the points of attacks, and defensive positions such as archery slits and kill holes cached with an ample supply of arms gave defenders a decided advantage.

Castle fortifications evolved over time with two key goals: increasing and strengthening the defensive barriers; and improving the defender's ability to actively fight back. A similar evolution is needed in the information security realm. It begins with the establishment of computing enclaves based on the value of the assets being protected, and it continues with the identification of specific security objectives for controlling the transactions within the enclave, as well as the inbound and outbound data flows with systems in other enclaves.

Three common information processing environments to consider are: in-house, fully hosted, and hybrid. In-house environments have an enclave that is under a single controlling authority governed by corporate policy. In a fully hosted environment, the consumer only has end-user systems that connect to service enclaves. One or more service providers supply all the applications and services the consumer needs to conduct his or her business. The services are governed by contract (service-level agreement). The hybrid model has both in-house and outsourced (service provider) applications and services under the control of different authorities, some governed by corporate policy and others by contract. In-house is the most costly, but also the most secure because it does not have to deal with shared risk. Fully hosted is the lowest cost option but does not allow for any security customization. The consumer must accept the provider's "one size fits all" security management scheme. Hybrid environments are a combination of in-house and hosted applications and services. There are hundreds of different hybrid configurations that fall into four major types: uncoupled, loosely coupled, fully coupled, and fully integrated. These types define the level of connectivity between the parties. Uncoupled is primarily a "push" connection that is always initiated by the consumer. Sending content updates to a website is an example of this type of connection. Loosely coupled involves two-way communications between the consumer and the service, but the connection is not full time and it is initiated by the consumer. Web-based mail is an example of this type of connection. Fully coupled is bi-directional communications that can be initiated by either party, and fully integrated is where the provider's enclave functions like an extension of the consumer's environment. Both of these environments are based on full-time dedicated connections between the consumer's and the provider's enclaves. The principal difference is the range of services using this connection; fully integrated environments may share a number of common services including naming, time, identity, monitoring, and backup services. The security objectives for each scenario are different for consumers and providers, and each scenario emphasizes the need for excellence in certain control structures over others. These factors must be taken into consideration when identifying defense-in-depth security objectives.

Today networks are the primary conduits of modern commerce, but their architectures remain remarkably similar to the ancient castle bastides (a fortified security perimeter with multiple openings to support trade with partners, vendors, and customers). There is this one important difference, however: There is no place to retreat to for better protection! Understanding this analogy is critical to the design and deployment of secure enclaves. "Bastide"-style enclaves are not now, nor will they ever be, defensible. IT environments must implement the strategies that made castle defenses so effective—layered defenses, limited access, outstanding observation and alarming (monitoring and alerting), preparedness, and rapid response. Defense in depth at every level of service means people, process, and technology.

Chapter 9

Did You See That!
(Observation)

If I were to prescribe one process in the training of men which is fundamental to success in any direction, it would be thoroughgoing training in the habit of accurate observation. It is a habit which every one of us should be seeking ever more to perfect.

Eugene G. Grace

Introduction

Observation is the central principle of security. It is both a deterrent and a detector. It is a deterrent because people are less likely to do something illicit if they believe someone will see them doing it, and it is a detector when an illicit act is seen. Observation is not limited to sight; it can be a function of any of the five senses or any number of mechanical or technological sensors. A magnetic switch on a door observes (senses) when the door is opened or closed; a motion detector observes something moving through a space and so on.

Strategy requires thought, tactics require observation.

Max Euwe

From a security standpoint, observation is the monitoring of activities to identify suspicious or malicious activity and invoke a response. These are the three components of observation: monitor, detect, and alarm. The monitor component observes the current state of something, detectors observe changes to the state, and alarm components generate an alert when the change to the state crosses one or more thresholds. A threshold is the point or value above which something is considered an event. A threshold can be binary (the door is open, the door is closed), based on multiple factors (the door is open and 300 milliseconds have passed) or a scale (the temperature is normal, the item is overheating).

Observation is a major component of facility design. Buildings are uphill from the parking area, landscaped with ground-level plants, have glass-walled reception areas, and well-lit entryways to facilitate the observation of approaching vehicles and people. Interiors are designed with open spaces filled with 5-foot walled cubicles, straight hallways, and windowed offices to facilitate the observation of staff activities. Observation in operations may include posting guards or using video surveillance to observe people's actions and monitor safeguards. Observation in operations also includes alarm systems such as smoke and fire detectors. Information systems are equipped with antivirus, intrusion detection, and other controls that observe what comes into the system to see if it contains any malicious content or represents an attack pattern. All of these examples are based on observation because observation is what invokes response and response is what is required to curb malicious activity. Preventative controls, locks on doors, chain-link fences, turnstile gates, and the like, are *not designed to stop malicious activity*; they're designed to retard the effectiveness of an attack so that it can be observed and responded to. The effectiveness of security is based on our ability to observe what is happening and invoke a response.

> Safes are not designed to keep people out, otherwise they wouldn't have doors on them; they are designed to make it difficult for some people to open the door!
>
> **Unknown**

Observation Objectives

A large portion of strategy in general is based on observation—for example, observing what the competition is doing, observing what customers want, and observing our capabilities. When we do strategic planning, we seek tools that improve our observation: business and competitive intelligence, surveys, focus groups, and the like. Why? Because observation is what gives us the ability to respond to changes in our business or technical environment and make good decisions on how to address those changes. The principle isn't any different when it is applied to the realm of security; the only thing that changes is the scope. The essence of our strategic security objectives is to have unsurpassed observation capabilities. Ideally, we want no gaps in our observation; we want to be able to observe and detect every instance of malicious activity. Of course, the ideal isn't obtainable, but keeping the ideal as the goal allows us to continuously close the gaps.

Observation is directly linked to the principles of timeliness and response. The better our monitoring, the quicker we will be able to detect something is wrong and raise an alarm. Real-time observation invokes real-time responses, but not all observation is real time. For example, the periodic review of a log file or an audit trail will detect security events from the past; reviewing video surveillance tapes is a similar example. The timeliness of our response is based entirely on the timeliness of our observation.

Observation is also key to the principle of economy from two standpoints. The first is economy of response. The quicker the response, the less the potential damage from the malicious activity. Second, is the economy of force. Superior observation provides the information required to make a reasoned response that only pulls in the resources required to effectively address the situation. Automation can also reduce the number of people required for observation tasks. For example, installing a continuously monitored camera may eliminate the need for a guard, or combining video feeds onto a single monitoring station can reduce the need for monitoring personnel. Superior observation also facilitates coverage because the information it provides helps the response commander make better decisions.

Observations frequently overlap, for example, when someone comes into work, the card reader observes the person's entrance into the facility, video surveillance records the entry, and the authentication server observes the person's log-on. This provides a level of redundancy, but it also improves the quality of the observation.

Finally, observation supports the principle of preparedness by providing an early warning of an eminent attack or, in the case of reconnaissance, helping prepare for future attacks.

Observation, whether defensive or offensive, is a critical component of security strategy and will always be one of our key objectives. All our tactics should include an observation element that can alert us when an attack is imminent or manifest. Furthermore, we should construct our observation capabilities so that we can use the information to effectively direct responses to the key points of attack.

Observation Elements

Observation can be divided into three elements: reconnaissance, sentry, and command. Reconnaissance provides early warning of potential danger so we can prepare defenses; sentry provides evidence of an existing attack so we can respond; and command provides the information needed to use our forces effectively against the key points of attack. Each of these elements has slightly different applications in facilities and IT security.

Reconnaissance

Offensive units use reconnaissance to learn about an enemy's strengths, weaknesses, plans, and schedules for the purpose of engagement (i.e., to attack them). Reconnaissance for defensive purposes focuses on learning what will be targeted in the future and what tools (weapons) and maneuvers will be used so that countermeasures can be put in place and personnel prepared for the potential attack. Reconnaissance (recon) is a critical component of a good defense. The more you know about your opponent's capabilities and attack plans, the better you will be able to plan and deploy the resources needed to minimize their effectiveness. During the early years of the Internet, reconnaissance was a lost art. Security and networking professionals were aware of dangers like Distributed Denial of Service (DDoS) attacks, but no one was actively working on defenses against those attacks, nor was anyone tracking what malicious code the hacking community was developing. Then one day in 2000 hackers hit eBay, Yahoo, Amazon, and E*Trade with a massive DDoS attack, and suddenly understanding DDoS attacks and defenses became a critical part of defensive security planning. The pattern was similar for other attacks as well: little reconnaissance, ineffective responses, and massive damage.

Today, that pattern has changed substantially; there is more emphasis on preparedness. Large software vendors and Internet Service Providers (ISPs) work together to quickly identify and thwart attacks, and several employ spies to recon hacker activities. One company even used a widely publicized hack of their website to "up" the notoriety of their staff spy in the hacker community. His (phony) achievement gave him celebrity status and access to a much broader array of hacking activities. Some might classify this tactic as an offensive rather than a defensive one, and that might be true if the purpose was infiltration. Infiltration tactics involve getting past the enemy's frontline defenses and attacking lightly defended rear areas. Paratroopers were used for this purpose in World War II. But that isn't what we are talking about here; we are only gathering intelligence. We are not trying to put them out of business; that's the work of law enforcement. Communications companies like AT&T do extensive traffic analysis to identify attack patterns; Microsoft and other vendors of security products track malware outbreaks. Still others employ Honey Pot Systems to recon potential exploits and intrusions, and to capture malicious code for submission to antivirus vendors. Honey Pots are basically decoy systems that do passive reconnaissance. When attacked, they respond like a real system would, but in the background they are capturing information about the attacker and the tools/exploits they are using.

Reconnaissance is a manual control; it requires someone to go out and observe the enemy. Some of this recon can be done through "Hacker" websites, but spy techniques that get you into the underground world of black-hats are far more effective. It can also be far more challenging; it takes time to make the necessary inroads and build a reputation. Hiring a hacker is one way to shortcut the process. Someone who is an active member of the hacker community has the ability to gather information about emerging exploits, targeted systems, and hacking trends. This is information that can be used to facilitate preparedness through the identification of potential exploits (something a hacker can also help with) and the deployment of appropriate countermeasures. Hiring someone full time to perform defensive intelligence gathering is cost prohibitive for most organizations, but a number of excellent subscription services such as the SANS Internet Storm Center, Security Tracker, and Symantec DeepSight provide excellent reconnaissance information. Some are free, and others have a yearly subscription fee (approximately $20–$30/month).

Sentry

Sentries are deployed along the perimeter of an encampment to provide attack or imminent attack notification. The amount of advanced warning is a function of the sentry's field of view. In medieval times, during the day a sentry at the top of a castle tower had a broad view of the surrounding countryside and could provide an early enough warning to get the gates closed and defenders in place before the attackers arrived. At night this capability was greatly diminished, and so the gates were kept closed at night and more sentries deployed. Sentry positions were often enhanced with noisemakers or other devices designed to alert sentries to movement along the perimeter. Today the military uses electronic sensors and night-vision goggles to improve sentry observation. Bill learned how effective this type of monitoring was while looking for a good place to eat lunch on a naval base. There was a nice grassy knoll near where he was working, so he headed across it to find a place to sit down. He hadn't walked 100 yards along the outside of the security fence when a jeep pulled up alongside him and a rather displeased officer asked him who he was and what he was doing. Little did he realize he was walking along the perimeter of the ordinance bunker setting off the motion sensors as he merrily strolled along!

Physical Security

Observation tactics in physical security focus on two areas: improving human surveillance and improving event detection. Surveillance means to continually observe or to watch closely. Not all surveillance is necessarily visual; it could be audio (i.e., eavesdropping) as well. And not all surveillance is human, some can be electronic—for example, a home confinement ankle bracelet continuously monitors the distance a person is away from the confinement sensor. We will not be covering the latter scenarios but will focus on human-based visual observation. The effectiveness of human surveillance is based on three factors: field of view, resolution, and training. These factors are the same for people looking directly at the scene or monitoring it with video.

Field of view is what is visible from a given observation point or perspective. The larger the field of view is, the more things that can be observed at one time. Cameras tend to have a more limited field of view than the human eye; consequently, they are equipped with pan and tilt functions that allow them to quickly change perspectives. Field of view is enhanced by elevation; for example, standing at ground level, a person can see approximately 2.75 miles, but standing in a 100-foot observation tower, a person's field of view increases to 12.5 miles. Buildings are elevated above parking areas to provide a better view of vehicle and foot traffic approaching the building.

Field of view is diminished by obstructions. Reception areas typically have glass doors and floor-to-ceiling windows, so that reception personnel have a clear view of people approaching the building. Landscaping uses low-lying shrubs and plants that do not obstruct the view. Field of view is enhanced by light and diminished by darkness so the walkways and the main entry to the reception area are usually well lit in the evenings. Resolution relates to the quality of detail in the image. For example, HDTV has a higher resolution than standard television. Resolution is diminished by distance, monitor size, lighting, and the optical characteristics of the viewing device. Things at a distance and things on a small video screen are difficult to distinguish; video cameras have a zoom feature to improve distance resolution. Most video viewing systems have an option to switch to a larger monitor to improve resolution.

Resolution is affected by low lighting, excessive lighting, and poor contrast. These three factors all make it difficult to distinguish details in an image. Driving a car on a rainy night is a good illustration of the first two. It's hard to see any details in the dark, and then someone comes around the corner with his high beams on and blinds you so you can't see anything in the light. The third factor, contrast, is what makes one thing stand out against another. People wear light-colored clothing at night so they can be better seen. Commandos wear black clothes and paint their faces black so they can't be seen. A great example of this factor was a company that kept having issues with people breaking in at night. Even with guards and good lighting, the black-clothed bandits were still able to climb over the fence and get into the building. The solution? Paint white stripes on the blacktop outside the fence line. The contrast between the white stripes and the black clothing made the bandit's movements easy to spot. Night-vision cameras, infrared projectors, and night-vision goggles can also help deal with low-level light or poor-contrast situations. Sunglasses help humans deal with excessive light, and cameras typically have aperture adjustments to deal with the issue. Each factor is a trade-off: When you zoom in, you reduce the field of view; when you increase brightness in one area, you reduce resolution in other areas. A great example of this is Bill's security review of a data center. The exterior of the building was monitored with video cameras. The parking lots were lit with moderate-level sodium vapor lights, and the sidewalks around the building were lit with bright halogen lighting. The cameras adjusted their aperture for the bright lights; consequently, nothing in the parking areas could be seen on camera. Quality of optical characteristics covers a couple of different things; in cameras it can refer to the quality of the lens, the color abilities, and the number or pixels in the receptor. A black and white camera with a low pixel count and a poor-quality lens has the worst resolution, and by contrast, the color camera with a high pixel count and a high-quality lens has the best resolution. For humans it is related to the physical characteristics of our eyes—nearsightedness, farsightedness, color blindness, and so on. The final factor is training. The effectiveness of surveillance is based on our ability to accurately interpret what we are looking at. Our life experiences help, but the only way to become proficient at identifying malicious activity is through training: classroom and on-the-job experience.

Event Detection

Malicious activity can be identified through the use of event detectors. In most instances, event detectors do not discriminate between good and bad events; they simply report a state change to a controller that decides whether or not to take action on the event. Most controllers are computerized devices that analyze and forward events to a responder; on some occasions, the event is sent directly to someone for analysis. Detectors can be deployed to monitor just about any physical state. Table 9.1 presents a list of the more common types of detectors and how they are used.

Table 9.1 Common Event Detectors and Uses

Detector	Usage
Opening switches	Open or closed door, window, or other opening
Carpet/item switches	Movement on a carpeted area, item being moved
Motion detectors	Movement in an area, item being moved
Heat/infrared detectors	Temperature change, fire, presence of a heated body/object
Smoke/gas detectors	Fire, hazardous vapors, hazardous gas
Vibration detectors	Wall penetration, earthquakes, explosions, movement across an area
Membranes (e.g., silver tape)	Wall penetration, glass breakage
Sound detectors	Glass breakage, explosions
Moisture detectors	Humidity change, flooding
Beam detectors (e.g., light, infrared, laser)	Movement across an area or through an opening, item being moved
Proximity detectors	Movement near or approaching something
Operational status	Failed, disabled, or sabotaged equipment

Detectors may incorporate multiple mechanisms to increase accuracy (i.e., reduce false detections). For example, a motion detector might be combined with an infrared detector so that a pet passing through an area would not set off the alarm. For coverage purposes, detectors are often redundant or overlapping. For example, a window switch combined with a glass-breakage detector covers someone opening the window or breaking the glass to crawl through it. A beam detector and carpet switch cover someone stepping over the beam. Detectors are often used to improve the effectiveness of surveillance; for example, the opening of a door or motion in an area causes the main video monitor to switch to that doorway or corridor. Detectors also have a resolution factor based on their false and true detection rates. For example, a door switch that claims the door was opened when someone merely bumps into it is a low-resolution device because it is sending out false positives. Conversely, a sticky switch that only reports some door openings also has poor resolution because it is not detecting all events. Too much resolution can also be a problem; for example, a smoke detector may be so sensitive that it goes off for ordinary events like burning a scented candle. The effectiveness of detectors is largely related to the controller to which they are attached. The controller must be able to properly interpret the detector signals and take the proper action. Programmable controllers that support multiple input types are best.

The importance of having written operational guides and procedures for responding to events cannot be overemphasized. The timeliness and effectiveness of our response depend on people's ability to take the right action quickly and to escalate those actions when necessary. The purpose of surveillance and event detection is to identify wrong or malicious behavior so that it can be responded to and corrected. Coverage is vitally important; people and cameras need to be placed so that they have an appropriate field of view and eliminate blind spots. Detectors need to be in place to cover all events associated with physical security (and safety). Event detection can be used to enhance the effectiveness of surveillance by tying monitor focus to specific events. Resolution requirements depend on what is being monitored; color is always recommended for video. Programmable controllers and detectors with sensitive controls are recommended for event detection. Even the best surveillance capability cannot improve security effectiveness if the observers don't interpret what they are looking at correctly and don't respond in a timely and appropriate manner. Training staff to be good observers and to correctly interpret detector events is essential. For additional information on physical security controls, please see the Appendix—Physical Security Checklists.

IT Security

In information technology (IT), controls are deployed along the perimeter to protect data repositories and processing installations. The sentry element in logical security focuses on two areas: malicious pattern detection and abnormal behavior detection.

Pattern Detection

Pattern detection compares activity to a set of signatures. A signature is one or more conditions that, when matched, are indicative of malicious activity. There are four different types of signature matching:

1. **Misuse (signature) detection**—detects malware and malicious activity by comparing the contents of an activity (e.g., file, message, packet, etc.) to a dictionary of signatures to detect a pattern that matches or closely matches malicious activity.
2. **Pattern matching**—detects malware and malicious activity by comparing the contents of an activity to a fixed sequence of bytes (characters) within a file, message, or network packet. Patterns can be combined to improve detection; for example, if this is a UDP (User Datagram Protocol) or TCP (Transport Control Protocol), IP version 4 packet with a destination port of 5554, it is very likely the Sasser worm.
3. **Protocol decode analysis**—detects malicious activity by finding patterns in a protocol that are inconsistent with the standard. For example, a single open and two closes might indicate a response splitting attack. Protocol decode analysis is often used with multiple patterns in a single packet or content; it is also used across multiple packets (stateful).
4. **Heuristic analysis**—detects malicious activity or content using a problem-solving algorithm and heuristic-based signatures. Heuristics typically takes the results of each analysis and accumulates them until the total crosses a specific threshold that represents a high likelihood of malfeasance. For example, an e-mail might have lots of misspelled words, be just images, come from a questionable-source domain, or have an odd subject line. One of these conditions by itself might not mean the message is spam, but a heuristics match for two or more would cause the mail to be classified as spam. Heuristics can detect unknown attacks; it is the only way to detect certain types of malicious activity.

The effectiveness of the tactic is based on the quality of the signatures. A signature that is not sufficiently unique will match legitimate content or activity and generate a false positive. The generation of a signature requires the analysis of the malicious code; until the analysis takes place, none of the pattern-matching techniques will work effectively except perhaps heuristic analysis. Heuristics may be able to detect the presence of malicious content based on its similarity to other types of malicious code. Pattern matching is commonly used in antivirus/malware solutions and network- or host-based intrusion detection systems (NIDS, HIDS).

Anomaly Detection

Anomaly (profile) detection detects activity that deviates from the "norm" based on a predetermined definition of normal (i.e., a profile). Detection can include an event, a state, a piece of content, or a behavior that is considered abnormal. The profile (baseline) is usually "learned" through a statistical analysis of normal operational patterns. Most anomaly solutions will also allow behaviors to be programmed or imported into the system. Examples of the types of behaviors that might be detected include the following:

- Protocol anomaly—nonstandard traffic on an assigned port, for example, SSL traffic on the DNS port (53)
- Service anomaly—nonstandard service on an assigned port, for example, peer-to-peer file sharing on the HTTP port
- Application anomaly—nonstandard content in a data exchange, for example, Java script embedded in an HTTP post
- Statistical anomaly—disproportionate activity, for example, an inordinate amount of DNS traffic

Anomalies may be combined to detect additional conditions. The effectiveness of the tactic is based on how well the profile is able to characterize normal versus abnormal behavior based on where this activity originated (internal or external network). The profile is a list of attributes and associated values specific to the device being monitored. In other words, a profile for a Web server would be oriented toward HTTP and HTTPS protocol attributes. The profile must be created and be stable before enabling the detection; otherwise a large number of false positives are likely to result. A false positive (or false alarm) is an erroneous detection of malicious activity, when in fact the activity was legitimate. The opposite—a false negative—is the failure to detect a malicious activity when it was taking place. Anomaly matching is commonly used in network- and host-based intrusion detection systems (NIDS, HIDS).

Intrusion Prevention Extensions

Intrusion Prevention Systems (IPS) are basically intrusion detection systems with proactive extensions. The extensions are designed to stop an intrusion before it can do any damage. Host-based IPS hooks into the operating system kernel and Application Programming Interfaces (APIs) in order to block malicious actions such as changing system files or configuration and creating a new account. Some versions have extensions that are designed to monitor applications as well. Controls to prevent unauthorized changes to website files or registry settings are one example. One of the best features of IPSs is their ability to block attacks that do not have a signature yet. On the downside, they are often so integrated into the operating system that doing OS upgrades becomes a problem. Along the same lines, they need to be impeccably designed and coded so that they don't interfere with system operations or performance. Bill saw an example of this at a company he worked with; the company had IPS running on its domain controllers, and every now and again the servers would blue screen (crash). When the memory dump showed the faulting module to be the IPS, it was removed and the problem went away. Unfortunately, the problem was difficult to find and fix, and after a couple of tries the vendor gave up and subsequently lost the account. Network IPS functions like an advanced firewall; intrusion detection (IDS) is passive—it just monitors traffic as it passes by—but there's no way to block malicious traffic. To block traffic it must travel through a device like a firewall. When network IPS detects malicious traffic, it refuses to forward it and usually resets the connection as well. Some devices also add the source to an Access Control List so that subsequent packets are dropped as soon as they arrive. The advantage of this configuration is that the malicious content never gets delivered to the target system. The downside is that traffic must go through the device, so it becomes a potential choke point and a single point of failure. Because IPS uses a signature-based detection system, its effectiveness is based on the quality of the signatures provided. Quality is a major issue because a poor signature will not only generate a false positive but will kill the session as well!

Resolution

False positives and false negatives are used to determine the resolution of pattern and anomaly detection solutions. Each detection method has its pros and cons. Misuse detection has a low false-positive rate, but signature-based approaches are not effective against new or unknown viruses. Pattern matching suffers from the same issue; the pattern must be known (and attack patterns tend to change a lot), and if the pattern isn't unique enough it produces a lot of false positives. Stateful pattern matching can improve this somewhat. Protocol decode analysis has few false positives if the protocols are well defined, but the rate can be high for protocols that are loosely defined. Heuristics analysis is remarkably good at detecting malicious activity, but it is very resource-intensive and can have negative performance impacts under a heavy load.

All the applications and appliances based on these detection technologies will generate alerts and log events. The question is one of accuracy and effectiveness. The closer the detector is to the asset it is protecting, the more effective it will be. The principle is easy to illustrate; if you put NIDS on the Internet side of your firewall, you see all the attacks coming at the firewall. If you place it on the inside of your firewall, you see all the attacks that are getting through! Detectors can also be tuned to the system or systems they are protecting when they are on the host or on the same network segment. The accuracy issue is related to good-quality signatures and the ability to tune those signatures to your environment. If you choose to use IPS, this is even more critical. Commonality is another consideration; you want a system that will use your standard protocols, record formats, and storage mechanisms. Solutions that have proprietary monitoring consoles add complexity to the monitoring environment; look for solutions that work well with your overall strategy.

Log-Based Detection

The processing of log or audit trail records is another method of detecting malicious activity. There are two ways to accomplish this. The first is periodic review; logs (or video recordings) are reviewed for activities indicative of malfeasance. A number of log parsing and reporting tools are available to assist with this process, but from a security perspective periodic review is not a very effective control because it detects events after the fact. Most of the malicious activity discovered by this method comes from the prevalence of repeated entries, something that would have easily been detected in real time with other technologies. Log-based detection can be improved using an automated collection and analysis system. Several commercial products do this type of analysis. Their accuracy depends on the quality of the information in the log or audit trail; false positives can be an issue. One of the advantages of these products is collation. Because these systems collect logs from multiple devices, they can match events from across the environment and identify activities that might otherwise go unnoticed. For example, collating physical access logs with logical access records can identify compromised or shared accounts. If someone isn't in the office but is logged on to the network locally, either he tailgated through an entrance or his account has been compromised; both events constitute unauthorized activity. Automated log analysis can be done in-house or outsourced as a Managed Security Solution Provider (MSSP). While this is not the best overall solution, it does provide both near real-time detection and a good stopgap measure until application- and data-intrusion detection solutions become available. (For additional information on these technologies see Chapter 11.)

Improving IT event detection involves people, processes, and technology. Intrusion detection systems, intrusion prevention, and antimalware are examples of commonly used real-time IT detection technologies. Automated log processing is another alternative that provides near real-time detection. Process-based periodic log and audit trail review is another option that provides after-the-fact detection. All these techniques have their advantages and disadvantages. The closer the detection is to the protected asset, the more effective and accurate it will be. It is best to employ technologies that have commonality with other security controls to make alert processing, data transfers, and reporting more effective. No matter which technologies you decide on, remember that a well-trained and skilled staff is essential to achieving the best operational results.

Alarming

Thus far we have concentrated on the first two components of observation: monitoring and detection. This section addresses the third component: alarming.

Whether our reconnaissance and sentry is human or electronic, the purpose is the same: to monitor the scene, note changes, and raise an alarm when malicious or potentially malicious activity is detected. Alarming is based on the severity of the event. Severity is determined from a number of different classes that are environment-dependent. For example, events that pose an imminent (or manifest) danger to safety or security are considered *critical events*. Events that affect a large number of systems or users are also critical events, as are events affecting high-value assets. These events require an immediate response, so alarms are sent directly to response personnel. In larger organizations, the response agency would typically be the security operations center; in smaller organizations, alerts may be sent to a text pager, cell phone, or other alerting device. For critical events it is best to have more than one communications channel for alerts and a positive acknowledgment system to verify the alert has been received. Critical events call for an immediate activation of the emergency or incident response function.

The second class of events is *important events*—events that pose an immediate danger to safety or security. Because these also require an immediate response, they are also sent directly to response personnel. Important events may require a partial activation of the emergency or incident response function. The difference between critical and important is the impact (loss potential) of the attack—such as an attack against a limited number of systems or lower value assets. An attack against systems in the DMZ is a good example. The attack may have the potential of compromising or defacing a Web server, but it will not impact the business operations of the internal network.

Moderate-level events are the third class of alarms. These events apply to attacks that are detected but have a limited potential of success or represent no significant impact to safety or security. Moderate events are forwarded to response personnel but do not require an immediate response. For example, the connection of an unauthorized system to the network is a violation of security policy that requires a response, but the system poses no immediate threat unless it is infected with malware and is actively attacking other systems. Even this event may qualify as moderate if other mitigating controls are in place; for example, if all the systems have been patched and are not susceptible to the attack.

The final classification is *low*. Low-level events pose a threat to a very small number of systems or users, and other mitigation controls are present. Depending on your environment, low-level events may or may not be forwarded to response personnel; some may simply be logged. Antivirus and malware alerts from a single system are examples of low-level events. The antimalware software on the local machine has already mitigated (quarantined) the threat, and the alert is mostly informational. These types of events usually point to training issues. Examples include someone opening an infected e-mail attachment or downloading an infected file from an unreliable source. The importance of establishing criticality is to prioritize response. Table 9.2 shows an example of

Table 9.2 Severity Rating Criteria

Rating	Definition
Critical	An event that poses an imminent danger to safety or security, including events that • Endanger the safety of people • Affect a large number of systems or users • Have a high-loss potential • Affect high-value assets or critical business systems
Important	An event that poses an immediate danger to safety or security, including events that • Pose a danger to the safety of people • Are limited in scope • Have a moderate-loss potential • Affect lower value assets or noncritical business systems
Moderate	An event that has a limited potential of success or represents no significant impact to safety or security, including events that • Pose no danger to the safety of people • Are limited in scope • Have a low-loss potential • Are mitigated by other factors such as default configuration and IPS agents
Low	An event that has a very limited potential of success and represents no threat to safety or security, including events that • Pose no danger to the safety of people • Are extremely limited in scope • Have a very low-loss potential • Are significantly mitigated by existing controls and other factors such as default configuration and patches

these ratings and their associated definitions. (Please note that this is only an example; the criteria for your environment should be established in your security standards based on your asset protection requirements.)

Alarms may be active or passive; that is, they may activate a warning device such as a bell or flashing light, or they may pass an alert silently to a response function. It is not uncommon for organizations that do not have full-time monitoring staff to configure audio alarms on security management systems.

Alarming is based on thresholds. Thresholds define the upper or lower limits of a particular condition; when the threshold is crossed, an alarm is generated. Determining what thresholds are appropriate for certain events is not always obvious; some monitoring and adjustment over time is usually required. Thresholds may be time sensitive too. For example, a scheduled streaming backup may exceed an established Denial of Service threshold. One organization Bill worked with forgot this and drove the graveyard shift staff crazy with audio alarms that went off every 15 minutes during server backups! It is not necessarily wise to accept the vendor's default setting either. Starting with low thresholds and adjusting them based on false positives is the better method.

Command

Command is the use of observation to make effective decisions when responding to an attack. In an automated attack scenario, the attacker may alter his attack approach, first trying one exploit and then another. He may change the source location of the attack or attempt the attack from a different path (e.g., dial-up, VPN, partner connections, etc.). The person directing the response needs to anticipate these changes and, when observed, react to them.

Commonality is one of the principles that greatly facilitate command because it consolidates alert information on a common monitoring console and collects log/audit trails in easily queried repositories. Systems that collate alert and log information from multiple systems are also advantageous because they give the response commander a broader view of the event across the environment in near real time. This enables the commander to direct resources to the points of attack for the fastest and best overall resolution. (For more information on response tactics, see the Rapid Response section in Chapter 11.)

SIDEBAR: CAMOUFLAGE AND SECURITY BY OBSCURITY

The term "security by obscurity" is often met with derision from security people, particularly those who like to consider themselves experts. Nearly akin to a four-letter word in some circles.

Jesper M. Johansson

Most security professionals will tell you that security by obscurity is a bad practice and will then go out and implement a bunch of it themselves. Camouflage is an ancient military measure designed to deceive opponents and protect one's forces—"protect" being the key word. The goal of the camouflage/obscurity tactic is to protect resources by limiting or confusing the observations of the enemy. The camouflaging of the Lockheed-Martin aircraft plant (Figure 9.1) during World War II is an excellent example. Network Address Translation, split DNS, encryption, and any number of other technologies are all designed to obscure an attacker's view of information and potential targets. You see the same principle in physical security; the data center has no special markings, rooms in the data center are not labeled, and so on. This is a valid component of any security management program.

The principal issue associated with security by obscurity in the IT realm has more to do with secrecy than anything else. Claude Shannon, one of the founding fathers of the computer age stated the problem this way: "The enemy knows the system" (Shannon's maxim). In other words, if your protection relies on keeping something secret, it's going to fail because secrets don't remain secret for very long. The simplest example would be changing the

Figure 9.1   Lockheed-Martin aircraft plant before and after camouflage.

port number of a service, for example, using port 8000 instead of port 80 for a Web service. If the Web service has an exploitable vulnerability (e.g., SQL Injection), changing the port number does nothing to mitigate the vulnerability; it simply obscures it from attackers looking for Web services on port 80. One good port scan and you're had. Microsoft's LAN Manager (NTLM) authentication protocol is another great example. Microsoft considered the protocol a trade secret and wouldn't release any detailed information about it to the industry. So a team of software engineers working on a UNIX-NT integration project (Samba) reverse-engineered it and in the process revealed a number of exploitable security flaws. Now the enemy knew the system and began to exploit it to the chagrin of many security and networking professionals. Tactics that use obscurity to increase protection are valid; those that simply try to hide a system from attack are not.

Summary

Observation is central to our security objectives. Observation is what gives us the ability to respond to suspicious or malicious activity. Ideally, we want to be able to observe and detect every instance of wrongdoing, but that simply isn't possible. Nonetheless, our objective should be to close as many gaps in our observation capabilities as possible. Observation is primarily a detective control that depends on the identification and proper interpretation of events. Real-time observation is best, but not all observation is real time. Some observation is reconnaissance—that is, observing your adversaries to determine their strengths, weaknesses, weaponry, and attack plans so that countermeasures and response preparations can be made. Other observation is postmortem—the after-the-fact discovery of malfeasance by reviewing recorded surveillance or IT logs and audit trails. This type of observation, from a security perspective, is ineffective because it does not support the principle of timeliness; our objectives should focus on preemptive reconnaissance and real-time observation because the timeliness of our response is based entirely on the timeliness of our observation.

Observation can be based on human surveillance, physical controls such as motion detectors and door and window switches, and logical controls such as antimalware, intrusion detection, and prevention systems. To reach your security objectives, these controls must be backed up with a solid set of procedures for when to raise an alarm (alert) and when to escalate alarms. Most importantly, a successful security management program must have observant people. You not only need to train security personnel but the entire organization to be observant. The best security person you can have is someone who asks, "What's wrong with this picture?" These are the people who ask questions before they take a potentially dangerous action like opening an attachment on an unsolicited e-mail or clicking a link on an attack website. These are the people who will pick up the handouts left behind in the conference room and pull security doors closed when they're ajar.

Moving from security as service to security as a culture needs to be an integral part of our security strategy. Security is everyone's job; it must be our goal to help our people be good at it.

Drivers and Benefits for Excellence in Observation

This section examines the benefits of observations as a whole. Observation improves most business practices. Business strategy is driven by vision and observation: observing what consumers need, what the competition is doing, what our capabilities are, and so on. Organizations set up metrics to observe progress toward specific goals. Good management exercises good oversight, and the list goes on. In the same way, observation improves security practices, effectiveness, and measurement. Since observation is the cornerstone of security, any benefit derived from security is a benefit that is ultimately derived from observation.

Observation improves security effectiveness through defense in depth. Observation monitoring, detection, and alerting capabilities can be deployed at the facility level (video, security officers, motion detectors, etc.) and IT perimeter (Gateway IPS), network (NIDS), host (host IDS/IPS, Antivirus), application (AIDS), and data (DIDS) levels. This is an extraordinary coverage capability as well.

The most prevalent benefit of observation is an economic one: loss prevention. Excellent surveillance capabilities deter people from performing illicit acts, and observing illicit acts helps people deal with those acts quickly, thus keeping damages to a minimum. Loss prevention in the context it is used here is more than theft losses; it also encompasses unrecoverable repair/restoration costs, notification costs, downstream liabilities, and legal liabilities from civil actions. These represent substantial loss liabilities that increase until malicious acts are observed, responded to, and resolved. Reconnaissance also helps prevent loss by providing early warning of potential attacks so defensive preparations can be made to prevent or limit damages.

Security is also becoming an important part of brand recognition and value. Companies that handle security well gain the confidence and trust of their customers. Brand value is earned over time, but can be lost in the heartbeat of a single security compromise. A Yale University study of people who received notification of a compromise of their bank account data found that 10% of surveyed customers had moved their account to another bank, and another 45% would definitely move their accounts if it ever happened again. No company can tolerate this kind of defection! The last thing a company wants to be recognized for is doing security poorly. Microsoft suffered this fate in the late 1990s. Microsoft had such a large share of the market that any exploitable vulnerability in their software resulted in devastating impacts on the industry. The "I Love You" virus hit 50 million systems in 2000, shutting down e-mail systems worldwide. Sasser sliced through the Internet in 2004, shutting down airline reservation systems, television broadcast systems, and just about anything else running Windows. It took Microsoft years to dig itself out of that reputation hole, and even today a survey of developer blogs still shows a great disdain for Microsoft "security."

Compliance is going to remain a driver for security functionality for years to come. Observation benefits compliance efforts by creating audit records of the malicious activities it detects. Some issues with the evidentiary quality of these records still exists, but this is bound to improve over time.

Excellence in observation also has a performance benefit. Good observation information dictates the proper level of response; people are not unnecessarily distracted from their primary job functions to deal with attacks. Both authors have sat in war rooms full of people waiting to do something while the response leaders tried to figure out what was going on. Good observation gets the needed people moving and lets everyone else get back to work.

Security also benefits innovation in that it allows innovation to move forward in a safe manner. No matter how innovative your idea, if it gets hacked it may be impossible to recover from bad publicity and reputational damage. Practices like Security Development Lifecycle, which includes proper security controls, application intrusion detections, and reactive measures, not only reduce the likelihood of adverse events but actually improve product marketability. People prefer to buy secure products and services.

Excellence in observation is a good fit for any size organization because it begins with people. Sophisticated controls like IDS or IPS may be cost prohibitive for smaller organizations, but training staff to be security minded is not. Antimalware is also economical. Medium-size organizations may find MSSP services an attractive alternative to in-house detection systems, and they may also benefit from the continued decrease in video surveillance equipment costs. Larger organizations and those dealing with high-sensitivity-level data may also realize cost reductions from MSSP solutions, especially when combined with in-house intrusion detection and prevention systems.

Observation is the cornerstone of security; any benefit derived from security is a benefit that is ultimately derived from observation. Observation tactics can be deployed at multiple physical and logical levels to provide defense in depth and comprehensive security coverage. The most prevalent benefit of a good observation strategy is the reduction of losses from malicious activities. Reconnaissance allows us to prepare for upcoming attacks. Surveillance deters people from committing illicit acts and aids in detecting illicit acts. Physical detectors help identify security-related events such as the opening and closing of a door into a high-security area or movement in a secured area. Logical detectors, such as IDS and Antivirus, use pattern and anomaly matching to identify malicious content or malicious activity in network traffic, files, and messages. The ultimate objective of observation is to identify (detect) unauthorized activities and raise alerts so that those activities can be responded to and resolved quickly. Done well, observation not only prevents economic losses, but also adds brand value, aids compliance, increases staff performance, and facilitates innovation. Good observation begins with observant people; we want an organization of people that asks the question, "What's wrong with this picture?" and takes the right actions.

SIDEBAR: NOT A VERY GOOD EXAMPLE OF OUR SECURITY, IS IT?

A few years ago we attended a meeting at a data center in northern California. Getting to the conference room involved a fairly long and detailed security process that included getting your picture taken and leaving your driver's license at the reception desk. Once we were properly registered, an administrative assistant escorted us to the conference room though a series of security doors, including one with a biometric device that measured hand geometry. Upon arrival, she asked if we would like a beverage and left to get our drinks and let her boss know we had arrived. In the interim, we were left alone in the conference room. Something from a previous meeting had been left on the table, so Bill took a look. It was a handout that contained some very sensitive business information. In fact, when the CSO came in and saw it laying there he grabbed it and said with a sheepish grin, "That shouldn't have been left there! Not a very good example of our security, is it?" No it wasn't, nor was it a good example of observation; not only had everyone at the previous meeting overlooked the document, so had the assistant who brought us to the conference room.

Observation Challenges

There aren't any real barriers to using the tactic of observation; everyone understands the principle at least in the context of physical security. We all survey the areas we are in for potential dangers—a stray dog in the park, an oddly dressed person in the parking garage, or a group of people in an alley. Unfortunately, this doesn't automatically carry over into the logical realm of information systems. The issue is not one of observation, but one of interpretation. We see the stray dog as a potential danger but don't think twice about opening an e-mail with "I Love You" for a subject line. Consequently, attackers are able to take advantage of our naivete, fear, confusion, or helpfulness to attack and damage our systems. "I Love You"—who wouldn't open a message with that subject line?

Interpretation and resolution are the two main challenges in observation tactics. Whether the monitoring is being done by a human, a physical device, or software, the detection of unauthorized or malicious activity is based entirely on the proper interpretation of changes in the scene or situation. The higher the resolution of the scene, the more information is available for interpretation. The accuracy of all observation is the result of this learned (or programmed) behavior; the effectiveness is based on resolution. Poor resolution or inaccurate interpretation means some malicious activity may go undetected (false negative) or some acceptable activities may be interpreted as malicious (false positive). Interpretation and resolution are the main control objectives for observation-based controls.

Excellence in observation extends beyond interpretation and resolution to include coverage. Excellent coverage means there are no "blind spots" (gaps) in our capabilities. This represents another challenge: We want to be able to observe and detect every instance of unauthorized or malicious activity. Though not completely feasible, this goal should be a driving factor in our efforts. The challenge of coverage is how to identify our observation gaps and understand the risks they represent so that we can prioritize our efforts to close them. A good place to start is with your past breaches; then you need to take a look at the current breaches the industry is experiencing. Understanding the root causes of these breaches not only shows you the failure of your preventative controls but also points to the gaps in your detective controls (observation). Once you understand the gaps, you can begin looking at which observation tactics will best address them.

Success Factors and Lessons Learned

Now let's look at some of the observation success factors and lessons learned.

Reconnaissance

Successful reconnaissance provides reliable information about pending attacks far enough in advance that preparations and countermeasures can be deployed. Reconnaissance information gathered from black-hats has questionable reliability. Vetting information with other reconnaissance efforts can improve reliability and can help with countermeasure preparations.

Surveillance

For surveillance to be considered successful, it should, at a minimum, record all security-related events such as building or secured area entry and exit. It should also provide monitoring of public areas such as lobbies, conference rooms, and parking areas, as well as the exterior walls and the roof. Blind spots must be minimized. Lighting must be sufficient for nighttime recording and consistent throughout the field of view so that the complete scene is recorded clearly during night surveillance. The same principles apply to the use of physical detectors. Make sure they provide overlapping detection capabilities and complete coverage of all exterior entry points, including windows, doors, load docks, HVAC vents, skylights, and so on.

CCTV Surveillance Lessons Learned

The following points are commonly employed as best practices for the deployment and use of CCTV:

- Plan holistically; design as if you are going to observe everything and cut the design back as required.
- With regard to overlapping fields of view, try to have at least two devices cover the same field of view to eliminate blind spots and to cover device failures or sabotage.
- Use tamper-resistant devices and locate them out of reach; protect all cabling to prevent tampering.
- Return devices to their default field of view after a period of inactivity.
- Use recorders that sense motion to reduce disk usage and speed up reviews.
- Use IP-based devices that support power over Ethernet (POE); avoid wireless devices, which can be jammed.
- Integrate physical sensors so that monitoring is switched automatically to high-priority scenes when activity is present.
- Use color cameras and color monitors to improve resolution.
- Watch your disk usage carefully on recording servers.

Physical Detectors Lessons Learned

The following lessons learned and best practices are fairly consistent throughout the industry:

- Use devices that have adjustable thresholds.
- Use devices that combine detections to increase accuracy.
- Use devices that are attached to the network.
- Have dedicated power sources for critical detectors.
- Use programmable controllers that can be expanded to support a wide variety of devices.
- Try to use devices and controllers that can report to a common console.
- Use high-resolution devices (low false positives and false negatives).

IT System Security

High resolution is the best measure of success when you are using logical detection applications and appliances. High resolution means low false-positive and false-negative rates. Systems that use multiple types of detections have higher resolution. Heuristic analysis appears to have the best overall results. Resolution improves the closer the detector is located to the asset it is protecting. No detection device is going to have perfect resolution; there must be good procedures for dealing with false-positive alarms.

IT System Security Lessons Learned

- Use software that allows signatures and patterns to be tuned.
- Use solutions with stateful detection for higher resolution.
- Try to find solutions that report to a common management platform.

- Stay with high-end vendors that produce high-quality signatures, automate updates, and have a quick turnaround on new threats.
- Use overlapping controls when possible.
- Do exhaustive testing on IPS agents and appliances, especially failover features for network IPS.
- Test the detection accuracy occasionally to ensure the solution actually detected malicious activity.

The final lesson learned is training. Ensure you have a knowledgeable and skilled staff managing your observation solutions and a company of observant people.

Excellence in Observation Control Objectives

Reconnaissance

This section covers the controls the reconnaissance tactic requires for successful operations. Table 9.3 maps reconnaissance attributes to specific baselines. The type (hard or soft) is used to denote how evidence is collected for each control. Soft indicates a procedure-based control, while hard denotes a technology-based (i.e., automated) control.

In-house reconnaissance capabilities are not cost effective for most organizations, especially in light of the low-cost availability of reconnaissance information from security vendors, service organizations, and government agencies. The success of in-house reconnaissance efforts is based on three factors: planning, operations, and effectiveness. Planning includes training personnel in reconnaissance techniques, as well as giving them time to study the black-hat culture. Spending time with other people who do black-hat reconnaissance is recommended. These contacts also assist in the vetting of information obtained during reconnaissance operations. Reconnaissance efforts should have specific operational objectives oriented primarily toward connecting with good sources of reliable information. Operations should be active (continuous). Efforts must be ongoing, and regular interactions with black-hat resources should be taking place. Operations must be flexible; be willing to break off contacts and change techniques or avenues of approach when the situation dictates (e.g., being discovered as a white-hat spy). It is also important to evaluate the effectiveness of your reconnaissance efforts from time to time. Successful reconnaissance provides accurate information about potential threats far enough in advance to allow countermeasure preparations to be made and to develop a good understanding of potential risk as well as the time line available for preparations.

Surveillance

Surveillance in the context of this chapter is human-based visual observation by viewing a scene either directly or remotely using video. There are two types of surveillance: active and passive. Passive surveillance is the review of recorded video; all other surveillance is active. The effectiveness of surveillance is based on interpretation and resolution. In surveillance these factors are expressed as field of view, resolution, and training.

Table 9.4 maps surveillance attributes to specific baselines. The type (hard or soft) is used to denote how evidence is collected for each control. Soft indicates a procedure-based control, while hard denotes a technology-based (i.e., automated) control.

These factors are the same for people either looking directly at the scene or monitoring it with video. The control objectives are intended to improve the viewing area or the resolution of the scene so that changes to the scene can be properly interpreted and malicious activity detected.

Table 9.3   Reconnaissance Control Objectives

Attribute/Control	Type	Risk and Requirements
Planned		
Prepared	Soft	Personnel performing reconnaissance activities should be trained in reconnaissance techniques and should become knowledgeable in black-hat culture before engaging in reconnaissance. Work with experienced reconnaissance agents is highly recommended.
Focused	Soft	Reconnaissance activities should have well-defined objectives designed to obtain the best and most current information.
Operative		
Active	Soft	Reconnaissance activities should be conducted continuously to gain all possible information about people (black-hats), planned attacks, and potential targets.
Connected	Soft	Reconnaissance activities should make every effort to gain and maintain contact with the black-hat community to provide continuous information on activities and changes in threat situations.
Flexible	Soft	Reconnaissance activities should be flexible, that is, able to break off contact, change techniques, etc., to prevent discovery and/or retaliation.
Effective		
Timely	Soft	Information obtained by reconnaissance activities should be reported as quickly as possible to maximize countermeasure preparations.
Developed	Soft	Personnel performing reconnaissance activities should analyze threat situations to provide threat-level ratings, potential attack time frames, etc., to help guide countermeasure efforts.
Accurate	Soft	Reconnaissance activities should endeavor to provide the most accurate information possible to ensure the best possible response.
	Soft	Information obtained by reconnaissance activities should be vetted to ensure accuracy.

Event Detectors

Event detectors are used to monitor changes to the physical state of a scene. The effectiveness of event detectors is based primarily on resolution. Event detectors typically do not differentiate between good or bad behavior; they simply report state changes. It is up to the device they are reporting to (i.e., the controller) to interpret those state changes. As a general rule, controllers do a good job of detecting events because events are based on changes in physical state.

Table 9.4   Surveillance Control Objectives

Attribute/Control	Type	Risk and Requirements
Coverage	Soft	Surveillance should provide, at a minimum, visual observation for all facility security-related activities, including building ingress and egress, entry or exit from secured areas, public access area (parking lots, reception areas, conference rooms, etc.) usage to facilitate the detection of unauthorized or malicious activities.
Field of View		
Properly scoped	Soft	Surveillance should, to the most reasonable extent possible, provide the broadest field of view possible.
	Soft	Surveillance must be configured so that the entire scope of activity is in the field of view (it should not be necessary to change the viewing perspective to see everything that is taking place).
Clear/unobstructed	Soft	The field of view should have no structural or landscaping feature that would allow someone or something to approach undetected, including frosted glass, works of art, plants, and posts.
Resolution		
Defined	Soft	Surveillance should have a resolution definition commensurate with the value of or risk to the monitored object to facilitate the detection of unacceptable activity. Definition depends on optical lens quality, receptor pixel count, and monitor size and pixel count.
Focused	Soft	Surveillance scenes must be in focus (have the best possible clarity) to facilitate the detection of unacceptable activity.
Properly lit	Soft	Surveillance scenes must be properly lit to ensure unacceptable activity within the field of view can be detected.
Contrasted	Soft	Surveillance scenes should be properly contrasted to facilitate the detection of unacceptable activity within the scene and to prevent someone or something from approaching undetected.
Colored	Soft	Surveillance should use color monitors and viewing devices to facilitate monitoring and detecting unacceptable activity.
Training		
Survey	Soft	Personnel performing surveillance activities should be trained in surveillance techniques, including the use of surveillance equipment and features to improve surveillance effectiveness.

Table 9.4   Surveillance Control Objectives (continued)

Attribute/Control	Type	Risk and Requirements
Detection	Soft	Personnel performing surveillance activities should be trained to recognize threat situations and take appropriate actions to reduce damages or loss of human life.
Alerting	Soft	Personnel performing surveillance activities should be trained in proper alerting procedures to ensure that alarms are reported to the proper responder and that people in immediate danger are properly notified.

Table 9.5 maps event detection attributes to specific baselines. The type (hard or soft) is used to denote how evidence is collected for each control. Soft indicates a procedure-based control, while hard denotes a technology-based (i.e., automated) control.

Pattern and Anomaly Detectors

Pattern and anomaly detectors are logic-based applications used in computer environments to monitor content or activity for the presence of malicious code. The effectiveness of pattern and

Table 9.5   Event Detector Control Objectives

Attribute/Control	Type	Risk and Requirements
Coverage	Soft	Event detection should provide, at a minimum, detection of all facility events related to security, including the opening and closing of doors, windows, skylights, HVAC vents, etc.; movement in secured areas, flooding, fire, glass or wall breakage, and so on to facilitate the detection of unauthorized or malicious activities.
Detectors		
Accuracy	Hard	Event detection devices must correctly report changes in state to facilitate the detection of unauthorized or malicious activities.
	Hard	Detection must be reasonable; that is, it must take place in a reasonable time frame and be within a reasonable range.
Sensitivity	Soft	Event detection devices should have adjustable thresholds to reduce false detections resulting from environmental variables.
Controllers		
Accurate	Hard	Event device controllers must correctly interpret detector inputs and report actual or potentially malicious activity.
Flexible	Soft	Event device controllers must be able to accept inputs from a variety of event detectors.
Programmable	Soft	Event device controllers should be programmable to improve detection accuracy and reliability.

anomaly detectors is based on their correct or incorrect detection rate (sometimes called resolution). Resolution is the average of the false-negative and false-positive events for any given number of events. Resolution for pattern detection depends on the availability and quality of the signatures used for matching. Resolution for anomaly detection depends on how well the detection profile is able to characterize normal versus abnormal behavior.

Table 9.6 maps these attributes to specific baselines. The type (hard or soft) is used to denote how evidence is collected for each control. Soft indicates a procedure-based control, while hard denotes a technology-based (i.e., automated) control.

These control objectives form the basis for timely, comprehensive, and accurate observation of malicious or potentially malicious acts. The control objectives begin with human observation and proceed to physical and logical detectors. The objectives support rapid response through the use of reconnaissance and real-time detection and alerting. Detection is improved through the use of high-resolution devices that facilitate scene interpretation.

The following actions are recommended to further security observation objectives:

1. Review existing reconnaissance activities and results to identify shortcomings in preemptive notifications and information accuracy.
2. Survey existing surveillance practices procedures to identify gaps in coverage, procedures, and staff knowledge, skills, and abilities (KSA) deficiencies.
3. Survey the existing surveillance equipment installation to identify gaps in coverage, resolution issues, recording shortcomings, and so on.
4. Assess the risks associated with existing reconnaissance and surveillance practices.
5. Survey the existing physical detector equipment installation to identify gaps in coverage or resolution issues.
6. Review existing antimalware, intrusion detection, and intrusion prevention practices and procedures to identify gaps in coverage, procedures, and KSA deficiencies. Review accuracy

Table 9.6 Logical Detector Control Objectives

Attribute/Control	Type	Risk and Requirements
Coverage	Soft	Logical detection mechanisms should be used to discover malicious activity or content on systems or network infrastructure.
Pattern Matching		
Accurate	Hard	Logical detection mechanisms should have the lowest possible false-positive and false-negative rates.
Timely	Hard	Logical detection mechanisms must be updated regularly and in the case of emanated attack updated immediately.
Tunable	Soft	Logical detection mechanisms must support the adjustment of signatures and profiles to provide better accuracy and more granularity detection.
Commonality	Soft	Logical detection mechanisms should integrate with existing alerting, transport, storage, and reporting solutions.

rates, including false negatives. Identify the primary assets these systems are designed to protect.

7. Update existing standards to conform to security strategic objectives for observation, including reconnaissance, surveillance, physical, and logical detection requirements.

8. Review and update application development processes (in-house or contracted) to incorporate observation (intrusion detection) guidance for all development efforts.

9. Review existing alert management equipment and procedures to identify gaps in commonality.

10. Review your corporation's data-retention policies to determine how they may impact your video recording and alert management schema.

11. Consider outsourcing reconnaissance to a third party.

12. Consider outsourcing log-based detection to an MSSP.

Conclusion

Observation is the cornerstone of security. It is both a deterrent and a detector. It is a deterrent because people are less likely to do something illicit if they believe someone will see them do it, and it is a detector when an illicit act is seen. Observation drives our outside and inside facility designs and campus layout. It guides operations, including the placement of security officers and the use of video surveillance. Observation extends beyond security to encompass fire, flood, earthquake, and other safety-related functions. Observation comes down to the desktop in the form of antivirus and intrusion prevention software. All security controls are based on the ability to observe an event, interpret what is happening, and detect malfeasance. Although not all security failures are directly caused by observation, it is ultimately our lack of observation that allows those failures to go unnoticed and damages to be done.

Excellence in observation must always be one of our principal strategic objectives. In this chapter observation was covered from three different perspectives: reconnaissance, sentry, and command. Reconnaissance is a preemptive tactic that focuses on learning what will be targeted in the future and what tools (weapons) and maneuvers will be used so that countermeasures can be put in place and personnel prepared for a potential attack. Reconnaissance is a critical component of a good defense. An in-house reconnaissance function is unusual; a number of services already perform reconnaissance, supplying information to the industry for free or for a modest subscription fee.

Sentry is an alarm tactic designed to detect imminent or manifest attacks. This chapter examined the sentry tactic from three different viewpoints: surveillance, physical event detection, and logical event detection. Surveillance means to continually observe or to watch closely. This chapter focused on direct or video-assisted human surveillance. The effectiveness of human surveillance is based on three factors: field of view, resolution, and training. Of the three, having observant people is the most important; the goal should be a culture of observant people.

Event detectors and controllers can be used to identify unauthorized or malicious activities. The effectiveness and accuracy of these devices are high because they are based on physical events such as the opening or closing of a door. Detectors can be deployed to monitor just about any physical state, including safety-related items such as fire, smoke, and flooding. Detectors often combine multiple mechanisms into a single device to increase accuracy. For coverage purposes, detectors are often redundant or overlapping. Physical detectors are frequently integrated with surveillance systems to switch the monitor focus to high-security events. The effectiveness of detectors is largely related to the controller to which they are attached. The controller must be able to properly interpret the detector signals and take the proper action. Written operational guides and procedures for responding to events is key to timely and effective response; people dealing with events must take the right actions and escalate alarms when necessary. Just like surveillance, a trained observant staff capable of correctly interpreting detector events is essential.

Logical event detectors come in two forms: malicious pattern detection and abnormal behavior detection. Pattern detection compares activity or content against a set of predefined signatures. A signature match indicates malfeasance. There are four different types of signature matching: misuse, pattern, protocol, and heuristics. With the exception of heuristics, pattern matching is only effective at identifying known malicious code. Heuristics can detect some types of unknown attacks if they have similar characteristics to other malware. The accuracy of pattern matching depends on the quality of the signatures that are produced. Poor signatures can result in false positives, which can be problematic when they halt legitimate work efforts. Pattern matching is commonly used in antivirus/malware solutions and network- or host-based intrusion detection systems (NIDS, HIDS).

Anomaly detectors are often referred to as profile detectors because they use a statistical profile of normal system activity to detect behavior that is abnormal. The initial profile is usually created during a learning period and is tuned over a period of time to resolve false positives. Anomaly detectors look for inordinate protocol, service, application, and statistical behaviors. Anomalies may be combined to detect additional conditions. The effectiveness of this tactic is based on how well the profile is able to characterize what is a "normal" system operation and what is not. One advantage of this approach is the ability to monitor applications. The downside is a high rate of false positives and the maintenance that goes with it. Anomaly matching is commonly used in network- and host-based intrusion detection systems (NIDS, HIDS).

Host and network intrusion prevention systems (IPSs) extend intrusion detection to include proactive methods that stop malicious activity or content before it can do any damage. A key benefit of IPSs is their ability to stop unknown attacks, but to accomplish this objective the IPS agent must be tightly integrated with the operating system kernel making it more susceptible to failure from OS patches and upgrades. In order for Network IPS to block malicious actions, all traffic has to pass through the device. The advantage of this configuration over IDS is that the malicious traffic never gets delivered to the target; the downside is that the NIPS becomes a potential choke point and a single point of failure. Intrusion Prevention Systems use signature-based detection, so effectiveness is based on the quality of the signatures provided. False positives and false negatives are used to determine the effectiveness of pattern and anomaly detection solutions. Each matching method has its good and bad points. Statistically, heuristics analysis is the best, but it can be very resource intensive. The closer these technologies are located to the asset they are protecting, the more effective they are. Commonality is another issue to consider; solutions based on proprietary monitoring and management consoles add complexity to the monitoring and response process; finding products that work with your existing management environment is the better overall strategy.

The processing of log or audit trail records is another method of detecting malicious activity. When done in real time using an automated collection and analysis system, it does improve detection of malicious activity. The accuracy depends on the quality of the information in the log or audit trail; false positives can be an issue. One advantage is collation; logs from multiple devices are collected so that events can be matched from across the environment. This can result in activities being identified that might otherwise have gone unnoticed. Automated log analysis is the current focus of the industry; there are many good products for use in-house, and many MSSPs offer this service as well.

Excellence in observation is a first principle in security tactics. Observation involves people, processes, and technology. Good processes and well-integrated technologies can fill many of the gaps in your observation strategy, but nothing will improve it more than a well-trained and skilled staff and a culture that fosters observant employees.

Chapter 10

Trust but Verify (Accountability)

Trust but verify.

President Ronald Reagan

Introduction

Accountability is the ultimate observation tactic.

Accountability ensures that actions taken on a system can be traced back to the individual or individuals who performed those actions. This is a huge deterrent against illicit activities and false claims. Properly executed, accountability makes it nearly impossible for someone to deny he performed a specific action or, conversely, to accuse others of doing something they did not do. Accountability can also support rapid response by detecting illicit activities, alerting security personnel, and taking preventative actions to stop or limit those activities. Accountability provides evidence of compliance to statutory, regulatory and contractual requirements, tracks the usage and distribution of intellectual property, and can be a significant market differentiator for organizations that do it properly. This chapter sets forth the control objectives for accountability and suggests ways in which these objectives can be achieved within various types of computing enclaves.

Unmatched Value of Accountability

The accountability tactic provides a number of important benefits that are applicable to most computing environments. The first is unprecedented observation. The tactic is based on two principal factors: (1) the collection and preservation of evidence and (2) the association of that evidence with the identity performing the action. This is a huge deterrent against insider threats or, for that matter, malfeasance in general. The premise behind observation is that people are not inclined to do something wrong if they believe someone will see them doing it (i.e., they will get caught).

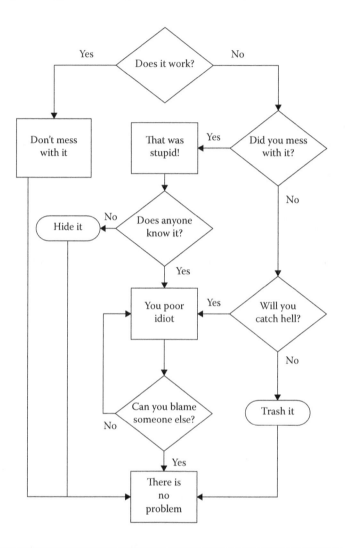

Figure 10.1   Problem-solving flowchart.

Accountability means you are going to get caught because accountability creates an irrefutable record of what was done under each account. Accountability means the answer to the "Does anyone know it?" question in Figure 10.1 is always YES! This is especially valuable for highly trusted (privileged) accounts; it provides a means to ensure that trust is not violated.

All computing environments require users with privileged access to build, configure, administer, and maintain systems and applications. The best access controls and administrative procedures will never eliminate the need for these users; at best, these controls can only limit who gets these privileges and where they are allowed to use them. An accountability control cannot stop a privileged user from performing a deliberate act of malfeasance, but it will certainly make them think twice because there is no avoiding the consequences.

The second benefit is compliance. Accountability ensures the proper collection and preservation of all the necessary information to satisfy legal, regulatory, industrial, and other external audits. The current regulatory and legal environment makes the retention of customer data a risky business. According to a Ponemon Institute study in 2007, data breach incidents cost companies $197 per compromised customer record, but this figure only accounts for notification and restoration costs; it does not include lost business opportunity, regulatory fines, or customer lawsuits that drive the costs even higher. For large organizations and service providers these are billion dollar figures. Accountability makes it possible to prove compliance and is designed to provide sufficient admissible evidence to ward off criminal or civil claims of negligence or malfeasance. Similarly, accountability aids in the resolution of contract and/or service delivery disputes by providing a chronological record of what was done, by whom, and when.

Third, accountability facilitates rapid response through the detection of illicit activities such as logging on with a generic (e.g., guest) account or using a service account for an interactive log-on, and the generation of alerts to security operations personnel. This is not limited to log-on events because accountability can track virtually any type of user action; it can be configured to detect all types of questionable behaviors, for example, database queries that return inordinately large amounts of data. In this instance, the accountability control could also be configured to take preventative action by limiting the number of records returned or by "filling" the returned data with randomly generated records. The accountability information collected also helps to focus response efforts by providing system and account specific records, as well as chronological records of all actions leading up to the alert and all subsequent actions.

A fourth benefit of accountability is intellectual property control. Accountability protects against intellectual property loss by tracking what individuals were in possession of any particular piece of information at the time it was compromised. This makes it possible to hold those individuals responsible for the breach and to take corrective action to reduce the likelihood of future disclosure.

The final benefit of accountability, especially for organizations that deal with financial and other sensitive data and for service providers, is marketing. Accountability is a huge market differentiator. Few organizations have the ability to provide high levels of accountability, yet in today's compliance-heavy climate there is a need to account for handling sensitive customer data. The ability to show potential customers an audit trail of every access and action taken to a particular piece of stored information is an incredible marketing advantage.

Accountability is a security function that ensures actions taken on a system can be traced back to the individuals who performed those actions. Assuming the records of these actions cannot be tampered with, accountability makes it nearly impossible for someone to deny having performed a specific action. Conversely, it makes it equally impossible to accuse people of doing something they did not do. Accountability improves the detection of illicit activity and facilitates rapid response through alerting and record retention. Accountability is also the vehicle for proving compliance with statutory, regulatory, and contractual requirements and avoiding sanctions for alleged violations. Finally, accountability is a huge deterrent to malicious behaviors and provides a way to track the actions of highly trusted individuals (i.e., administrators and other privileged users) to ensure they are not violating that trust.

SIDEBAR: OF AUDIT AND EVIDENCE

Before delving into the challenges and control objectives for accountability, it is necessary to discuss one other topic. Compliance has caused one of the biggest shifts in system auditing since the invention of the computer. Originally, system audit functions were designed for troubleshooting purposes; sufficient information was collected to track system behaviors and faults but little else. Often, standard audit records were augmented by debugging functions that produced incredibly detailed logs of system activity. From a compliance standpoint, these two functions were part of a "too little or too much" scenario. In order to prove compliance, audit mechanisms must create records containing compliance evidence—proof of adherence to legal, regulatory, and industry requirements.

Understanding the difference between the standard information an audit function provides and the evidence that is required to prove compliance is critical to the success of your compliance efforts. *Evidence is a collection of relevant and sufficient information to verify a fact.* Unlike troubleshooting information, evidence has very specific attributes; it must be:

- **Sufficient**—containing enough information to lead others to the same conclusion
- **Appropriate**—containing information that is relevant, valid, and reliable enough to support the claim
- **Quality**—containing information that is easily discernible and supportive of the claim

SUFFICIENT EVIDENCE

From an accountability standpoint, this means audit records must contain information about the entity performing the action, the IT resource acted upon, the type of action or actions taken, and (if the action involves a change) the old and new values. Standard event logs typically do not collect enough information to meet the sufficient requirement, and debug logs collect too much to meet the quality requirement. This isn't just an issue with operating system capabilities; many services and applications have equally limited audit mechanisms. Having sufficient information is essential, but it isn't everything; the information must meet the appropriate and quality bars as well.

APPROPRIATE EVIDENCE

The information collected must be relevant to the action taken. For example, if a change is made to the system, the data must accurately reflect what was changed as well as the changed values. In the case of a *create* action, the name of the created object, as well as the value or values associated with the object, must be recorded; for a file creation, the object would be a file and the value would be the file's fully qualified name (i.e., drive:\path\filename. ext). This level of detail is required for accountability. If only the directory (path) where the file was created was recorded, additional information would have to be accumulated to determine what file was created. This situation is completely unacceptable in large environments because of the quantity of data that would be generated (the goal in large environments is to minimize, not increase, data collection).

This requirement is equally applicable to subjects; the subject must represent the individual entity that originated the action. This account cannot be one that was delegated to do the action or a generic account such as guest or administrator because there is no way to validate the subject. This requirement can be problematic for multitier applications where service accounts are used for transactions between systems.

Finally, the appropriate attribute means the records are reliable. Records that are subject to unauthorized modification are not reliable and therefore are not admissible. In other words, security-related audit records must be written to a tamperproof container such as a centralized audit collection service managed by the security team. Since the information is written to devices that are accessible only to security personnel, the integrity and reliability of the audit information is assured.

QUALITY EVIDENCE

The quality attribute refers to the presentability of the evidence. Quality evidence is structured in a way that is easy to understand and simple to correlate with the other pieces of evidence being presented. And, of course, it must support the claim; quality-irrelevant evidence is still irrelevant. At odds with quality are the numerous places where audit records are stored and the different formats of those records. Some sort of common measurement collection capability is needed to address this issue. The goal is to force audit records into a common format and store them in a structured database for the analysis and reporting of quality evidence. This capability is valuable only if it is supported by infrastructure and by an enclave's systems and applications. Ideally, all services should use a common format and storage location for the audit records they generate.

Comprehensive Accountability Challenges

Implementing a comprehensive accountability control structure is no trivial pursuit. Accountability relies on two factors: identity and audit. Actions must be traceable to a unique identity, and sufficiently detailed records (i.e., audit trails, logs) must be kept to support the claim that the identity performed the actions. Both factors have their challenges.

Identity Challenges

A generic account is an account that cannot be associated with an individual identity. Examples are the guest account, the root or administrator account, and service accounts. Two other types of accounts also qualify as generic: shared accounts (accounts used by multiple people) and Anonymous. None of these accounts allows you to trace an action back to an individual. Eliminating the use of these accounts, however, isn't always possible. For example, a poorly designed application may require interactive log-ons for its service account. Management scripts may require interactive log-ons for generic accounts as well. For example, a script to join systems to the domain may require an interactive log-on by the SysPrepAdmin account to make sure it can be run successfully by a less privileged user. Replacing or restricting the use of generic accounts in a computing environment requires a thorough understanding of what each account is used for and the type or types of authentication it requires. This sounds easy, but it takes a lot of effort to track all this functionality down. It's worth it in the end to have this level of understanding, but getting there, especially in complex environments, is a major effort.

Audit Challenges

The sidebar presented earlier in this chapter highlighted a number of technological challenges regarding the structure and content of system-generated audit records. The issue extends to applications as well. Take Active Directory (AD), for example, beginning with Microsoft Windows Server 2008, changes to AD settings create two audit records: one containing the old value and one containing the new value. From an accountability standpoint, this improvement is an important one; yet, at the same time, it demonstrates the vendor's lack of proficiency. Why is this only a feature in AD? Why isn't it a standard audit feature in DHCP, DNS, and other domain services? What is lacking in Windows 2008 and other major operating systems is a consistent audit architecture. In fact, so disparate are the audit log formats in the 2008 operating system that an XML schema function was added to the event (log) viewer application so that it could display them in a readable format. These are major evidence issues within a single product manufactured by a single vendor. Imagine what happens when you incorporate multiple vendors. A great example of this is SYSLOG, a UNIX logging facility. SYSLOG is a model of simplicity; it contains just five fields of information: time, facility, priority, source, and meaning/description. Three of these fields have a fixed format; the other two (time and meaning) do not; consequently, there is no consistency for these fields across vendors. This makes it nearly impossible to collate records across multiple systems or applications without a sophisticated parser.

The emphasis on compliance in recent years has put pressure on manufacturers to provide better auditing facilities, but the rate of change has been dismal. Instead, a number of companies have introduced products designed to fill the gaps left by existing vendor audit functions. Most of these products install an agent on the system capable of collecting detailed audit information and converting it to a standard format for processing and reporting. Most have the ability to identify and flag unauthorized or questionable actions, and some have the ability to generate alerts as well. The main limitation of these products is processing time; usually a significant amount of time elapses between when the action took place and when it is detected and reported. In other words, these products do not support rapid response. The rapid response issue is somewhat understandable because the products are designed primarily for auditing and most environments have other systems dedicated to detecting malicious activity. However, from an operations standpoint, combining these two functions into a single system makes perfect sense. It contributes to the principle of economy (force conservation) by reducing complexity and simplifying operations.

Coverage is another limitation; the audit application may not have the ability to collect audit information from one or several applications within an enclave. The operational impact of this functionality must also be considered. First is the issue of maintenance (updates, patches, etc.); second is the issue of compatibility with other products running on the system. One organization Bill worked for could not identify a conflict between Active Directory and the IDS agent they were using. Every so often the agent caused the domain controller to blue screen. To resolve the problem IDS was removed from the one system where it was needed most! Performance is the other impact issue. How will the collecting and processing of audit information impact the response time of a system? Years ago a friend of Bill's at Digital Equipment Corporation told him that the auditing capabilities of VMS were so extensive that turning them all on meant the system didn't have time to do anything else! It is doubtful the effect would be that severe, but it is going to have an impact and that impact must be known for proper system planning. Ideally, you want a function that has a fixed impact; for example, the function will never exceed 7% processor usage or 25 megabytes of memory.

The quantity of data is another issue that must be considered, especially in large environments. There are two aspects to consider: processing and storage. Accountability produces an audit record for a large number of security-related actions each user performs. If you are an online service provider with a million users, that's a lot of audit records—probably close to 9 million records a day for log-ons and log-offs alone. Collecting that number of records is challenging enough; getting them into a searchable store is even harder. Bill remembers working on a Trivoli management system that monitored 65 or so machines. On average, the system had between 15,000 and 20,000 management records in the import queue. The system only imported about 1,000 records an hour, so this represented close to a day's worth of delay between the event and the processing of the event. Even worse, for every record taken out of the queue, one was added. This kind of delay is totally unacceptable for detecting and responding to unauthorized actions; those responses need to be in near real time. Database capacity and processing impacts may also need to be evaluated if the system is using SQL Server as a backend.

The benefits that accountability provides to the organization in the areas of risk reduction, compliance, and liability management are obvious, but providing a high level of accountability is challenging. Eliminating or restricting the use of generic accounts can be difficult and with some applications impossible, but conforming the content of audit records to a common and comparable format is a bigger challenge. Individual vendors don't even use the same formats for their products; crossing vendor product lines only exacerbates the problem. In large environments, the volume (quantity) of data can be both a storage and a processing issue. If the goal is to have near real-time responses to illicit activities, long processing delays cannot be tolerated. Making accountability a reality in any computing environment takes a lot of planning; organizations must expect that changes will need to be made to existing controls, new controls will have to be added, and enhancements made to development processes and applications. Having identified those challenges, we can now begin to look at how organizations can overcome them.

Best Uses for the Accountability Tactic

Financial organizations and organizations that deal with classified secrets already use this tactic. Banks, brokerages, and trading companies have to ensure that transactions cannot be reputed. This requires the collection and preservation of records that prove a particular action was taken (or approved) by a specific individual. Government agencies, the military, and military suppliers must account for the use and distribution of classified information to protect national security. They must ensure not only that actions can be assigned to an individual but also that the individual has the proper clearance to perform those actions. Financial organizations and government agencies require accountability to be a part of their operational structure, but any organization that is subject to compliance auditing can benefit from the application of this tactic.

Any structure that reduces the overall time and effort required for compliance reporting is beneficial. Manual reporting is a costly, time-consuming resource hog; any degree of automation is of value. Accountability, however, provides a number of other long-term benefits that are difficult to ignore. For example, the ability to prove compliance through accountability could be used to reduce the overall scope of audits. Accountability can also reduce malicious conduct, legal or regulatory sanctions, and liabilities from false accusations or claims. Every organization stands to benefit from these capabilities. The question is, "Will it be cost effective?" Given the state of today's audit technologies, the cost of achieving high levels of accountability for small to medium-size businesses is prohibitive. Large enterprises, especially those with in-house application development, will find this tactic much easier to implement for two reasons: (1) the ability to build missing functionality and (2) the ability to incorporate accountability functionality into their applications. These allow the gaps between existing technologies and accountability control objects to be closed. Service providers have the most to gain from this tactic. Accountability is not only a viable way to reduce liability, it also improves availability by discouraging illicit behaviors and identifying operational deficiencies. Finally, a high level of accountability is a major market differentiator.

Comprehensive Accountability Identity Objectives

Accountability is an information security tactic that assures actions taken on a system can be traced back to the individual or individuals who performed those actions. The U.S. National Institute of Standards and Technology (NIST) definition notes that accountability "supports non-repudiation, deterrence, fault isolation, intrusion detection and prevention, and after-action recovery and legal action." This section covers accountability controls and control objectives. Accountability relies on two functions: identity and audit. It isn't possible to trace actions back to an individual unless the individual has a unique identity, nor is it possible to trace actions back to an individual without sufficiently detailed records (i.e., audit trails, logs) of those actions.

The primary accountability attributes for identity are unique, specific, and exclusive. *Unique* means only one occurrence of this identity exists within the system. *Specific* means that the identity references a real person or process as opposed to a generic entity such as anonymous, guest, or testuser1. *Exclusive* means the identity is used by a single entity as opposed to being shared with multiple entities. These three requirements should be part of your information security policy for systemwide (domain) identities as well as local system identities, and these policies should be backed up with the appropriate procedures for identity issuance, monitoring, and revocation.

The goal is high assurance identity management beginning with properly vetted identity requests, assuring the requestors are who they claim to be and have been properly authorized to receive an identity. It continues with an incorruptible process for validating a presented identity such as multiple factor or third-party authentication. And it concludes by assigning the appropriate permissions to data and computing resources (i.e., authorization).

Ideally, the user should only need to log on once (single sign-on) and be able to gain access to all their assigned resources. When this isn't possible, the ideal is to be able to use the same identity (alias) for all log-ons. It is not unusual to find multiple identity management solutions in today's IT environments, but from an accountability perspective this creates problems. Although it is possible to implement accountability on a system-by-system basis, collating information across systems is less than ideal. The best solution for high-assurance identity management is to have a single identity for each user. The best alternative, if no single system meets all your identity needs, is a meta-directory that associates multiple system identities to a single-user meta-identity.

Identity Control Requirements for Accountability

This section covers the controls this tactic requires for effective operations. Table 10.1 maps the identity attributes to specific accountability baselines. The type (hard or soft) is used to denote how evidence is collected for each control. Soft indicates a procedure-based control, while hard denotes a technology-based (i.e., automated) control.

Domain and Local Account Management

The identity management system needs to provide coverage for local and domain account management across all platforms. This includes the establishment of an identity-naming convention that will reduce the likelihood of identity collisions, support "no identity reuse," and facilitate the automation of identity management across the enterprise. Possible actions include:

- Updating the identity management strategy to include accountability controls
- Developing identity-naming standards across all platforms and services
- Updating existing operations procedures and development practices to reflect identity naming requirements

SIDEBAR: NAMING STANDARDS

Two factors need to be considered when developing naming standards: management and usernomics (i.e., the human factor). Names should be constructed in a way that facilitates system management. For example, service identities ought to clearly identify the infrastructure or hosted service with which they are associated, as well as the role of the identity within the service. This is equally true for human identities; they should be easily associated with a specific organization or service. These associations make it easier for service and support personnel to quickly identity the environment they are serving.

Usernomics relates to the usability of services from a human perspective. Accountability requires uniqueness of identity but the introduction of complexity or ambiguity that negatively impacts users in order to achieve uniqueness must also be avoided. Examples include users that end up with multiple identities to access different resources or users that end up with disassociated or convoluted identities like John Smith ending up with the alias KTmith or JnSmith2a14.

Name Collision

Collision detection is inherent in most identity management systems, but clear procedures for resolving collisions, especially when multiple technologies are involved, must be established. Table 10.2 contains examples of potential name collision scenarios.

Name Collision Scenarios

A clear procedure must be in place for resolving name collision issues. Under no circumstances should it be possible to write an ambiguous identity to an audit record. The procedure must contain

Table 10.1   Identity Requirements for Accountability

Attribute/Control	Type	Risk and Requirements
Unique		
Domain and local account management	Soft	Controls must apply across all domains and systems.
Name collision detection	Hard	Identity creation or mergers/consolidations that would result in multiple entities with the same identifier must be detected.
Collision remediation	Soft	The user ID is altered based on established creation or migration practices.
Identity retention	Soft	Process to ensure an identity is never reused.
	Hard	Process is in place to detect and disable accounts that have not been used within a certain period of time.
Specific		
Identity verification	Soft	Prior to the creation of any account, the identity of the requestor MUST be verified.
Generic account detection	Hard	Prior to production, all systems must have all generic accounts disabled.
	Hard	Regular account scans are made to discover generic accounts (i.e., accounts not attached to a real person or process).
No local system accounts enabled (exc. administrator)[1]	Soft	Prior to going into production all systems must have local accounts removed (if possible); all other accounts except administrator must be disabled.
Generic and local account detection (creation or enabled)	Hard	During production operations, the creation or enablement of any local or generic account must be detected and an alert generated to security operations.
Generic or local account remediation/ disablement	Soft	Any detected generic domain or local account (other than local administrator) must be deleted or disabled.
Generic or local account usage detection	Hard	During production operations, the successful or failed use of any local or generic account for any type of activity must be detected and an alert generated to security operations.
Exclusive		
Multiple log-ons from disparate locations	Hard	Simultaneous usage of an identity from disparate locations should be detected and reported.
Out-of-band log-on (nonwork hours)	Hard	Frequent log-ons outside of the entity's normal working hours should be detected and reported.

[1] Local administrator is retained for emergency recovery when access to the identity management system (IMS) is not available.

Table 10.2   Identity Requirements for Accountability

Scenario	Description
Customer merger	A customer through acquisition or reorganization merges two identities into a single domain, causing user aliases common to both domains to collide.
Technology integration	An identity in one technology (e.g., AD) requires an associated identity in another technology (e.g., Live ID), but the proposed identification from the initiator collides with an existing identity in responding technology.

an expedient way to notify the parties involved to prevent a user from being locked out of their account. A well-defined process aided by a universal naming standard for identities should provide the necessary foundation for automating the remediation process. Possible actions include the following:

- Ensuring that information security standards require name collision detection and remediation
- Updating identity management procedures to ensure compliance with the name collision detection and remediation policy
- Developing technologies to detect and automatically resolve name collisions, including appropriate operations and where necessary end-user notifications

Identity Retention

Identity retention is another risk that must be addressed, including the reuse of identities and the elimination of stale accounts. Identity reuse refers to the establishment of a new account with an identifier that was previously used to grant access to system or service resources. Stale accounts are identities that have not been used for some predetermined amount of time. These accounts can result from troubleshooting/problem resolution efforts, periodic audits (i.e., auditor access), vendor maintenance access, personnel reassignments, leaves of absence, and the like. Table 10.3 contains risk scenarios associated with identity retention.

Table 10.3   Identity Retention Scenarios

Scenario	Description
Identity reuse	A person is incorrectly associated with actions in an audit record performed by the previous owner of the identity.
	A person is inadvertently granted access to resources based on authorizations associated with the previous owner of the identity.
Stale account	A person reassigned to a different job function (role) uses an old (stale) account to access resources they are no longer authorized to access.
	A person granted access for a specific period of time (i.e., an auditor or vendor service personnel) uses the account outside of that time frame to access resources they are no longer authorized to access.
	An attacker gains unauthorized access to resources using a brute force or other type of attack to compromise the account password because it is not changed at required intervals.

There must be a clear procedure preventing the reuse of identity. Under no circumstances should it be possible to attribute an action to an entity that did not perform the action. Different identity domains usually provide sufficient context to identities, so reuse is not an issue across these identity boundaries. For example, *MyDomain\MyUserID* is sufficiently unique so that the identity *YourDomain\MyUserID* is not a collision. However, within these domain boundaries identity reuse is an accountability issue that must be addressed. Possible actions include the following:

■ Ensuring that information security standards prohibit the reuse of identities within a native identity domain
■ Updating identity management procedures to enforce the reuse of identities within a native identity domain policy
■ Extending reuse prohibitions across all identity domains
■ Developing automated technologies to manage identity reuse requirements

SIDEBAR: REUSE AND COLLISION

The reuse control is really an extension of the name "collision control"; if identities are inactivated but never deleted, an attempt to reuse an identity will always result in a name collision. Online services like Hot Mail have already demonstrated that it is technologically possible to efficiently manage identity reuse in very large identity stores using this technique.

• Creating a common automated technology (control) that can identify and disable stale accounts across all infrastructure and enclave systems
• Updating procedures and requirements to assure all systems integrate with the above control

Identity Verification

Identity verification is critical to accountability. If no direct relationship exists between the identity and a party that can be held responsible for the actions taken by that identity, accountability is lost. Different operating system identity management functions have different identity verification processes. Table 10.4 contains risk scenarios associated with identity verification.

There must be clear processes and procedures for verifying the identity of the requesting party before an account is created or activated. Under no circumstances should it be possible to create or activate an account for an unknown (unverified) party. Face-to-face validation is best.

Table 10.4   Identity Verification Scenarios

Scenario	Description
Social engineering	An attacker or other unauthorized person convinces the identity management function to create or activate an identity for them.
Spoofed identity	An attacker or other unauthorized person uses an assumed name (e.g., the name on a stolen credit card) to create or activate an identity.
Workflow corruption	An attacker or other unauthorized person corrupts the identity creation or activation process to bypass or spoof the identity verification function.
Identity flooding	An attacker attempts to clog or convolute the identity process by programmatically requesting/establishing enumerable identities on the system.

Hosted and hybrid scenarios where user accounts are managed by the customer's identity management function require service providers to guard against workflow corruption and attempts to bypass or spoof the identity verification function. Possible actions include:

■ Ensuring that information security standards incorporate identity verification requirements for user accounts
■ Updating identity management procedures to comply with the above policy
■ Reviewing current identity management processes and procedures for proper identity verification functionality
■ Updating procedures and requirements to ensure operations has integrated identity verification controls addressing social engineering, identity spoofing, and process corruption attacks
■ Creating an automated process for detecting unauthorized accounts—for example, a process that compares existing accounts in AD with an authoritative database of personnel or account creation/activation requests
■ Updating requirements for user account creation to include a mechanism that prevents the programmatic creation of accounts

Local System Accounts

Local machine (system) accounts are problematic for accountability because anyone with sufficient authority can create or activate a local account without going through the standard identity management process. Some built-in local accounts are required for the proper operation of the system; others are necessary for the building, restoration, or maintenance of systems when access to a domain Identity Management System (e.g., a Windows Domain Controller) is not available. By policy, all local accounts (except administrator) must be disabled before the system can be placed into production. Furthermore, the use of local accounts must be subject to auditing. At issue is the ability to directly relate the actions taken by a local account to a specific person either because a generic account (e.g., administrator, test, temp, etc.) is being used or the entity associated with the local account has not been verified. Table 10.5 describes the threats associated with local/generic system accounts.

Table 10.5   Local Account Scenarios

Scenario	Description
Generic account	A generic local account is used to perform unauthorized activities on a system.
	An attacker uses a generic local account (e.g., guest) that was left enabled to gain unauthorized access to a system.
	A generic local account (e.g., guest) is enabled and used to grant unauthorized access to a system.
Local account	A local account is used to perform unauthorized activities on a system.
	A temporary local account created for system build/rebuild, troubleshooting, or maintenance purposes is used to perform unauthorized activities on a system.
	An attacker uses a temporary local account that was left enabled to gain unauthorized access to a system.
	A local account required for system monitoring, security, or other function is used to perform unauthorized activities on a system.

There must be clear processes and procedures controlling the creation and use of local system accounts. Under no circumstances should it be possible to create, enable, or use a local system account without attributing that usage to a known party. Therefore, it is necessary to have a process in place to identify and disable (or remove) all unauthorized local accounts before a system is placed into production, and to detect and monitor the creation, activation, and/or use of local system accounts. Possible actions include:

■ Ensuring that information security standards require local account creation or activation via the standard identity management process
■ Updating identity management and service operations procedures to comply with the above policy
■ Ensuring that final security and operational review procedures for all systems include the disablement or removal of all identified local accounts (except administrator)
■ Defining procedures to enforce accountability for local administrator account usage that associates the actions taken with an individual that can be held accountable for those actions

Note: A number of existing methods can be used to provide this functionality—for example, generating complex local administrator passwords and storing them in a secure container. When someone requires the use of this account, the process for checking out the password can enforce accountability.

■ Creating an automated control to implement accountability for local administrator account usage
■ Creating an automated control to detect the creation of a local account on any production system and to report this activity in near real time to security operations and the service owners
■ Creating an automated control to detect the enablement of a local account on any production system and to report this activity in near real time to security operations and the service owners
■ Creating an automated control to detect the usage or attempted usage of a local account for any type of activity on any production system and to report this activity in near real time to security operations and the service owners
■ Updating procedures and requirements to ensure all systems and applications are integrated with the above controls

Shared Accounts

Identities that are used by multiple entities defeat accountability. A shared account is an identity that is used by more than one party. It is often created to support common work functions (e.g., controlling a process that is run on day, night, and graveyard shifts). Another instance of a shared account is where the account log-on information has been compromised either by intentional disclosure or unintentional compromises. Most information security policies prohibit the sharing of accounts for any purpose, and user awareness training should emphasize the need to maintain the confidentiality of account log-on information. There is only one risk scenario for shared accounts (see Table 10.6).

Table 10.6 Shared Account Scenario

Scenario	Description
Shared account	An unauthorized system activity cannot be attributed to a single individual because the account used to perform the activity is shared by multiple users.

A shared account is the antithesis of accountability. Under no circumstances should it be possible for an action to be taken that cannot be attributed to an entity that can be held responsible for the action. The ability to identify instances of multiple usages is particularly valuable for detecting account compromises, but the process, especially in the system support and maintenance arena, can be difficult. One way to enforce exclusive use is to limit users to a single log-on, but this limitation isn't acceptable for most support and maintenance personnel. A better method is to use two-factor authentication. Possible actions include:

- Reviewing and reducing exemptions to two-factor authentication requirements
- Requiring two-factor authentication for all production log-ons
- Creating an automated control to detect multiple log-ons from disparate locations

Note: The assumption is that no person can be in two geographical locations at the same time; however, node hopping (i.e., Telnet to Telnet to Telnet) might make this appear to be so.

- Creating an automated control to detect temporal abnormalities such as frequent log-ons outside of the entity's normal working hours
- Updating procedures and requirements to ensure that all systems and applications are integrated with the above controls

These controls require the collation of data from disparate sources across the enterprise, making it difficult to provide any type of real-time alerting. This does not, however, reduce the value of these controls, particularly in the area of compromised account detection.

Comprehensive Accountability Audit Objectives

The second accountability function is audit—the construction of evidentiary records of the actions taken on a system. Evidentiary is the key term here. The records must contain the information required to prove a fact or a claim (e.g., compliance to a regulatory requirement). These audit records have three primary attributes: They must be *sufficient,* display *quality,* and be *authentic.* Sufficient means the record or records contain enough information to lead others to the same conclusion about the facts being presented. Quality means the record information is applicable, valid, and reliable enough to support the claim. Authentic means the record information is in the same state at the time of its presentation as it was when it was written (i.e., unaltered).

Current State

Most IT environments rely on a patchwork of audit solutions including system, service, and application-level audit trails. Few organizations have established information security standards defining what information must be contained in these records or how that information will be formatted or setting out the requirements for where these records will be stored, how long they will be retained, or how the authenticity of the records will be preserved. Consequently, in most organizations the majority of the audit records being created are inadequate and unusable for accountability purposes. For example, not uncommonly audit facilities are configured to overwrite audit records when the file reaches its maximum allowed size. Even when logs are retained, it is unusual for them to be reviewed with any regularity.

Information security policies and standards must contain requirements for the auditing of specific operating system-level actions and specify a periodic review of these records. Requirements must be evidentiary based and address requirements for infrastructure, system, and application-level auditing. Finally, standards must ensure that these records are properly stored, safeguarded, and retained for the appropriate period. Furthermore, operational procedures must guarantee that audit controls are operational prior to a system being placed into production and periodically checked for proper operations while in production.

The centralized audit record collection capability is very important to accountability. Access to this system must be tightly controlled to ensure the integrity of the records written there. A complete separation of duties between infrastructure and enclave administrators and owner/operator of the audit collection is recommended. Anyone with sufficient privilege can tamper with locally retained audit records, but records written to an isolated centralized audit collection service cannot be maliciously altered. Most commercially available audit and compliance systems provide this capability.

Audit Requirements for Accountability

The second set of control objectives for accountability is based on auditing functions. Tracing actions back to an individual requires sufficiently detailed records (i.e., audit trails, logs) of those actions. Most organizations require some level of auditing, but it usually is not comprehensive enough for accountability; much of the data collected is not relevant to legal, regulatory, or industry compliance. Effective accountability requires stringent audit processes and technical controls. Table 10.7 maps the audit attributes to specific accountability baselines. The type (hard or soft) is used to denote how evidence is collected for each control. Soft indicates a procedure-based control, while hard denotes a technology-based (i.e., automated) control.

Domain and Local Audit Management

The audit strategy needs to include comprehensive evidentiary audit management for infrastructure components, host/server systems, and applications across all platforms. This includes the establishment of a consistent format and naming conventions for audit records and data fields. Possible actions include:

■ Ensuring that accountability requirements are incorporated into all infrastructure, system, and application work streams
■ Updating work stream strategies to include accountability controls for evidentiary auditing
■ Developing audit record formatting and field-naming standards across all platform and services
■ Updating procedures and standards to reflect evidence-based auditing requirements

Table 10.7   Audit Requirements for Accountability

Attribute/Control	Type	Risk and Requirements
Sufficient		
Domain and local audit management	Soft	Records must be collected across all domains and systems.
Comprehensive	Soft	It is possible to collect audit information for all objects that can be acted upon, including infrastructure components, systems, and applications.
Complete	Hard	Audit records must contain all the elements required to prove accountability.
Temporal	Hard	Records must be associated with a global time source.
Quality		
Consistent	Soft	Records have a common format across all objects.
Relevant	Hard	The information collected supports all associated compliance and legal claims.
Understandable	Soft	The information in the record is easy to assimilate.
Simple	Hard	The records do not contain extraneous content.
Sequential	Hard	The records are in chronological order.
Correlated	Soft	The relationship between the records is apparent.
Authentic		
Tamperproof	Hard	The records have not been altered from their original state.
Traceable	Hard	The records have a consistent chain of custody.
Retained	Soft	The records are retained for a sufficient time frame.

Complete

Audit records must contain all the information required to prove compliance with applicable statutory, regulatory, and industry requirements; this includes at a minimum:

■ The identity of the subject taking the action
■ The name (identity) of the object being acted upon
■ The action being taken
■ The result or status of the action (success, failure)
■ The old value and the new value (if the object was created, deleted, or otherwise changed)

Possible actions include:

■ Mapping existing control objectives to evidentiary requirements
■ Identifying gaps between existing audit capabilities at all levels (network, host, service/application, etc.)

- Updating existing security standards to reflect evidentiary auditing requirements
- Updating procedures and standards to reflect evidentiary auditing requirements
- Promoting company and industry changes that will improve and unify auditing capabilities supporting accountability

Temporal

Records must be date and time stamped using a global time source so that they can be accurately associated with other activities that occurred within the same time frame. Possible actions supporting this objective include:

- Ensuring that security standards require audit records to be date and time stamped based on a common global time source
- Reviewing existing audit functions and identifying all instances of audit facilities that do not meet the above requirement
- Updating procedures and standards to reflect temporal auditing requirements supporting accountability

Consistent

The quality of audit records is highly dependent on the format of the data contents. This is one of the major issues associated with existing logging facilities; they are written in so many different formats that correlating information across platforms, services, and applications is nearly impossible. The SYSLOG facility is an excellent example. Although the records have well-defined fields, the information in those fields does not have a common format. Consequently, correlating SYSLOG records requires additional parsing. The Windows 2008 logging facility improves on record consistency somewhat by providing an XML-based record parser. However, the facility does not contain a standard naming convention for defining the XML content. Possible actions supporting this objective include:

- Developing a common taxonomy for the data content field within audit records that includes at a minimum consistent naming for the data elements in the "Complete" section above
- Ensuring that security standards require the use of the common taxonomy for all audit records
- Updating procedures to specify the use of a common auditing taxonomy supporting accountability
- Promoting company and industry changes to improve and unify auditing capabilities supporting accountability

Relevant

Complete records contain the relevant information needed to prove a fact or claim. The relevant attribute actually relates to the other information contained in the record. It is possible for a record to contain so much information that it is nearly impossible to discern what is relevant to the fact or claim. The use of progressive logging controls is one way to ensure that extraneous information does not dilute the relevance of the record. Progressive logging establishes levels of logging based on the nested levels of application calls. For example, level 1 logging would only capture events related to the entry point and main application procedure, level 2 would capture events for the methods and the main procedure call, level 3 for methods, level 2 calls, and so on. Possible actions supporting this objective include:

- Developing guidance for the development team on the use of progressive logging techniques
- Updating procedures and development standards with auditing relevance guidance

Understandable

The information contained in each record should be presented in such a way that a reasonably intelligent person would be able to read and understand it. Audit records written for troubleshooting purposes often contain information that is only meaningful to the developer or a service technician. For accountability purposes, the information in the record must be understandable by the average person. Thus, when codes are used, they should be accompanied by a verbal explanation. For example, "The call returned 1 (Successful)." Possible actions supporting this objective include:

- Ensuring that standards require audit records to be constructed so that they can be easily assimilated by an average person
- Reviewing existing audit functions and identifying all instances of audit facilities that do not meet the above requirement
- Updating procedures and development standards to reflect the understandable auditing attribute supporting accountability

Simple

Records are designed to convey one or two pieces of information. The more complex a record is, the more difficult it is to understand or to explain. Records that use the same event code to convey different pieces of information are particularly troublesome because the information conveyed in the description field must be parsed to figure out which piece of information this record refers to. Microsoft IPSec events logs are a great example. During negotiation, if the connection falls back to a clear (non-IPSec protected) connection, the event number will be the same as any clear connections. The only way to determine whether the clear connection was the result of a fallback to clear action is to parse the information in the description field of the record. Possible actions supporting this objective include:

- Developing guidance on the use of simple logging techniques
- Updating procedures and development standards with auditing simplicity guidance

Sequential

The order of the records is the same as the order of the events. Record sequence is seldom an issue on a single host. The issue comes into play when records are being centrally collected and processed. There is a potential for the records to get out of order and thereby paint a faulty picture of what actually took place. For example, Alice accesses and changes a record; then Bob accesses and reads the record. If these records are misordered in the audit collection system, it would appear as if Bob was the one making the change. Possible actions supporting this objective include:

■ Reviewing existing audit functions and collection technology to ensure that records are ordered the same as the events. The ability to index records by the date and time stamp is sufficient to meet this requirement.
■ Updating procedures and development standards to reflect sequential auditing requirements supporting accountability.

Correlated

When multiple records from the same or different sources are used to support a fact or claim, the relationship between the information in these records must be obvious. This is one of the driving forces behind a common taxonomy. It is important to keep the "average person" scenario in mind; labeling the same piece of information with two different names will make it more difficult for the average person to understand the evidence being presented and may cause them to come to the wrong conclusion. Possible actions supporting this objective include:

■ Reviewing existing audit functions across all platforms to ensure that records contain information that is consistent in content and format so that it can be easily correlated with records from other platforms
■ Updating procedures and development standards to reflect correlation auditing requirements supporting accountability

Tamperproof

This attribute, together with the next two, are related to the admissibility of records. A tamperproof record is one that cannot be altered from its original state without the alteration being detected. If a record can be tampered with, it can be argued that the information contained therein is not reliable. Two mechanisms are commonly used to ensure tamperproof records: access controls and integrity controls. Privileged use creates issues with the access control approach; that is, a person with sufficient privilege can tamper with the records. Sending events to a centralized log server can resolve this issue provided the privileged use does not extend to this server as well. However, integrity controls such as digital signatures or record hashing is much more difficult to defeat. The records can be erased, but they cannot be altered without detection. Possible actions supporting this objective include:

■ Ensuring that security standards require audit records to be tamperproof
■ Reviewing existing audit functions and identifying all instances of audit facilities that do not meet the above requirement
■ Updating procedures and development standards to reflect the tamperproof auditing attribute supporting accountability

Traceable

It is also necessary to ensure that a verifiable chain of custody is maintained for each record. Traceable means that looking backward we can account for all entities that have control over or access to this record from the time of its creation. Any point in time when control over the record cannot be accounted for means it could have been replaced or otherwise tampered with; such a record is therefore unreliable. Possible actions supporting this objective include:

- Reviewing existing audit procedures to ensure that audit records required for accountability have a management process that maintains a viable chain of custody
- Updating operational procedures to reflect traceability auditing requirements supporting accountability

Retained

Large computing environments generate large volumes of audit information that quickly becomes impossible to manage. At the same time, not having the necessary evidence to prove compliance with legal, regulatory, and industry requirements can be a major liability. There must be a balance. At the very least, audit records must be retained long enough to be duplicated (i.e., backed up). Second, they must be maintained for as long as legal and/or regulator actions are possible. Possible actions supporting this objective include:

- Reviewing existing audit facilities to ensure that accountability-related audit records are being retained for a period commensurate with legal and/or regulatory requirements
- Updating operational procedures and standards to reflect retention auditing requirements supporting accountability

Conclusion

The accountability tactic is not easy to fully implement with today's technology, but good account-ability controls give you the ability to defend against accusations of malfeasance or negligence surrounding an unauthorized disclosure or loss of data.

> The ancient Romans had a tradition: whenever one of their engineers constructed an arch, as the capstone was hoisted into place, the engineer assumed accountability for his work in the most profound way possible: he stood under the arch.

> **Michael Armstrong**

Accountability controls are also a way to prove compliance with regulatory requirements, thus avoiding regulatory sanctions for alleged violations. Similarly, accountability controls help resolve contract and/or service delivery disputes by providing a chronological record of what was done, by whom, and at what time. Finally, accountability controls are a strong deterrent against "insider threats" because the actions of highly trusted individuals (i.e., administrators and other privileged users) are monitored to ensure they are not violating that trust. For large companies and service providers, properly implemented accountability is a huge market differentiator. Effective account-ability begins with an understanding of the problem and what needs to be done; hopefully, this section provides a good start down that path.

Chapter 11

SDL and Incident Response

Security suffers from one principal problem—it has nothing to show for itself! When security controls work properly nothing bad happens.

Unknown

Introduction

This chapter covers two interrelated tactics: software security and incident response. The relationship between the two may not seem obvious at first, but consider this point: According to the Gartner Group, more than "75% of hacks [breaches] happen at the application." The majority of attacks are aimed at applications; the majority of compromises are via application exploits. In other words, the majority of security incidents organizations are dealing with are related to applications. So from a security strategy standpoint, addressing this issue must be one of our principal objectives. The shift of attack focus from networks and systems to applications is based on two factors. First, attacking networks and hosts has become much harder; operating system security has improved considerably, and a plethora of security products is aimed at mitigating network and host attacks. The second factor is the huge increase in application targets. Millions of applications are running on the Internet that for all practical purposes are one hop away from the nearest attacker.

> You cannot code your way out of an insecure design.
>
> **Michael Howard**

Combine that fact with poor development practices, insecure protocols, and readily available automated attack tools and you have a field ripe for exploitation.

> The most damaging targeted attacks—those against specific businesses—have focused on vulnerabilities in Web applications and custom-developed software.
>
> **The Gartner Group**

Another aspect of the problem is access. The majority of these applications can be accessed anonymously, and when credentials are required, the mechanisms for verifying user identity are weak. For the price of a stolen credit card number, an attacker can gain direct access to online applications using encrypted connections that completely bypass network and host-based controls, thereby gaining access to applications containing valuable data from tens of thousands of other users. Is it any wonder that the number of compromised records reported in Verizon's "2009 Data Breach Investigations Report" is nearly three times what it was the previous year and that the Privacy Rights Clearinghouse totals for compromised records containing sensitive personal information for 2009 is 10 times what it was in 2008? This represents more than a failure of application security; it also represents a massive failure of our detection and response mechanisms, and this is why we have chosen to combine these two tactics into a single topic of discussion.

> Audits performed [...] on over 100 leading Web sites simulated hacker attacks and revealed that over 97 percent of the sites had major application-level problems that could be exploited in only a few hours.
>
> **TechRepublic (Yahoo News)**

A large body of knowledge has grown up around developing secure applications thanks to the pioneering work of Steve Lipner (Microsoft), Michael Howard (Microsoft), Gary McGraw (Cigital), John Viega (McAfee), and David LeBlanc (Microsoft). Consequently, we will only give a brief overview of SDL and focus our efforts on the challenges that initiatives like SaaS (software as a service) and cloud computing have created. Likewise, a large body of knowledge has developed around incident management and incident response, so we will only explore the tactical aspect of this subject and focus our efforts on the detection and alerting gaps that exist between the two.

Terms Used in This Chapter

Directed (accurate) response—a response that brings resources to bear on the point(s) of attack based on observation and supplied intelligence.

Malicious activity—any intentional, accidental, or coincidental act that could or does result in damage to a computing resource or the bypass of a system security mechanism.

Near real time—within a short interval of time from the event trigger. The actual time frame defined as part of a service-level agreement or in a standards document; an interval of less than one minute is common for automated responses.

Programmatic—functionality implemented in the source code of an application (as opposed to being a call to an external library or process).

Real time—the actual time when an event occurs or the duration of time required for a computer system to complete a particular task.

Security incident—any adverse event, real or suspected, that violates or threatens to violate any facility, product, system, or network security provision.

The usage of MUST, SHALL, SHOULD, and MAY in control objective requirements conforms to Internet Engineering Task Force (IETF) Request for Comments (RFC) 2119 "Key Words for Use in RFCs to Indicate Requirement Levels," S. Bradner, Internet Engineering Task Force, March 1997.

Security Development Lifecycle (SDL) Overview

Security Development Lifecycle (SDL) is a component of the overall software development process. There are many different models for software development, but they all can be broken down into six basic parts or phases: envisioning/requirements, design, build, test/verify, release, and support/maintain.

SDL contains security-specific requirements for each of these application lifecycle phases. Three basic principles drive SDL: (1) software should be secure by design; (2) software should be secure in implementation (development); and (3) software should be secure in deployment. (See Figure 11.1.)

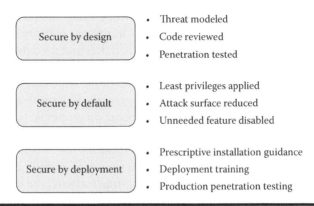

Figure 11.1 Security development lifecycle principles.

These principles constitute a set of tactical practices or software design and development standards. These standards specify the SDL requirements in each phase of the development lifecycle—for example, training and education for software designers and developers; threat modeling for application designs and functional components; and design and source code reviews, security testing, release planning, and security response planning for post-release vulnerability management. The goal of SDL is to reduce or eliminate flaws in software applications that cause security controls to be weakened or bypassed. It also has the added benefit of improving the overall quality of software as a result of improved review and testing practices.

Security Development Lifecycle was designed to be used for the development of large packaged software products with long development time frames, and this is actually one of its downfalls. As the focus of applications has moved toward Web-based products, the ability to use SDL in a meaningful way has diminished. Factors such as smaller development teams, the tendency to reuse "free" code or prepackaged functionality (giblets), short development time frames, and the need to maintain/service code on a continuing basis also contribute to the problem. These factors have shifted SDL into the realm of system lifecycle management, which adds two additional phases to the product lifecycle: operate and retire. We'll talk about these phases and their impacts in greater detail in the SDL section.

Security Incident Response Overview

Response is one of the first principles of security tactics. The ability to rapidly respond to and resolve potential or actual security threats is an essential part of every security strategy. Security incident response is the process used to evaluate suspected violations of security policy or controls, and take the appropriate actions to contain, eradicate, and recover from said violations. The effectiveness of incident response is based on three principles: preparedness, timeliness, and accuracy. The 13 soldiers at Carmarthen Castle were able to repel 300 attacking Welsh rebels because they were well prepared and could move quickly to the points of attack based on the accurate information their commander had. This isn't any different for a cyber-castle. Well-trained people, a seasoned commander, prestaged weaponry, preemptive or real-time observation, rapid application of resources, and concise information—all are essential. The story of the Three Mile Island Nuclear Power Plant incident in 1979 is not one of failed procedure, poor training, or slow response; it was the lack of reliable (concise) information that hampered good response decisions. The operator observing the alerts could not accurately convey to the chief engineer what was happening; consequently, the commander made the wrong decision, and a situation that could have been contained became a major defeat for the nuclear power industry. The principles of preparedness, timeliness, and accuracy drive the tactical practices and procedures found in an organization's security incident response plan. The plan specifies the actions taken during each stage of the response process. Response is a progressive process in the sense that the results of one stage determine progression to the next response stage. For example, if the evaluation stage determines that the suspected violation is a hoax, the incident response progresses no further. The goal of the security incident response is to limit the potential damages or liabilities that might result from a security violation. People tend to associate security incidents with computer hacker break-ins and data losses, but "violation" covers a much broader spectrum, including sabotage, espionage, property damage, hardware thefts, misuse of resources, virus/malware, and denial of service events perpetrated by internal or external forces. Violations against Web applications are actually one of the easier security incidents to deal with, so why is the industry suffering so much loss from these attacks? The issue is one of observation; response begins when someone or something detects a possible violation. If this happens after the fact, it is called passive detection (e.g., finding an unauthorized access in the RADIUS accounting log); active detection is the real-time observation of a violation (e.g., the detection of a virus-infected file at the time it is copied to your computer). Active and passive detection and the resultant alerts are the gaps we will focus on in the incident response section below.

Before moving on to the actual topics, it is worth reiterating the basic attack scenarios that can be used against systems and networks because these also apply to applications. There are six basic system-style attacks against computer applications. These are:

1. **Application flaws**—Exploit a weakness in the application software, including coding errors (e.g., buffer overflows) or design flaws.
2. **Configuration flaws**—Exploit errors in the application software configuration, including unsecure functions (e.g., SQL admin stored procedures), default or missing passwords, enabled anonymous or guest access, or incorrect file, instance, or record permissions.
3. **Unsecured trusts**—Exploit the trusts that the application has with other components, including the underlying operating system or service, called dynamic link libraries (DLLs), system settings, or interactions with other application tiers (e.g., ODBC or DCOM connections).
4. **Malware infection**—Implant a piece of malicious code in the application software during development or distribution or during an operational event such as a patch download, an e-mail read, or a Web access to an attack site.
5. **User impersonation**—Compromise the credentials of a legitimate user by guessing or cracking their password, getting them to disclose it (e.g., phishing), or by capturing it with a man-in-the-middle system or a sniffer.
6. **Process flaws**—Become a user of the application software by gaming the provisioning process or convincing (or coercing) someone to create an account for you (i.e., social engineering).

Applications that use networking may also be subject to some additional attack scenarios against the network connections. These include:

1. **Networking system flaws**—Exploit a weakness in the operating system, hardware, firmware, protocol, or network services to gain access to application data in transit or to disrupt application data transfers.

2. **Passive wiretapping**—Capture data or credentials in transit on a link using a sniffer or a man-in-the-middle system.
3. **Data insertion**—Write data to the link such as a cookie or a packet with credentials to gain access to a resource or to modify application data or configuration.
4. **Node impersonation**—Become or compromise a transit node on the link to capture application data or credentials passing through it or to redirect traffic to another system.
5. **End-point Impersonation**—Appear to be a legitimate end point of the application (e.g., a fat client, Web server, backup server, etc.).
6. **Process flaws**—Become a permitted application component by convincing or coercing someone to add your node to the network or application configuration. Once attached, it can be used to capture data and credentials.

Despite all the claims of increased threats and attacks, these 12 scenarios have remained constant. Table 11.1 illustrates the point by mapping Windows attack vectors to these scenarios. These are the attack scenarios application security controls must be able to observe and mitigate. Observe in this context means that attempts to bypass any mitigating control in the application are detected and logged, and where appropriate an alert is generated. There are innumerable ways to carry out these attacks, but the attack methods are not what's important. Rather, understanding the scope (boundaries) of the attack scenarios is the important consideration. By focusing our tactics on the attack scenarios and not on the attack methods, we can address the issue of threats across a broad range of attacks. Keeping these attack scenarios and the "big picture" in mind, let's now move on to the main topics of discussion.

Tactical Objectives

The problem we are experiencing is one of observation: We cannot see the attacks when they are happening, and consequently we cannot respond. Therefore, improving our observation capabilities is the first objective, but in reality, secure applications and good incident response touch on every security tactical principle in one way or another. Least privilege is a standard SDL design pattern. SDL threat modeling practices adhere to the coverage principle by required application designs and functionality to address the threats posed by all attack scenarios. This includes internally and externally instigated attacks. The second part of coverage is response; when controls fail or are intentionally violated, incident response assures a prompt and consistent mitigation across the entire environment.

The chapter introduction referenced preparedness in the context of incident response, but preparedness also applies to applications; secure applications and well-designed security controls enable (prepare) the business to take on new markets, mergers, partnerships, and so on, without a lots of unnecessary retooling of IT systems. This is a security strategy that anticipates the future and builds applications that can adapt to new business demands and requirements. Building secure applications makes good economic sense. The Gartner Group estimated "the cost of removing a security vulnerability during testing to be less than 2 percent of the cost of removing it from a production system." Fewer application security flaws means fewer vulnerabilities, fewer fixes, less patching, less downtime, and greater reliability; which translates into fewer incidents, fewer responses, less damage, and lower recovery costs. This also equates to more security bandwidth for planning and supporting business initiatives. The savings that come with these advantages apply if you are buying software, building it, or having it built for you. The commonality aspects of secure software development are also cost savers because they eliminate complexities and promote

Table 11.1   Windows Attack Vectors and Scenarios

Attack Vectors in Windows	Attack Scenario
Open sockets	Exploit a weakness in the operating system, hardware, firmware, protocol, or network services.
Open RPC (Remote Procedure Call) end points	Exploit a weakness in the operating system, hardware, firmware, protocol, or network services.
Open named pipes	Exploit a weakness in the operating system, hardware, firmware, protocol, or network services.
Services	Exploit errors in system software or service.
Services running by default	Exploit errors in system software or service configurations.
Services running as SYSTEM	Exploit errors in system software or service configurations.
Active Web handlers	Exploit errors in the application software.
Active ISAPI (Internet Services API) Filters	Exploit errors in the application software configuration.
Dynamic Web pages	Exploit a weakness in the operating system, hardware, firmware, protocol, or network services.
Executable virtual directories	Exploit errors in system software or service configurations.
Enabled accounts	Exploit errors in system software or service configurations.
Enabled accounts in admin group	Exploit errors in system software or service configurations.
Null sessions to pipes and shares	Exploit a weakness in the operating system, hardware, firmware, protocol, or network services.
Guest account enabled	Exploit errors in system software or service configurations.
Weak Access Control Lists (ACLs) in file systems	Exploit errors in system software or service configurations.
Weak ACLs in registry	Exploit errors in system software or service configurations.
Weak ACLs in shares	Exploit errors in system software or service configurations.

the free flow of data between systems. This improves operations, business intelligence, reporting, and customer satisfaction. Secure application development (i.e., SDL) also has a set of very specific tactical objectives around the reduction of attack surface and attack paths (vectors) to enable better attack management.

Carmarthen Castle was designed so that it could only be attacked on two of its four walls, and attack paths were limited and well guarded. Attackers really had just two choices: They could attempt to break through a heavily fortified gate, or they could climb over the walls. Both options subjected an attacker to well-prepared defenders with big stockpiles of weaponry. Similarly, incident response has specific tactical objections built primarily around time and information quality. The speed with which attacks proliferate requires real-time engagement and the parlay of defenses to squelch the attack quickly. Too much incident response is currently based on passive detection—which is the equivalent of telling the Carmarthen soldiers the rebels broke into the castle and stole everything of value and then asking, what are they going to do about it? The problem is often compounded by the poor quality of the attack information being supplied. A good response requires quality information. Although detection systems have improved over the years, the "cry wolf" (false-positive) rate is still remarkably high. False alarms just waste people's time, but poor detection is only part of the issue. Often the information supplied in a valid alert is not sufficient to coordinate a smart directed response.

Elements of Application Development and Response

The emphasis of this chapter is on the relationship between applications and incident response. Figure 11.2 depicts the three core components covered: application, interface, and response.

Application covers the Security Development Lifecycle and associated software design and development standards, including a review of the environmental changes that drive new requirements into the SDL process. Interface covers the tactics used to transfer security-related information generated by the application to the response component. Response covers two areas: tactics for incident response and responses to customer inquiries. The overall goal is to identify tactical ways to bridge the existing gaps in application capabilities and transfer (interface) mechanisms that result in poor responses to malicious activity and customer service requests.

Application

As noted earlier, SDL is a component of the software development lifecycle and is driven by a set of software design and development standards that specify requirements for security functionality within applications. These standards are typically developed and maintained by the security group in cooperation with application development leads. The standards are based on industry requirements, government regulations, and vendor-specific best practices. Applications

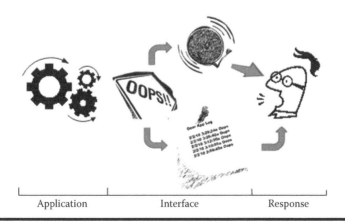

| Application | Interface | Response |

Figure 11.2   Chapter elements.

that do not meet these standards are considered unfit to be run in a production environment. The standards help application designers and developers avoid design and coding practices that result in application security vulnerabilities. The standards also contain guidance for testing security controls and functionality, including the application's default installation configuration. In addition to guidance, the standards specify what security controls are approved for usage and how those controls should be implemented to ensure proper operation and compatibility (commonality) with other components—for example, what cryptographic algorithms can be used and how cryptographic keys are to be managed. The standards further define the security "bug" bar, the criteria used to determine the severity of an application security flaw. The bug bar criteria are similar to other risk evaluations: How exploitable is the flaw? What is the potential impact if it is exploited? Exploitability is based on how much opportunity an attacker would have and how difficult the flaw is to exploit. Impact relates to the value of the asset (potential loss liability) or the scope of the attack (potential number of users or systems affected). (For additional information on these ratings, see the section Threat Modeling later in this chapter.) The idea behind a "bug bar" is that it can be adjusted up or down based on the production environment of the applications. If you are producing a widely distributed piece of software (e.g., Windows OS), you want the bug bar to be fairly high because a single flaw has the potential to affect millions of systems. For example, the Remote Procedure Call (RPC) flaw in Windows exploited by Blaster affected more than 15 million computers and generated over 3.3 million support calls to Microsoft in a single month!

Software development has six basic phases, and SDL has a component in each of these phases. Figure 11.3 shows these phases and the associated SDL tasks and processes.

Phase 1—Requirements

Security Development Lifecycle begins at the onset of a software development project. It gives the development team an opportunity to consider the big picture security aspects of the proposed application. For example, can the application be secured? What controls will be required? Can the application use existing security controls, or will it require new functionality? The effort

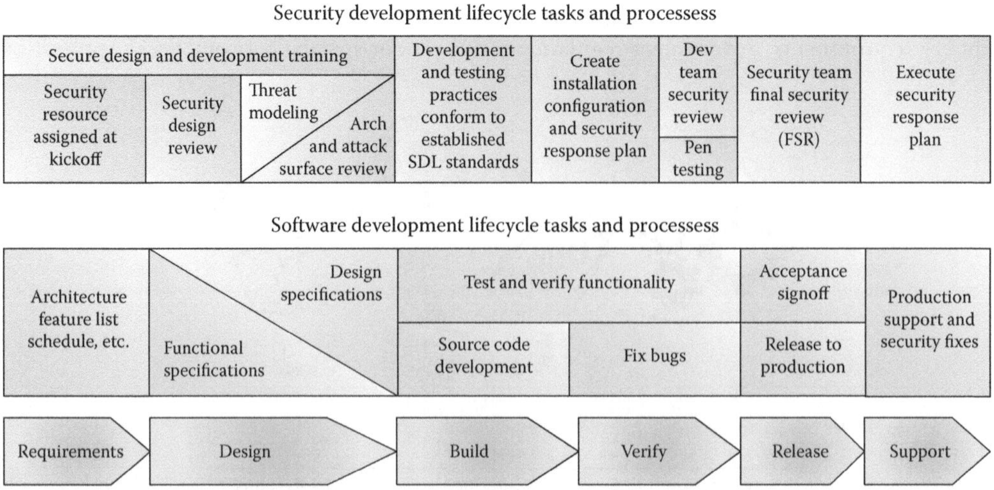

Figure 11.3   Development lifecycle processes and tasks.

is collaborative: The development team and a security resource work through product plans to identify security requirements and feasibility. Another element of this phase is ensuring that the development team has prepared properly—that is, that all team members have completed all SDL training and educational requirements.

Phase 2—Design

During the design phase, the security architecture for the product is defined, and the security critical components are identified. Threat modeling is one of the major activities of this phase. A threat model identifies the major components of the system as well as the interfaces between those components, and evaluates the risk to application's assets based on the threats to which each of these components is subject. For example, a Web application that allows anonymous access from the Internet has a high threat of attack against the Web server and client connections. The threat model helps the development team to identify what countermeasures must be employed, which in turn drives the security design techniques (e.g., managed code, least privilege, attack surface minimization, etc.) and the testing tools requirements.

Threat Modeling

Threat modeling is a structured way to identify threats to the assets managed by the application. The original threat models are built during the design phase, but additional models are built throughout the development process to assess the effectiveness of employed controls. The original model is built without mitigation (worst case), and as the application is developed, mitigations are added to the overall model. The end goal is a threat model in which all identified threats have been appropriately mitigated. The threat model drives the security work that will be done during the other phases beginning with the designs to mitigate the security risks, the development (build) phase of security requirements and features, and the security testing requirements.

Phase 3—Development

It is at the development or build phase that SDL standards are applied to the coding and testing of the application. The goal is to use and enforce safe coding practices through testing and review practices. These include having static code analysis tools that look for unsafe functions or methods, and peer code views to ensure standards compliance and the application of development best practices. Testing may also include the application of fuzzing tools to validate the strength of protocol and file-parsing functions.

Phase 4—Verification

The verification phase starts once the application functionality is complete (i.e., code complete) and the code enters into a second round of testing. Previous testing focused on the newly developed code. Now testing shifts to include both new and legacy code. For the first time the application is tested as a whole entity, including its default installation configurations. This phase may include external code reviews and penetration testing. The goal is to identify any remaining vulnerability and get them fixed before the application is released.

Phase 5—Release

Release is where the rubber meets the road. The Final Security Review (FSR) is the security component of this phase; it is an in-depth review of all the SDL evidence that has been collected during the development process. Security and product managers review training records, threat models, testing tool usage, and so on, to ensure that the development team has complied with all SDL requirements. Any unfixed security bugs remaining in the code are thoroughly reviewed, and decisions are made on their final resolution (fix, grant an exception, accept the risk). The ultimate goal of this effort is to answer the question, "Is this software, from a security standpoint, ready to be delivered to customers?" There is another benefit of FSRs, however: The review can often reveal weaknesses in the overall SDL process that need to be addressed. For example, to pass FSR at Microsoft, teams had to submit records showing that all team members had completed all mandatory training, but the SDL did not specify when the training had to be completed. Consequently, team members were attending training between the time they had completed writing the code and the FSR! This clearly was not the intent of the SDL training requirements, so the SDL standards were updated to require the completion of training prior to the build phase. The FSR may also include a review of newly reported vulnerabilities that may be applicable to the new application, and when necessary, additional testing may be conducted. For example, the FSR team may specify additional testing from a third-party penetration testing company.

Phase 6—Support/Service

The final phase of SDL is support or service—preparing for future security issues regarding this application. It simply is not possible to anticipate every conceivable security issue that could be manifest in an application. The development team is going to make mistakes, and some of these mistakes will get through to the final release. Moreover, new kinds of vulnerabilities will manifest themselves over time. New requirements will emerge from changes to laws and regulations. The environment in which the application is running will be changed by advancing technology, and your users will likely find ways to use the application that the product team never anticipated. These all equate to the same thing: Updates to the application will need to be issued in the future, and an effective plan for doing this is going to be needed.

$(SDL)^2$—Software as a Service Extension (SaaS)

Under the SaaS, or Online Services model, SDL is no longer a stand-alone process that stops at release; now it is paralleled by a Secure Delivery Lifecycle (SDL'). We choose to designate the combination $(SDL)^2$. The service component of $(SDL)^2$ begins at the requirements phase and proceeds through the design and build phases, determining requirements and planning for the operational aspects of the service environment, including facilities (physical space, power, processor, storage and pipe/network, etc.), build-out (pilot, solution stabilization, acceptance criteria), operations (staff, tools, training, operation guides, help desk procedures, etc.), and retirement procedures. Figure 11.4 shows the security tasks and processes associated with the services delivery lifecycle. The two processes converge at the stabilization phase, which extends the SDL Verification Phase to include environment build-out and implementation verification. The SDL release phase becomes part of the deploy phase, which takes the released version of the application into pilot and then full production. The SDL Support/Service becomes a small component of a much larger Operate and Support phase, and one new phase is added to complete the lifecycle: retire. Retire specifies how the application will be taken out of service or migrated to its replacement.

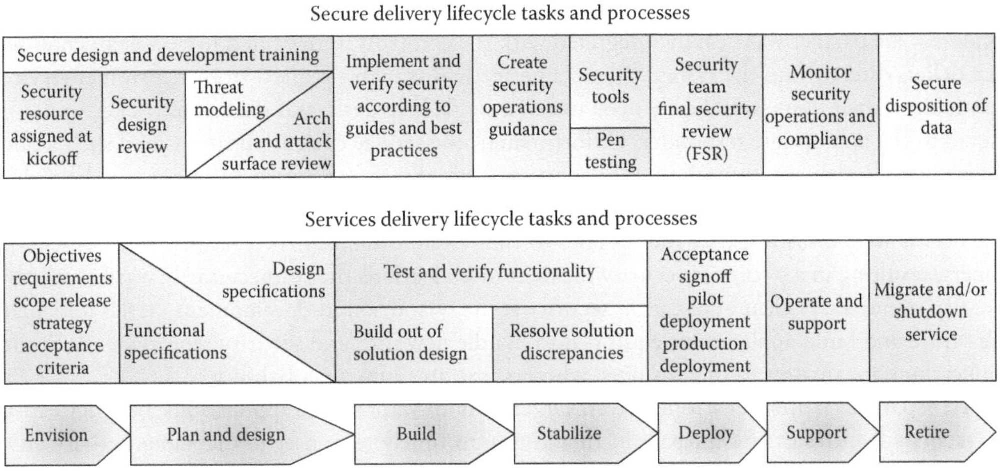

Secure delivery lifecycle tasks and processes

Secure design and development training			Implement and verify security according to guides and best practices	Create security operations guidance	Security tools	Security team final security review (FSR)	Monitor security operations and compliance	Secure disposition of data
Security resource assigned at kickoff	Security design review	Threat modeling Arch and attack surface review			Pen testing			

Services delivery lifecycle tasks and processes

Objectives requirements scope release strategy acceptance criteria	Functional specifications	Design specifications	Test and verify functionality		Acceptance signoff pilot deployment production deployment	Operate and support	Migrate and/or shutdown service
			Build out of solution design	Resolve solution discrepancies			

Envision → Plan and design → Build → Stabilize → Deploy → Support → Retire

Figure 11.4   Secure delivery lifecycle processes and tasks.

Security Development Lifecycle Drivers and Benefits

Secure software is a major tactical component of a good security strategy. The application layer is where the majority of attacks are taking place and the majority of damage is being done. We must have a strategy for curbing this activity or bear the liabilities failure imposes upon us. The business world has experienced more than enough damage from security failures and now finds itself struggling to keep the compliance requirements that grew out of those failures from putting them out of business. Compliance is probably the biggest driver for application security from two perspectives: first, having the ability to prove compliance and second, stemming the tide of increased regulatory oversight. The more we fail, the more the powers that be will try to force us to do better. SDL standards are built around industry best practices as well as legal and regulatory requirements. Applications built with SDL are designed to be compliant from the start. Avoiding compliance liabilities is only one of the economic advantages, however.

Applications built with SDL not only have fewer security flaws, but they are better quality products in general because the mandatory reviews and testing requirements of SDL also catch other flaws. Better quality and fewer security flaws means less downtime, fewer incidents, and lower costs. It also allows security personnel to focus on planning and supporting business initiatives. The standards that SDL introduces to support the security management process further reduce costs by eliminating complexities, duplication of effort, and manual processes. Commonality is an important aspect of incident response because it promotes the efficient flow of information from security controls to responders, making it possible for them to quickly repel malicious activity. Quick response has its economic advantages; the faster the response, the less the damage; the less the damage, the less recovery time and resources required. Consider this fact: An automated attack can compromise something on the order of 20 systems every minute, and the proliferation rate increases with every infected system. Waiting to respond is not an option.

> Gartner estimates that if 50 percent of software vulnerabilities were removed prior to production...enterprise configuration management and incident response costs would be reduced by 75 percent each.
>
> **The Gartner Group**

Secure applications and well-designed security controls are business enablers. Poor application security practices are quite the opposite. A company Bill worked with had a homegrown help desk application it used extensively to service internal users, external partners, contractors, and vendors. One partner was heavily integrated with the company and wanted to be able to enter service tickets directly into the system. It was a perfectly reasonable request from a customer services standpoint: Their users would only need to call a single help desk, and the service ticket would be routed to the appropriate responder. Unfortunately, the service desk applications had such a poor security design that accommodating the request required major software reengineering. Foolishly, the company decided to "patch" a few functions so that the software could be accessed remotely. The results were disastrous; partner queries to the system often returned records from other customers, resulting in a stream of security incident investigations that unnecessarily wasted valuable security resources. A clear application security strategy and sound development tactics anticipate the future and build applications equipped to handle new uses and security requirements. Secure applications are an asset to the business, whereas insecure apps are a liability.

Transparency is another strong driver. Organizations want secure applications, but they expect the security features to be transparent. In addition to timely responses to malicious activity, SDL objectives must include timely performance (usability). Some of the major complaints against the Vista operating system were related to usability. Vista had great security controls but slow performance and unfriendly (intrusive) processes. Microsoft lost sight of this customer expectation, and they paid for it with one of their lowest ever adoption rates.

Compliance remains the primary driver for security controls in general. Application security is one tactic that has significant promise for improving organizational compliance efforts. The improvements SDL brings to application security and quality in general greatly reduce maintenance and support cost, as well as potential loss liabilities. The improvements SDL standards drive into common supporting processes improve not only incident response capabilities but also operations, support, and customer service in general. The improvements it can bring to incident response are a win–win for organizations that leverage this tactic. In the next section we will look at some of the barriers to adoption.

SIDEBAR: THE SECURITY DEVELOPMENT LIFECYCLE SUCCESS STORY

Microsoft began applying the SDL process to all major products in 2004, and the results have been very impressive. No one at Microsoft is willing to claim SDL is the security "silver bullet," but the Return on Investment (ROI) has been huge. The simplest measure of success is product vulnerabilities. There was a 45% decline in reported vulnerabilities in Vista over Windows XP for the same reporting period (the first year after the release of the product); Internet Explorer 7 had a 65% decline; and SQL Server 2005 had a 90% decline. These products also had the lowest vulnerability counts of all competing products in the marketplace. SDL obviously works and works well.

Microsoft takes a lot of criticism for some of the things it does, but SDL is one for which they deserve a lot of praise. Not only did they develop a great process for improving software security, but they gave it away to the industry for free so that everyone else could do the same.

Security Development Lifecycle Challenges

Why try to [hack] Vista when you have [easier, non-Microsoft targets like] Acrobat Reader installed, some antivirus software with shoddy file parsing, and the latest iTunes?

Halvar Flake
Security Researcher,
BlueHat Conference Speech

Although the benefits of SDL are undeniable, there are some challenges, one of which is the rate of change in the IT world; new requirements are constantly surfacing from legal and regulatory changes, and new storage, processing, and connectivity technology are completely changing the face of IT infrastructure. Cloistered in-house enclaves have morphed into interconnected online and outsourced services, manned data centers have become power and pipe hubs for plugging in computer and storage containers (modules), and locally loaded client applications are quickly becoming browser-based Web apps. Suddenly the skimpy pieces of information dropped in the audit trail are insufficient to meet evidentiary requirements, and the disparate sources and formats of audit trails are hampering compliance efforts. Gone are the perimeter, network, and host security defenses applications relied on to reduce security threats; now the user comes directly to the application. Gone are the physical barriers that kept data isolated and safe; now thousands of users share the same processor and storage facilities in the cloud infrastructure. All of these factors impact SDL, which for most organizations (if they are using it at all) is a fairly new practice. Adapting SDL to these different environments is a stretch, to say the least. SDL was designed for large packaged products. It isn't well suited to Web applications that are constantly being updated and changed. Logging and audit standards haven't caught up with statutory and regulatory reporting requirements, and application intrusion detection is practically nonexistent. Not only is it a problem with lagging or missing standards, but it is also a problem with coverage. The process for packed application development begins with product envisioning and ends with product release. In the online world, product release is when the real work begins. Once the service goes online, it is a continual process of fixes, updates, and enhancements; you don't get to walk away and start on the next version. This is a major shift in the development paradigm, a shift many developers are not finding easy to make.

Getting application developers to change their mind-set and incorporate mandatory functionality (performance, management, security, etc.) into their design and coding practices is not easily accomplished. Microsoft's trustworthy computing initiative kicked off in 2000 with a security stand-down that many both inside and outside the company considered a joke and a complete waste of time. It took years of training, reinforcement, process refinements, and tooling to finally get everyone on board, and 10 years after the fact, Microsoft is still struggling to make SDL work well in its services business. SDL was designed to be used in the development of large packaged software products with long development time frames. Many environments have very short development and testing time frames where existing SDL processes do not work well. To address that issue internally Microsoft developed a version of SDL for agile development methodologies. After refining it for a while in-house, Microsoft made it available to the public in the fall of 2009. Change takes time: Change impacts development schedules, and it takes time for people and organizations to assimilate the new elements that change brings. Unfortunately, time is not always a luxury organizations have.

SIDEBAR: STRANGER IN A FOREIGN LAND

I (Bill) used to do security code reviews and, believe me, developers do not like to be told their babies are ugly. People tend to think development is a technical skill. To some extent it is, but mostly it is an art. As a reviewer, I was constantly amazed at the creative ways that developers came up with to solve very complex problems. You can teach an artist technique, but when you start telling her you want structure and order to what she is doing, you are going to get resistance. Anyone who thinks Bill Gates stood up one day and said, "Okay from now on we're doing to develop trustworthy code," and everyone said, "Yeah and amen," you are kidding yourself. It takes time to become skillful and productive at something, whether it is painting or programming; the more skillful you become, the less interested you are in change, unless there is a compelling reason. Technology drives change, but unlike painting, technology consumes the old when it produces the new. There have been thousands of improvements to paint, but I can still buy a canvas; technology consumes the canvas and forces you to use a graphics pad. You can spend 10 years learning how to be proficient in a computer programming language, only to find that it's no longer available and no longer supported. Consider this: In my 25 plus years working with computers, I have developed reasonable proficiency in eight different programming languages, four of which are obsolete. I still have code in my development library that I couldn't compile and run on any current technology if my life depended on it. The point I'm making is that technology introduces more than enough change into the environment for developers to deal with. For example, multiple 64-bit processors are now the standard for PCs; learning to leverage the capabilities of this type of CPU architecture takes new skills that single-processor 32-bit programmers have to acquire. Adding more stuff (that also changes constantly) such as mandatory performance, reliability, management, and security functions only makes their jobs more difficult.

Have you ever tried to learn a foreign language? Imagine what it was like for the Visual Basic and Java developers at Dell Computers when the company decided to standardize on C# and dotNet for all future development. Gone are all the tools, shortcuts, code samples, and everything else they had that helped make them great developers. Suddenly, 300 proficient productive developers are relegated to newbie status while they try to assimilate and use a whole new language, new techniques, new libraries, and so on. Time to forget what made you a great developer; you are now a stranger in a foreign land—welcome.

Assimilation is not just a question of training and practice; it is also a matter of tooling. If you want specific functionality within an application, there needs to be a library of methods to implement that functionality. Sometimes an existing library can be modified to suit the need; other times, a new library needs to be created. Developers are not going to build this functionality into everything they create; they want to use a tool with this functionality. The lack of tools becomes a challenge to adoption.

Cost can be another challenge. Microsoft experienced about a 15% impact to their development process when they implemented SDL, 15% in cost and 15% in time. Depending on the size of your project, that can be a pretty substantial hit. According to "Microsoft SDL: Return on Investment" (Microsoft Corp., iSEC Partners, Inc., September 15, 2009), the approximate start-up and run costs for the first year of SDL would be $350,000 for a small development team (50 people). For small and medium-size companies, that's a pretty challenging number, and for larger organizations looking to cut expenses, it could be a hard sell as well.

Cost and competency can also be major factors for incident response. Creating an effective response capability that extends to the application and data management levels is going to require some major retooling. Small and medium companies may not have the in-house expertise to do this and hiring an external resource may be cost prohibitive. Even larger organizations may bristle at the costs, despite the potentially good ROI.

The major barriers to SDL adoption are the start-up costs and the ability to assimilate new processes and requirements into existing development efforts. The lack of tooling can be another challenge. Making the process work requires good tooling, and making the new functionality work requires the software tools (libraries) implementing those functions. The impact and expertise required to make SDL work may not make it a good fit for every organization. Implementing good tactical security practices at the application development and response level can be a challenge, especially for small and medium-size companies, but the return of investment makes it worth the effort in the long run.

SDL Success Factors and Lessons Learned

Security Development Lifecycle has been a hot topic in the industry for a number of years. It has its critics, but for the most part it has been praised for its effectiveness and positive impact on the industry. The organizations that have been successful with the implementation of SDL have a number of success factors in common. The first factor, not surprisingly, is the need for executive sponsorship. Security Development Lifecycle will not be successful if it is not mandatory, and development teams are not required to attend mandatory training. The only way this is going to happen is to have an executive leadership directive. Development standards are the second factor; there must be a well-defined set of development standards and metrics for all phases of the development process. The development of standards should be a cooperative effort between development leads and security, and standards should be based on industry best practices and the legal and regulatory requirements applicable to the organization. Program continuity was another major success factor; assigning the same security resource ("buddy") to work with the development team throughout the development process improves communications and produces better results.

The most consistent lesson learned was the need to get "everyone's head in the game." Mandatory training isn't going to do the job; you are changing a culture and that takes consistent reinforcement. Weyerhaeuser tied security incidents to people's bonuses—how's that for incentive! Making the process cyclic is another important lesson: Learn from your failures and mistakes. The final lesson is never compromise good security practices, be security by default, always fail to the most secure condition, enforce least privilege, and practice defense in depth.

Michael Howard's blog also contains this advice:

■ Model your threats before you start coding.
■ Keep on top of the security news.
■ Use DCOM/RPC security.
■ Make your samples secure too.

> We have undertaken a rigorous "engineering excellence" initiative so that our engineers understand and use best practices in software design, development, testing and release. We're doing this because software vulnerabilities are not just a Microsoft issue; they're an industry-wide issue.

Michael Howard

Application Control Objectives

The control objectives at the application layer are observation based. There is a need to improve the ability of applications to recognize malicious activity and to take action to capture activity information, notify operations, and/or take mitigation actions. Let's begin with the observation/recognition attribute.

Observation/Recognition

There is a general security principle that states: The closer a control is to the target of the attack, the more effective it is at preventing, detecting, and/or responding to that attack. If you think of this principle in terms of layered security, perimeter controls (e.g., firewalls) would be the least effective, network-based control a little more effective, host based more effective, application based even better, and data controls the best. Unfortunately, controls in the last two layers are oriented mostly toward protection, not detection. In terms of effectiveness, this is actually a backward approach. What is more effective at keeping someone from breaking through a door, a good quality door or an armed guard? The guard is more effective because he or she can detect the attack and move to prevent it before the door can be damaged. The current SDL approach is to build a really high-quality door and let people beat on it until someone finds a way to bash it open! Don't take this in the wrong way: We are not saying we shouldn't build quality doors, just that our primary focus should be on detecting malicious behavior because it is the more effective control.

Passive Detection Control Objectives

Today most detection functionality in applications is passive: the patrolling guard scenario. Every so often, someone comes by and looks at the door. They may note some damages to the door and investigate how it got there, or even worse they may find that the door has been broken down! Periodic application log review is the same scenario (assuming application logging is turned on and subject to periodical review). Occasionally, some abnormal activity may be noted, investigated, and result in the discovery of a breach. The effectiveness of this scenario depends largely on the quality of the information recorded in the logs. Developers are interested in catching problems with code execution, not detecting malicious activity. Sometimes, these are one and the same (the malicious activity is the cause of the problem), but more often, this isn't the case. Audit trails designed for debugging seldom contain the quality of information required to identify malicious activity. Error codes are frequently used to identify where the fault took place rather than why it took place. Determining the why requires parsing the text—not a trivial activity for unstructured data. Quantity is another issue; reviewers are forced to wade through hundreds of irrelevant events to find security-related information, and when it is found, it is often insufficient to detect malicious activity or to facilitate investigation, not to mention provide evidence for compliance reporting. This situation is completely unacceptable. Audit trails must contain quality information sufficient for the detection and investigation of malicious activity, as well as the prosecution of the perpetrator.

Table 11.2 maps audit trail attributes to specific baselines. The type (hard or soft) is used to denote how the metric for each control objective is collected. Soft indicates a procedure-based control, while hard denotes a technology-based (i.e., automated) control.

These requirements are essentially the same as the audit control objectives for accountability. For a detailed description of these control objects, see the Audit Requirements for Accountability section of Chapter 10.

Active Detection Control Objectives

From a response perceptive, passive detection is an ineffective security control because the detection takes place after the fact. As the interval of time between the event and its review increases, the potential damage the attacker can do also increases. Passive detection alone is not sufficient to meet strategic security objectives; real-time (active) detection is required. Active detection enhances the detection process by generating an alert when the event takes place. There are two possible scenarios; the audit trail can be reviewed in real time or the application can generate the alerts. The first scenario is the current approach the industry has taken; audit records are forwarded to a central collection point and evaluated (reviewed) against a set of predefined rules, and alerts are generated for activities that violate one or more rules. The effectiveness of the control depends on the quality of the information in the record, the accuracy of the rules, and the processing efficiency of the evaluation system. One advantage of this approach is the ability to collate records from multiple systems to get a broader understanding of the event, thus facilitating the accuracy of the response. The downsides of this approach are a propensity for false detections (false positives) and processing lag under high record volumes.

The application-based intrusion detection system (AIDS) doesn't suffer from these shortcomings because detection is based on programmatic security functionality; not on the interpretation of a recorded event. At a security conference in 1991, Bill presented the concept of

Table 11.2 Audit Trail Control Objectives

Attribute/Control	Type	Risk and Requirements
Sufficient		
Coverage	Soft	Audit/logging mechanisms must be enabled for all applications and subject to review at established intervals.
Complete	Hard	Audit records must contain all the information required to detect and investigate malicious activity and prove compliance with all applicable legal, regulatory, and industry requirements.
Temporal	Hard	Records must be associated with a global time source.
Quality		
Consistent	Soft	Records must have a common format that complies with established standards.
Relevant	Hard	The information collected must support all associated compliance and legal claims.
Understandable	Soft	The information in audit records should be easy to assimilate.
Simple	Hard	The records should not contain extraneous content.
Sequential	Hard	The records must be in chronological order.
Correlated	Soft	The relationship between the records should be apparent.
Authentic		
Tamperproof	Hard	Records must be protected against malicious alteration.
Traceable	Hard	The records should have a consistent chain of custody.
Retained	Soft	The records must be retained for a sufficient time to assure proper review and to facilitate investigations.

exceptional logging as the basis for application intrusion detection. The concept was based on the idea that in the normal course of operations certain things should never happen, and when they do happen they are an exceptional event that should be logged and where appropriate should generate an alert and/or take corrective action. The process diagram in Figure 11.5 is an example. Web-based applications verify data on the client side because it is quicker and it reduces the amount of traffic that passes back and forth between the client and server. However, any data transmitted from an application that is outside of your control (i.e., the Web page and associated scripts on the client) cannot be trusted, so data submitted to the server is checked a second time to ensure its validity. How many times should this validation fail? ZERO! The only way for this validation to fail is for someone to deliberately disable the checks on the client side. Disabling these checks is indicative of malicious activity. Therefore, the event should be logged and the session with the user terminated. If the user has to log back on the next time he or she accesses the server, it won't take long to realize you can't access the system with a hacked client!

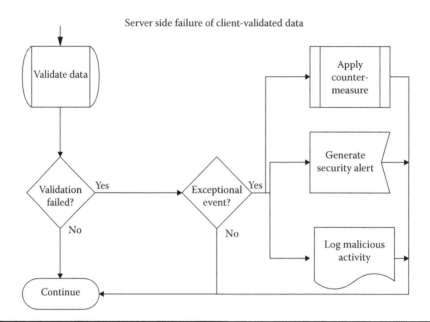

Figure 11.5   Exceptional event example.

Assuming there is an ExceptionalEventHandler class, the process requires the insertion of a line or two of code to provide real-time alerting for malicious activity. Exceptional logging also encompasses the audit component of this control objective. All events must be logged using the same criteria as passive detection.

Alert generation should also be a call to a predefined set of methods (class). The details of this functionality will be discussed in the Transition Objectives section later in this chapter. For now just remember that AIDS requires an alerting capability. The final component is corrective action (intrusion prevention): the application of a countermeasure or mitigating control. The use of this response mechanism depends on a number of things, including the value of the data on the system, the severity of the event, the application interface, and the response processes you have in place. In some instances, a programmatic response from the application makes sense; in other cases, allowing the alert management process to decide on countermeasures is more appropriate. The level (intensity) of response is also a judgment call; in the example above, the user's session was killed. A more graceful approach might be to return a Web page informing the user their client is corrupted and they need to download a new version.

Table 11.3 maps active detection attributes to specific baselines. The type (hard or soft) is used to denote how the metric for each control objective is collected. Soft indicates a procedure-based control, while hard denotes a technology-based (i.e., automated) control.

These control objectives form the basis for AIDS, and when applied to a database management application, they become the basis for data intrusion detection. The control objectives are designed to ensure the timeliness and effectiveness of this tactic, including minimizing false detections and providing flexible intelligent alerting to facilitate event management for application-level instances of malicious activity. These control objectives also include an intrusion prevention option design to proactively invoke countermeasures that will reduce or eliminate the risks associated with certain types of malicious activity. This capability is particularly valuable for systems processing or storing high-value or high-sensitivity data.

Table 11.3 Active Detection Control Objectives

Attribute/Control	Type	Risk and Requirements
Coverage	Soft	All applications must have a means of detecting malicious activity, logging such activity, and generating an alert (notification) for event management purposes.
Audit		Detection processes shall conform to passive detection audit record control objectives.
Detection		
Timely	Hard	Detection must be in real time and result in the immediate creation of an audit record.
Accurate	Hard	Detection to the best extent possible shall: - Identify all known types of malicious activity (i.e., minimize false negatives). - Be based on actual malicious activity (i.e., minimize false positives).
Alerting		
Intelligent	Soft	Alerting mechanisms whenever possible should have features that improve the accuracy and efficiency of alert processing such as the ability to: - Consolidate multiple occurrences of an event within a certain time frame into a single alert message. - Generate alerts based on threshold triggers (e.g., too many events within a certain time frame) instead of on every occurrence of an event. - Filter (ignore) certain events. - Confirm the delivery of alert messages. - Direct alerts to multiple destinations. - Be remotely configurable
Timely	Hard	Alerts shall be generated in real or near real time according to established alerting standards.
Consistent	Soft	Alert messages must have a common format that complies with established standards.
Sufficient	Hard	Alert messages should contain sufficient information to support a directed response.
Understandable	Soft	The information in alert messages should be understandable by a person of normal intelligence.
Simple	Hard	Alert messages should not contain extraneous content.
Temporal	Hard	Alert messages must be associated with a global time source.

(continued)

Table 11.3   Active Detection Control Objectives (Continued)

Attribute/Control	Type	Risk and Requirements
Sequential	Hard	Alert messages should be in chronological order.
Correlated	Soft	The relationship between alert messages should be apparent.
Authentic	Hard	Alert messages should have a means for proving authenticity to prevent message tampering or spoofing.
Countermeasures		
Coverage	Soft	Countermeasures may be included in applications to provide proactive protection against malicious activity.
Callable	Soft	Programmatic countermeasures should have an interface that allows them to be invoked by an external management process.
Timely	Hard	Countermeasures shall have a means for setting the time interval between an event and the countermeasure execution.
Accurate	Hard	Countermeasures shall only mitigate the threat associated with a specific instance of malicious activity (i.e., the countermeasure should not adversely impact overall system performance or usage).
Effective	Soft	Countermeasures should mitigate the threat associated with the malicious activity to an acceptable risk level. **Note:** SHOULD is used because mitigation to acceptable levels is not always possible, and to acknowledge that any measure reducing risk is better than no action at all.
Comprehensive	Hard	Countermeasures should ensure that all actions taken result in the return of all related resources to the system (i.e., no open files, allocated memory, etc.) to prevent a potential Denial of Service from repeated attacks.
Reporting	Hard	Countermeasures shall generate an audit trail of actions taken and when possible the results of said actions.

The following actions are recommended to facilitate the observation and recognition of malicious activities at the application level:

1. Survey existing application detection and alerting mechanisms and associated interfaces to determine application requirements and identify gaps in capability.
2. Review existing alerting message formats and content to identify gaps in information completeness, clarity, and the like.
3. Assess the risks associated with existing time interval standards for generating alerts.
4. Update existing standards to conform to security strategic objectives.
5. Build a knowledge base of exceptional events patterns.
6. Review and update application development processes (in-house or contracted) to incorporate AIDS requirements into all development efforts (in-house and contracted).

7. Define and incorporate AIDS requirements for commercial off-the-shelf (COTS) products into procurement standards.
8. Review your corporation's data-retention policies to determine what retention cycles must be established for data stored at a service provider.
9. Review your corporate data destruction standards to determine what data destruction capabilities will be required for your providers.
10. Review and update security policies to require application auditing to be enabled and to establish mandatory periodic review of the same.
11. Consider outsourcing audit record process and alerting to an MSSP.

Detection addresses the existing gap in our observation capabilities at the application level. Passive detection identifies malicious activities through the periodic review of application logs. The method from a response perspective is ineffective because it identifies events after-the-fact, thus giving the attacker more time and opportunity to damage or compromise assets. Active detection identifies malicious activity in real time, records it, and generates an alert to facilitate response. The control objectives in this section represent an application intrusion detection system; they can also be used for data intrusion detection when applied to data management applications.

As the focus of attacks has shifted to the application layer, the need for an effective AIDS tactic has increased. Unfortunately, the industry is struggling to effect the basic development practices needed for SDL. Compliance-level audit practices and application intrusion detection are advanced SDL requirements. Changing culture and mind-set takes time; getting developers to think in terms of secure coding practices is an uphill battle, and getting them to think in terms of compliance audits and intrusion detection isn't even on the road map for most organizations. In the interim, organizations should consider real-time automated log (audit trail) review as a stopgap measure. Several commercial products perform this function, and these services are also available from MSSPs.

Transition Objectives

The control objectives in the previous section resulted in two outputs: audit trails and alerts. This section defines the control objectives for the interfaces used to distribute these outputs to other systems. It is based primarily on the principles of commonality and timeliness, and in that sense it isn't a security-specific function. It can be utilized by any process to facilitate the intelligent forwarding of alert messages and audit information. The goal is to convey information in a timely manner and to present it in a form that facilitates good decision making, including directed incident responses. We call this functionality Common Collection and Dispatch.

Common Collection and Dispatch

Common Collection and Dispatch (CCD) provides a simple, scalable, and automated way to transfer audit records and alert messages to various consumers, such as the IT help desk and security operations, as well as data collection systems (e.g., Business Intelligence, data warehouse, etc.) and reporting systems (financial, compliance, customer, etc.). CCD is based on the commonality of

- Data storage engines
- Transfer mechanisms for audit data and alerts
- Formats for audit data and alerts

The three principal components are a collector service, a consolidator service, and a reporting service. Figure 11.6 illustrates how CCD might be implemented in an enterprise environment.

Collectors receive alert and audit records from system logs, application logs, and other sources through the collection and alert API. Collectors reduce, consolidate, and process the collected data into a format suitable for reporting. Collectors may also generate alerts if a threshold is crossed during data processing. To ensure the timeliness of responses, alerts are sent to the dispatcher function for immediate distribution to the designated responder or responders. Consolidators receive periodic data transfers from collector systems or other consolidators. Consolidators store data for use by reporting systems. They may also have a dispatcher service for transferring data to consolidators in other service areas (e.g., business intelligence). Collector and consolidator services are used for transit functions and dispatcher services are used for response.

Transition Drivers and Benefits

> The computer programmer is a creator of universes for which he alone is responsible. Universes of virtually unlimited complexity can be created in the form of computer programs.
>
> **Joseph Weizenbaum**
> *Computer scientist and creator of the AI program "ELIZA"*

Information transfer is essential to the operation of computing technology, but this is more than moving pieces of data from one point to another; it also encompasses the concept of usability. Much of the complexity in technology is the result of thousands of information transfer solutions, none of which has any commonality. This results in a tremendous amount of unnecessary churn to manipulate data from various sources into usable information. Eliminating just

> Complexity is not a cause of confusion. It is a result of it.
>
> **Jeff Hawkins**

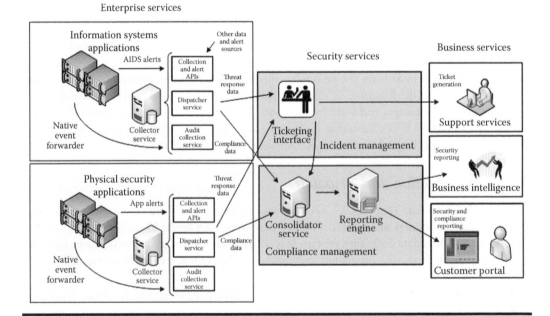

Enterprise services

Figure 11.6   Common collection and dispatch architecture.

a small portion of this churn would produce tremendous improvement in system efficiency. This is the primary driver for CCD: a level of commonality that substantially improves the efficiency of information management, resulting in better enterprise, IT, and business services. One of the biggest benefits for security management is the ability to converge information from facility management and access control systems with IT security data, enabling better security monitoring capability and the centralization of security operations. Another major benefit is the ability to see all the alert data related to a particular event on a single system instead of having to go from system to system gathering data and manually collating it. The benefits are similar for other business processes, including the convergence of financial data, business intelligence data, planning data, and the like, and perhaps the biggest benefit of all is the ability to easily report on that data.

In addition to the cost benefits from improved operational efficiencies, CCD provides other economies as well. CCD is designed to keep network utilization to a minimum by processing raw data locally and only transferring relevant data summations to the consolidators and reporting engines. This means it works efficiently over leased lines. CCD can be implemented using standard COTS (commercial off-the-shelf) software; little custom programming is required. Use of a standard alerting protocol (SNMP) and standard extensions (Inform Trap, SMUX, and AgentX) means alert messages can easily be forwarded, received, and processed by existing management systems. Stored procedures can also be used to forward data in any number of other formats. It is the commonality and compatibility of these components and their scripting capabilities that facilitates the entire transition element. CCD also leverages the native event-forwarding capability of the Windows operating system to send security-related events and system logs to a central collection point (e.g., ACS). No customized solutions are required.

CCD is adaptable to any size organization. The hierarchical layout of components allows CCD to be incrementally scaled to accommodate additional enterprise service environments and permits the addition of parallel collectors and consolidators to accommodate higher volumes of data. For smaller organizations with lower volumes of traffic, consolidators may not be required, and functionality (e.g., consolidator and reporting) can be combined on a single server.

The ability to deliver information in a common format, using a common transport, and to store it in a common data management solution greatly improves the efficiency and effectiveness of security processes and benefits a number of other business processes. This section proposes one method for the common collection and dispatch of transition data that organizations can use as a model for building a simple, scalable, and automated way to transfer audit records and alert messages to various consumers.

SIDEBAR: IN A MATTER OF MINUTES

A simple illustration of the efficiency gains that result from commonality comes from a consulting engagement that Bill had with a major cell phone provider. Bill went there to demonstrate a network mapping technology. The company used an Asset Inventory Management System based on Microsoft SQL Server. The network mapping application also used SQL Server. After completing a scan of their network, the inventory manager came by to take a look at the results; then he took a screen print of one of the records and left. Returning to his workspace, the inventory manager proceeded to write an SQL query that joined the two databases and gave him a list of all the nodes on the network that weren't in his inventory. He was ecstatic! In a matter of minutes he was able to solve a problem he had been working on for months. The data he needed was present in other systems, but he couldn't get it in a form that he could use. Commonality provided the fix.

Transition Challenges

A wise man once said, "Simplicity can be very complex to achieve." Establishing a common format for data elements, common transport, and storage management across multiple platforms and applications is no trivial pursuit. In many instances, it will be impossible to substitute a common storage platform for an existing solution. When this happens, custom procedures must be written to "blackboard" the data so it can be transferred. The task has been made somewhat easier because of the adopt XML, but it is far from perfect. In some instances, changes or updates to existing applications and data stores may be required. These are usually nonintrusive extensions of existing formats, but vetting these changes to ensure they do not impact application performance takes time. The volume of data that needs to be processed by the CCD architecture can also be a challenge. Data previously distributed by multiple systems is now converged onto a single solution. Processing lag may also come into play. Collection and consolidation services process and reformat data before storing it; under heavy volume, this processing could introduce unacceptable lags.

Transition Success Factors and Lessons Learned

The key to the success of any major change like this one is executive sponsorship. Make transition a part of your overall security strategy and implement it as such. If at all possible, make facility management and access control data your first integration—it will not only enhance your security management capabilities but it will give you the experience you'll need to make other integrations successful. Once you have your CCD architecture fully operational, extend it to a couple of high-profile business initiatives. It won't take long for leadership to see the value of commonality, and this will help you expand the architecture to other systems. The other key is a flexible and scalable architecture like CCD. Single-level black-box solutions may work well for smaller implementations, but scalability is essential for performance in larger installations, especially when other business functions begin using it.

Lessons Learned

- Anticipate the need for customization and choose products that support scripting or other forms of customization.
- Anticipate the need to blackboard data and choose products that support industry standards and best practices for data translation (e.g., XML).
- Plan for data growth two or three years ahead.
- Watch your data growth, have a good retention management plan, and spool records off the system when they have outlived their usefulness.

Transition Control Objectives

The control objectives for this tactic are based on commonality and timeliness.

Table 11.4 maps transition attributes to specific baselines. The type (hard or soft) is used to denote how the metric for each control objective is collected. Soft indicates a procedure-based control, while hard denotes a technology-based (i.e., automated) control.

These control objectives form the basis for a Common Collection and Dispatch service capable of transferring application intrusion detection alerts and security-related application audit records, as well as other, similarly formatted data related to other business functionality. The control objectives are designed to ensure the commonality of data, transfer protocol, and storage management solutions. Control objectives also enforce the real-time delivery of alerts through process prioritization, transmission failure detection, and system redundancy. This tactic includes a set

Table 11.4   Transition Control Objectives

Attribute/Control	Type	Risk and Requirements
Coverage	Soft	Transition mechanisms must be able to: - Import/receive, assimilate, process, and store security-related audit records from any source. - Receive, assimilate, process, and forward security-related alerts from any source.
Commonality		
Data format	Hard	Transition mechanisms must conform all audit records and alert messages to a common format in accordance with established standards.
Transfer protocol	Hard	Transition mechanisms shall use a common set of protocols in accordance with established standards for all data transfers between systems.
	Hard	Protocols should support protective capabilities that assure the confidentiality and integrity of transmissions.
Data storage		Transition mechanisms shall store all data using a common storage technology (e.g., SQL Server) to facilitate the transfer of data between systems.
Timeliness		
Timely	Hard	Transit mechanisms shall process and forward alerts in real time and create an audit record of this action and when possible the results of the action.
	Hard	Transit mechanisms shall process, store, and forward audit records in a timely manner and in accordance with established time frames.
Prioritized	Hard	Transit mechanisms shall have a means of prioritizing the processing of alerts and audit records to ensure alerts are processed in real time.
Redundant	Hard	Transit mechanisms shall have the ability to act as a backup destination to accommodate system failures.
	Hard	Transit mechanisms shall have the ability to select alternate destinations to ensure that alerts reach response resources in a failed system scenario.
Verified	Hard	Transit mechanisms shall have the ability to detect and recover from forwarding failures to ensure that alerts reach response resources in a failed system scenario.
Scalable	Soft	Transit architecture should be designed for the simple addition of resources to accommodate increased usage requirements and to ensure that alert forwarding is not impacted by excessive system load (resource starvation).

(continued)

Table 11.4 Transition Control Objectives (continued)

Attribute/Control	Type	Risk and Requirements
Correlated	Soft	The relationship between the records should be apparent.
Economy		
Intelligent	Soft	Transit mechanisms, whenever possible, should have features that improve the accuracy and efficiency of alert and audit record processing and distribution such as the ability to: - Consolidate multiple occurrences of an event within a certain time frame into a single record. - Generate alerts based on threshold triggers (e.g., too many events within a certain time frame) instead of on every occurrence of an event. - Filter out irrelevant audit events. - Be remotely configurable.

of intelligent processing capabilities to reduce network bandwidth utilization, facilitate accurate responses, and improve reporting. The following actions are recommended to facilitate the transition of application-level alerts and audit trails:

1. Survey existing application log (audit trail) collection and processing mechanisms and associated interfaces to determine application requirements and identify gaps in capability.
2. Review existing alerting message formats and audit record formats to identify gaps in information completeness, clarity, and the like.
3. Assess the risks associated with existing time interval standards for alert forwarding.
4. Update existing standards to conform to security strategic objectives.
5. Build a database of existing security-related audit record formats.
6. Review and update application development processes (in-house or contracted) to incorporate transition requirements into all development efforts (in-house and contracted).
7. Create or update your CCD architecture and component requirements.
8. Define and incorporate transit commonality requirements for commercial off-the-shelf (COTS) products into procurement standards.
9. Review your corporation's data-retention policies to determine how they will impact your data management schema for collector and consolidator systems.
10. Review and update security policies to require all application auditing and alerting functionality to conform to CCD control objectives.
11. Where applicable, form a team to work on CCD-based processing and reporting for logical and physical access control systems.

Rapid Response

This chapter began with a discussion of the existing gaps in application-level security, including missing or ineffective preventative and detective controls and how these gaps have led to massive data losses. Hopefully, the previous sections of this chapter have provided some solid tactics to attack and close these gaps. This section will address two additional types of controls: corrective and restorative. Corrective tactics are used to respond to and resolve security incidents to reduce or eliminate potential damages. Actions may be people, process, or technology based—for example, a guard stopping someone who tailgated through a security access point, a manual procedure for removing malware, or a programmatic countermeasure that kills an attacker's TCP/IP session. Restorative controls are controls that return systems to normal production operations after they have experienced an incident. This includes system rebuilds, restores from backup, as well as business continuity planning (BCP) and disaster recovery planning (DRP) procedures. This section will also touch on nonincident-related responses, such as compliance and security status reporting.

A large body of knowledge surrounding incident management and incident response already exists, so this section contains just a brief overview of the process and a discussion of the tactical aspects of response. Response is one of the two most important tenets of security (observation is the other) and a key component of any security strategy. In most instances, incident-related responses will be triggered by a detective control such as a guard observing a shoplifter, a call to the help desk, server operations noting the failure of a security process, or antivirus programs finding a Trojan mail attachment. These responses may also be initiated by external sources such as the reporting of a product flaw or third-party notification of suspicious activity or downstream damage. Nonincident-related responses are usually scheduled but may be triggered by a random customer inquiry.

Incident Response Procedures

A security incident is defined as any adverse event, real or suspected, that violates or threatens to violate any facility, product, system, or network security provision. Incident response is typically divided up into progressive stages (phases). The stages are progressive because results from the current stage determine whether or not the process will proceed to the next stage. The stages are:

1. Evaluate
2. Contain
3. Resolve
4. Restore

The evaluate stage begins when *Transition* delivers a security alert to the designated responder. The first part of the evaluate stage is triage—a quick assessment of the authenticity and severity of an event based on predefined risk or threat criteria. Triage is often facilitated using a short checklist, flowchart, or error code lookup procedure. In larger organizations, triage may be carried out by help desk and system management personnel, and the results forwarded to security operations. The first question triage addresses is the authenticity of the threat; did the alert come from a valid source, and is the threat real or a hoax? If the alert is invalid or a hoax, the information is noted and sent to security operations in an informational message. If the threat is valid, an incident ticket is created and the alert is forwarded to security operations. The key to successful triage is timeliness; the alert must be processed when it arrives, validated, and forwarded as quickly as possible. The creation of an incident ticket initiates the formal (structured) incident response process. In some organizations ticket generation is automated; a program or script uses the information contained in the alert to create and route the incident ticket. (An incident ticket is used to track response and resolution time and the actions taken.) Now the real evaluation work begins. The evaluation process must determine the type and severity of the incident so that responses are commensurate with the risks and costs associated with the incident. This varies considerably with every incident. Gaining privileged access and sharing a password with a co-worker are both unauthorized access incidents, but the former carries a much higher level of risk. The evaluation process may involve reviewing video surveillance, audit records, or other sources of information. Establishing the severity of the incident determines the resolution actions that will be taken, the time lines for those actions, and the priority given to those actions. The final task in the evaluate stage is notification. Once an incident has been confirmed and severity established, notifications should be issued to all parties responsible for the management or execution of the response. For example:

- The chief security and technology officers
- The manager(s) responsible for the personnel, facilities, or systems involved
- The director of human resources when staff personnel are involved or staff safety is at risk
- Legal counsel when legal, regulatory, or contractual requirements are involved
- Customer/end-user representatives when customer data are involved
- The director of public relations when customer data is involved
- Response team members (when severity warrants it)

The process then proceeds to the contain stage. There isn't necessarily a hard-and-fast point where this transition takes place; containment actions may occur during evaluation, especially when critical assets are involved.

The containment stage is designed to limit the scope and magnitude of an incident, especially those involving malicious activities. Not all incidents require containment; for example, a security process that fails is an incident that is already contained to a single device. A product vulnerability is another example of an incident with a fixed scope. Malicious code, on the other hand, does not have a defined scope; it can spread very rapidly, incurring massive liabilities and costs as it does. Containment procedures include actions such as:

- Cordoning off a facility or partitioning the network to block the spread of the malicious activity
- Applying additional protections to critical business assets such as locking down the data center, updating antimalware software, or adding host firewall rules
- Taking precautionary measures such as transporting valuable assets to another location, backing up critical business systems, and running diagnostics to verify the operational integrity of critical systems
- Removing compromised systems from service or monitoring them for evidence collection and investigation purposes

Once the scope of the incident has been contained, the process of repairing or eradicating the cause of the incident can begin in earnest.

The resolve stage entails the repair or removal of the cause of the incident, for example, removing a virus from all infected systems and media. In the case of facility or IT systems, the resolve action may be as simple as revoking someone's access or as complicated as tracking, arresting, and prosecuting the attacker. The success of the resolve stage is based on preparedness: having and maintaining the tools required to repair faulty equipment or software, and eradicating malicious software or other behaviors. Once the incident has been resolved, the process transitions to the restore stage or the restorative control. Security groups that have Business Continuity and Disaster

Recovery functions will often consider this a separate control, so catastrophic event recovery can be included in the control objectives.

The recovery processes restore compromised systems to normal system operations. Recovery requirements vary depending on the incident. Relatively benign incidents such as port scans only require verification that all services are still operating properly. Complex attacks involving root kits, Trojan Horses, or backdoors may require a complete reload of system and application software and the restoration of data from backups. The recovery process must include verification of normal operations.

There are three additional items related to incident response. The first is escalation. Escalation procedures define the time frames for additional measures to be taken to ensure incidents are resolved as quickly as possible. Often in emergency situations the required personnel are not always available to make corrective changes. Escalation procedures address these shortcomings and help to reduce the risks and costs associated with prolonged security exposures.

The second item is evidence preservation, which is an important part of incident investigation and a required component of any legal action. The evidence preservation process should include the following minimum elements:

- **An incident investigation log**—All activities related to the incident should be entered into the log, including interview notes, observations, actions taken, and list of subsequent suspicious or abnormal events and the time at which they occurred. The chain of custody of evidence for all evidence gathered during the investigation should also be maintained in the log book.
- **Backup**—A full backup of any system involved in or suspected of being involved in the incident should be taken as soon as possible after the incident has been confirmed to preserve critical log and audit information. Disk imaging is the preferred method for this backup.
- **Photographs**—Photographs should be taken of the scene, including the system, video screen contents, and surrounding facilities, in addition to any video surveillance of the scene captured and preserved.

The third item is follow-up or postmortem review. All incidents should include a review process designed to determine root causes and identify what actions can be taken to eliminate further occurrences. The review should include response actions (what worked well and what needs improvement), as well as an analysis of the incident costs (personnel time, lost revenue, hardware damages, etc.). These metrics are an important part of your security strategy. The ability to equate incident response to direct costs provides leverage for security initiatives and helps to demonstrate the return on investment for those solutions.

It is also important to remember that incident responses will vary depending on the source of the attack, the value of the asset, the severity of the attack, customer involvement, and so on. It is wise to build process diagrams and procedures for each instance to ensure the best possible response.

Automated Responses

Some response procedures can be automated to improve the timeliness and effectiveness of responses. For example, an automated response to a building intrusion alert might activate alarm bells, turn on lights and surveillance cameras, and switch the video monitor at the guard station to the affected area. A network-generated alert might cause an access rule to be added to a firewall or router to block the source of a denial of service attack. The possibilities are endless, and so is the potential for unintended consequences. Automated responses of a retaliatory nature are discouraged. Responses that make changes affecting a large number of systems are also discouraged. The best automated responses are those that resolve a specific problem and clean up everything that is left behind (i.e., open files, allocated memory, etc.). A common use for an automated response is to retrieve information related to the alert. The person doing the alert evaluation is going to need it, so automating the retrieval makes perfect sense. Automation is a key economic principle, and we encourage the use of automation to improve the effectiveness and efficiency of security processes. We also encourage careful planning and thorough testing.

Nonincident-Related Response Procedures (Reporting)

Replying to customer inquiries is not commonly thought of as a security response mechanism, but it is precisely such a mechanism. Mandatory legal, regulatory, and industry compliance reporting requirements are directly related to security controls and operations. Requests for compliance information require a timely response; failing to comply with reporting deadlines can result in fines and other potential sanctions. Customers also expect that the information they request will be supplied to them in a reasonable time frame; when responses take an inordinate amount of time, customers become disgruntled. By contrast, when customers can query information directly (i.e., via a portal), it becomes a brand-enhancing value added.

Reporting as a Response

The Common Collection and Dispatch (CCD) architecture has a reporting component. The reporting service extracts a subset of information from one or more consolidators to produce various types of reports for internal and external customers. For customer-facing reports, the reporting engines can use a Web interface (i.e., a Customer Portal) to give customers direct access to the information they seek. The two primary types of reports are:

1. Vertical for management reporting
2. Horizontal for customer reporting

You could look at these reports as summary versus detailed. We advocate a balanced scorecard (BSC) approach to management reporting because it is an excellent way to report security metrics to executive management; the framework supports tangible metrics as well as intangible or difficult-to-monetize goals. BSC makes it possible to highlight strategic progress on risk reduction without resorting to monetized risk assessments and estimated Annual Loss Calculations (ALC). Another advantage of the BSC approach is that it communicates strategic security objectives in terms that align with corporate strategies. This helps improve enterprise strategic planning and provides management decision support. The report in Figure 11.7 shows the general layout for a BSC report.

Each section of a BSC report begins with an element from the security strategy, followed by one or more "perspective" subsections based on the objectives of that element. Each perspective has specific metrics, as well as targets and initiatives that can be reported in percentage of completion. This provides management with a better understanding of security progress against goals and of where additional planning and support will be required. The typical interval for balanced scorecard reporting is quarterly.

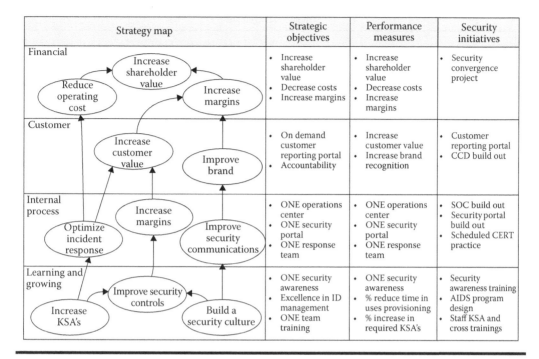

Strategy map	Strategic objectives	Performance measures	Security initiatives
Financial — Increase shareholder value; Reduce operating cost; Increase margins	• Increase shareholder value • Decrease costs • Increase margins	• Increase shareholder value • Decrease costs • Increase margins	• Security convergence project
Customer — Increase customer value; Improve brand	• On demand customer reporting portal • Accountability	• Increase customer value • Increase brand recognition	• Customer reporting portal • CCD build out
Internal process — Optimize incident response; Increase margins; Improve security communications	• ONE operations center • ONE security portal • ONE response team	• ONE operations center • ONE security portal • ONE response team	• SOC build out • Security portal build out • Scheduled CERT practice
Learning and growing — Increase KSA's; Improve security controls; Build a security culture	• ONE security awareness • Excellence in ID management • ONE team training	• ONE security awareness • % reduce time in uses provisioning • % increase in required KSA's	• Security awareness training • AIDS program design • Staff KSA and cross trainings

Figure 11.7   Balanced scorecard sample.

Another type of vertical reporting is dashboarding. Summaries of information are presented in graphical format with deltas from previous reporting periods noted. The dashboard in Figure 11.8 shows three summary categories: business risk profile, update compliance, and baseline privacy compliance.

The report contains an overall business risk profile as well as updated compliance and baseline compliance values. Each is accompanied by a summary of the elements contributing to the measurement result. In this example, changes from the previous report are shown as deltas, and the results from the 12 previous reports are presented as average values. The reporting interval for vertical reports will vary based on organizational needs; monthly is common. The distribution of the report will also vary. At a minimum, it should be distributed to senior and executive IT management and department heads.

Horizontal reports are more technical in nature than vertical reports. They typically contain details on specific activities that can be used for postmortem assessments, compliance proofs, process improvement, planning, and so on. The sample horizontal report is a list of incident tickets with calculated response and resolution times (see Table 11.5).

Incidents are listed in chronological order and criticality. The reporting interval for horizontal reports depends on established reporting time lines for legal, contractual, and regulatory compliance and other business requirements. The distribution of horizontal reports will also vary depending on content.

Rapid Response Drivers and Benefits

The biggest driver behind response is loss prevention; alerts are generated because malicious or potentially malicious activity is taking place. The faster that activity can be squelched, the less the

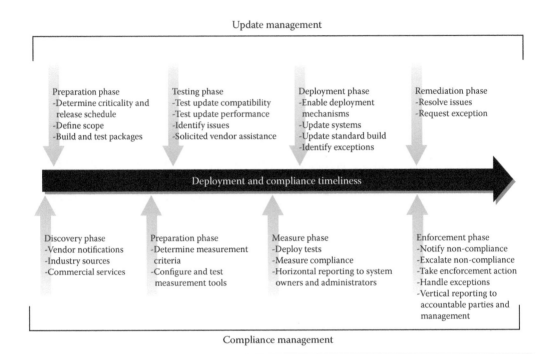

Figure 11.8 Sample vertical report.

resulting damage. In this context, loss prevention is more than the loss of assets; it also encompasses loss of reputation and customer confidence, unrecoverable restoration costs, notification costs, downstream liabilities, and legal liabilities from civil actions. These represent a substantial loss liability that increases until the incident is resolved. The second driver is compliance; compliance reporting has very specific time lines. A good response capability allows compliance

Table 11.5 Sample Horizontal Report

Updated Compliance Report, May 15, 2010					
Date	*Node*	*Service*	*Owner*	*Status*	*Check*
May 15, 2010 1400	Mtg0-TL5EXFE01	Web Mail	macssupport@ elensolar.com	Failed	AP-Parent paths disabled
May 15, 2010 1402	Mtg0-TL5EXHUB01	Business Intelligence	macssupport@ elensolar.com	Failed	UP-Critical updates installed
May 15, 2010 1411	Std0-TL5SPWS01	SharePoint	macssupport@ elensolar.com	Failed	OS-Supported version
May 15, 2010 1412	Mtg0-TL5OCS01	OCS	macssupport@ elensolar.com	Failed	SQL-Restricted CmdExec
May 15, 2010 1418	Std0-TL5EHS01	Exchange Hosted Service	ehssupport@ elensolar.com	Failed	AP-Signatures current

information to be quickly compiled and reported on. This capability also applies to customer satisfaction because it provides timely responses to customer queries, and it also increases the value of security services to the organization when query capabilities are directly available to customers (e.g., a reporting portal).

Another rapid response benefit is preparedness. A well-designed and practiced response capability assures an effective accurate response to incidents. All the tools and resources required are available at the time the alert is received; all the information required to make good response decisions is present. Instead of throwing the organization into chaos, the situation is dealt with quickly and professionally, demonstrating the added value security brings to the organization.

Response Challenges

The major challenges to this tactic are quality of information and the lack of existing tools and commonality. Response accuracy and effectiveness are based on good weaponry and high-quality information. The lack of commonality scatters information across multiple platforms, making the collection and collation of data difficult. The lack of commonality in transfer protocols and record formats only exacerbates the problem, hampering response timeliness and accuracy. The lack of quality information is more prevalent at the application layer because audit trail and intrusion detection functionality are not present nor are they likely to be present in the near future. This lack of commonality and information quality also affects compliance. Compliance is based on proof, but the majority of existing audit mechanisms are designed for debugging; the information captured is insufficient to meet the evidentiary requirements of compliance.

Response Success Factors and Lessons Learned

Success is when you have 13 soldiers fighting off 300 rebels without a single loss of life or a breach of Carmarthen Castle perimeter defenses. We need that type of prepared, practiced, and organized response. It is undoubtedly one of the best ways to demonstrate the value security adds to the organization.

Incident response requires the cooperation of many different business functions and the availability of multiple resources throughout the organizations. The only way to guarantee this level of cooperation is to have executive sponsorship. Along with acquiring the cooperation of various business groups for incident response, it is also wise to have clearly defined roles and responsibilities so that business leaders know exactly what they are committing to.

Other lessons learned include the following:

- Overcome denial and blame—Past failures and finger pointing often make it difficult to garner the cooperation needed to build a good response capability. Get over it! Response is not about who did what in the past, but about preventing loss. Fix the problem and move on.
- Identify the internal expertise you have and make friends with them.
- Have well-defined evaluation criteria and escalation time lines.
- Be prepared! Practice the plan regularly and keep your stockpile of weaponry (tools) up to date.
- Have prearranged external resources (e.g., a red team) that can assist when needed; retained services are recommended.

Table 11.6   Response Control Objectives

Attribute/Control	Type	Risk and Requirements
Coverage	Soft	Response mechanisms must: - Be able to import/receive, process, and respond to security alerts from any source. - Have required expertise (knowledge, skills, and abilities) available at all times.
Incident Responses		
Timely	Hard	Response mechanisms shall process alerts in real time. The interval of time between the receipt of an alert and the creation and routing of an incident tracking ticket shall be kept to a minimum and escalated in accordance with established standards.
Accurate	Hard	Responses shall, to the best extent possible, apply response actions to the specific system that generated the alert (i.e., not respond to or interfere with any other system).
Comprehensive	Hard	Responses shall be comprehensive, identifying and containing all instances of an event.
Prioritized		Responses shall be prioritized to ensure critical threats and threats to high-value assets are resolved first.
Economic		Responses shall be in stages and should only proceed to the next stage when necessary. Reponses to the greatest extent possible shall make the most efficient use of internal expertise (not pull people away from their duties unnecessarily).
Prepared		Response mechanisms shall remain in a high state of readiness: - Procedures shall be current. - Personnel shall be trained. - Personnel shall be drilled in response procedures. - Tools and supporting equipment shall be maintained and up to date.
Nonincident Responses		
Timely	Hard	Response mechanisms shall process customer inquiries in a timely manner and generate responses in accordance with established schedules or time lines.
Comprehensive	Hard	Responses shall be to the best extent possible comprehensive, containing all of the information requested in the inquiry.

Response Control Objectives

The control objectives for this tactic are based on timeliness, quality, and preparedness.

Table 11.6 maps response attributes to specific baselines. The type (hard or soft) is used to denote how the metric for each control objective is collected. Soft indicates a procedure-based control, while hard denotes a technology-based (i.e., automated) control.

These control objectives form the basis for timely, comprehensive, and accurate responses to incidents and customer inquiries. The control objectives enforce rapid response objectives through a structured process of evaluation, containment, resolution, and restoration. The control objectives also guard against false alarms and protect against things "slipping through the cracks" by using incident tracking tickets. The following actions are recommended to facilitate security responses:

1. Survey existing response plans and procedures to identify gaps in coverage for different sources of incidents (e.g., insider, partner connections, external hacker, etc.).
2. Survey existing response resources (tools) and expertise to identify KSA deficiencies, missing coverage, and training requirements.
3. Assess the risks associated with existing response and resolution time lines including escalation time lines.
4. Update existing standards to conform to security strategic objectives for security responses including criteria for triage evaluations and severity ratings.
5. Create a threat knowledge base to facilitate triage efforts.
6. Compile a list of all resources that may be required to facilitate incident response including network and server administrators, engineers, and team leads.
7. Review and update application development processes (in-house or contracted) to incorporate automated response guidance for all development efforts (in-house and contracted).
8. Survey existing reports and report-generating mechanisms to identify gaps in vertical, horizontal, and compliance reporting.
9. Define and incorporate reporting commonality requirements for commercial off-the-shelf (COTS) products into procurement standards.
10. Review your corporation's data retention and security labeling policies to determine how they may impact your data management schema for reporting systems and report generation.
11. Form the basic teams responsible for managing responses to facility and IT security incidents (i.e., Incident Response Teams) and beginning planning training and practice sessions to ensure that personnel are proficient at dealing with incidents both quickly and accurately.
12. Consider outsourcing event triage and evaluation to a MSSP.

Conclusion

The two interrelated tactics covered in this chapter—software security and incident response—are grouped together because the majority of attacks and security compromises take place at the application level. Addressing this issue must be one of our principal strategic objectives. The shift of attack focus is due to the huge increase in application targets and the lack of good application programming practices. There are a limited number of attack scenarios against applications. We have focused this chapter on tactics that address attack scenarios, not attack methods, because it is a better way to examine threats across a broad range of attacks. Our efforts have concentrated on tactics that best address current application-level deficiencies, including Security Development

Lifecycle (SDL), detention and alerting mechanisms, and a Common Collection and Dispatch (CCD) architecture supporting the commonality of data formats, transport protocols, and storage technologies.

SDL promises improved application security through the use of a set of development practices designed to reduce or eliminate exploitable vulnerabilities. However, the industry is just beginning to adopt it. The results from the use of SDL at Microsoft have been impressive. However, SDL does have to overcome some challenges: First, it has substantial start-up costs, and second, existing SDL standards don't address the application functionality needed for generating evidentiary audit trails, or the active detection of malicious activity at the application level. Without this functionality, our ability to respond to incidents in a timely manner is seriously hampered, as is evidenced by the number and extent of breaches.

Most existing responses to application-level attacks are based on passive detection (the review of application logs); this is ineffective because it is based on after-the-fact information. The attacker has a prolonged period of time to cause damages. Applications need to be updated to support active detection, so responses can be in real time; this is the most effective way to limit damages. This may be some time in coming; in the interim, the real-time scanning of application logs for malicious activity is a way to improve response times. Response is also hampered by a lack of commonality in data formats, transfer protocols, and storage technology. We have proposed a conceptual architecture (CCD) to address this issue. CCD facilitates security responses by collecting data, making it conform to a standard format, and storing it on a common platform. CCD enhances the responder's ability to understand events and direct accurate responses. CCD also enhances security reporting capabilities to management and customers.

Response is a first principle in security tactics. The ability to respond to and resolve security incidents rapidly is essential to effective security management. Most organizations have an organized incident response capability. But response is only as effective as the detection and alerting mechanisms that drive it and the quality of information that is being provided to it. Rapid response must be one of your key security strategies for two simple reasons: It is a first principle of security, and it is the most visible function that security provides. When security controls work well, nothing bad happens, and it is hard to show value based on nothing! Response is the one component of security that is very visible. If done well, it's one of the best demonstrations of the value security brings to the organization.

Chapter 12

Keep Your Enemies Closer

Keep your friends close, and your enemies closer.

Sun Tzu

Introduction

This chapter focuses on two personnel-related tactics: hiring a hacker and countering insider threat. The "hire a hacker" tactic is based on the idea that hiring someone good at finding security flaws in systems provides a defensive advantage. The assumption is that these individuals are more likely to find flaws in a system before it is released or goes into production and hopefully, before one of the bad guys does. The reviews on this strategy are mixed. Most security professionals say no, while some security service companies would say yes. One example that stands out is @Stake, which hired a number of hackers from L0pht Heavy Industries (a band of well-known Boston-based hackers). Whether or not this is a good tactic really depends on the objectives you are trying to achieve. Some in the industry say hiring a hacker is too risky and increases the threat of insider attacks.

Insider threat (the threat of malicious activities by internal staff) has become a major topic of concern in the industry since the terrorist attacks against the United States in September 2001. Much of it is focused around the protection of critical infrastructure, but the problem is systemic. Incidents of insider malfeasance costing millions of dollars are present in every business sector. Insiders that go bad typically cause three times the damage that external attackers cause, including damages resulting in permanent data loss. Despite the dangers, most organizations do not actively manage their insider risks. Hopefully, the information contained in this chapter can help reverse that trend.

Before we delve into those objectives, it is probably worthwhile to define the various definitions applied to "hacker." The term *hacker* is typically broken down into three categories: white-hats, black-hats, and gray-hats. These terms do not have hard and fast definitions; instead they characterize the types of activities these individuals are involved in. Before Hollywood and the media turned hackers into people who illegally broke into computer systems (e.g., *War Games*), the term *hacker* referred to someone who was a clever programmer. *The New Hacker's Dictionary* (Raymond,

1996) puts it this way: "A person who enjoys learning details of a programming language or system; A person who enjoys actually doing the programming rather than just theorizing about it; A person capable of appreciating someone else's hacking; A person who picks up programming quickly; A person who is an expert at a particular programming language or system, as in Unix hacker." Today, such persons fall into the white-hat category: security researchers, ethical hackers, and others who use their skills to benefit information security and to protect the public.

The opposite are black-hat hackers. These are people who use their skills to commit malicious or illegal acts, usually for personal gain or notoriety. Crackers (people who illegally break into computer systems), as well as spyware and virus authors, fall into this category.

In the middle are the gray-hats, people whose activities may result in an illegal compromise of a system but not for malicious purposes. Instead, the goal is to better protect the public by identifying flaws and helping system owners to close them. It is not unusual for gray-hats to have an active presence in the black-hat community, having gained some notoriety from their exploits. We use the term *hacker* to refer to someone in any of these groups, security researcher or white-hat to reference well-intended professionals, and black-hat to designate persons with nefarious intent. The use of the term *gray-hats* is contextual.

Another aspect of hacking worth understanding is motivation. While white-hats and gray-hats may have different reasons for pursuing their craft, both are ultimately interested in protecting the public through improved information security. This is clearly NOT the motivation of black-hats. In the black-hat community there are three primary motivations: reputation, profit, and intelligence. Many hackers start out motivated by reputation; they desire to demonstrate their technical prowess and gain acceptance within the hacking community. The story of Phantomd (recounted in @ *Large: The Strange Case of the World's Biggest Internet Invasion*) is a great example. Phantomd's primary motivation was curiosity; he wanted to see what he could gain access to. Aided by a few "friends" in the hacking community and tremendous persistence, Phantomd managed to break into computer systems at hundreds of university, military, research, and business sites. Although his intentions were not particularly malicious, his "experiments" did cause some of the systems he broke into to malfunction or crash, and when he broke into the system controlling the central California dams, he put thousands of lives at tremendous risk. Phantomd gained notoriety and contributed to the exploits of other hackers by sharing his techniques and code, but he wasn't criminally motivated. This brings us to our second class of black-hats: profit-motivated hackers or cybercriminals. Their activities are primarily computer- or electronic-based versions of scams, forgeries, extortions, and thievery that have been prevalent in other forms for years. Prominent examples include the following:

- Russian hacker Vladimir Levin, who managed to steal some $10 million from Citibank in 1995
- Barry Schlossberg's extortion of $1.4 million from CD Universe in 2000
- Brian Salcedo's installation of a program at Lowe's headquarters in North Carolina to capture credit card numbers in 2004
- The millions of dollars of false credit card charges that resulted from CardSystems loss of 14 million credit card numbers in 2005
- The shutdown of E-Gold online payment services for money laundering in 2006
- John Schiefer's use of illegally installed botnets to steal the online banking identities of 250,000 Windows users in 2008
- The Hannaford Supermarket hack who stole 4.2 million debit card and credit card numbers from its computer systems, resulting in a minimum of 1,800 incidences of credit or debit card fraud in 2008

Though spectacular, none of these examples comes close to the $500 million lost in phishing attacks in 2008 in the United States alone.

A second class of "for-profit" hackers comes under the title of "exploits for sale." These are people who find exploitable flaws in products, and rather than notify the vendor of the flaw so it can be fixed, they sell the flaw to someone who will use it for illicit purposes. One example of this type of activity is WabiSabiLabi (WSLabi) in Switzerland. WSLabi is a website that conducts eBay-style auctions for exploits. Some contend that this is not necessarily black-hat activity; for legitimate security researchers (white-hats), this can be a potential revenue stream for the flaws they discover (especially if the vendor refuses to provide renumeration). Most security experts would disagree; the more probable result of this activity is the fast tracking of dangerous code (i.e., zero-day exploits) into the hands of criminal or espionage groups. This leads us to our third class of black-hats: spies.

Hackers who compromise systems for intelligence gathering or cyberwarfare fall into this class of black-hats. This activity is usually limited to government agencies but can be used for corporate espionage as well. One of the best examples of government-sponsored activity is Titan Rain—a ring of Chinese hackers accused of breaking into computer systems at U.S. military bases, defense contractors, and aerospace companies between 2003 and 2005. Examples of cyber-based corporate espionage are numerous; one recent example is Starwood Hotels' lawsuit against Hilton Worldwide alleging the theft of some 100,000 electronic files containing proprietary and confidential company information by two employees just prior to their defection to the Hilton group.

These hacker types (white-hats, gray-hats, and black-hats) and motivations (public good, reputation, profit, and espionage) provide the basis for understanding the majority of the material in the remainder of this chapter.

Hire a Hacker Objectives

Not all hackers are spies per se, but they all have something in common with spies: They all gather intelligence. Spying is a long-standing military tactic for meeting both offensive and defensive objectives. On the offensive side the intelligence gained from spying on an enemy can be used to identify enemy positions, armament, and defensive weaknesses. This information is used to execute attacks and other offensive movements more effectively and successfully. On the defensive side, the intelligence gathered can be used to plan and deploy countermeasures that will reduce the effectiveness of enemy attacks against your position. This is equally true in the IT arena.

Offensive Objectives

Hiring clever people (i.e., hackers) to fight cyberwars against other cyberoperatives may indeed be a good tactic, especially from a military perspective. Military forces are increasingly dependent on computers and network infrastructure for command, control, and communications (C^3). The ability to disrupt or destroy this capability gives an enemy significant advantage. Furthermore, if one can cripple the civilian critical infrastructure (power, telecom, transportation, etc.), you can shut down entire cities or regions and cause massive civil unrest. A government dealing with internal strife has less time to focus on external (international) activities such as military actions and diplomacy. Today, the vast majority of this infrastructure is computer controlled and network connected, including power grids, traffic signals, radio towers, subway systems, and so on.

The ability to distract a commander or divert forces by causing catastrophic events like flooding (opening dam flood gates), explosions, and fires (power grid overloads) is equally as effective. In the past these attacks required physical access; today, they can be carried out from anywhere due to the wonders of the Internet and computerized control systems. These types of offensive activities are usually confined to military and government intelligence agencies where time, effort, and costs are not significant factors. Information warfare has three primary attributes: reconnaissance, acquisition, and disruption. Reconnaissance in offensive terms is learning about your enemy's strengths, weaknesses, plans, and schedules. Information can be gathered by compromising e-mail accounts, eavesdropping on Web conferences, intercepting message transmissions, and the like. Acquisition is gaining access to an enemy asset for sabotage, theft, tampering, or monitoring purposes. Attacks include password cracking, buffer overflow exploits, SQL injection, and others. Disruption is using an acquired asset or other means to disrupt or deny your enemy access to critical information or functions. Destruction of data, logic bombs, equipment shutdowns, and falsification of critical data are some of the options. When these activities are controlled by the military or government agencies (e.g., the CIA), a fair number of checks and balances can be in place to prevent abuses. Outside of the military and government purview, these skills can be used for corporate espionage.

Corporate espionage is the gathering of intelligence that can be used to maintain or gain competitive or financial advantage. According to the Society of Competitive Intelligence Professionals (SCIP), corporations spend more than $2 billion annually to keep tabs on one another. While SCIP promotes ethical techniques for information gathering, there are many less ethical techniques that can produce more desirable results. Hacking into computer systems to acquire client lists, personnel records, financial data, trade secrets, pricing information, production plans, and research and development data is one such technique that is well suited to a hacker skill set. Other "softer" techniques such as social engineering can be used to gain entrance into online corporate conferences (i.e., NetMeeting, WebEx, etc.), social networks, and collaboration shares. While the world tends to view hacking as illustrating technical skills, Kevin Mitnick is more famous for his social engineering skills. In his book *The Art of Deception*, Mitnick points out how worthless firewalls, encryption, and other technical controls are against a gifted social engineer. Ira Winkler, in his book *Corporate Espionage,* details a number of different techniques he has used to exploit human targets.

Although we certainly do not advocate unethical techniques for intelligence gathering, if this is one of your strategic objectives, hiring a hacker may be a good tactic. There is one caveat, however: Make sure you keep a good eye on their activities lest their efforts be turned inward and you become the target.

How to Use This Tactic for Offense

Maintaining an offensive hacking capability is an expensive proposition and the primary reason why these activities are usually confined to military and government agencies. Part of the expense is related to hiding the activity from the ones being targeted, and the other is providing the means necessary to properly monitor agent activities to identify and thwart potential abuses. Most non-government entities outsource offensive intelligence gathering to a competitive intelligence (CI) professional (i.e., an ethical corporate spy); the exception might be large enterprises involved in highly competitive endeavors. These organizations may choose to keep some intelligence gathering activities in-house. It really depends on the level of intelligence needed, the effort required to gather it, and the costs involved.

SIDEBAR: AUTOMATED ATTACK SCENARIO

Observing offensive intelligence gathering isn't difficult. On any given day, an Internet-connected firewall will log hundreds, if not thousands, of packets attempting to exploit the latest discovered vulnerability or any number of older ones. These types of attacks are easy to automate across a range of IP addresses, and once they are set in motion all the attacker needs to do is wait for notification of a vulnerable system and follow up on the exploit. One wouldn't think that this technique would be terribly effective, but it is.

Far too often the procedures for deploying and maintaining Internet facing systems fail to adequately address security. This was the case with a defense contractor Bill helped a few years back. Someone built a new Windows 2000 Server system for database management in the DMZ. They did a good job of securing the sequel (SQL) database application but failed to properly configure security on the host operating system, including leaving the default Web service unpatched and fully operational. Needless to say, one of these offensive sweeps found the vulnerability, and the attackers followed it up by exploiting a buffer overflow in the Web service, gaining system (root) access to the box and proceeding to compromise every system in the DMZ, as well as a number of systems on the internal LAN that connected to the DMZ. It's difficult to say how much damage was done, but the price tag for investigating and repairing the breach exceeded half a million dollars.

Defensive Objectives

Most security groups use intelligence gathering for defensive purposes. Defensive objectives have three principal attributes: reconnaissance, preparedness, and assessment. Reconnaissance for defensive purposes focuses on learning what is being targeted, attack tools and techniques, and emerging threats. Preparedness focuses on countering planned attacks, and assessment focuses on reducing potential attack avenues (vectors).

> In preparing for Information Warfare, one must fortify his castle with proactive layers of security, thereby creating his defensive paths and direct the defense instead of following the dictates of the attacker.
>
> **Richard Forno and Ronald Baklarz**

Reconnaissance is a critical component of a good defense. The more you know about your opponent's capabilities and attack plans, the better you will be able to plan and deploy the resources needed to minimize their effectiveness. During the early years of the Internet, reconnaissance was a lost art. Security and networking professionals were aware of dangers like Distributed Denial of Service (DDoS) attacks, but no one was actively working on defenses against those attacks—nor was anyone tracking what malicious code the hacking community was developing. Then one day in 2000 hackers hit eBay, Yahoo, Amazon, and E*Trade with a massive DDoS attack, and suddenly understanding DDoS attacks and defenses became a critical part of defensive security planning. The pattern was similar for other attacks as well: little reconnaissance, ineffective responses, and massive damage.

Today, that pattern has changed substantially; there is more emphasis on preparedness. Large software vendors and Internet Service Providers (ISPs) work together to quickly identify and thwart attacks, and several employ spies to recon hacker activities. One company even used a widely publicized hack of their website to "up" the notoriety of their staff spy in the hacker community. His (phony) achievement gave him celebrity status and access to a much broader array of hacking activities. Some might classify this tactic as offensive rather than defensive, and that might be true if the purpose was infiltration. Infiltration tactics involve getting past the enemy's frontline defenses and attacking lightly defended rear areas. Paratroopers were used for this purpose in World War II. But that isn't what we are talking about here; we are only gathering intelligence. We are not trying to put them out of business; that's the work of law enforcement. Communications companies such as AT&T do extensive traffic analysis to identify attack patterns. Microsoft and other vendors of security products track malware outbreaks. Still others employ Honey Pot Systems to recon potential exploits and intrusions, and to capture malicious code for submission to antivirus vendors. Honey Pots are basically decoy systems that conduct passive reconnaissance. When attacked, they respond as a real system would, but in the background they are capturing information about the attacker and the tools/exploits they are using.

Reconnaissance is one potential reason for hiring a hacker, although this has more to do with a hacker's social connections than it does with their technical skills. Someone who is an active member of the hacker community has the ability to gather information about emerging exploits, targeted systems, and hacking trends. This information can be used to facilitate preparedness through the identification of potential exploits and the deployment of appropriate countermeasures.

Assessment, hiring hackers to find flaws and potential exploits in your systems, is also a good defensive tactic, especially for systems exposed to the Internet. Assessment efforts include hiring code reviewers and security testers during product development, as well as employing penetration testers when the original and subsequent revisions of the code are placed into production. Microsoft's Security Development Lifecycle (SDL) is a great example of this tactic. SDL incorporates a number of different processes designed to improve the quality and security of code. The SDL process includes security testing at multiple levels. Development teams perform regular security testing during the development cycle, and the Secure Windows Initiative (SWI) team performs additional testing when the product is code complete. When Microsoft built the initial SWI team, it actively recruited a number of well-known security researchers to work on the team. While SWI focuses on product security, other teams within the company manage SDL for programs used internally and for customer-facing services, including Xbox Live, Microsoft Online, MSN, and Microsoft.com. In addition to these code review and testing teams, Microsoft maintains its own penetration test team and hires third parties to perform testing and product security reviews.

How to Use This Tactic for Defense

Hiring someone full time to perform defensive intelligence gathering is cost prohibitive for most organizations, but there are a number of excellent subscription services such as the SANS Internet Storm Center that provide excellent reconnaissance information. Source code reviews and penetration testing services are readily available from a number of third-party firms, and the results tend to be more comprehensive because of the breadth of experience of the people involved. The exceptions to this rule would be government agencies and some larger enterprises. These organizations have the resources, time, and motivation needed to do in-house testing. Microsoft's SWI team is one example. Microsoft also maintains a reconnaissance capability through its relationships with security researchers and hacker communities. In addition to cost, the time and effort involved can be substantial. It is rumored that in addition to costing millions of dollars to perform security reviews for Vista, the time those reviews took also contributed to the lengthy delay of its initial release.

There are also some real advantages to hiring hackers for certain types of security engagements. For penetration testing, the real-world experience of a former hacker is particularly valuable. Compromising the security of a system requires the application of multiple techniques. Books can explain the techniques; real-world experience can apply them. Hackers are also very adept at developing the tools required to exploit systems. Once, while doing a code review on a system, Bill pointed out a potential security flaw to a colleague (a former kernel developer for the Santa Cruz Operation). In less than an hour, the developer generated the proof-of-concept code needed to prove the flaw was exploitable.

SIDEBAR: SECUREPOINT HIRES A BLACK-HAT

Microsoft restricted its hiring for the Secure Windows Initiative to white-hat hackers, but in the past few years, a number of companies have hired "reformed" black-hats to help improve the security of their products or to increase the effectiveness of their services. SecurePoint's hiring of Sven Jaschan (the confessed creator of the Sasser virus) is a notable example. SecurePoint builds firewall appliances with antivirus and anti-spam capabilities; if SecurePoint's objective is to improve the effectiveness of their products, hiring someone credited with creating 70% of the world's viruses seems to be a reasonable course of action. Not every professional would agree, including the CEO of H+BEDV who canceled the company's partnership with SecurePoint the day they hired Jaschan.

Summary

The use of "hackers" within an IT security context is entirely dependent on the objectives you are trying to achieve. The use of criminal agents (black-hats) is justified only if your objectives are clandestine in nature and the agents can be closely monitored to ensure their efforts are not turned inward. Clandestine activities tend to be offensive in nature and support the tactical principles of observation and preparedness. This activity also supports rapid response in the sense that it allows a targeted entity to respond with equally devastating blows. Furthermore, this type of activity involves a small force, concentrated on limited targets and usually not in harm's way. On rare occasions, the use of black-hats to improve the effectiveness of security products may be justified, but, in general, the use of criminal elements to protect information systems is discouraged. The time, effort, or costs involved in clandestine activities is not a factor for government-sponsored activities, but corporations need to weigh the cost and benefits before funding such efforts. Reconnaissance is probably the best benefit of hiring a black-hat hacker, but expecting a black-hat to do full-time reconnaissance is probably a little unrealistic.

The contrasting alternative is the use of security researchers, code reviewers, and penetration testers (i.e., white-hats) to improve the defensive capabilities of systems and products. This is considered to be a sound practice. With the exception of organizations with a large Internet presence or highly sensitive data, outsourced services seem to be the better and more cost-effective way to accomplish these objectives.

Gray-hat hackers are an enigma. Although their intent is not malicious, some of their activities are nonetheless criminal and could result in harm to the party they are purporting to help. The level of trust you put in someone who is willing to break the law on the pretense that it achieves a greater good is really a judgment call. Gray-hats also provide a reconnaissance benefit because of their reputation and contacts within the hacking community. Caution in hiring and a strong monitoring program seem to be the best overall approach.

The Hire a Hacker Controversy

The main controversy in the industry surrounding the use of hackers is primarily related to the question of trust. White-hat (ethical) hackers and security researchers are considered trustworthy and smart hiring decisions. Hiring "reformed" black-hat hackers is generally considered unacceptable. For all practical purposes, you are hiring a former criminal to maintain the security of your company's or customer's information. It's hard to justify that thinking to your partners, customers, and stakeholders unless you have an ironclad way to monitor exactly what that person is doing.

Mitnick Security Consulting serves as a good example. Here's a security services organization owned by a convicted hacker who, according to the company's website, never did anything wrong (or at least didn't deserve to be convicted of doing anything wrong). The company offers a large array of security consulting services, but other than Kevin Mitnick's experiences compromising system security, it's difficult to understand how this organization has anything more to offer than those staffed by experienced white-hats. The question becomes one of trust. Which is more trustworthy, a company run by a convicted criminal or a company run by certified security professionals?

Misplaced trust can prove disastrous. The best way to deal with this risk is to have an ironclad way to monitor what people are doing and to validate that those activities are appropriate for their assigned duties. This includes technical activities, as well as personal behaviors such as moods, attitudes, and interactions with other people. Ideally, this level of technical and supervisory monitoring should be standard practice for all employees because they all represent an insider threat. When you hire a former black-hat, technical and supervisory monitoring is mandatory; unfortunately many organization are not equipped to do this competently. This can be less of an issue if the activities of the individual can be limited or isolated—for example, they do not have access to internal systems or resources. Separation of duties is another alternative. In this scenario, a person is not given enough authority to accomplish a high-risk transaction by themselves; rather, the transaction requires the participation of another party to be completed.

Another potential challenge is connectivity. If your operations are designed to be clandestine, it will be necessary to develop a means of hiding the identity of your organization and operatives. This may involve the development of custom code or the engagement of external services. This is equally true for some of the tools you may require for these activities.

Hiring gray-hats has its own challenges. How much trust can you put in someone who is willing to break the law on the pretense that it achieves a greater good? Such logic is questionable at best; it is seldom necessary to actually compromise a system to demonstrate that a flaw exists. If the goal is to be able to prove there is an exploitable flaw, the better course would be to wait until after you have notified the system owner. If they don't believe you, then you have an opportunity to demonstrate the exploit to them. Take this scenario, for example: A gray-hat discovers a flaw in a system at a law firm. After compromising the system, he runs a directory listing of the files he can access and sends it to one of the partners of the firm. When the partner looks at the list of files, he comes unglued because this "well-intended" gray-hat has just compromised the integrity of thousands of pieces of evidence!

Another consideration has to do with a person's willingness to extend gray-hat logic beyond information security. Suppose such a person discovered a business practice within the organization that he considers "injurious" to the public. Could you trust this person to abide by the nondisclosure agreement, when he is perfectly willing to violate the law for "the greater good"? Again, it is hard to justify that thinking to your customers, stakeholders, and partners if you do not have a strong way of monitoring their activities. (See Chapter 9 for further discussion on monitoring and compliance.)

Another challenge to reconnaissance is corroborating the information gleaned from hacker communities. The information may be incomplete, inaccurate, or overstated, making it difficult to determine what, if any, response is needed and, if needed, what is appropriate. A similar issue is true of any hacking tools sourced from a black-hat community; they must be checked for malicious code before they can be used. If hackers are willing to put attack code on their websites, they are certainly willing to put it in the software they build.

Trust is the main issue involved with the hiring of hackers. White-hat (ethical) hackers are considered trustworthy, but "reformed" black-hat hackers are generally considered to be unwise hires. As suggested earlier, it's hard to justify hiring a former criminal to maintain the security of your own or your customer's information. This is equally true of gray-hats because of the questionable logic behind breaking the law on the pretense of achieving a greater good. A high level of technical and supervisory monitoring is the only sensible way to address these risks, but competence in these areas is lagging in many organizations. The reliability of the information gathered from hacker communities is also of concern, as is the reliability of tools sourced from black-hat sites.

Success Factors and Lessons Learned

Good intelligence, whether it is gathered for offensive or defensive purposes, is complete and accurate, and can be corroborated. This includes information about existing systems, products, and services, as well as information about pending attacks and attack trends gathered from hacker and nonhacker resources. The success factors aren't that much different for offensive intelligence gathering except for the stealth factor (not getting caught doing it) and the exploit factor (using the information to successfully "acquire" an enemy resource).

Being able to fix security flaws in products and services before they become exploitable vulnerabilities is an important cost-reduction measure in both patching and updating costs and liability avoidance. It is also a major competitive advantage. Building products and taking steps to prepare for and counter the next wave of attacks are other great results that can be realized from hiring a hacker. Just remember, however: Misplaced trust can be disastrous if you are dealing with people of questionable character.

The best lessons learned in this discussion are from Microsoft's Secure Windows Initiative (SWI). SWI is credited with finding and helping to fix over 500 security flaws in Microsoft Windows products since its inception in 2004. Microsoft's SDL process has reduced major vulnerabilities approximately 50% generation after generation of their product releases. One of the most outstanding examples is the Internet Information Service, which has suffered no significant security issues since the version 6 release. Much of this success can be credited to the outstanding work of the SWI team of white-hats.

SIDEBAR: HIRED HACKER GONE BAD

Ethics appears to be the primary concern when the industry talks about hiring gray- and black-hats. Despite this concern, the authors were unable in all our research for this book to find any examples of a hired hacker gone bad. That's not to say it hasn't happened, but just that we were never able to find a news story or any article corroborating the notion that hiring a former gray- or black-hat to do security-related work represents an inordinate risk. In fact the research is actually tilted in the other direction. National Infrastructure Advisory Council (NIAC) research into employee screening practices concluded that the presence of a criminal history record was not in or of itself a clear indicator of risk. NIAC did find a consensus among experts that for some types of convictions broadly applicable risks are present. However, "for other types of convictions, research on recidivism indicates that risk diminishes with age and time." In other words, the "I was a stupid kid" argument seems to have some merit. The NIAC report also points out, "Currently, there is no research available that directly correlates criminal conviction history with employee risk." However, when combined with other factors such as a propensity for pushing boundaries, breaking rules, substance abuse, and antisocial behavior, criminal history definitely contributes to the appraisal of someone's overall trustworthiness.

Control Objectives

There are four primary risks associated with the hire-a-hacker tactic: malicious insider, target retaliation, target deception, and malicious code implantation. These risks apply equally to the offensive and defensive elements, although the attributes may be slightly different. The offensive element also carries with it a risk of being caught. In the government arena, this is the threat of diplomatic or legislative repercussions. In the business world, it is the threat of criminal prosecution.

Our definition of a malicious insider is based on the NIAC definition of insider threat. We prefer the NIAC definition because it encompasses both IT and physical security. A malicious insider is "someone with the access and/or inside knowledge of an organization that would allow them to exploit the vulnerabilities of the entity's security systems, services, products or facilities with the intent to cause harm." "Someone with access" encompasses current or former employees, contractors, partners, and anyone else within the organization's "circle of trust" that at some point in time had legitimate access to these assets. Target retaliation is the threat of reprisal for your offensive actions against a target or for your deception in defensive actions. Target deception is the reverse: The target attempts to bait you into some kind of action by appearing as something it is not, feeding you phony or unreliable information or supplying you with bogus or malicious software. The threat of malicious code is always a concern when dealing with black-hats. Drive-by attacks when visiting hacker websites as well as malicious code in downloaded hacker tools are two common methods used to implant malicious code on a system.

Countering Insider Threats (Malicious Insider)

The "insider threat" has been a major topic of discussion in the security community for a number of years. Insider threat is a trust issue: People are entrusted with certain assets at the time they are employed or associated with the firm. Different degrees of trust exist based on the sensitivity or value of accessible assets. Highly trusted individuals, such as system administrators, are given control over a broad spectrum of resources. When someone deliberately betrays that trust, the results can be devastating to the organization, its employees, and its customers. Hiring someone with a nefarious background only heightens the potential for malicious insider activity. While this is a legitimate concern, insider threat extends beyond hacker hires; it applies to all employees because all employees have the ability to commit malicious insider acts.

SIDEBAR: ROGUE ADMINISTRATOR

One of the most difficult situations for an organization to deal with is a rogue administrator. A few years ago the company Bill worked for was called in to investigate an attempted compromise of an executive's mailbox. No data had been compromised; the real concern was who had gone bad. Either the administrator account had been compromised or one of the 13 people in the organization who knew the administrator password had used that knowledge to alter an e-mail security file. Based on the logs and file permissions, the latter was the more likely scenario. As security professionals, the first question that comes to mind is, why were they allowed to log on using the administrator account in the first place? That's a good question, but it pales in comparison to, "Who can I no longer trust?" Yes, best practice says to eliminate or very carefully control the use of the administrator account, and going forward this would be the standard practice at this firm. But the question the IT director still had to deal with was, "Who can I no longer trust?" We entrust our administrators with full access to our systems and system content; when that trust is violated, it's a devastatingly serious situation. Today it was a mailbox; tomorrow it could be all the credit card records.

As security consultants, one of the oddest questions we get asked is, "How can I restrict administrator access to a system?" You can't! This is why it's called the administrator account. You can change file permissions and encrypted data, and you can do any number of other things to try and limit what the system administrator can access on a system, but at best it only slows the user up. An all-powerful user has the ability to circumvent any control and to cover up the fact that he or she did it. This is why a rogue administrator is such a serious problem: If you cannot trust your administrators with the "keys to the kingdom," who can you trust?

There doesn't seem to be a consensus on the percentage of attacks that are insider driven (estimates range from 20 to 80%), but there is no doubt that insider attacks do the most damage.

The Verizon 2009 "Data Breach Investigation Report" shows that insider attacks have three times the impact of external attacks, and the CERT 2009 "Common Sense Guide to Prevention and Detection of Insider Threats" details damages from sabotage and theft that extend into the millions of dollars range.

> [A] hostile insider with access to vulnerable critical systems, potentially combined with knowledge of that system has the potential to cause events that would far exceed the consequences of an intrusion or attack.
>
> **The Insider Threat to Critical Infrastructures**
> *NIAC Report, April 2008*

One other thing existing research underscores is just how poorly the industry is dealing with the situation. Most companies do not actively manage their insider risks. Corporate culture, organization, and leadership are three big factors. Companies want to trust their employees (especially long-timers), and they find it distasteful to "spy" on them. The lack of convergence in security management also hampers mitigation efforts by limiting data exchanges between access control systems and IT identity management functions. A study group sponsored by the Computer Security Institute in 2007 concluded, "Surveys have shown corporate leadership understands that insider incidents occur, but it appears corporate leadership neither completely appreciates the risk nor realizes the potential consequences." The problem extends to supervisors as well. Supervisors seldom have the time or the training needed to identify and mitigate employee issues before they become malicious. This was another interesting finding in the research: Virtually all inside attackers manifest the same behavior patterns leading up to their malicious actions (e.g., stress, anger, disrespect, etc.), but, for the most part, their supervisors ignore these patterns. Enforcement is another management problem. The enforcement of security policies and standards at most organizations is inconsistent or lackadaisical at best, and security is seldom granted the authority to enforce compliance. Another major challenge to insider threat mitigation is technology. The technologies we need to hold people accountable for their actions are lacking, including the ability to:

■ Manage and maintain employee identities across multiple platforms
■ Create and preserve audit trails of employee actions
■ Consolidate and collate data
■ Detect patterns of malicious insider activities

Nonetheless, accountability remains the best tactic for dealing with malicious insiders; followed by competent supervision and comprehensive employee screening. (Accountability tactics and control objectives are covered in detail in Chapter 10 and will not be repeated here.)

Competent Supervision

Supervision and supervisory controls have been in place in the banking industry for decades. Separation of duties, forced vacations, job rotation, and other measures are all designed to reduce the likelihood of fraud, theft, or other types of malfeasance in environments with sensitive and high-value assets. Good supervisory controls in other environments are almost unheard of. Unlike banking where real money is involved, managers in other industries tend to be complacent about insider threat; that is, they do not associate malicious insiders with high-value losses. But a privileged user (one with root or admin access) can cause irreparable damage to company-owned information assets and cause huge downstream damages to company employees, customers, and other innocent victims—not to mention the hit the company's brand image and reputation will take. One incident reported by CERT involved a terminated employee who launched a logic bomb that deleted over 10 billion records from his former employer's servers. The restoration costs exceeded $3 million, and many records were permanently lost. It's amazing to think that in most companies, people with this level of access receive less supervision than a bank teller.

There are a number of contributing factors to this dilemma. Management complacency (or lack of awareness) is one; lack of proper training is another. The move away from command and control structures to empowered employees and self-directed teams is another. Cost cutting, work from home, and geographic dispersions are others. When cost-cutting measures are in place, managers end up supervising an increasingly larger number of employees. While government ratios remain in the 7 to 1 range, private industry ratios are double that and climbing! It's not unusual to have a "distant" manager in today's connected and geographically diverse work environments. When Bill worked at Predictive Systems' California office, the boss's office was in Reston, Virginia. He never actually met the boss in person: Meetings were by telephone, and he was even laid off by phone when the dot-com bust hit in 2000. Given the realities of today's business environment, it's unlikely these things are going to change, and for many job functions that's okay. But for high-privileged positions, that's not only dangerous but just plain stupid. Virtually every malicious insider attack we reviewed was discernible, but how do you discern bad behaviors when you don't actively engage with your workforce? The lack of direct (face-to-face) interaction can also be one of the causes for illicit behavior. People require care; we believe that fully one-third of a leader's time should be devoted to the people working for him or her. When mangers are swamped with duties and overloaded with people, people are the ones who suffer. Requests go unanswered, one-on-one meetings get canceled, and the attention and recognition people need get lost. Is it any wonder that employees get stressed out, dissatisfied, and disgruntled?

Competent supervision is a combination of supervisor and supervisory control objectives. Table 12.1 maps the attributes of these control objectives to specific user threat baselines. The type (hard or soft) is used to denote how evidence is collected for each control. Soft indicates a procedure-based control, while hard denotes a technology-based (i.e., automated) control.

Supervisor Attributes

Supervisor attributes apply to the managers and other personnel charged with the oversight of other workers, including employees, contractors, vendors, and partners working within their sphere of responsibility. This combination of workers is generally considered to be the organization's *staff*.

Trained

The "trained" control objective ensures that the supervisor has the proper knowledge, skills, and abilities (KSAs) to hire trustworthy individuals for security-sensitive positions and to properly monitor the activities of their staff against company requirements. Supervisors, especially those responsible for personnel with highly privileged access to company assets (i.e., servers, data warehouses, etc.) or access to high-value assets (i.e., bank accounts, payroll, etc.), need to be trained in

Table 12.1 Control Objectives for Malicious Insider Threats

Attribute/Control	Type	Risk and Requirements
Supervisor		
Trained	Soft	Supervisors of personnel with highly privileged access or access to sensitive information must be trained in: 1. Employee monitoring techniques 2. The recognition of behaviors indicative of malicious or potentially malicious acts 3. Proper response procedures for dealing with bad behaviors 4. Proper screening techniques for hiring
Observant	Soft	Supervisors of personnel with highly privileged access or access to sensitive information must consistently observe employee behaviors to detect illicit acts.
Enforcing	Soft	Supervisors must consistently enforce security policies and controls, including applicable sanctions for illicit employee acts.
Cautious hirer	Soft	Supervisors must exercise "due care" when hiring people for highly privileged or sensitive positions.
Supervisory		
Separation of duties	Soft	High-value or highly privileged actions cannot be completed by a single person; actions must require the participation of two separate persons for completion.
Least privilege	Hard	Privileged and high-value accesses must be confined to the specific assets the user requires to accomplish his or her assigned tasks.
Isolated	Hard	Personnel with highly privileged access or access to sensitive information must be physically and logically isolated from the systems used to monitor and record their activities.
Rotated	Soft	Personnel may be periodically moved to different positions, work locations, or shifts to reduce the likelihood of collusion with others for actions requiring multiple actors.
Rescreened	Soft	Personnel with highly privileged access or access to sensitive information must be periodically rescreened to identify factors related to their trustworthiness.
	Soft	Internal transfers and temporary staff transitioning to permanent positions must be rescreened to high-privilege/high-value position standards.
Forced leave	Soft	Personnel with highly privileged access or access to sensitive information may be required to take leave of a specific duration each year to facilitate the detection of illicit behavior.

proper staff-monitoring techniques, including technical and people-oriented sources of information. Supervisors must be able to recognize and respond to behaviors that violate company ethics, policy, or human resource standards. This includes internal and external behaviors that are common precursors to malicious acts such as co-worker abuse, repeated policy violations, and arrests. Supervisors must also be trained in proper screening techniques when hiring or contracting for positions with highly privileged access or access to high-value assets. Techniques may include additional background investigations, written assessments, and advanced interviewing procedures.

Observant

The "observant" control objective ensures that supervisors are doing "due diligence" in their management of staff security performance. As noted earlier, supervisors should devote one-third of their schedule to the oversight of their staff. Oversight includes both personal interactions and the review of technical control information (e.g., logs, alerts, video, etc.). Supervisors need to regularly review staff activities to identify violations of company ethics, policy, or human resource standards. Supervisors may choose to solicit additional information from other staff members as well. When personnel know that their activities are being observed (monitored), they are less likely to commit an act of malfeasance. In addition, regular reviews help the leadership identify areas where additional training or controls may be needed.

Enforcing

The "enforcing" control objective assures consistency in the application of policy requirements across the enterprise. Supervisors must actively manage policy violations by their employees. Disciplinary actions must be applied equally across the organization to avoid the appearance of favoritism. Employees must understand the value the organization places on security. When employees are subject to disciplinary actions, they are more diligent in adhering to policy requirements. Conversely, poorly enforced policies create an environment that is more susceptible to attack.

Cautious Hirer

The "cautious hirer" control objective ensures that supervisors have exercised "due care" when hiring people for highly privileged or sensitive positions. Due care implies that all reasonable and prudent measures were taken in the screening of a candidate for highly privileged or sensitive positions. Background checks should include fingerprint checks whenever possible to assure the positive identification of the applicant and a full-disclosure of criminal history. Other forms of evaluation that are recommended include psychological assessment questionnaires and drug testing.

Supervisory Attributes

Supervisory attributes apply to the management or limitation of personnel activities, for example, limiting their physical access to company facilities.

Separation of Duties

The "separation of duties" control objective ensures that high-value or high-impact actions cannot be carried out by one person, thus reducing the likelihood of malicious high-impact events.

Approvals are a simple example of this control, provided the approval is required before the transaction can be completed. This is a common source code control; new versions of the code cannot be checked into the source safe without the review and approval of the change control manager. More sophisticated versions of this control involve multiple parties to complete single tasks, for example, requiring two parties to simultaneously turn the keys to arm an ICBM (Intercontinental Ballistic Missile). This control object can be implemented as a procedure or a technical control. When the control is procedural, supervisors must make sure that the persons involved in the transaction are sufficiently isolated from each other to prevent collusion. Separation of duties is most commonly used for transactions involving money, intellectual property, source code, security devices, and backup and restore operations.

Least Privilege

The "least privilege" control objective makes sure that users and processes do not have access to assets that are not required for the proper execution of their assigned job or function. Least privilege is a very old security principle. Inside a castle compound, people were restricted to the area where they worked, and access to the lord's chambers was controlled by armed guards. Least privilege means you are explicitly allowed access to a specific set of assets and nothing else. However, the practical application of least privilege using today's general-purpose operating systems and business applications is extraordinarily difficult. Poorly designed applications, inadequate tools, and poor identity management practices all contribute to problems. The best compensation for the lack of technical controls is supervision. Supervisors should regularly monitor the activities of employees to ensure that they are not violating acceptable use guidelines by accessing information they have no legitimate need for. Accountability controls that record user access are useful for this purpose and often have configurable rules that can detect unauthorized activity. Today, least privilege in general-purpose computing is really a trade-off between functionality and protection; when protection cannot be achieved with technology, competent supervision is required.

Isolated

The "isolated" control objective ensures that personnel with highly privileged access or access to sensitive information are physically and logically isolated from the systems and processes used to monitor and record their activities. For example, access to system logs and logging services is restricted. When dealing with privileged users, isolation can be difficult to achieve. System administrators have the ability to disable audit/logging services and destroy or alter audit records. There is no practical way to prevent this, but it is possible to use a centralized monitoring and/or log collection service to capture these events to an incorruptible system (e.g., configuring systems to forward log entries to a Syslog server). While this tactic may not prevent a malicious user from disabling log forwarding, it will record the disablement event for future investigation. When technological controls are not in place, the best compensating control is competent supervision. Supervisors should regularly monitor employee activities for events indicative of "hiding"—that is, attempts to conceal their activities by deleting, falsifying, or altering audit records.

Rotated

The "rotated" control objective ensures that personnel with highly privileged access or access to sensitive information are periodically assigned to different positions, work locations, or shifts to reduce the likelihood of collusion and to highlight suspicious activities. Collusion between insiders is extremely high in attacks motivated by financial or business advantage. Moving people into different work environments helps break up opportunities for collusion and may provide other benefits, including better coverage from cross training and improvement in morale and performance for employees with tedious or boring jobs. In addition, rotating people facilitates the detection and correction of misbehaviors because the acts either cease once the person is gone or they follow the person to his or her next assignment. Rotation is a process-based control objective suitable for medium to large organizations where sufficient staff is present to make the practice effective or beneficial. Supervisors can plan the practice around skills management and security monitoring requirements and then use regular monitoring to correlate suspicious or unauthorized activities.

Rescreened

The "rescreened" control objective ensures that personnel with highly privileged access or access to sensitive information continue to have the trustworthiness commensurate with their job position. It also ensures that the internal resources for moving someone into a position of trust meet all applicable hiring standards. Management oversight is not limited to internal (job-specific) performance. Good supervision means involvement in the social aspects of people's lives, including events that are external to the workplace. The vast majority of insider attacks we have examined were associated with "stressor" events, some of which were internal but many others were external, including divorce, debt, addiction, and illness. Periodic rescreening provides supervisors with an opportunity to observe shifts in circumstances, attitudes, or behaviors that may affect a person's trustworthiness.

Forced Leave

The "forced leave" control objective requires that personnel with highly privileged access or access to sensitive information take leave for a specified duration each year to facilitate the detection of illicit behavior. Forced leave and rotation have similar control objectives. Forced leave can be used to facilitate the detection and correction of misbehaviors because the acts cease once the person is gone and return when they resume their duties. Forced leave is a process-based control objective suitable for organizations in which staffing limitations make rotation impractical. Supervisors may plan the practice around cross-training and security monitoring goals and then monitor actions to correlate suspicious or unauthorized activities. The following actions are recommended for competent supervisor control objectives:

1. Improve supervisory skills so that managers are cognizant of issues leading up to insider malfeasance and are equipped to take appropriate action before issues result in malicious activities.
2. Incorporate insider malfeasance into employee awareness training.
3. Update employee screening practices to include additional measures for sensitive or high-privileged positions, including a means to positively identify the applicant and get a complete criminal history. Improve hiring practices, including the addition of interview questions or questionnaires to evaluate ethical or moral attitudes. Create specific disqualification criteria when hiring for sensitive and high-privilege positions.
4. Improve the process and scope of account deactivation procedures to ensure a quick, comprehensive account deactivation upon termination.
5. Improve HR management policies and procedures to reflect changes in the hiring and termination processes.

6. Update the incident response plan to include procedures for malicious insider activities, such as procedures for the preservation of evidence on live systems (i.e., step away from your computer procedures).
7. Improve or initiate supervisory processes to mitigate insider threats, including supervisor monitoring, consistent policy enforcement, separation of duties, mandatory approvals, mandatory change control, job rotation, and forced leave.
8. Add insider threat to all audit and assessment criteria.
9. Improve or enable strong accountability controls, including stringent identity management and evidentiary-based audit trails for systems and applications. Use technologies to enforce isolation to preserve the content and integrity of log and audit data. Consider outsourcing log management and analysis to ensure isolation and improve detection and response to malicious activity.
10. Improve physical security controls and tracking (audit) mechanisms and collate physical and logical access records to detect suspicious or anomalous activities.

Employee Screening

The previous section touched on employee screening in the hiring process and for ongoing monitoring efforts; this section covers those attributes in greater detail. Employee screening is used for three basic scenarios: new hire, internal transfer or promotion, and periodic rescreening. Screening criteria will vary depending on the access privileges and the sensitivity or value of the data being accessed. The matrix presented in Table 12.2 is an example of how employee screening might be applied to various internal positions. Table 12.3 maps employee screening attributes to specific baselines.

In this example, all positions are subject to a baseline set of screening criteria; positions with privileged access or access to sensitive or high-value information are subject to an addition (superset) of screening criteria.

Baseline screening for all employees must be completed before they are granted access to company information systems and assets. Superset screenings should be completed before privileged or high-value access is granted, although granting access while the screening is completed may be acceptable for internal promotions.

Background Checks

Although listed as separate attributes, criminal, driving, and credit checks are common components of a standard employee background check, which typically includes employment, education,

Table 12.2 Screening Matrix

Scenario	Standard Access	Privileged Access	High Value Access
New hire	Baseline	All	All
Internal transfer or promotion		Super set	Super set
Temporary to permanent employee transition	Baseline	All	All
Periodic rescreening		All	All

Table 12.3   Control Objectives for Employee Screening

Attribute/Control	Type	Risk and Requirements
Baseline Screening		
Completeness	Soft	Baseline screening shall be conducted for all new hires, including temporary employees transitioning to a permanent position.
Criminal history check	Soft	A criminal history check shall be conducted using local and regional (state, providence, etc.) police records to verify full disclosure of criminal history and to identify patterns of conduct impacting trustworthiness.
Driving history check	Soft	A driving history check shall be conducted using local and regional (state, providence, etc.) records to identify patterns of conduct (e.g., recklessness, habitual offense) impacting trustworthiness.
Credit history check	Soft	A credit history check shall be conducted using a reliable credit-reporting source to identify patterns of conduct or financial impropriety impacting trustworthiness.
Employment verification	Soft	Employment history shall be verified, including employment dates and compensation claims to identify falsifications, omissions, or other facts impacting trustworthiness and to ensure that the applicant meets the minimum work experience requirements of the position.
Education verification	Soft	Postsecondary education claims, including degrees and professional certifications, shall be verified to identify falsifications or other facts impacting trustworthiness and to ensure that the applicant meets the minimum education requirements of the position.
Eligibility checks	Soft	Eligibility claims for preferential hiring such as veteran, disabled, displaced worker, and security clearance shall be verified to identify falsifications or other facts impacting trustworthiness.
Superset Screening		
Completeness	Soft	Superset screening shall be conducted for all new hires, internal transfers, promotions, temporary to permanent employee transitions to positions with privileged access, or access to sensitive or high-value information such as financials, intellectual property, and source code.
Disqualification	Soft	Disqualification criteria shall be developed to assist with the evaluation of superset screening results.
Identity check	Soft	The identity of the applicant shall be verified using the best possible means to ensure information pertaining to the trustworthiness of the applicant is not being concealed behind an alias.

Table 12.3 Control Objectives for Employee Screening (continued)

Attribute/Control	Type	Risk and Requirements
Criminal history check	Soft	A fingerprint-based criminal history check shall be conducted to verify full disclosure of criminal history and identify patterns of conduct impacting trustworthiness.
Preemployment testing	Soft	Testing, including lie detection and psychological assessments, may be conducted to supplement or verify applicant claims and trustworthiness.
Rescreening		
Completeness	Soft	Rescreening shall be conducted at prescribed intervals for all positions with privileged access, or access to sensitive or high-value information.
Review	Soft	Rescreening results shall be evaluated in accordance with established superset disqualification criteria to confirm that the employee meets the trustworthiness standard for the position he or she holds.

and eligibility verifications too. Most companies have screening practices that are sufficient for positions requiring ordinary user access to company resources. However, these screening standards are not usually applied to temporary (contracted) staff, vendor, or partner personnel. It is assumed that the agency or organization supplying the resource has screened them appropriately. *This is a bad assumption*; temporary staffing agencies do cursory checks at best and no checks at worst. Vendor-supplying services with high turnover rates (e.g., cleaning and moving) are not incentivized to conduct background checks. Partner organizations' screening practices may be subpar. It is in your organization's best interest to make sure that all parties requiring access to your assets meet your minimum screening criteria.

Secondary screening procedures for positions with high-privilege or high-value access are unusual in most business environments. This situation must be improved upon. Postmortem reviews of insider malfeasance often reveal criminal histories that were undisclosed and undiscovered during the hiring process. An additional area of concern is the failure to apply secondary screening when transferring or promoting internal employees. Behaviors exhibited in the current position may point to trust issues that are not acceptable for the new position. Failing to do secondary screening may promote someone into a position with a greater opportunity to do harm.

Identity Check

Nearly 12% of all fingerprint checks conducted by the FBI for employment and licensing purposes return names different from the ones provided. People wishing to hide their criminal history, illegal status, or nefarious trade (i.e., terrorist, spy, etc.) often use assumed names or stolen identities. When hiring to positions requiring high trust, a positive identification is essential. A skilled social engineer with privileged access can rob a company blind in a matter of days.

SIDEBAR: HOW I STOLE $30 MILLION

A number of years ago we read a story recounting the assessment of a computer chip manufacturer's security controls by a penetration testing team. The engagement included "hiring" one of the consultants as a temporary clerk in the IT department. Within hours of arriving for work, he had set up a number of interviews with department heads to discuss their security concerns. Posing as a senior security analyst, he charmed his way onto three departmental servers to "assess" their security controls. He then applied (online) for remote access privileges, which he received the following day. Using this access and the credentials he had on the departmental servers, a team of penetration testers went to work compromising a slew of internal systems. Meanwhile, the "temporary clerk" remained late one evening to walk the building with the CSO and see what he could "discover." It didn't take long; entering the office of one of the senior design engineers, he accessed an engineering workstation that was left logged on. Using a portable storage device, he then proceeded to download an entire set of engineering plans, at which point the CSO put an end to the exercise. In a span of three days, someone hired as a temporary clerk had orchestrated the root compromise of 24 computer systems and the theft of data valued at over $33 million!

Positive identification and full disclosure are essential components of trust and should not be bypassed or compromised for a position requiring a high level of trustworthiness.

Preemployment Testing

Preemployment testing can be used to supplement or verify applicant claims and trustworthiness. Drug screening tests are common, lie detectors less so. In between, there are a number of psychological tests, including tests designed to assess reasoning abilities, personality, and moral sense (ethics). Most are designed to be administered by professionals who can accurately assess the results, but this is a pretty expensive proposition. The alternative is self-assessment tests. The results for these tests tend to be broader and less reliable. Results are mapped against information collected from thousands of other test takers, and conclusions are generally accurate but not specific. We do not oppose the use of psychological testing as a supplemental factor in your trust evaluation; we only suggest that tests not administered by professionals be weighted appropriately.

Disqualification

Multiple people can look at the same data and come to very different conclusions. This isn't a particularly good scenario when you are trying to make hiring decisions for positions of high trust. A consistent means of evaluation is key to the success of the process. Not only do organizations need to establish good screening criteria, but they also need to define the metrics associated with those criteria. Since the process assumes trustworthiness and looks for patterns of conduct impacting that trust, these are, for all practical purposes, disqualification metrics. These metrics will be different depending on the organization and business sector. In general, candidates for positions of high trust who falsify, omit, or misrepresent facts on their application form or résumé would be disqualified. Egregious criminal or vehicular offenses or a pattern of fiscal irresponsibility are other disqualifiers. Defining your disqualification criteria assures a consistent screening result and may help guard against claims of favoritism or prejudice.

Rescreening

Rescreening, as already noted, is a periodic reaffirmation of an employee's trustworthiness. It is usually carried out in the background; that is, it does not require the employee's participation, but it is wise to inform the employee that rescreening is taking place. Getting notification that your company just pulled your credit history can be a little disconcerting if you weren't expecting it. Rescreening follows the same processes used above to collect and evaluate data except static information such as education and veteran status, which do not need to be reaffirmed. Regular rescreening is a standard process for personnel holding government security clearances, but, outside of government, it is very uncommon. The use of rescreening is really a judgment call; in organizations with competent supervision, the need to rescreen is diminished by supervisor interaction, monitoring, and care.

The following actions are recommended for the employee screening control objective:

1. Improve supervisory skills so that managers are cognizant of issues leading up to insider malfeasance and are equipped to take appropriate action before issues escalate into malicious acts.
2. Incorporate insider malfeasance into employee awareness training.
3. Update employee screening practices to include additional measures for sensitive or high-privilege positions, including a means to positively identify the applicant and get a complete criminal history. Improve hiring practices, including the addition of interview questions or questionnaires to evaluate ethical or moral attitudes. Create specific disqualification criteria when hiring for sensitive and high-privilege positions.
4. Improve the process and scope of account deactivation procedures to ensure a quick, comprehensive account deactivation upon termination.
5. Improve HR management policies and procedures to reflect changes in the hiring and termination processes described above.
6. Update incident response plans to include procedures for malicious insider activities, including procedures for the preservation of evidence on live systems (i.e., step away from your computer procedures).
7. Improve or initiate supervisory processes to mitigate insider threats, including supervisor monitoring, consistent policy enforcement, separation of duties, mandatory approvals, mandatory change control, job rotation, and forced leave.
8. Add insider threat to all audit and assessment criteria.
9. Improve or enable strong accountability controls, including stringent identity management and evidentiary-based audit trails for systems and applications.
10. Use technologies that preserve the content and integrity of log and audit data. Consider outsourcing log management and analysis to ensure isolation and improve detection and response to malicious activity.
11. Improve physical security controls and tracking (audit) mechanisms and collate physical and logical access records to detect suspicious or anomalous activities.

Target Retaliation

When you are conducting offensive maneuvers, there is always the chance that the entity you are targeting will discover your activities and retaliate. Hacker defacements of the entertainment industry's websites for actions against Napster, The Pirate Bay, and other music-sharing sites are noted examples. In cyberwarfare the stakes are much higher because the retaliating force may be able to affect critical resources and functionality. Defensive reconnaissance efforts (i.e., cyberspying), if discovered, may also invoke a retaliatory response. Massive denial of service attacks is not unusual; the attacks are generally short-lived, but they get the point across. The best tactic against retaliation is anonymity. It's difficult to be the direct recipient of a retaliation attempt if the target cannot identify you. This, incidentally, is the biggest issue associated with proactive defenses that launch counterattacks. Often they are targeting an innocent party and an unwitting participant.

Their system has been compromised and is being used to disguise the attackers' actual location. Depending on your jurisdiction, a retaliatory response may subject you or your organization to criminal charges and/or civil liabilities.

There are a number of ways to achieve anonymity, including hidden Internet Assigned Numbers Authority (IANA) registrations for specific IP ranges, but the more popular method is exploitation. Exploitation is the compromise of third-party systems or communications channels that is subsequently used to target other systems. Botnets are a great example; hackers and cybercriminals using various exploits implant a zombie on a victim's computer system and send it remote commands to carry out their illicit activities. For example, the Cimbot zombie uses the victim's e-mail accounts to send spam. Cimbots accounts for some 15% of the world's spam; that's about 13% of all e-mail! Botnets are also used for Distributed Denial of Service (DDoS) attacks. But exploitation doesn't necessarily have to involve remote control zombies; any access that allows the attackers to disguise their actual source address is sufficient, and it is not unusual for attackers to use multiple hops to make it more difficult to trace their actions back to the source.

In the popular book *The Cuckoo's Egg: Tracking a Spy through the Maze of Computer Espionage*, Markus Hess, a West German hacker, used up to 10 intermediate sites to disguise his hacking efforts against U.S. military sites, national laboratories, and NASA. It took more than two years to backtrack this maze of connections to Hess's telephone line. Another means of achieving anonymity is through account compromise or hijacking. Various means are used to capture a user's credentials (userID, password, session ID), which are then employed to conduct illicit activities. Because such usage is readily traceable to the source, hackers may use this technique in combination with a compromised system or a publicly accessible system (e.g., library computer, Internet café) for greater anonymity.

Defensive anonymity can use the same techniques to disguise the actual location of the agent, but the interactive nature of digital reconnaissance (i.e., chat rooms, blogs, etc.) makes it harder to maintain. Like any clandestine operation, there is always a possibility that the agent's cover will get blown. Black-hats tend to be smart intuitive people; they are not easily fooled or taken in, and they are not at all nice when they discover they've been had. Anonymity is the only real control objective associated with the target retaliation risk, and getting caught is the only real metric. Even with good anonymity controls, it is smart to prepare for massive retaliation attacks just in case your true identity is uncovered.

The following actions are recommended for the target retaliation risks:

1. Train your people. Spying, intelligence gathering, reconnaissance, whatever you choose to call it, is a craft. In fact, the CIA calls it "the craft." Training people in the craft, including how to maintain anonymity, build and promote a persona (cover), and avoid detection or tracing, are all important to their effectiveness. Natural ability, attitude, intelligence, and experience are the other ingredients.

2. Maintain separation. To the greatest extent possible, try to keep your reconnaissance activities completely separate from the agency or organization sponsoring them. There should be nothing on the systems used for reconnaissance associating it or the operator with the sponsor. If someone is going to retaliate, you want him to retaliate against the agent, not the organization.

3. Prepare for retaliation. Whether you are doing offensive or defensive intelligence gathering, when people discover what you are doing they are likely to retaliate. Be prepared for it by creating a good incident response process capable of managing the attack. You should be able to "pull the plug," rebuild the system, and be back in business as a different entity in a half hour or so.

4. Prepare an isolated environment. This is the technical side of maintaining separation. Systems used for reconnaissance should be completely isolated (physically and logically) from internal resources. This includes a separate dedicated Internet connection, preferably one that does not have a permanent IP address associated with it.
5. Identify, gather, and deploy tools that make it possible to quickly rebuild reconnaissance systems and to change identifiers, including system and account SIDs and MAC addresses.

Target Deception

The old proverb, "There is no honor among thieves," is certainly applicable to the black-hat world. Notoriety is one of the major motivators for hacking; money and espionage are the other two.

> It is important that you recognize your progress and take pride in your accomplishments. Share your achievements with others. Brag a little. The recognition and support of those around you is nurturing.
>
> **Rosemarie Rossetti**

Consequently, there is a propensity for bragging and exaggeration within the hacking community. Organizations may end up on expensive wild-goose chases if the information they gather is not properly vetted. In some instances, this misinformation may be intentional or retaliatory, designed to divert resources unnecessarily or lure you into a trap. Verification is the only real control objective associated with this risk. Before taking action on any piece of information from a black-hat source, it is best to confirm the contents first. Cross checking with reliable knowledgeable sources such as the Carnegie Mellon CERT and other white-hat reconnaissance efforts is the first step. Investigating the claim itself is the second step. Is it plausible? We get one of our favorite laughs when we see movie depictions of hackers sitting at computer consoles watching graphic displays of their hacking agent breaking through firewalls and other protections. Possible? Yes. Plausible? It's a stretch to say the least. Of course, vetting isn't all that it's cracked up to be either. The other parties could be deceived as well, so it is wise to be prepared, but only proceed when the evidence is compelling. If this approach had been taken for the DDoS threat, the attacks on eBay, Amazon, and E-Trade in 2000 would have had less impact. The weaknesses in the protocols were well known, brags in the hacker community abounded, and even some examples of attack zombies had been captured, but for some unexplained reason, the industry made no concerted effort to prepare for the attack.

SIDEBAR: LEVERAGING THE BRAG

Bragging has an interesting reconnaissance benefit. As Ralph Waldo Emerson points out, "There is also this benefit in brag, that the speaker is unconsciously expressing his own ideal. Humor him by all means, draw it all out, and hold him to it." In other words, it is possible to use a person's bragging to draw out additional details that will help you determine the legitimacy of his or her claim. Such efforts can also help you determine the type of hacker you are interacting with. Accomplished black-hats are not inclined to brag or readily advertise their tools of the trade. If you bait someone and get a cold response, you may want to pursue the conversation with a different tact.

The following actions are recommended for the target deception risks:

1. Identify resources that supply reliable, timely information, including organizations such as the Carnegie Mellon CERT and the SANS Internet Storm Center.
2. Collaborate with others doing the same type of reconnaissance and with security researchers who can perform proof-of-concept on new exploit claims.

3. Maintain separation. Never disclose your cover identity to anyone. Just because someone says he is a good guy doesn't make it so—black-hats do reconnaissance too!
4. Create a triage process for quickly vetting the information you gather so that you can prioritize what further actions will be taken.
5. Create a multistage set of procedures for evaluating threat information you gather to help you make appropriate decisions concerning defensive preparations. Triage should establish whether the information has merit or is simply a hoax (nonsense). Other stages should evaluate the potential impact, how imminent the act is, and how existing controls can be used to mitigate an attack. A staged procedure allows you to review results at the end of each stage to determine whether or not to proceed to the next stage.

Malicious Code Implantation

If you tease the bull, you're going to get horned.

Spanish proverb

The black-hat community is not a friendly one; exploiting newbies, script kiddies, and curious spectators is not unusual. Many hacking sites have drive-by and other Web-based attacks installed on them, and downloadable tools and utilities on these sites frequently contain malicious code. The primary control object for this risk is containment. Reconnaissance efforts will undoubtedly subject our systems to these types of attack attempts. If our goal is to understand these attacks and how they are executed, it's not necessarily wrong to allow this code onto our systems as long as we are able to contain it and prevent any significant damage. Table 12.4 lists a number of different attributes of the containment control objective.

Isolated

The last thing we want is to have our reconnaissance efforts cause a security incident in our internal business network. The best way to mitigate this possibility is to completely isolate the systems used for reconnaissance from internal resources. This includes physical and logical separation. Strongly recommended is a separate dedicated Internet connection, one that does not have a permanent IP address associated with it. One of the tricks we used to conceal our identity when doing penetration testing was to periodically force the Dynamic Host Configuration Protocol (DHCP) server to assign us a new IP address by altering the Media Access Control (MAC) address of the machine and then renewing the DHCP address. This is a useful technique if you come under a retaliation attack as well. Strong isolation is one of the best ways to contain the potential damages from implanted or downloaded malware.

Hardened

General-purpose operating systems, especially those intended for end-user systems, are designed for usability, which usually equates to a relaxed security configuration. This configuration isn't, however, acceptable for reconnaissance. Every reasonable precaution needs to be taken to ensure that systems used for reconnaissance cannot be compromised. Standard hardening practices apply. We recommend the NSA/CIA and NIST guides. Select the high-security option. Microsoft also has excellent security configuration guides on TechNet for their operating systems.

Table 12.4   Containment Control Objective

Attribute/Control	Type	Risk and Requirements
Systems		
Completeness	Soft	All systems used for reconnaissance shall be hardened to prevent and/or contain the effects of malicious code implantation.
Isolated	Soft	Systems used for reconnaissance shall be physically and logically isolated from the business network and systems.
Hardened	Hard	Systems used for reconnaissance shall be hardened to minimize potential attack vectors to include (but not limited to): - Removal of nonessential services and applications - Removal of nonessential network protocols - Disablement of nonessential accounts - Configuration of OS strong security features - Installation of all applicable security patches - Installation of protective mechanisms to ensure system integrity and detect malicious code and/or activity
Malware protected		Systems used for reconnaissance shall have protective mechanisms installed to detect, contain, or restrict the execution of malware; for example: - Antivirus protection - Anti-spyware or adware protection - Root kit and zombie detectors - File integrity checkers - Intrusion prevention agents
Privilege restricted		The operators of systems used for reconnaissance shall log on using standard (nonprivileged) user accounts and use OS utilities to escalate privileges when necessary.
Software		
Source code formatted	Soft	The preferred format for all externally acquired applications is source code. Binaries, including executables and linked libraries, are to be avoided whenever possible.
Scanned	Hard	All software acquired from external sources shall be scanned for malicious content using multiple scanning engines.
Execution restricted	Hard	All software acquired from external sources shall be restricted (e.g., in a sandbox) in its execution, including its ability to access or modify critical system components or configurations.
Execution reviewed	Both	Software acquired from external sources may be monitored during its execution to identify the presence of potentially malicious or dangerous functionality.
Code reviewed	Soft	All software acquired from external sources shall be code reviewed for malicious content. Software in binary formats shall be decompiled and the resulting source code reviewed for malicious content.

Malware Protected

Malware can be detected in multiple ways beginning with the content of the code (signature recognition), the behavior of the code (behavior recognition), or the results of the code's execution (modified files, running processes, open ports, etc.). Since the goal is containment, not prevention, tools that scan content need to be configured to quarantine not "clean" or reject malicious code. Behavior controls need to be configured to block potentially dangerous behaviors (e.g., attempting to modify a system file or configuration), and result-based tools need to be configured to detect anything that slipped through the previous two controls. Look for single-purpose, efficient, and accurate signature-based scanners. With over 2 million malware signatures to check, efficiency is critical. The same thing goes for behavior controls. You're looking for a self-contained, accurate intrusion prevent agent—in other words, something that works without a separate control console and does a good job of blocking bad behaviors. Finally, use tools that do a comprehensive job detecting unauthorized changes to files (i.e., Tripwire), as well as tools that can accurately detect running instances of malware, including root kits.

Privilege Restricted/Execution Restricted

The best privilege restriction is no privilege. Microsoft has an add-in for Windows (AppSec) that controls application execution. It can be somewhat challenging to use if you have a lot of scripts and external tools, but there is no better mechanism to prevent downloaded malware from doing damage. Sandbox solutions are the next best mechanisms; Java and DotNET have configurable privileges (permissions) controlling what executed code inside the sandbox is allowed to do. Vista and subsequent versions of Microsoft operating systems also have an integrity control that prevents downloaded code from accessing and modifying other files or system configurations.

Scanned

Any compile code (binaries) acquired from any external source should be subject to malware scanning by three separate scanning engines. E-mail scanning products typically use three out of a selection of five scanning engines to check messages and attachments for malware. If you don't have a separate system you can set up for scanning, you may be able to get the same results by attaching the code to an e-mail message and sending it to yourself. If the message loops through the mail system, chances are the code is clean, or at least free of any known malware.

Execution Reviewed

When source code is not available, it is prudent to perform an execution review of the code. An execution review captures the files and configuration data the program accesses, as well as any network traffic it generates. Reviewing the captured data can reveal suspicious or dangerous behaviors, for example, attempting to contact an external website. A good network sniffer is sufficient for the network capture; capturing file and configuration activities are platform specific, but good tools are available for most popular operating systems.

Code Reviewed

The preferred format for all tools acquired externally is source code. We are not saying it's impossible to hide malicious code in source code, but it's certainly a lot more difficult and it's nearly impossible to hide from a skilled code reviewer. Code reviews are your best defense against logic bombs, backdoors, and other types of malicious code in tools you acquire from black-hat resources—so much so that we recommend decompiling binaries and reviewing the resulting source code if source code is not available for a particular tool. The issue involved in doing code reviews is usually one of resourcing. Code reviews are tedious and time consuming and require a rather sophisticated set of skills, so there is a trade-off. Smaller utilities and tools should be source code reviewed. For larger applications, an execution review combined with other mitigation controls such as sandboxing and IPS may prove to be more cost effective.

The following actions are recommended for the malicious content implantation control objective:

1. Identify resources that can assist with code reviews and tool evaluations.
2. Develop appropriate procedures for dealing with malicious content to ensure that it is at all times contained to include management and custody controls for all media containing malicious code.
3. Gather and test the recommended best practices for high security hardening of the platforms you are using for reconnaissance.
4. Determine the equipment and resources required to set up an isolated reconnaissance capability, including capital and run expense estimates.
5. Acquire and test potential security controls for malicious content, behavior, or results detection.
6. Acquire and test system recovery or rebuild tools that permit quick recovery from a system that has been compromised.

Conclusion

This chapter covered two important personnel-related tactics. The first, hire a hacker, discussed the merits of hiring clever people to assess security controls, improve security products, and recon future threats or exploits. The second tactic, countering insider threats, discussed control objectives for mitigating risks associated with malicious insider activities. The use of "hackers" in the context of IT security is entirely dependent on the objectives the organization is trying to achieve. The use of white-hats to improve the security function of your products and service is a good practice. Security professionals generally consider employing "reformed" black-hat hackers to be a bad idea, although there doesn't appear to be any body of evidence to support the notion that this practice substantially increases risk. In truth, all employees have the potential to commit malicious acts, and insiders typically will do three times the damage that an external attacker might do.

Malicious insiders have authorized access that bypasses most network and host-based controls; weaknesses in operating system and applications controls exacerbate the problem by granting users access to inordinate amounts of data. Management complacency, corporate culture, empowerment, erratic enforcement, and missing supervisor skills also add to the problem. Company processes, including audit, hiring, and termination practices, supervisory controls, and incident response, are often inept and require technologies to manage user identities, collate physical and logical accesses, and detect unauthorized activities. The problem is systemic; the industry is just now starting to recognize the tremendous risk that insider malfeasance represents to companies, agencies, and the public. This isn't a hired hacker problem; it's an "everybody problem," and until technology catches up with the need, the best mitigation we have at hand is competent supervision: Nurture and promote it.

Chapter 13

Hire a Hessian (Outsourcing)

He is at this time transporting large armies of foreign mercenaries to complete the works of death, desolation and tyranny...totally unworthy the head of a civilized nation.

Thomas Jefferson
Declaration of Independence

Introduction

In early 1776, King George III of England hired 20,000 soldiers from his German brethren to help suppress the growing rebellion in the American colonies. The majority of these troops were supplied by Friedrich II ruler of Hesse-Cassel in northern Germany, hence the name Hessians. The Hessians represented about one-third of King George's troops in the Americas. Outsourcing the war to foreigners had its benefits; being able to keep a reserve force in England to protect against his French nemesis Louis XVI was one. It also had its drawbacks; for one, it gave the American leadership a powerful propaganda tool to inflame patriotic passions.

Outsourcing portions of IT operations is a fairly standard practice in most companies today. A study conducted by RTI International shows the financial sector leading the charge with 100% of the participants outsourcing something, followed by manufacturing with 83%, then small business and healthcare with 67%. IT outsourcing has its benefits and its drawbacks. We define outsourcing as a contractual agreement between two organizations by which one organization pays the other to conduct certain activities on its behalf.

In terms of offensive or defensive objectives, outsourcing is fairly neutral. It's possible to hire out just about any activity, including offensive maneuvers such as cyberwarfare and competitive intelligence. The more common scenario is outsourcing defensive objectives. Security may be a major concern when one is outsourcing, but it is seldom the primary objective of the practice. The three most common objectives of the outsourcing of services are cost savings, business focus, and productivity. Risk mitigation is a distant fourth. By offloading commodity services, companies are able to focus on their core strengths and key business initiatives. Productivity is gained from access to the latest technologies and business tools available. Collaboration and business intelligence tools, once too costly for small and medium companies to implement, are now delivered as cost-effective services. Provider expertise and contractual obligations can also serve to reduce business risks, but these are often countermanded by risks inherent to outsourcing in general. The degree to which outsourcing can help a business achieve these objectives depends largely on the sensitivity or value of the data involved, and on the legal and regulatory requirements the business is subject to.

From a security perspective, outsourcing supports the principles of economy, redundancy, and preparedness through lower control and personnel costs, high reliability, and provider expertise. Outsourcing may also improve coverage by forcing the enterprise onto a common application platform. However, if your strategy is dependent on excellence in observation and response timeliness, outsourcing may not be a good tactic to use. Once your data is out of your direct control, it is much harder to observe how it is being used. Furthermore, your responses become wholly dependent on provider notifications, which may not be generated in a timely manner. These and other factors, such as shared infrastructure, introduce new business risks that must be accounted for.

In this chapter we will examine the use of this tactic from two security perspectives. First, we will examine the security aspects of outsourcing IT services in general—that is, how to deal with security requirements for data that is transferred, processed, and stored by an outsourced provider. Second, we will address requirements that are specific to the outsourcing of security services, such as penetration testing, security monitoring, and facility security.

Security in the Outsourcing of IT Services

Let's begin by defining the different outsourcing solutions used in today's IT environments. These fall into two major divisions: fully hosted and hybrid. A fully hosted environment, as the name implies, means the customer has no in-house IT; all services are delivered to the consumer (end user) through a networked connection. Microsoft's Business Productivity Online Standard Suite (BPOS) is an example of this type of service. BPOS provides e-mail, instant messaging, Web conferencing, and collaboration services via the Internet; no in-house systems (other than end-user laptops or PCs) are required.

Hybrid environments employ some in-house and some hosted systems. The solutions can be characterized by the systems' level of integration. We have classified these as follows:

1. **Uncoupled**—Services where the consumer initiates a connection usually across a public network for the purpose of pushing data to the provider (e.g., updating a hosted website).
2. **Loosely coupled**—Similar to uncoupled, except that once the consumer is connected the provider may request the consumer take a specific action (e.g., update the client software), but the provider cannot initiate that action. Web-based e-mail is a good example of this type of service.
3. **Fully coupled**—Services delivered through a dedicated connection (e.g., a VPN) that allows either party to initiate an action (i.e., a connection or data transfer). The connection is bi-directional; the consumer can push and pull information, and so can the provider. A good example is an application with a federated identity. Federated identity is the use of a userID in one security realm to securely access systems and data in another security realm. The end user initiates a connection to the service; the service initiates a connection to the customer's authentication service to verify the user's permissions.

4. **Fully integrated**—Services that are characterized by full-time dedicated connections and bi-directional data exchanges that can be initiated by either party. An example is a hosted backend database server that regularly queries the customer's authentication server and other services such as DNS, Time, and WINS.

Outsourcing Pros—Benefits

The primary benefit of using outsourced services is cost savings. Service providers can deliver commodity services such as e-mail, instant messaging, and Web conferencing at a lower per user cost than the equivalent in-house service. Savings result from lower equipment, personnel, recruiting, operations, and support costs. Customers also benefit from higher reliability (availability), fault tolerance, no-cost technology transitions (always on the latest release of software), and the security expertise of the provider's staff. Other security-related benefits can be realized by the transition to services. For example, the transition may require infrastructure changes that benefit other security functions. These include the consolidation of user identities and the convergence of Active Directory domains. Getting all users on a common platform and having the ability to securely extend services to partners are two other potential benefits.

Outsourcing commodity services allows companies to focus on their core business and business initiatives instead of expending resources on the supervision and management of routine tasks, including some help desk and security-related functions. Some modest risk reductions can result from the provider's contractual obligations, high availability, Business Continuity and Disaster Recovery capabilities, and security management expertise, as well as transitional changes to security-related infrastructure services. These benefits apply to both fully hosted and hybrid environments.

SIDEBAR: LEVERAGING TECHNOLOGY TRANSITIONS

Major technology transitions are one of the hardest things for IT departments to accomplish. Moving from one version of an operating system to the next, or from one version of MS Office to the next, often requires months of preparation and even more time to roll everything out. Such was the case of one organization that wanted to transition to Microsoft Online Services. The company had been struggling for years with an Active Directory that had over 20 different domains and hundreds of domain trusts. The IT department had an ongoing consolidation project that had made little progress in the past year; that changed when the CEO decided to go online. The transition required a consolidated domain structure, so the Online migration team went to work solving the problem. Five months later, the company was not only saving money on e-mail, instant messaging, conferencing, and collaboration tools, but it also had an expertly designed and implemented Active Directory to help it manage its in-house computing resources. The cost? Less than what was budgeted for the original consolidation project.

Outsource Cons—Challenges

Outsourcing can provide some modest risk reduction, but it also has a number of inherent security risks that must be considered. The first is the security of the data transferred, stored, and processed by the provider. Once the data leaves your control, your ability to observe how it is handled or used is lost. Your ability to detect and respond to security violations concerning that data becomes wholly dependent on the provider's notification process, which may or may not be done in a timely manner. *However, your liability for the proper management of the data has not changed.* You are still the owner of the data, and you are still the party that is ultimately responsible for its protection. You cannot transfer this responsibility to the provider, nor is the provider likely to accept it.

Service providers achieve profitability by delivering commoditized services to a large audience. The approach leaves little room for customization, especially when it comes to customer-specific security requirements. Provider security is, for all practical purposes, a "one size fits all" solution. You either accept the provider's security management practices and controls or you don't. It becomes your responsibility to ensure that the provider complies with your requirements. For some services this can be a straightforward exercise; for example, a service like Instant Messenger that does not store data at the provider is limited to network attack scenarios. For services such as e-mail that store large quantities of data at the provider, the task is more difficult. The best strategy is to take your requirements and map them to the practices and audit measures of the provider. This may require some translation of terms, but chances are the provider already meets the vast majority of your requirements. If there are any gaps, there are two possibilities for resolving the disparity: The vendor can add the requirement to their standard practices or you can accept the risk.

Service providers also introduce new threats to data confidentiality and integrity from unauthorized staff accesses, data leakage across customer boundaries, commingling of data in help desk and other support systems, data exports to test/staging systems, and poor media transport or disposal practices. Compliance is another issue. You are responsible to prove compliance to all applicable laws and regulations. When you outsource services, the process now involves the provider on two fronts. First, whether or not the provider's practices meet your compliance requirements, and second, can they can supply you with the information you need to prove compliance within a reasonable time frame. It is also possible that your organization will be subject to additional statutes and regulations based on where the provider stores your data and what international borders it crosses during transfers and processing.

These challenges apply equally to fully hosted and hybrid environments. However, hybrid environments have some additional challenges as a result of shared risk. Systems that cross connect company and provider computing enclaves have a certain level of trust extended to them. It is possible that one or more of the systems involved in these connections will develop a vulnerability that exposes the other systems to potential attack. The simple example is a worm infecting a customer laptop. Because the provider's e-mail server trusts that laptop, it becomes a potential target for the worm to exploit. The simplest way to address shared risk is to limit inbound and outbound traffic to very specific services and systems. This works fine for connections classified as uncoupled and loosely coupled, but it can become very challenging for fully coupled and fully integrated environments. These may be better served by application-based firewalls.

Outsourcing presents a number of challenges that may make certain services unsuitable for the processing and storage of sensitive/high-value data. Services such as Instant Messenger and Web conferencing that do not store data at the provider have the fewest issues, e-mail and collaboration services the most. Acquiring the necessary information to prove compliance can also be a challenge, and in some instances the storage location and the movement of data across international boundaries may increase compliance requirements. In addition, shared-risk issues resulting from the cross connection of customer and provider systems must be mitigated. The provider's standard security management practices and controls will usually suffice; the challenge is reconciling the differences in grammar and terminology between the parties.

Success Factors and Lessons Learned

The success of outsourcing IT services, from a security perspective, comes down to compliance. Are you continuing to meet your legal, regulatory, and business information security requirements, and can you prove it? For this tactic to have been successful, the answer to this question must be "yes." Getting to yes requires a well-executed vetting process and excellence in contract management.

Setting your strategy and objectives up front is the first priority. Your outsourcing decisions must be tied to the business's mission, strategic direction, and core competencies. The next most important factor is to get executive sponsorship and stakeholder involvement. Getting executive management support for outsourcing is usually not difficult because of the potential cost savings. In fact, the executives are often the initiators of outsourcing efforts, which at times makes it difficult to get them to step back when security objectives cannot be met. Nonetheless, the input from executives and key stakeholders is critical to the planning and vetting portions of the process. The third major success factor is good engagement and governance processes (i.e., Excellence in Service Provider Management). This includes frequent evaluations and face-to-face interaction, especially in the first year of engagement. Manfred Immitzer, CIO of Nokia Siemens Networks, suggests that companies "do even more due diligence on IT outsourcing."

> Overall, outsourcing is a viable and sustainable strategy for companies, as long as their objectives are clear.
>
> **Matthew Ricks**
> *Sun Microsystems*

During the vetting process, make sure to do a good job of mapping your security requirements to the provider's security practices and audit requirements. Ensure that the provider can supply you with all the information you need to prove your compliance with legal, regulatory, and business security requirements. Also make sure the time lines for the delivery of this information are established and agreed upon (get them into the contract if possible). Make sure to fully evaluate the provider's incident management process and establish reasonable time lines for incident response, resolution, and notifications. Data breaches warrant near-time notification, but you should be able to get a monthly report of all the incidents affecting your services as well.

Outsourcing is a business process that takes some time to mature. Expect the first year to require a lot of hands-on management as expectations, outcomes, and schedules are clarified. Using the outsourcing tactic successfully will depend on your ability to properly vet the provider's security practices and controls against your requirements and reconcile the differences. If this cannot be accomplished, this may not be the right vendor, or outsourcing may not be the right tactic for your organization. Once engaged, active monitoring and the oversight of a good management team (governance body) will help ensure that security, cost, and operational efficiency goals are achieved. (Also see Chapter 7.)

Outsourcing Control Objectives

This section makes a number of assumptions about the level of services being contracted, including geographical, equipment, and connection redundancy, vendor expertise, and coverage. Some of these attributes may not be present, nor do they necessarily have to be present in all outsourcing solutions. You should select those attributes and control objectives best suited to your circumstances.

Security in IT services outsourcing has the follow attributes:

■ Services have high availability because of redundancy (equipment, connection, site, etc.), staff expertise, and monitoring coverage.
■ Services conform to security standards and comply with applicable legal, regulatory, and industry requirements.
■ The provider has a limited liability; the customer is subject to liabilities for provider security failures.

■ Customer compliance, incident management, and contract management are based on trust (that the vendor is providing accurate and relevant information and proofs).
■ Parties are subject to shared risks.

The primary attack scenarios in IT services outsourcing are based on shared risks. These include logical attacks against network connections and system interconnects between the parties. They also include attacks against provisioning, identity management, and support processes (i.e., social engineering). There is a secondary concern as well. Since the customer is ultimately responsible for protecting the data entrusted to its care, any attack scenario against the provider represents a potential liability.

Assuming the outsourcing arrangement does not permit customized security options, you only have direct control over two security aspects of an outsourced service arrangement: data placement and shared risks.

1. Data placement means you control what types of data will be handled by the provider either by limiting the services used, restricting what data is transferred to the provider, or limiting how the provider may use the data. Some services do not require storing data at the provider, for example, Microsoft's Office Communications Server (OCS). OCS is an instant messaging product that distributes messages over secure (e.g., SSL/TLS) connections. All OCS message content is encrypted during transit, including any caching done by the message servers; consequently, the risk of data disclosure is minimal. Web conferencing is similar. Conference participants use secure (SSL/TLS) connections to access a conference session. The content can only be accessed as long as the meeting exists. To prevent unauthorized disclosure, conference content is deleted immediately after the conference concludes (or after a predefined period designated by the conference leader or coordinator). Once the content expires, users can no longer access resources associated with the meeting, and the conference system does not retain any of this content either. A third scenario is also possible; encrypt the data before transferring it to the provider. One of Bill's clients used Microsoft's Rights Management Server (RMS) to protect business sensitive documents. The documents were stored on a SharePoint server for distribution and collaboration purposes. In this instance it was a local implementation of SharePoint, but it could have just as easily been an outsourced service because the content is encrypted. Figure 13.1 depicts the RMS workflow. Note how RMS encrypts and decrypts content (data) at the end points; during transit and storage, the data is AES (Advanced Encryption Standard) encrypted so that the risk of disclosure is minimal. However, the cost associated with the RMS service will offset some of the original outsourcing savings. The key to making this control work is a thorough understanding of how the service handles data. Some providers are willing to supply this information, whereas others are not, in which case you are better advised to walk away than risk a disclosure of business-sensitive data.

   The ability to restrict what data is transferred to the provider depends on what services are being contracted and how the two computing environments are interconnected. Simple IP address restrictions may be sufficient in some instances—for example, a router ACL to restrict all finance systems from using an outsourced backup solution. Other situations may require application-level controls, such as a content monitoring tool. As the restrictions grow in complexity, the cost of implementing and maintaining them starts to offset the original cost savings objectives. The complexities in all likelihood will grow. Unless there is a particularly compelling reason for using this alternative, it should probably be avoided. Data

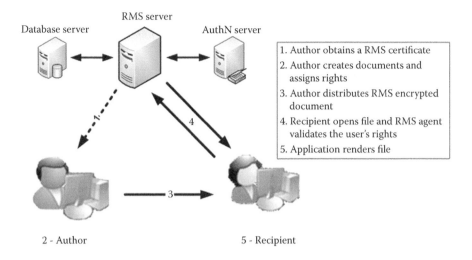

Database server   RMS server   AuthN server

1. Author obtains a RMS certificate
2. Author creates documents and assigns rights
3. Author distributes RMS encrypted document
4. Recipient opens file and RMS agent validates the user's rights
5. Application renders file

2 - Author   5 - Recipient

Figure 13.1   Rights Management Service (RMS) workflow.

placement can also help mitigate unexpected compliance liabilities based on data location and international transfers by restricting where the provider may store and process information. Most service providers, especially global providers, have features that allow the consumer to designate where data is stored and processed.

2. Shared risks at the network level are usually mitigated with encryption. S-tunnel (SSL) is common for uncoupled and loosely coupled connections, IPSec for VPNs, and link encryption devices for dedicated connections. Assuming standard host security controls (i.e., antivirus, patches, etc.) are in place, the shared risk that must be mitigated at the host level is unsecured trust. Service/port restrictions on system interconnects are the most common controls for this mitigation. Fully integrated environments may require the use of application-based firewalls or similar content-based filtering technologies. An explicit requestor verification process and staff training are the best ways to mitigate social engineering and other process-based attacks.

Some outsourcing arrangements may allow you (usually for an additional cost) to implement other direct controls over information security. For example, you might implement system management agents that report security-related information if you are only outsourcing rack space or server management.

Effective outsourcing of IT services requires good data placement control and shared-risk mitigation. Table 13.1 maps these controls to specific security baselines. The type (hard or soft) is used to denote the type of metric used for each control. Soft indicates a procedure-based control, while hard denotes a technology-based (i.e., automated) control. Both imply that the metric could be either one or a combination of both.

Because it isn't possible to observe the provider's actions, the remaining attributes (i.e., availability, compliance, liability, etc.) are based on trust, that is, contractual obligations and vendor performance monitoring. The two control objectives are:

1. Excellence in contracting
2. Excellence in service provider management (see Chapter 7)

Table 13.1 Control Objectives of Outsourcing of IT Services

	Type	Risk and Requirements
Data Placement		
Limited services	Soft	Only use services that do not store or only store data for a short duration at the provider to prevent disclosure from a provider security breach.
Restricted transfer	Hard	Block certain types of information from being transferred to the service provider to prevent disclosure from a provider security breach.
Restricted use	Soft	Set data storage and processing locations to prevent inadvertent statutory or regulatory compliance liabilities.
Encrypt local	Hard	Encrypt all data before transferring it to the provider to prevent disclosure from a provider security breach.
Host Shared Risk		
Standard measures	Soft	Ensure that systems meet DMZ (externally exposed) security standards, including but not limited to patches, permissions, anti-malware, log on restrictions, and the like.
Unsecured trusts	Hard	Restrict trusts to specific addresses (hosts), protocols, services (ports), and/or content.
Network Shared Risk		
Standard measures	Both	Ensure that local communication nodes meet current security requirements including, but not limited to, an approved version of software/firmware, up-to-date patches, secure log on, anti-DoS configuration, and so on.
Passive wiretapping	Hard Both	Encrypt data in transit to prevent eavesdropping. Use secure key distribution to thwart man-in-the-middle attacks.
Data insertion	Hard	Encrypt data in transit to prevent data alterations.
Node impersonation	Hard	Encrypt data in transit to prevent disclosure when traversing a counterfeit node.
End-point impersonation	Hard	Encrypt data using end-point authentications (i.e., TLS) to prevent disclosure when connected to a counterfeit end point.
Process Shared Risk		
Standard measures	Soft Soft Soft Soft	Excellence in operations - Written identity management procedures - Mandatory change control procedures - Properly trained and supervised staff - Sufficient resources to adequately manage identity provisioning
Unauthorized account	Soft	Implement explicit requestor validation for all account requests related to interconnected system.
Unauthorized system	Soft	Encrypt data in transit to prevent disclosure when traversing a counterfeit node or host system.

The following actions are recommended to facilitate the secure outsourcing of IT services:

1. Review any existing policies and procedures the organization has for outsourced services of any kind (e.g., janitorial services) to get an understanding of the company's expectations and requirements.
2. Review existing security and operations policies and procedures to identify applicable requirements and find areas where policies and procedures will need to be updated to support outsourcing.
3. Garner the support and participation of key stakeholders. Get their help defining the objectives for this outsourcing solution. Solicit their help filling the policies and procedure gaps identified above and finally, get their inputs to and reviews of the transition plan. Make sure you involve legal personnel as early as possible, for they are crucial to the contracting process; also make sure to involve HR if the outsourcing will result in any layoffs.
4. Build the processes you will need for vetting potential providers and managing contracted providers (engagement process).
5. Prepare the materials (forms, questionnaires, surveys, etc.) required for the vetting, contracting, and engagement processes.

Security in the Outsourcing of Security Services

> We outsource things that have one of three characteristics: they're complex, important, or distasteful. Computer security is all three.
>
> **Bruce Schneier**

All the elements, attributes, and control objectives identified in the previous section are also applicable to the outsourcing of security services. Consequently, this section will only address attributes that are unique to this type of outsourcing.

Commonly Outsourced Services

Let's begin by identifying the types of security services that are commonly outsourced. From most to least common they are:

1. Security auditing
2. Penetration testing, vulnerability assessment
3. System and facility monitoring
4. Consulting
5. Incident support
6. System management/administration
7. Security officers

Security Auditing

Compliance with legal, regulatory, and industry requirements makes third-party security audits mandatory for most businesses. Statutes such as Sarbanes-Oxley (SOX) and industry requirements such as the Payment Card Industry (PCI) security standards require companies to hire external auditors to verify compliance. Companies also rely on external audits for security certifications (compliance with generally accepted security standards and practices) and to meet specific customer security expectations. Audits are typically conducted on an annual or bi-annual basis.

Penetration Testing, Vulnerability Assessment

Companies frequently hire external parties to look for security flaws in their products or services. These include design and architecture reviews, code reviews, and security testing. The assessments are frequently mandated by the company's risk management or internal audit function as part of "due diligence" in managing enterprise risk. Penetration testing is typically performed just prior to the system going into production and periodically thereafter to ensure that changes to the system have not weakened the system's security profile. One could view penetration testing as a mock hacker attack, in that the penetration testing team attempts to compromise system security controls using the same techniques and attack scenarios the system will be subject to in its production environment.

Systems Monitoring

The two types of services offered in the systems arena are typically performed by a managed security service provider or MSSP. The MSSP may offer other services (e.g., consulting, penetration testing services), but the core business is system monitoring. The first type of service is automated vulnerability monitoring/scanning. The monitoring company continuously scans systems in the customer's environment for the presence of vulnerabilities. The simplest version of this service just scans systems exposed to the Internet via the Internet. More sophisticated versions use dedicated connections or appliances to scan a larger contingency of systems. The QualsysGuard (Qualsys, Inc.) service is an example of this type of monitoring. Qualsys maintains an up-to-date database of vulnerabilities and threats. It uses this database to assess client systems and report security states. The service includes comprehensive reports on vulnerabilities, threats, and potential impacts.

The second type of system monitoring uses automated assessment. The MSSP collects security-related information from multiple systems and analyzes it for malicious or unauthorized activity. The information may be provided by software agents installed on the monitored systems, by appliances attached to the network or gleaned from system logs and audit trails. BT Managed Security Solutions (formerly Counterpane Internet Security) is an example of this type of service. BT gathers log information from security devices and evaluates the information in real time against a comprehensive rule set to detect and generate responses to malicious or potentially malicious activities.

Facilities Monitoring

Remote facility monitoring includes 24/365 intrusion detection and control, video surveillance, electronic access control, and GPS asset tracking services. Most organizations offering these services are facility management firms that offer maintenance, moving, and many other services including safety-related monitoring such as fire and smoke detection, power failures, overheating, and flooding. Services can range from simple surveillance to complex interactive access control management. For example, a credit card company Bill worked with used an outsourced service to remotely manage their data center mantraps. When entering a data center, you step into the mantrap, close the outside door, and scan your identity badge. The scan signals the service provider, who remotely locks the outside door, checks that you are alone in the mantrap, verifies your video image against your stored image, and then remotely unlocks the inside access door. ADT and Sentor are examples of companies that offer these types of services. Monitoring and control is typically based on vendor-supplied on-site appliances that communicate alerts to redundant monitoring center.

Incident Support

Firms commonly supplement their in-house incident management capabilities with third-party resources when dealing with security, fraud, and other IT-related malfeasance. Employing a red team to assist with the containment and resolution of a major compromise is not uncommon. "Red Team" is the military term used in war games for the opposing force or OPFOR. In incident response, it is the team opposing or countering the attacker. Some organizations use the term in reference to penetration testing. For example, the NSA Red Team is essentially a penetration testing team that acts "like our country's shadowy enemies…attempting to slip in unannounced and gain unauthorized access." This is a misuse of the term: Penetration testing uses attack techniques, whereas incident response uses defensive techniques; these are two very different functions. Calling them by the same name creates more of a confusion factor than anything else. Companies are also prone to use external resources for forensics work and security investigations, usually for the expertise, but impartiality is also a factor. A third factor is cost: Forensic tools and training are expensive to purchase and maintain. Digital Intelligence and Encase are probably the two best known vendors; their products range in price from $6,000 to $20,000 for hardware and $3,000 to $6,500 for software. Training for a primary and backup operator will run another $3,000. This is a pretty stiff entry fee for a system that will likely sit idle most of the time. Outsourcing this function for most organizations is more cost effective. Most MSSP consultancies offer forensic and investigative services.

System Management/Administration

This class of security services also falls into the MSSP realm. Services include the installation, configuration, and operation of security devices such as firewalls, VPN servers, intrusion detection appliances, and content filters. Small and medium-size businesses are most likely to use these services because the cost of maintaining in-house expertise for these functions is difficult to justify. SecureWorks' Firewall Service is an example of this type of service. The service provides full administration (i.e., configuration, patching, software updates, and performance tuning) as well as real-time monitoring of firewall logs for malicious activity.

Security Officer Services

Outsourcing security officer (guard) services is another common practice. Service providers offer a variety of services based on industry sector and client need. These services include reception/concierge services, video (CCTV) console monitoring, vehicle and foot patrols, inspection services, visitor badging, new employee orientation, campus access control (gates) and parking control/coordination. Securitas and Wackenhut are examples of companies that offer outsourced guard services. It is not uncommon for these companies to offer investigation, executive protection, and secure transport services as well.

Outsourcing of Security Services Objectives

The primary driver for outsourcing security services remains cost savings, but savings will vary depending on the size of the organization and the kind of services contracted. The overhead involved in keeping security expertise in-house for small and medium-size companies can be burdensome; IT salaries are high, but the turnover rates are relatively low. By comparison, security officer compensation is modest but turnover rates are high. For large enterprises, the cost of in-house expertise is a less important factor, and so savings are less pronounced. Compliance is another big driver because many statutes, regulations, and industry standards require third-party verification. For example, Section 404 of the Sarbanes-Oxley (SOX) Act requires annual financial reports for publicly traded companies to contain an assessment of the effectiveness of the internal control structure and procedures for financial reporting. The act specifically calls for the attestation of a registered public accounting firm. The Payment Card Industry Data Security Standard (PCI DSS) requires an annual on-site review performed by a Qualified Security Assessor (QSA). Businesses may also use external auditors to certify their compliance with a set of international, national, or industry standards, for example, ISO 27001 or ISO 17799 accreditation. There are also a number of commercially available trust seal attestations. For a fee the vendor will assess the security and privacy features of a company's online services and attest that they are trustworthy if they meet the vendor's criteria. The customer may then display the vendor's trust seal on their websites. TRUSTe requirements include ongoing compliance monitoring, reporting of key changes in data management practices, and periodic reviews by a certified Client Services Manager.

Coverage is another driver. Most businesses do not have 24/7 security monitoring capabilities, and on-call staffing management can be problematic. It is for this very reason that hackers attack at night and on weekends. Coverage can be an issue for small and large companies alike. A large retailer Bill worked for in North Carolina had one of the best implementations of SNORT he had ever seen, and the young lady who operated the system was very proficient. Unfortunately, she was it: If she wasn't sitting at the console monitoring events, the events didn't get monitored. When she wasn't at work, alerts were sent to her pager, and when she was on vacation the alerts were forwarded to one of the network technicians. The lack of coverage severely limited the effectiveness of the tool, and, sure enough, they got hacked when no one was watching. Improved coverage leads to improved incident management, another driver for security service outsourcing. In Chapter 6 we talked about timeliness and its effect on potential damages; the prompter the response the lower the damage. MSSPs monitor and analyze events in real time and provide immediate notification for critical (high-risk) events. Not only does this facilitate response, but it also eliminates false responses (a major headache for on-call personnel). MSSP personnel evaluate events to establish criticality; false alarms detected during this process are not forwarded, and on-call personnel get a full night's sleep.

Incident response points to another benefit of MSSP outsourcing: expertise. MSSPs gather data from multiple customer sites and have a highly skilled staff analyzing attack trends and attack methods. Their assessment of an event as well as the information they provide in a notification will be more comprehensive than anything you could generate in-house. Their recommended actions and support will be more focused and effective because their knowledge base and experiences are broader. When you combine all of these factors, the net result is improved security, which is an obvious driver for any security outsourcing effort. Security improvement is also the main driver for outsourcing security assessment services.

The majority of hacker attacks are now aimed at the application layer. SQL injection, cross-site scripting, and response splitting are some of the most prevalent attacks. SANS listed application attacks as the second biggest cybersecurity risk in 2009. Citing attack and vulnerability data collected by TippingPoint and Qualsys, SANS concluded, "During the last few years, the number of vulnerabilities being discovered in applications is far greater than the number of vulnerabilities discovered in operating systems. As a result, more exploitation attempts are recorded on application programs." This shift can be partially attributed to improvements in operating system and network security controls, but the prevalence of targets and the lack of effective application patching are the more likely culprits. In addition to employing secure development practices, companies will hire third parties to assess the security of their applications. Pre-deployment assessments may include security architecture and design reviews, code reviews, and security testing. Outsourcing a penetration test on a fully staged deployment is a common practice. Penetration testing is also a popular post-deployment assessment used to verify security controls after system changes are deployed.

Organizations outsource security services in seven distinct areas (auditing, assessment, monitoring, consulting, incident support, device management, and facility security) primarily for defensive purposes. The largest driver is cost savings, followed by compliance mandates, broader coverage, improved incident response, and a better overall security posture. Cost savings tend to be more modest because of the narrower scope of the services; small and medium companies realize the best benefits from not having to keep in-house expertise.

Challenges to Outsourcing Security Services

Losing in-house expertise can be a downside to outsourcing from two different perspectives. The first perspective is availability: Vendor resources are shared across multiple customers; you may need to "wait your turn" to get a qualified resource, especially when you need them the most (e.g., when the region is getting hit by a major worm attack). The second perspective is validation: When changes are made, you don't have the ability to confirm they were done correctly. A great example of this is an assessment Bill did for a law firm in Phoenix. The firm had a Cisco PIX firewall that was managed by an external provider. The IT director asked him to review the configuration, which he did; he found more than 20 configuration errors, including seven exploitable "holes" in the firewall rules. Some of those holes had been there for years, but the firm had no way of knowing because no one in-house knew how to evaluate a PIX configuration. Another issue associated with outsourcing expertise is, how expert is that expertise? You don't really have a good way to assess the knowledge, skills, and abilities of the provider's staff. During an IT services bid review for the U.S. Navy, Bill noticed, based on the submitted resumes, that the vendor had assigned a relatively inexperienced resource to a senior-level task. When he raised the question, the contractor indicated that the resource was one of their top performers and that one of their most senior resources (he was sitting in the room at the time) was on call to assist if necessary. The vendor won the contract, the senior resource was never seen again, the primary resource was completely overwhelmed, and ultimately the U.S. taxpayers footed the bill for his lack of expertise! Anyone who has done much outsourcing likely has similar stories. When outsourcing security consulting and assessment services involving individual contributors, resume and training record reviews are a good way to assess expertise; interviews are even better. Microsoft contracts resources from a number of vendors to staff spikes in workloads. While interviewing a potential vendor resource for a security engagement, Bill asked about his CISSP and his job experience leading up to his certification. The man had falsified his application! He may have had the requisite skills, but he certainly didn't command trust—and without the interview no one would have known the difference. When outsourcing to a MSSP for monitoring or system management, the best way to deal with the question of expertise is to stick with name-brand vendors, check out what the industry analysts say, or talk with other customers of the service.

Using name-brand vendors also alleviates two other common outsourcing challenges: longevity and performance. A lot of small companies offer a variety of security services, some of which are solid value propositions and some are not. The industry has already seen a number of unprofitable MSSP ventures fail, including Pilot Network Service and Salinas. Name-brand vendors stick to what they know, do it well, and remain in business. With the exception of consulting services, the performance of small service providers can also be an issue because you don't have a viable means of observing their operations. Smaller companies don't always have the luxury of planning things in advance; attrition, absenteeism, recruiting, and other staffing issues may cause a provider to shirk their obligations, take shortcuts, employ unqualified staff, and the like. This is less of a concern with providers that have a brand name to protect and promote. Consulting services are the exception; a number of highly skilled professionals work in small consultancies that specialize in specific security disciplines (e.g., architecture, strategy, forensics, code review, etc.). For short-term and specialty projects, these firms deliver exceptional results for substantially lower rates. This makes them a good option for small and medium-size companies. Large businesses can also benefit from this expertise but usually prefer the stability and brand recognition of larger consultancies.

The shared-risk issues were addressed earlier in this chapter but bear additional mention here because a number of outsourced security services involve elevated user privileges and/or access to sensitive data. Consequently, the potential damage from malicious or erroneous vendor behavior can be substantially greater. Security device management has the highest risk, auditing probably the lowest.

Realizing expected cost savings for outsourced security services is also a challenge. Some outsourcing versus in-house costs are difficult to quantify. Loss of in-house expertise is also a concern from both a resource availability and a configuration/change verification standpoint. Organizations can avoid longevity, expertise, and performance issues by using brand-name providers. When outsourcing system management and other tasks involving elevated privileges or high-value data (e.g., source code), organizations must ensure that share risks are properly mitigated.

Success Factors and Lessons Learned

Companies reporting the best results are those that outsource for expert assistance. Firms outsourcing management haven't fared as well, especially those impacted by vendor failures (e.g., Pilot Network Services).

> Stay clear of outsourcing any activity that's critical to policy development, or that has a critical impact on your business. Those are the company jewels and they're too valuable to trust to strangers.
>
> **Jonathan Gossels**
> *CEO of SystemExperts*

Avoiding conflicts of interest in security outsourcing is also important. Self-auditing is not a good security practice. If you are outsourcing device management, monitoring should be done by a different provider. This resolves the conflict of interest issue and also supports the "four-eyes" principle for change validation.

SIDEBAR: THE TRADE-OFF BETWEEN CONFLICT AND INTEGRITY

Assuming someone is lying because there's a possible conflict of interest is a slippery slope. Attesting to your own work has never been considered a sound practice; Accenture spun off from Arthur Andersen for this very reason. Andersen consulting was providing IT services to clients, and those services were subsequently being audited by

Andersen accounting services. Conflicts of interest result when telling the truth or making the best decision has negative impacts on you or your employer: for example, Andersen accounting finding fault with Anderson consulting work or Microsoft Consulting Services (MCS) recommending an IBM software solution. Where conflicts of interest exist, the integrity of both parties is tested. Presenting a biased conclusion or making a biased recommendation lacks integrity. Ignoring or devaluating the same on the assumption it is biased also lacks integrity. There is a balance. A few years ago I (Bill) was working with Telco to improve its patch management processes. The company was using an old Tivoli system to distribute and install software patches to 6,000 desktops. The process involved manually creating a Tivoli distribution package for each patch, then placing it on the Tivoli system for distribution and installation. The process took 10 or 11 days to reach an 80% completion mark; the remaining systems had to be manually patched. The Tivoli system was slated for an upgrade, but I recommended replacing it with Microsoft System Management Server (SMS). The system was only used to manage Windows workstations, and SMS (being a Windows product) did the better job. The decision looked like a no-brainer, but I was "biased," and so my recommendation was invalid. Instead of doing her due diligence (comparing the features and costs of the two products), the manager took the "unbiased" opinion of the IBM representative and stayed with Tivoli! The funniest part of the whole story is that her company actually paid me for the privilege of ignoring my advice!

If cost savings is one of your objectives, it's important for you to know your run costs up front; otherwise, you can't make a valid comparison to the vendor's fees. Most vendors have cost/value models that are heavily skewed in their favor. Don't be too optimistic. You may not see any cost savings, but there are still a number of other advantages that make the effort worthwhile.

Outsourcing Security Services Control Objectives

Because of the sensitive nature of the information involved in security services outsourcing, some additional control objectives are warranted in order to:

- Maintain the confidentiality of results
- Prevent the disclosure of events
- Preserve evidence
- Avoid retention/discovery liabilities
- Prevent the loss of intellectual property
- Mitigate elevated privilege risks

Maintain the Confidentiality of Results

The unauthorized disclosure of security-related information is a risk in all outsourced security services. The biggest risks involve the disclosure of assessment results from code reviews or penetration testing because they expose potentially exploitable vulnerabilities. The disclosure of firewall, IDS, and appliance results (logs) can facilitate attacks because the information allows an attacker to map the internal network topology, protocols, and access control (i.e., firewall, router) rules. The disclosure of audit results can create legal liabilities as well; it proves you were aware of a security flaw. If the flaw is exploited and damages result, you can be held culpable if you didn't make a reasonable effort to fix the problem. Verizon Communications learned this lesson the hard way when they were fined for a late FCC filing that Verizon attributed to a worm infestation. The court found in favor of the FCC because a patch of the vulnerability the worm exploited had been available for six months prior to the attack, and Verizon had failed to do "due diligence" in getting it deployed. Loss of customer confidence and reputation are two other potential liabilities. The risks are similar from the disclosure of monitoring and incident response information, especially if these disclosures are not consistent with what the organization has been saying publicly.

These scenarios are essentially the same shared-risk issues found in nonsecurity outsource scenarios only with an elevated risk. Furthermore, you don't have the option to limit the services or the sensitivity of data transferred, processed, or stored at the provider. All the services deal with sensitive data; there is no getting around that. At best you may be able to limit the length of time the data are retained by the provider. Network shared risks will be mitigated with mandatory encryption, including end-point authentication (i.e., TLS, IPSec, etc.). One can expect the provider's host security to be tight, with services restricted to a limited number of ports and protocols. Prudence calls for a thorough verification, however.

Another shared risk involves the provider's support systems and applications. Data from multiple customers is commingled on these systems. An operator error, system failure, or misconfiguration could result in some data being disclosed to the wrong party—for example, an alert like this, "fs01.de.abccorp.com breach, Downadup variant C exploit, status: critical" being sent to the ABC Corporation instead of its Germany subsidiary. This makes verifying the provider's operations and personnel process equally important. Table 13.2 maps result confidentiality objectives to specific baselines. The type (hard or soft) is used to denote how the metric for each control objective is collected. Soft indicates a procedure-based control, while hard denotes a technology-based (i.e., automated) control.

Prevent the Disclosure of Events

The disclosure of actual events can have a much stronger impact. In addition to exposing an exploitable vulnerability, the disclosure may cause the attacker to break off the attack, hampering investigative and law enforcement efforts. The disclosure may also subject the organization to unwarranted notification requirements or fines. Actual security breaches also have a much higher impact on customer confidence and company reputation. These risks are more prevalent in system monitoring, incident support, and system management services, but auditing services may also uncover event information.

The control objectives for this risk and the Maintain the Confidentiality of Results risk above are the same (see Table 13.2).

Table 13.2   Control Objectives Maintain the Confidentiality of Results

Attribute/Control	Type	Risk and Requirements
Data Placement		
Limited retention	Soft	Service provider must securely delete data containing customer-specific information (aggregation for statistical analysis is permitted) within a specific time frame to prevent disclosure from a provider security breach or operator error.
Process Share Risk		
Extended measures	Soft Soft Soft	Excellence in operations: - Data separation in shared support systems and application - Notification and report routing controls - Operator accountability controls
Training	Soft	Provider has mandatory training and skills tracking process.

Preserving Evidence

Security events carry with them a potential for legal action, including prosecution of the perpetrator, prosecution of company officials (à la Sarbanes-Oxley), civil penalties, and lawsuits for downstream damages. This makes the collection and preservation of evidence a critical component of incident management. When security services are outsourced, some of that evidence may end up being stored or generated at the service provider; therefore, controls must be in place to ensure that the integrity of the data is maintained. There are two major risks here: loss of evidence and inadmissibility. The first issue is obvious: We want our provider to retain the evidence we need. Second, we want our provider to preserve the integrity of the information in a traceable way. Evidence has some very specific attributes. It must be sufficient, relevant, and reliable. Records that are subject to unauthorized modification are not reliable and therefore not admissible. There are two aspects to integrity: One is the integrity of the data, and the second is the protector/custody of the data (i.e., what parties had control over the information from the time it was collected until it was presented in court?). This record is called the chain of custody, and it can be a real challenge to maintain for civil suits that take up to five years to complete! Since the outcome of legal actions depends on the evidence presented, submitting insufficient, irrelevant, or unreliable information will increase potential liabilities. Evidence collection and preservation processes are usually part of an organization's *Incident Response Plan*. When security services are outsourced, the plan must be revised to include an interface with the provider or providers. Most MSSPs will already have this interface defined; some may provide automated tools for selecting the data you want preserved and to digitally sign or create ICV (Integrity Check Value) for data integrity purposes. The management of evidence is a standard skill set for security consultancies and incident support vendors. Table 13.3 maps the management of evidence objectives to specific baselines. The type (hard or soft) is used to denote how the metric for each control objective is collected. Soft indicates a procedure-based control, while hard denotes a technology-based (i.e., automated) control. Both indicates either or a hybrid control.

Avoiding Retention/Discovery Liabilities

This issue is almost the opposite of preserving evidence. We want to retain evidence that supports our cause, but we do not want to risk retaining information that may prove to be a future liability. Most organizations have a data-retention policy based on industry

Important Note

The authors wish to make it clear that we are not under any circumstances suggesting that companies should destroy any information subject to discovery under a pending legal action.

Table 13.3 Control Objectives for the Management of Evidence

Attribute/Control	Type	Risk and Requirements
Evidence Preservation		
Retained	Soft	Excellence in operations - Formal process and provider interface to designate specific data as evidence to prevent it from being altered or deleted by the provider
Reliable	Both	A means of ensuring that retained evidence is admissible must be in place, including tamperproofing the data and maintaining the chain of custody.

requirements and standards. When an organization is outsourcing security services, these require-ments must be reconciled with the provider's capabilities. Most providers will not retain informa-tion for any extended time. The quantity of data MSSPs collect is too massive to retain for any length of time. Assessment, consulting, and incident support providers prefer not to retain data because of its sensitive and potential disclosure liabilities. Auditors are more likely to retain data supporting their attestation.

The "reasonable man" standard is used in U.S. law to determine culpability for damages. The question is, "What would the reasonable person of ordinary prudence have done under the same or similar circumstances?" In other words, given the knowledge and skills the person (or organiza-tion) had at the time, did they exercise due care to prevent people (or other entities) from being damaged? For example, if you know the brakes on your car aren't working and you drive it anyway and crash, you didn't exercise due care because any reasonable person would know you don't drive a car without brakes! Now think about this in terms of hundreds of records of system vulnerabili-ties or breaches. If someone sues you and subpoenas those records, you've got a lot of explaining to do! That's not to say that you didn't do the right thing each time, but now, you have to *prove* you did, and that could be a very costly endeavor in both directions: internal investigation costs and civil penalties if you can't prove due care. The best way to manage this risk is to destroy this data when it is no longer useful. What is and is not "useful" is something you'll need to negotiate with your provider; their definition may require a longer retention period than yours. Table 13.4 maps retention/discovery liability avoidance objectives to specific baselines.

Elevated Privilege and Intellectual Property Loss

These two issues are combined because they share the same control objectives. Some outsourced security activities involve access to valuable intellectual property, for example, software architecture and design reviews and source code reviews. Other activities, incident support and security device management, for example, require elevated privileges that also grant access to intellectual property. These activities increase the risk of loss from the theft or disclosure of the organization's intellectual property. When Bill first went to work at Microsoft, he was a contractor doing security assessments and source code reviews. He remembers poking around the network for internal tools he could leverage for his assessments. He was utterly amazed at the level of access he had to proprietary intellectual property, including a substantial amount of Windows 2000 source code. That certainly wasn't the case when he left, however. In today's world of high-capacity portable storage devices and miniature cameras, exposing any quantity of high-value data to strangers is dangerous.

Table 13.4 Control Objectives for Media Retention

Attribute/Control	Type	Risk and Requirements
Retention Liability		
Destroyed	Soft	Excellence in operations
		- Adjustable retention time frame for data stored at the provider to ensure that it is not subject to legal discovery
		- Formal process to securely delete all copies of data exceeding the retention period to ensure that it is not subject to legal discovery

Good accountability controls are the best way to deal with this risk. Accountability protects against intellectual property loss by tracking what individuals are in possession of which pieces of information at any given point in time. This makes it possible to hold those individuals responsible for any misuse of that data. Unfortunately, there aren't a lot of good accountability controls available. Good oversight and monitoring is another possible mitigation; limiting I/O (input/output) is a third. The problem with oversight is that it is resource intensive. Mandatory escorts were not uncommon when Bill worked for the U.S. Navy, but while he was standing outside the men's room one day waiting for his consultant, nothing productive was getting done! If you have video surveillance capabilities in the areas where external resources are working, you may be able to leverage it to reduce the amount of one-to-one time required. Limiting I/O capabilities works better. This was the approach one brokerage house took for their source code review. They allowed the external auditor to bring a laptop on-site for note-taking purposes but nothing else. They furnished a workstation that had no USB ports and a read only CD drive. No system documentation or source code could be taken off premise. The downside of the arrangement was that work could only be conducted when a member of the staff was there; the upside was that on Friday they all headed off to the pub at 4 PM! Most modern systems are equipped with USB connections. Depending on the operating system, limiting their use can be challenging. We like the Navy's solution: Fill the connector with epoxy! Somehow disabling the device driver seems to be a better approach. Table 13.5 maps the intellectual property management objectives to specific baselines. The type (hard or soft) is used to denote how the metric for each control objective is collected. Soft indicates a procedure-based control, while hard denotes a technology-based (i.e., automated) control. Both indicates either or a hybrid control.

The following actions are recommended to facilitate the outsourcing of security services:

1. Review your incident response and investigation processes and establish what interfaces and data exchanges will be required for outsourcing.
2. Review your corporation's data-retention policies to determine what retention cycles must be established for data stored at a service provider.

Table 13.5 Control Objectives for Intellectual Property Management

Attribute/Control	Type	Risk and Requirements
Intellectual Property Loss		
Accountability	Both	Records of all accesses to intellectual property for each outsourced entity are captured and protected against alteration to discourage illicit activities and alert staff of unauthorized activity.
Supervision	Soft	Internal staff is assigned to monitor outsourced personnel to discourage and/or report unauthorized activity.
Surveillance	Soft	Security staff is assigned to observe the actions of outsourced personnel to discourage illicit behavior and report prohibited or suspicious activities.
Limited I/O	Hard	All unnecessary output devices are removed or disabled to prevent loss of intellectual property.

3. Review your corporate data destruction standards to determine what data destruction capabilities will be required for your providers.
4. Review your service areas (e.g., U.S., EU, Asia, etc.) to determine the best outsource data storage and processing scheme. Make sure your storage and processing scheme does not subject you to any additional statutory or regulatory compliance requirements.
5. Garner the support and participation of key security stakeholders. Get their help defining the objectives for each security outsourcing solution. Also get their help filling the policies and procedure gaps and modifying processes to accommodate security outsourcing risks.
6. Modify existing processes for vetting potential providers and managing contracted providers (engagement process) to include security specific checks.
7. Prepare the materials (forms, questionnaires, surveys, etc.) required for the vetting, contracting, and engagement processes.

Conclusion

King George's outsourcing efforts ultimately failed (he lost the war), although history would tell us it wasn't the service provider's fault. By all accounts, the Hessians were well-trained, disciplined, and valiant soldiers. If anything could be blamed, it was the language barrier between the British and Hessian commands and the arrogance of their commanders. They discounted the will and determination of the rag-tag continental army. Hopefully, in our outsourcing efforts we won't make the same mistakes.

Outsourcing portions of IT operations is a fairly standard practice. From a security standpoint, most outsourcing has defensive objectives. Data security is always a major concern when outsourcing, but cost savings is the major driver, followed by better business focus and increased productivity. Risk mitigation is a distant fourth. Outsourcing supports the security principles of economy, redundancy, and preparedness through lower control and personnel costs, high reliability, and staff expertise. If your organization depends on excellence in observation and response timeliness, outsourcing may not work well for you.

In this chapter we examined outsourcing from two perspectives: general IT services outsourcing and security services outsourcing. The general requirements and risks are applicable to all IT outsourcing; security outsourcing has some additional risks to address. The majority of IT outsourcing arrangements create a hybrid or shared infrastructure; some services remain in-house, whereas others are external. This cross connection of computing enclaves creates shared risks that must be mitigated. *It is important to remember that you can transfer data and processing to a service provider, but you cannot transfer responsibility; you are ultimately responsible for the protection of the data resources entrusted to your care.*

Small and medium companies seem to realize the biggest benefit from outsourcing because they get to use the latest versions of software and have access to advanced technologies they couldn't afford to keep in-house. They also benefit from reduced labor costs because they do not need to retain in-house expertise. Companies have the best success when outsourcing commodity IT services (such as e-mail, instant messaging, and conferencing) and expert assistance (i.e., incident support, consulting, security monitoring). Firms that outsource management functions haven't fared as well.

The biggest security challenges in outsourcing are data protection and compliance. Companies can mitigate the risks associated with external processing and storage by carefully managing data location, limiting the types of services used, or encrypting sensitive information before sending it to the provider. Company compliance requirements may involve data inputs from the service provider; to avoid potential fines and liabilities, companies should specify compliance requirements and time frames in outsourcing contracts. The provider's standard security management practices and controls are usually sufficient to meet your legal, regulatory, and business security requirements; the challenge is reconciling the differences in grammar and terminology between the parties.

Data protection risks are increased in security services outsourcing because the data is of a sensitive nature, and sometimes vendors require elevated privileges to perform their tasks. Disclosure of security information can lead to a number of financial liabilities as well as damage to the company's reputation and brand image. Increased vendor monitoring and accountability controls are the best ways to deal with these risks.

The world continues to move toward specialization in just about every modern endeavor, the IT world is no different. Outsourcing IT services to highly skilled and specialized service providers is a good tactic. It allows companies to focus on their core competencies while reducing costs and improving performance. Understanding your objectives, compliance/security requirements, and current (in-house) run costs are necessary to properly evaluate potential providers. Vetting is the most critical piece of IT outsourcing; you must ensure that the provider is capable of meeting all your critical requirements and that those requirements are accurately reflected in the service contract. Once contracted, vendor monitoring and excellence in service provider management are crucial to the ongoing success of an outsourcing business partnership.

Chapter 14

Security Awareness Training

Security is always excessive until it's not enough.

Robbie Sinclair
Head of Security, Country Energy, NSW Australia

Introduction

As security budgets flatten or diminish in economic downturns, the monies available for training shrink. The challenge for any training is determining what training, where, and for whom, as well as what technologies and methods to employ for best impact and ROI (return on investment). Meanwhile, security compliance requirements are increasing; penalties, fines, and lawsuits for breaches of security seem to fill headlines; and security issues are increasingly a high-priority issue for many businesses (most notably of late, data security). The requirements for training remain a primary focus for all security groups. The question now more than ever is how to do it efficiently with greater impact, especially in compliance domains. Whether your security group is responsible for security awareness training and education, or requirements have been sourced to an enterprise training group or an external supplier, the discussions in this chapter should help you refine security training requirements.

> The mantra of any good security engineer is: "Security is a not a product, but a process."
>
> **Bruce Schneier**

We have more than 50 years of combined experience as teachers, trainers, and consultants, and both of us are avid, lifelong learners. Our sojourns have taken us into many cultures, as well as into organizations of business, education, government, and nonprofit groups around the globe. In our careers, we have helped design, deliver, and evaluate literally hundreds of courses to learners of every kind and stripe, while having the good fortune to work with brilliant minds from major universities around the globe. Training is not adequate to describe what is required for organizations to remain relevant and credible in the marketplace today. We're not sure even transformational learning, learning organization, or collaborative learning are enough to describe what is needed today.

> If you spend more on coffee than on IT security, you will be hacked. What's more, you deserve to be hacked.
>
> **Richard Clarke**
> *White House Cybersecurity Adviser*

In this chapter we will review the basic standards required for awareness training, and we will also consider some of the issues that security must address as enterprises continue to strategically transform the way they do business.

As organizations begin moving toward a commitment-based security model, as outlined by the American Center for Strategic Transformation, the educational requirements for security become increasingly important. A commitment-based security group provides employee training that well verses employees in potential security threats and the actions they should take. In the commitment-based model, the security group regularly shares information with employees and seeks feedback on how to enhance their performance. Ideas for implementation into security strategy and practice can come from anywhere in the organization. The security function collaborates with the enterprise to determine what combinations of technology and people practices best provide the appropriate level of security. And most importantly, the security function is seen favorably as a critical player and true business partner. In essence, security has become part of the enterprise DNA, and security functions are continuously improved by learning together how to get better.

Regardless of the current model your security group functions in (or the model you are working toward), there are several major categories of training that security groups need to manage well. The first category is staff development for present and future skill requirements. This includes security staff requirements (present and future skills), as well as enterprise staff security training requirements. Security staff requirements include:

- Security training requirements and certifications required by outside agencies
- Training requirements and certifications required internally
- Future training requirements (caused by technology changes, organizational changes)

Enterprise staff training includes:

- Orientation training
- Annual training
- Issue training for general population or specific groups

The second major category is security awareness training, which includes:

- High-level executive awareness of prime security issues
- Awareness programs for engaging specific groups
- General security awareness training for employees
- Security awareness segments included in employee orientation programs

In many security groups, awareness training may also be mandated by outside agencies that require various types of awareness training to be deployed in conjunction with international, federal, state, or local agency policies.

For the purposes of this chapter we will focus on security **staff development** and security **awareness training** efforts. First, let's take a moment to articulate the differences between awareness and training.

Awareness is simply the efforts of security to focus people in the organization they serve on security issues. By focus we mean how to identify common risks and how to appropriately respond to that risk. For example, awareness efforts may involve topics such as recognizing and responding to suspicious behavior, phishing attacks, or social engineering attempts to gain access to organizational information, property, or people. Awareness training is normally aimed at a broader audience and uses marketing tactics and selected communication technologies to deploy the message.

Training focuses on how to produce relevant and needed security skills and competency. Training is a more formalized approach to building the knowledge, skills, and abilities (KSAs) to help employees do their jobs in a way that does not compromise organizational assets. In training, the audience is typically much more engaged in the process and expected to be an active participant. Training may also be much more specific to the audience group and require more segmentation of KSAs required for a particular organizational group (i.e., International Sales vs. Engineering and a security training session in thwarting industrial espionage attempts).

Staff Development Training

> This job is a test. It is only a test. If this had been a real job you would have had:
> - Recognition for good work
> - Pay commensurate with your expertise & results
> - Promotions to greater responsibilities.
>
> **Unknown Author**

There are several levels of staff training to consider for both the security staff itself and the organizational staff that is expected to perform security functions themselves (beyond a general awareness of security issues and reporting them).

As we discussed in prior chapters, as an organization moves down a security model continuum from compliance- to commitment-based security, a change occurs for all staff members regarding their responsibility for security, which usually involves specific training for additional skills (just as quality and productivity movements did in prior decades). All too often security training for enterprise staff is met with universal groans and sighs of "Here we go again." Security training must be timely, applicable, interesting, and enjoyable to matter. Let's look at techniques that work.

> I hated every moment of training, but I said, "Don't quit. Suffer now and live the rest of your life as a champion."
>
> **Muhammad Ali**

General Staff Security Training

> Creative minds have always been known to survive any kind of bad training.
>
> **Anna Freud**

Typically, there are some general training requirements for all staff in an enterprise and some nonsecurity personnel that require specialized training because of the security requirements of the organization. Requirements for general staff are as follows:

1. Knowledge of the general structure and operation of security—Where to find information, who to call, as well as information about policies and standards, compliance expectations, and penalties for noncompliance.
2. Training on proactive security techniques—Detecting malicious activity, answering the question, what's wrong with this picture?
3. Training for a security role if their work is associated with security but not in the security department.

4. Security Development Lifecycle training for IT application designers, testers, and developments.

Here are some examples of shifts in training requirements for organizations that are moving toward a security aware culture—a culture where security is Job 1 for all employees.

1. In an article titled "Staff Training Crucial to Successful Security Program," Bill McShane, director of loss prevention and life safety at Affinia Hospitality, stated, "Security used to be a stepchild of the hotel. It has not only become an important issue, but it is a competitive advantage because guests are so much more concerned with security. We educate all of our staff in security basics," he said. "We hope to have the entire staff working as a protection team."
2. In another example cited in a *Network World* article titled "Security Training 101" New York State developed a hands-on anti-phishing exercise in conjunction with the Anti-Phishing Working Group, AT&T, and the SANS Institute. This exercise included some 10,000 employees, who were unaware they were participating in the exercise. If participants fell victim to the phishing attack in the exercise, they were immediately routed to a brief tutorial on phishing scams. Two months later, they followed up with a different phishing scam and saw a 50% improvement in employee response.
3. Many security breaches are also identified and reported by nonsecurity personnel. Let's take industrial espionage attempts, for example. In our experience working with international sales groups, many of the specific incidents utilized in the security training we helped design came from sales representatives, executives, support personnel, and in-country offices that had reported either foiled or successful espionage attempts.

Attempts ranged from laptop thefts, communications intrusions, cybertheft, and more. Some incidents were also reported by the extended enterprise (including suppliers, customers, and in some cases, even competitors) who provided either evidence or suspicions of industrial espionage attempts. Other incident data came from security group personnel audits and observations, from government groups monitoring the industry, and from other organizational audits that turned up suspected incidents.

From this compiled data, security worked with an outside vendor to design and deliver specific training for executives, sales personnel, and enterprise employees likely to be the target of espionage attempts with specific information regarding the tactics employed, how to best thwart those tactics, and how to report incidents. In addition, individual executives and sales force representatives, as well as in-country focus groups, were conducted to better assess how to deliver an effective program to enterprise personnel.

Besides just telling employees about security attacks that have proven successful, other training techniques such as mock scenarios to interact with, role-based training, and computer simulations can be used to improve effectiveness. The key to effective training is taking a blended approach that utilizes active involvement techniques, as well as awareness and information techniques.

Security Staff Training

Security staff training requires careful, systematic planning for developing staff knowledge, skills, and abilities for both today's and tomorrow's security work. When you think of your security staff and training requirements, questions such as these should arise: What is the depth of current staff skills, and will they be relevant tomorrow? Are they getting the required ongoing training? Are they familiar with security policies, procedures, and their roles and responsibilities? Are regular readiness exercises and awareness sessions scheduled? Among some of those training considerations that must be considered are the following.

Security Staff Training Requirements

1. Training necessary to keep certifications
2. Training necessary to maintain skills (includes practice drills for incidents and disasters)
3. Training necessary to prepare for the introduction of new technologies
4. Training necessary for employees to gain a new perspective and develop additional skills (keeps employees growing and learning and prepares them to better manage multiple sections of security)
5. Training required to show due diligence
6. Training to ensure coverage (cross training so that two people are always available for any given security technology or function) and reduce audit findings of insufficient training records
7. Training for technology migrations/upgrades (not new stuff but changes enough that getting a handle on the new features is needed)
8. Training for social networking with other professionals, learning what is working for others, latest trends, benchmarking, and so on
9. Training so that managers of high-risk staff positions have the skills to properly oversee staff and deal with bad behaviors and other issues before they spin out of control

Compliance, risk management, and business continuity requirements drive expanding training considerations among security departments as well. Increasingly, organizations must ask if their security systems, people, and procedures are all aligned. For instance, it is important to consider operational and physical security measures while accomplishing information security tasks. Your business continuity and crisis management plans must also include operational and physical security elements and the training requirements that are part of fulfilling security's responsibilities.

Depending on the complexity of your enterprise, you may have a lot of job types to manage under very different requirements. These may range from industrial security job types, which require many U.S. Department of Defense (DOD) certifications, to all types of security professionals ranging from investigators, security guards, firefighters, closed circuit television (CCTV) personnel, badging, lobby services, protective services, security dog handlers, international security groups, not to mention IT security categories such as specialists, consultants, operations managers, security analysts, engineers, identity access managers, and more.

Working with Human Resource (HR) departments helps determine the job categories and responsibilities in greater detail and specificity. Developmental tracks across multiple sectors of security are also important to consider for developing cross-functional capabilities and management bandwidth. It is not our intention to provide specific details regarding how best to detail the levels within a security career grouping or how best to approach cross-functional training. But we do want to emphasize the importance of both of them, as well as building in a plan for future skill requirements for your security group. Too often, organizations employ new technology without providing the prerequisite training that allows security personnel to successfully manage that deployment. Training plans and budget should be part of the overall planning for new technology.

Security Awareness Training

Security awareness programs have the highest payback compared with all other countermeasures.

Ira Winkler

Security awareness isn't one of those things that organizations do for fun. It's 24/7, and accountability starts with the CEO and is pushed to all corners of the organization.

Larry Ponemon

Security awareness training should be an integral part of your organization's strategic plan. These training elements require an even stronger strategic focus if your organization is engaged in moving security from a compliance paradigm to a holistic, commitment-based security paradigm. It's important not to overlook the opportunity to engage all employees as a first line of defense against current and emerging threats to organizational infrastructure, people, property, and information. The preferred goal of security awareness training involves a focused effort to ensure that every organizational employee has an understanding of their responsibility and accountability for protecting organizational resources. A holistic approach to security will revolve around people, not programs. Cultural change requires all employees, contractors, and suppliers to understand their security responsibilities and to take them seriously.

Awareness Training Objectives

An organization's ability to learn, and translate that learning into action rapidly, is the ultimate competitive advantage.

Jack Welch

The number one benefit of information technology is that it empowers people to do what they want to do. It lets people be creative. It lets people be productive. It lets people learn things they didn't think they could learn before, and so in a sense it is all about potential.

Steve Ballmer

A learning organization is one that seeks to create its own future; that assumes learning is an ongoing and creative process for its members; and one that develops, adapts, and transforms itself in response to the needs and aspirations of people, both inside and outside itself.

Navran Associates Newsletter, 1993

This chapter discusses ways to shape the goals of security training and awareness programs, the process used to develop and deploy awareness and training programs, methods for delivering, industry trends and best practices regarding training. However, training and awareness programs are not enough for a security group to be successful. Learning is more than staying compliant. Learning is more than making people aware of security policies, processes, and procedures. Learning is more than acquiring the next set of skills required for new technology or the new processes for conducting business. Training isn't enough. Learning is now a required core competency for staying relevant and working. Today learning has to occur at individual, team, profession, and learning organization levels continuously. Becoming a learning organization as a security group requires a different set of skills and competencies than remaining a group that simply performs security training. It's more than just knowing security; you need to understand your business and what it's trying to do, and you must know how you can help them accomplish their objectives.

There is a strong movement in business, education, and government toward the concept of a learning organization. Since the early 1980s, a whole field has been dedicated to the definition, the hows, and the benefits of creating a learning organization. Long ago, large companies like General Electric (GE) followed a defined course for helping create an organization that learned faster than its competition. In all cases, information flows more easily when organizations:

- Place a strong emphasis on team learning.
- Move toward employee learning to identify mental models and question the assumptions behind them.
- Engage in personal mastery of the disciplines required to create a learning organization.
- Seek a more complete understanding of systems thinking and the resultant need for the creation of a "shared vision."

The intent is to create an organization that is better able to manage change, garner independent thought, improve quality, establish a more dedicated workforce, and create new boundaries in thinking and execution. The result is a more competitive and fulfilling work environment.

It doesn't take very long for any security professional to see a number of security challenges for an organization that wants to embrace this model, which to be sure, has many attractive qualities. The first challenge is usually to IT security: How do you to create an information management system that is designed for learning, from an IT structure designed for the control and security of information? IT in much of the early literature on the learning organization was seen as a hindrance and not a help to the essential elements required to create a learning organization like adaptive or "double-loop" learning. IT, however, is not the only challenge; businesses today employ people from all over the globe. In addition, up and down the supply chain, from customers to suppliers, are users who need access to information 24/7. Other factors complicating the requirements include constant mergers, acquisitions, and plenty of outsourcing; these bring additional demands for adaptive learning, integration, and access to information. Hierarchical structure is seen as another impediment to team learning and access to information, and yet, most security is based on hierarchy and structure. Another element of learning organizations is that they must fully embrace change; that is, be open to new possibilities and be willing to learn from trial and error or mistakes. In a risk-averse, audit driven-role, security employees will not easily move toward a learning organization model. A dialogue is required between security and the enterprise to better understand the business drivers that lie behind both sets of mental models and to discover a way forward between seemingly conflicting goals and requirements.

We have both worked in security groups with over a thousand personnel that helped support multiple business models all operating simultaneously. A security group may have to be incredibly flexible to adapt to the business models that are being followed, while being ever mindful of its governance responsibilities. What is most important is to clearly understand the business philosophy and model being used and to bring an informed discussion about how to best move forward together without compromising the requirements for a safe and secure work environment. It is also important to be active in business discussions when new business units, products, or services are being created. When you learn to fly at the 50,000-foot level, you help frame potential risk implications and help think through how best to protect organizational assets while moving the enterprise into new territories.

Awareness Training Elements

The requirements for speed in developing training and awareness programs increase exponentially, based on the need for quick reaction to many of today's security challenges. Educating users about security issues is difficult, demanding, and more necessary today than ever before. While development and deployment cycle time requirements are increasing, the basic elements of a security awareness and training program remain the same. Those elements are as follows:

1. Put in place a basic structure for programs.
2. Analyze and understand existing vulnerabilities.
3. Conduct needs assessment for the audience.
4. Prepare training strategy, plan, and priorities.
5. Sell the plan, communicate the plan, and create organizational value with the plan.
6. Develop material (including an acceptable use policy).
7. Deliver training.
8. Monitor compliance.
9. Evaluate results and gather feedback, allow for dialogue with end users, listen well.
10. Manage organizational change, revisit policy when necessary.
11. Incorporate ongoing improvements into the program.
12. Monitor success indicators.

The basic training development process can be summarized in the process flow shown in Figure 14.1. Throughout this process, keep in mind that the goal is to create a partnership between the employee or end user and the business in regards to security issues and employee commitment.

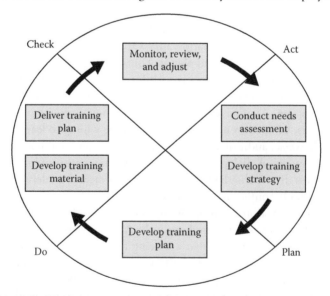

Figure 14.1   Training development process.

Awareness Training Drivers and Benefits

If you think you are worth what you know, you are very wrong. Your knowledge today does not have much value beyond a couple of years. Your value is what you can learn and how easily you can adapt to the changes this profession brings so often.

Jose M. Aguilar

Two drivers for security personnel training are particularly important to understand when you are designing training programs: current and future needs. Let's examine each driver and some of the associated implementation challenges.

Current training requirements are usually determined by a combination of outside agency and internal training requirements. Security positions may require ongoing certifications, yearly renewal training, enterprise required training, and functional and cross-functional job training. Security supervisors require training in high-risk employee management and oversight. Several issues can impact the success of these efforts to keep your security workforce current with required training. Critical to security training program success are the following considerations:

■ Determine cost-effective training delivery systems (particularly with workers who must work on varied shifts or employee populations that are dispersed over large geographical areas).
■ Clear job and task analysis to link job requirements to needed training (what specific KSAs—knowledge, skills, and abilities—are needed?).
■ Link strategic outcomes to job performance specifics and tasks.
■ Stage training to coordinate with new technology deployment and integration into the organization.
■ Standardize training design and delivery where appropriate between like occupations to reduce overall cycle time and costs regarding training (quality, standards, and measurement).
■ Design the training system to fit the environment. (What training methodology fits? Which training tools, job aids, templates, wizards, etc., are most useful?)
■ Include new technology or technology systems training requirements in the budget planning cycle for security personnel that will be performing those duties.
■ Standardize the methodologies used to track training requirements and fulfillment of those requirements, especially where the fulfillment is audited by external agencies (quality, standards, and measurement).
■ Track training results, identify and measure superior performance (quality, standards, and measurement).
■ Utilize lessons learned for process engineering, benchmarking, and productivity measurements, build in high-performance recognition and below-standard performance corrections.

Often awareness training is addressed after risk assessments are conducted and security policies and measures have been implemented. Before creating another new awareness training program, organizations can benefit by looking at what is already in place. Performing a systems check of ongoing training efforts can provide these benefits:

■ Eliminate redundancies.
■ Reduce audit findings related to security training.

- Identify and inventory training systems already in place.
- Discover gaps in ongoing awareness training efforts.
- Coordinate awareness training efforts with the larger organizational architecture.
- Create and implement policies that support the awareness training being developed.
- Consider the use of available technology solutions to deploy training.
- Learn how to make better use of audit, compliance, and enforcement activities to determine how effective the training is.
- Determine whether or not other awareness training is needed.

Once you have performed a systems check of your greater organization, you now have a baseline to identify areas that need a security awareness focus. A systems check should also help you identify gaps in your security training, such as inconsistent tracking of required awareness training or disparities between security policies and enforcement. This information will help security leadership develop their training targets.

Industry Training Trends and Best-Practices Examples

> The difference between theory and practice is that in theory, there is no difference between theory and practice.
>
> **Richard Moore**

> Companies spend millions of dollars on firewalls, encryption and secure access devices, and it's money wasted, because none of these measures address the weakest link in the security chain.
>
> **Kevin Mitnick**

Case Scenarios—An adult education technique that has been used for successful staff awareness training where there is either lack of knowledge or a resistance to security initiatives is the case scenario. We have seen this technique used effectively for ethical, safety, and security issues. In an article titled "Staff Training on Computer Security," Joni Rose of Career Minded Consulting Services discusses how to create case scenarios for such IT security issues as malware risks and infection protection. Keys for success with this method include presenting multiple options to choose from for each scenario, increasing the interactiveness of scenarios, and management support and involvement in the discussions.

Video and Web Analytics—Another example cited in *SC* magazine for IT security professionals, in an article by Rob Buckley titled "Employee Education Key to Successful Enterprise Security," is that of Cisco's security program organization. Paul King, a member of the Cisco program that coordinates worldwide training, describes Cisco's approach to awareness training. This approach utilizes an internal Web page that hosts well-produced security videos and uses Web analytics to monitor who is accessing them. Cisco has top management support for this type of training from the CEO on down, and if managers' employees are not watching these important security videos, they will be asked why. Another important aspect of the training was an immediate link from the video to the required resources (e.g., a privacy screen order form to help reduce shoulder surfing that was linked to the departmental budget). A recent video effort by Cisco suggests that employees think of themselves as "security champions" who keep the company safe.

Extended Enterprise Approach to Awareness Training—Liz Claiborne, Inc., summarizes the lessons learned from its deployment of a program dedicated to the issue of domestic violence. (This is an example of an organization taking security issues out into the extended enterprise, the personal and work lives of employees.) In the program called "Women's Work," which is designed to generate awareness of the pervasiveness of domestic violence, Liz Claiborne, Inc., states that its intent is to give back to those who have made the company successful—their consumers and employees. The primary lessons Liz Claiborne learned from over a decade of running this awareness program are as follows:

- Make a genuine commitment to the issue. Liz Claiborne credits the success of the program to the company's genuine passion for and commitment to the issue.
- Get senior-level buy-in. It is critical to have the support and commitment of senior management. In particular, it is helpful to have someone with decision-making authority champion the cause.
- Acknowledge the contribution of all partners. Liz Claiborne makes a concerted effort to recognize the contributions of the nonprofit partners and acknowledge the benefits of partnership to the corporation.
- Enlist experts. It is important that companies partner with experts in the field when taking on an issue.

Just as Liz Claiborne successfully linked a security awareness program to its brand both internally and externally, so too, can security groups link efforts like Workplace Violence and other employee awareness issues to organizational core values for the benefit of employees, consumers, and the extended enterprise.

Simulations—The military has made use of simulations for thousands of years to better prepare their forces. Simulations are now used at war colleges, in national emergency preparedness exercises for Top Officials (TOPOFF) in government and industry, and in national and international communities and within private industry and universities. Tabletop exercises are becoming more common from the CSO level to the first-line security professional as a means of honing responsiveness to crisis plans and the like.

CSO magazine, in an article titled "Security Simulations: This Is Only a Test," written by Deborah Radcliff, reported on 2004 conferences hosted by Homeland Security and the Secret Service. These workshops utilized a two-day simulation for top officials in financial, IT, and oil and gas industries. Simulations now blend both physical and online attacks throughout the experience, giving respondents the chance to build detailed responses. Although simulations are not inexpensive to create and implement (they cost $250,000 per session), they are being used increasingly in training people in many aspects of security responsiveness (cybercrime, terrorist attacks, business continuity, first-responder preparedness, industrial espionage, data protection, and more). One of the key advantages of simulations is the interagency cooperation that is required in order to be successful.

Both of us have worked with many vendors to produce various simulations for both national and international use. The simulations we have worked with have included computer simulations, social gaming simulations, business simulations, virtual simulations, table top, interactive, immersive, and war gaming simulations. Eric worked for years in a building where multimillion dollar flight simulators were housed for pilots to learn to fly in various models of airplanes. Those were amazing simulators to say the least. From our experience, we would underscore the need for careful planning, budgeting, and beta-testing of simulations prior to roll out. The consistency of experience, participant immersion, and analysis possible in a simulation are strong attributes of this approach. Many simulation suppliers can help craft high-quality simulations. Visual Purple, Skybox, Xenon, CAE Professional Services, and Pregasis are just a few of the companies that can provide simulation expertise.

Training Resources

Myriad security training resources, as well as companies, consultants, and other organizations, are available that can help a security group design training and awareness programs. Strategically, building security practices into the fabric of any extended enterprise can help decrease costs in terms of software developmental cycles, costs of security incidents, and intellectual property and data loss, and can also create strong elements of customer value in an enterprise's products and services. Choose partners who can assist you in developing security training and awareness programs that are integrated into enterprisewide security values, ethics, and cultural norms. Training and awareness programs should be built to create high-level employee commitment to creating a safe and secure workplace. While budgets for security may be understood more as an investment and not just as a cost in creating an organizational brand, it remains important for security leadership to make wise use of training dollars for education and awareness efforts that include not just training but enforcement, posters, bulletins, newsletters, and so on. Following is a discussion of some of the most recognized national and international organizations in the security training and certification business.

ASIS International, established in 1955, has been helping security professionals develop through its extensive educational programs and materials that address broad security interests. ASIS has more than 200 chapters worldwide that also sponsor educational programs and focus on local security professional issues. ASIS is continuously involved in setting national and international standards for security practices worldwide.

CSO Executive Programs/Seminars/Perspectives is another great networking opportunity with the additional benefit of in-depth discussions and seminars with other senior-level security professionals. If you are one of the security industry's best and brightest, you'll find your way to these forums.

International Information System Security Certification Consortium (ISC)² touts its certifications as the "international gold standard" against which all other certifications are measured. (ISC)² was founded in 1989 as a nonprofit organization dedicated to the creation of stringent global standards and certifications for IT professionals. Its accreditations have been formally approved by the U.S. Department of Defense. In 2002 these accreditations were adopted as the baseline for the U.S. National Security Agency's Information Systems Security Engineering Professional (ISSEP) program. Professionals may also obtain certifications in three distinct IT arenas:

1. Information Systems Security Architecture Professional (ISSAP)
2. Information Systems Security Engineering Professional (ISSEP)
3. Information Systems Security Management Professional (ISSMP)

(ISC)² credentials require 40 hours of ongoing learning (CPEs) each year and must be renewed every three years.

The Conference Board has been operating as a global, independent, nonprofit membership organization working in the public interest for nearly a century. Currently, the Conference Board has over 2,000 member companies. It is a great source for learning the latest trends about management and the marketplace. While geared toward organizational leaders, security professionals can glean much from this organization's research, conferences, forecasts, trends analysis, and white papers. Their topic areas cover security-related subjects such as risk management, operations and business processes, corporate governance, ethics and compliance, C-Suite forums for chief privacy officers, and leadership development. Attendees to conferences will hear firsthand what their peers are doing in multiple industries.

ISACA (the Information Systems Audit and Control Association) is a recognized leader in the global IT governance. Begun in 1967, ISACA is a global organization for information governance, control, security, and audit professionals. Its IS auditing and IS control standards are followed by practitioners worldwide. ISACA currently has 86,000 members from around the world and provides a lively forum for its membership to share widely divergent viewpoints on a variety of professional topics. IT professionals can also obtain certifications through ISACA's educational programs in Certified Information Systems Auditor (CISA), Certified Information Security Manager (CISM), Certified in the Governance of Enterprise IT (CGEIT), and the soon-to-be-rolled-out Certified in Risk and Information Systems Control™ (CRISC™) designation.

The **NSI (National Security Institute)** was founded in 1985 by Stephen S. Burns and David A. Marston. Marston and Burns are two leading-edge security practitioners who have had many years of experience in government and corporate security environments. The NSI has become one of the leading organizations in assisting contractors in understanding threats to U.S. national security. Burns and Marston's employee security awareness programs are also widely used by America's top corporations to educate employees to the risks of critical information loss from hackers, spies, and data thieves.

The **SANS (SysAdmin, Audit, Network, Security) Institute** is one of the largest sources for information security training. It was established in 1989 as a cooperative research and education organization. SANS has over 165,000 security professionals from around the world working together to help the entire information security community. You will find many of the SANS resources free for the asking, as well as many educational and training resources available, including the largest collection of research documents about various aspects of information security.

The **Transglobal Secure Collaboration Program** (TSCP) is a government–industry partnership focused on mitigating risk in the aerospace and defense (A & D) industry. TSCP is a relatively new organization that was begun with a number of aerospace and defense companies in Europe and the United States to solve the problems of information sharing between governments, companies, and individuals. TSCP works with vendors, supply chain participants, defense and aerospace agencies, and trade associations to ensure and provide more secure collaboration throughout the extended enterprise of the A&D industry. One of the important aspects of TSCP is its provision for a collaborative environment for elements of an extended industry value "system" to discuss mutually beneficial rules and requirements to create a secure working environment.

Innumerable U.S. government organizations including the following are also helpful for security personnel involved in defense contracting or related security issues:

- (DISAM) Defense Group of Security Assistance Management
- The U.S. Department of Transportation's Federal Transit Administration (FTA)
- Federal Emergency Management Administration (FEMA)
- Transportation Security Administration (TSA)

- U.S. Department of Homeland Security
- Customs and Border Protection (CBT)
- Customs Trade Partnership Against Terrorists (CTPAT)
- Port and Maritime Security
- National Technical Information Service (NTIS)
- National Institute of Standards and Technology (NIST)

Many other government groups exist that have national and international training or information that will provide the knowledge, skills, and certifications needed in the many sectors of security that interact with these agencies and their policies.

In addition, many international organizations provide global scope regarding similar issues, including the International Security Industry Organization (ISIO), World Customs Organization (WCO), International Standards Organization (ISO), International Air Transport Association (IATA) and others that may be relevant depending on which industry or government sector you work in.

Many more resources are to be found in any number of forums, organizations, consultant groups, and issue-related seminars sponsored by nonprofit, academic, government, and private interest groups. These can be helpful in gaining additional insight into security training issues and complexities at a local, state, national, and international level. Here are a few examples of these types of resources:

- **Fuld Gilhad Herring Academy of Competitive Intelligence (ACI),** which is an educational institution dedicated to training managers and companies in better managing risks and anticipating new market opportunities through the use of superior competitive intelligence. ACI is recognized for its expertise in competitive intelligence by *Business Week,* CNBC, *The Economist,* Fast Company, Forbes, Fortune, Fox News, *The New York Times,* the United Nations, and *The Wall Street Journal.*
- **Wharton/ASIS Program for Security Executives** is an example of a well-regarded mini-MBA-type academic program that is a collaboration among the Wharton School, the University of Pennsylvania, and ASIS International. These shorter programs can be ideal for security executives who need to sharpen skills in managerial and strategic perspectives and develop their bottom-line business instincts. These types of two-week to month-long programs can be ideal for security leaders who have limited time, and yet want to continue to hone their ability to maximize organizational impact and model continuous learning.
- **The Rand Corporation** is another nonprofit organization dedicated to improving policy and decision making through research and analysis. It offers many educational and informational resources that are cutting edge in many fields, including many of the major security issues that currently face the world. Rand makes many workshops, internship opportunities, tools, and seminars available for the security professional interested in gaining insight and understanding of many crucial issues of the times. If you desire a learning track with independence, rigor, discipline, and an interdisciplinary approach, you will find a broad range of subjects of interest to a security practitioner.
- **CERT** is part of Carnegie Mellon's Software Engineering Institute dedicated to studying Internet security vulnerabilities and researching long-term changes in network systems. CERT has developed many training programs for organizations to improve security. Started in 1998 at the request of DARPA (the Defense Advanced Research Projects Agency), CERT is dedicated to developing and promoting the use of appropriate technology and systems

management practices to resist attacks on networked systems, to limit damage, and to ensure continuity of critical services.

These are a few of the resources available for continuous learning for those who consider themselves security professionals. This is not meant to be an all inclusive list; many other organizations are available in education, government, private business, and nonprofit sectors that will benefit anyone trying to keep abreast of the security field. The important thing is to have a plan for personal development that lasts throughout your career.

Awareness Training Challenges

The user's going to pick dancing pigs over security every time.

Bruce Schneier

Good security training should begin at and remain throughout a person's employment. From the first day of orientation until the last day on a job, an employee is part of organizational security with responsibilities and requirements. From hiring, job description, orientation, and training program to promotion and career, an employee is part of your organizational culture and how you do things. It's important from the start to link security into the very organizational DNA of group identity and organizational values.

Creating security training and awareness programs throughout an employee's life cycle is integral to establishing security as a competitive advantage. Here are a few of the challenges that must be considered in that undertaking.

- Cultural security blinders that prevent the adoption of best practices (mental models in place prevent seeing new options)
- A piecemeal security training and awareness approach instead of a systemic approach
- Nonalignment of security training with enterprise core values
- No clear understanding of the barriers or resistance to security principles in employee groups
- Boring security training
- Irrelevant content to the audience
- Training not memorable
- Too many security topics covered, can't be absorbed by the audience
- Training not applied to the workplace
- Too time consuming for the employees
- Not enough depth
- Costs too high
- Not effective at changing behavior
- Security training not integrated into the extended enterprise's learning management system(s)
- Too many competing enterprise initiatives

Security training and awareness should not be aimed at a one-time event. Any security and awareness training should be part of a holistic approach to creating a security-committed culture. Martin Smith, chairman and founder of the Security Company, puts it this way, "You need to change the culture of the organization over several years. There's an awful lot that users need to know—too much," Smith adds. "They're overloaded with information they're not really interested in—it's boring." Smith suggests building constant reinforcement and places for getting how-to information for creating a security culture rather than creating countless check-the-box type courses or bad awareness training.

Often cultural shifts also require a change in mental models. An example is the shift from making the security department responsible for security to seeing that security is everyone's job. The security group itself must learn to examine its own mental models as well to determine when it might be getting in the way of a required change. In 2006, Eric attended a course titled "Predictive Profiling and Terrorist Threat Mitigation Seminar" put on by Chameleon Associates. The training seminar was well attended by various federal government agencies, private industry, and a few consultants. The course utilized Chameleon staff members and included former El Al security personnel. Although the simple mention of the word "profiling" sends many groups into diversity hysteria, the approach of the course was really not about profiling groups of people at all. Its approach, rather, was all about using very subtle communication skills to determine the modus operandi of passengers regardless of background. Many of the examples of apprehended threats would not have fit any racial profile typically thought of for terrorists.

As the group spent several days examining and learning the techniques, it was interesting to Eric to hear the stories of typical U.S. law enforcement agencies' resistance to using the more subtle communication skills being demonstrated in the course. One of the trainers illustrated those skills while on an elevator ride down one of the hotels where attendees were staying; he began speaking with a guest who was wearing a lot of jewelry and obviously headed out for the evening. She was quite engaged and seemingly quite charmed with him as he walked through a typical subtle questioning pattern without her even being slightly aware of his use of the questioning techniques he had been teaching in the course.

The stumbling point for many security groups in the United States seemed to be the mental models assumed in approaching questioning as a security technique. The techniques used were based closely on communication skills and fit into a much-layered security stance (that included well-armed and ready personnel). Many U.S. law enforcement agencies, when asked to practice these communication skills, quickly resorted to more heavy-handed questioning techniques, badge flashing, and other authoritative measures. The El Al approach to security was quite different from that used by many U.S. law enforcement employees. A whole security system that had been developed and tested repeatedly and had proven quite successful in deterring attacks was not easily transferable to our law enforcement communities. Part of the challenge in learning the Chameleon Associates approach seemed to involve mental models—learning to see the mental models that you use without being aware of it and then learning how to adapt to another set of mental models. Just as it can be difficult for a security professional to learn to adjust his own mental models to better implement an effective security practice, so too, it can be difficult for an employee to adapt a "personal responsibility for security" mental model.

Critical to creating employee motivation is helping employees really understand the organizational impacts and ramifications of unsafe behavior. Another requirement for effectiveness is using training delivery methods effectively whether they are face-to-face, e-learning, or paper. Learn to keep training events short, involving, and interesting with questions interspersed throughout the training. Effective messages can be crafted in many formats, well-prepared videos, screen saver reminders, online intranet case scenarios, articles, handbooks, or engaging enterprise events. Be sure to involve other departments that can assist you in both the educational and compliance elements of creating a security culture. Human resources, legal, ethics, intellectual property, communications, training, and education, and even marketing departments can all be very help-ful in planning security training and education.

Success Factors and Lessons Learned

As training professionals, we have spent many years in the trenches in many types of training situations. Eric has worked in educational sectors most of his career and has witnessed spectacular successes as well as failures at many levels, including organizational, company, enterprise, and institutional. Here are a few of the things you will want to consider for training and awareness types of security training modules.

Success Factors for Design of Training and Awareness Modules:

- Use the layperson's language and create training that is easy to understand with common-sense steps of application.
- Keep your messages short, simple, and easy to understand.
- Use well-designed stories, scenarios, case studies, and examples to illustrate your training.
- Use multiple methods of getting training to end users that have impact and are adapted to their environment.
- Describe and prioritize desired security behaviors.
- Get buy-in from upper management, what leaders practice, others notice, and may follow especially if they are led with integrity.
- Choose people to lead educational efforts who manage relationships extremely well, who understand how to market, persuade, and build relationships with people and groups.
- Understand your target audience and culture and adapt your message to them.
- Continue as a security group to build strong relationships with other elements of the enter-prise in order to engage influencers.
- Create security ambassadors who are good at influencing organizational behavior change.
- Work continuously to update and adapt organizational policy to reflect new security requirements.
- Communicate well by identifying enterprise events, methods, and media to share your security stories (go where the people are in cyberspace).
- Collaborate with training professionals to create training materials (whether inside your organization, the extended enterprise, or hired training consultants).
- Use credible sources for your material cites that are known, trusted, and respected by your intended audience.
- Create a "security culture" by implementing yearly "security rituals" or "security events" and have fun!
- Design security training for all levels and sectors of the extended enterprise your security group is responsible for.
- Consider having managers deliver security training to their own staff.
- Build toward a security "systemic" culture by working toward individual awareness, respon-sibility, accountability, and transparency regarding security.

Building a security culture gets done the same way that building a quality culture or a produc-tivity culture does—through careful planning, communication, passionate implementation, and constant learning.

How Do You Know if Your Training Is Successful?

I had been told that the training procedure with cats was difficult. It's not. Mine had me trained in two days.

Bill Dana

Training efforts should be creating value in the eyes of various stakeholders. Often many extended enterprise and external stakeholders are interested in security training efforts and their resulting metrics. Developing useful training metrics and tracking them can be a challenge. You can greatly bolster your department's results and reputation by developing good measures for your training program. Training success should mirror similar metrics as your strategic objectives. Metrics for training may include:

■ Scorecard metrics that are linked to strategic plan.
■ Financial metrics or targets
  – Per student cost.
  – Return on investment. (ROI is the most difficult training metric; if used, look for an ROI formula that sponsors agree on.)
■ Delivery metrics, which may include:
  – End-user satisfaction/value metric.
  – Instructor performance metrics.
  – Content metrics.
  – Training volumes (throughput of target audience).
  – Percentage of completion for target audience.
■ Behavior change metrics
  – Could result in operational efficiency measures.
  – Customer satisfaction/value or service metrics.

Before implementing a training program, you should have already determined what metrics you will be using by working carefully with training sponsors and/or training vendors. Usually, training efforts are aimed at closing some sort of performance gap or preparing employees for efforts in the near future. Metrics will be different for a performance gap than for future implementation efforts. There may also be larger questions for training organizations to include in some sort of metric. Questions include:

■ Are we focusing our training dollars on the right security issues?
■ Are we truly impacting our business performance?
■ Are our overall training efforts helping to develop and retain security personnel?
■ Are we achieving the right balance between strategic and tactical or operational training? (Present performance gap and future needs question.)
■ Are we efficiently delivering training requirements? (Consistent, well-designed, appropriate platforms, etc.)
■ Do our end users have easy access to training content where and when they need it?
■ What are the training benchmarking standards we should be paying attention to (both internal to the enterprise and external)?

■ Have we developed training from a wide-angle cultural perspective (diversity)? This is especially true for global enterprises that have a presence in multiple cultures or for multiple cultures that have a presence in security.

■ Do our training requirements and compliance metrics stand up to audit?

Track and refine your training metrics over time to both improve your overall training efforts and increase your program's credibility and reputation. If you are using a balanced scorecard approach to tracking your training metrics, you may have multiple sectors for each element of training such as training efficiency, training execution, and strategic objectives (which may include staffing retention rates and more). Strategic goals may range from **time** dimensions such as number of training hours per employee per year or **quarterly** goals such as the number of employees who have gone through the training. Other goals may include **user needs** (i.e., who needs the training versus who has gone through the training) and perhaps **fiscal efficiency** of the training. You may also have performance indicators created from **learning** progress, **behavior** progress, and **business** progress. Typically, the results will be compiled and rolled up from local levels to strategy maps and ultimately to Training and Development Balanced Scorecards that will be integrated into enterprise-level strategic goal metrics. There are various software products and metrics specialists that will assist any organization in learning to construct its own metrics templates for developing balanced scorecards. In addition, the **Balanced Scorecard Institute** will assist organizations in improving their strategic focus and performance by helping them develop balanced scorecards aligned with their strategic plans. Many Web-enabled tools and templates are available as wells. Usually, Human Resource departments will coordinate the training aspects of a balanced scorecard approach to tracking training metrics at an enterprise level.

The key for a security department is to align whatever metrics it is creating with enterprise metrics. If you aren't aligned with the company or enterprise in which you work, then you are creating confusion. Once you have determined what metrics are important for the organization and developed a metrics package for your training efforts. The last important element is to communicate what the metrics are and why they are important to employees. Be sure to highlight the benefits of an aligned organization, reduced audit findings, and the increased ability of your department to determine opportunities for employee career development, to measure their progress, and to improve the satisfaction and efficiency of training efforts. Keep the message clear and positive about why metrics are important and about how they will help and move your security group toward a better performance.

Conclusion

The great aim of education is not knowledge but action.

Herbert Spencer

This chapter was meant to stimulate your thinking and broaden your approach to the main facets of the training, awareness, and learning objectives in your security group. Although there are many objectives to accomplish in each of these arenas, the primary objective should be to create a lifetime learning culture among security professionals. Learning organizations focus on building learning capacity, knowledge accessibility, and professional development; security has a part in all three of these domains. We hope you are left asking, "How can I dramatically increase my organization's ability to learn?" Don't relegate this chapter to a training department. Own it, then get started, get energized, get committed, get perspective, get talking, get together, and get consistent. You owe it to your group, your organization, your discipline, your customers, and yourself.

References

Chapter 1

The Alliance for Enterprise Security Risk Management. 2005, November 8. Booz Allen Hamilton, *Convergence of enterprise security organizations.* http://www.asisonline.org/newsroom/alliance.pdf (accessed January 9, 2010).

Belgard, William P., and Steven R. Rayner. 2004. *Shaping the future: A dynamic process for creating and achieving your company's vision.* New York: AMACOM.

Bryson, John M., and Farnum K. Alston. 1995. *Strategic planning for public and nonprofit organizations: A guide to strengthening and sustaining organizational achievement.* San Francisco: Jossey-Bass.

Bryson, John M., and Farnum K. Alston. 2005. *Creating and implementing your strategic plan.* San Francisco: Jossey-Bass.

Hermann, Ned. 1990. *The creative brain.* Lake Lure, NC: Brain Books.

Kiely, Laree, and Terry Benzel. 2006. Systemic security management: A new conceptual framework for understanding the issues, inviting dialogue and debate, and identifying future research needs. Institute for Critical Information Infrastructure Protection (ICIIP), USC Marshall School of Business. http://www.marshall.usc.edu/assets/004/5347.pdf (accessed December 16, 2009).

Pironiti, John P. 2010. Information security governance: Motivations, benefits and outcomes. ISACA. http://www.isaca.org/Template.cfm?Section=Home&CONTENTID=35597&TEMPLATE=/ContentManagement/ContentDisplay.cfm (accessed Feb. 04, 2010).

Schonn, Donald, and C. Argyris. 1996. *Organizational learning II: Theory, method and practice.* Reading, MA: Addison-Wesley.

Sibbit, David. 2008. Strategizing with visual metaphors. DavidSibbit.com. http://www.davidsibbet.com/david_sibbet/2008/01/srategizing-wit.html (accessed February 8, 2010).

Silverstone, Ariel. 2009. Clear metrics for cloud security? Yes, seriously. *CSO:Data Protection-Industry View.* http://www.csoonline.com/article/507823/Clear_Metrics_for_Cloud_Security_Yes_Seriously (accessed January 21, 2010).

Taylor, Doug. 2005. Ten dangerous myths about strategic planning. The Business Blog at Intuitive.com. Intuitive Systems: Leadership for the 21st century: Online strategies and communications. http://www.intuitive.com/blog/ten_dangerous_myths_about_strategic_planning.html (accessed January 10, 2010).

Whittle, Ralph, and Conrad Myrick. 2004. *Enterprise business architecture: The formal link between strategy and results* (White paper). http://www.enterprisebusinessarchitecture.com/documents/EBA_The_Formal_Link.pdf (accessed February 15, 2010).

Chapter 2

Cooperrider, David L., and Diana Whitney. 2007. Appreciative Inquiry: A positive revolution in change. In P. Holman, T. Devane, and S. Cady (eds.), *The change handbook.* San Francisco, CA: Berrett-Koehler.

DeSilver, Drew. 2009, December 23. Reckless strategies doomed WaMu. *Seattle Times.*

Hurley, Edward. 2002. Does your CSO need to be a techie? *Security News: SearchSecurity.com.* http://search-security.techtarget.com/news/article/0,289142,sid14_gci858301,00.html (accessed January 5, 2010).

Johnson, Gerry, Kevin Scholes, and Richard Whittington. 1998. *Exploring corporate strategy.* Essex, UK: Pearson Education.

Kim, W. Chan, and Renée Mauborgne. 1997. Value innovation: The strategic logic of high growth. *Harvard Business Review: Best of HBR 1997.* http://innovationarsenal.pbworks.com/f/HBR_Value%20Innovation.pdf (accessed December 28, 2009).

Laban, Jake, and Jack Green. 2003. Communicating your strategy: The forgotten fundamental of strategic implementation. *Graziadio Business Report: A Journal of Relevant Information and Analysis,* 6, Issue 1. Pepperdine University, Graziadio School of Business and Management. http://gbr.pepperdine.edu/031/communication.html (accessed February 10, 2010).

Pitts, Damian "Skipper." 2007. *Building great teams: Charting the path of organizational politics.* Danvers, MA: BookSurge.

Prahad, C. K., and G. Hamel. 1990. The core competence of the corporation. *Harvard Business Review: The Magazine.* http://hbr.org/1990/05/the-core-competence-of-the-corporation/ar/1 (accessed December 28, 2009).

Prahad, C. K., and G. Hamel. 1994. *Competing for the future.* Boston: Harvard Business School Press.

Rowley, Anna. 2007. *Leadership therapy: Inside the mind of Microsoft.* New York and Houndmills, Basingstoke, Hampshire, UK: Palgrave Macmillan.

Scalet, Sarah D. 2005. Five steps to an effective strategic plan: Stop lurching from crisis to crisis. Take the long view to find business value in security by forming a strategic plan. *CSO: Security Leadership.* http://www.csoonline.com/article/220459/Five_Steps_to_an_Effective_Strategic_Plan (accessed January 7, 2010).

Senge, Peter M. 1990. *The fifth discipline: The art and practice of the learning organization.* New York: Doubleday/Currency.

Senge, Peter, Art Kleiner, Charlotte Roberts, Richard Ross, and Bryan Smith. 1994. *The fifth discipline fieldbook: Strategies and tools for building a learning organization.* New York: Doubleday/Currency.

Chapter 3

Galbreath, Jeremy. 2002. Building success in the relationship age: Building quality relationships assets for market creation. *The TQM Magazine,* 14, Issue 1.

Javelin Strategy and Research. 2009. Consumer willingness to share responsibility for security allows financial institutions to cut losses and increase profitability. https://www.javelinstrategy.com/news/787/92/Consumer-Willingness-To-Share-Responsibility-for-Security-Allows-Financial-Institutions-To-Cut-Losses-and-Increase-Profitability/d,pressRoomDetail (accessed June 21, 2010).

Javelin Strategy and Research. 2009. *Understanding consumer willingness to fight fraud: What industry leaders need to know about security partnerships, zero liability protection, and consumer preferences.* http://www.javelinstrategy.com (accessed January 7, 2010).

LeClaire, Jennifer. 2009, December. Protecting CRM customer data takes vigilance. *Enterprise Security Today: Network Security:* 1–3. http://www.enterprise-security-today.com/story.xhtml?story_id=0310012HJOBR (accessed January 27, 2010).

The metrics quest: Under pressure from the CFO to quantify security benefits, a CSO finds measures that matter. 2004. *CSO Security Leader November Newsletter,* http://www.csoonline.com/article/219799/The_Metrics_Quest (accessed January 7, 2010).

Senge, Peter, Art Kleiner, Charlotte Roberts, Richard Ross, and Bryan Smith. 1994. *The fifth discipline fieldbook: Strategies and tools for building a learning organization.* New York: Doubleday/Currency.

Chapter 4

Belgard, William P., and Steven R. Rayner. 2004. *Shaping the future: A dynamic process for creating and achieving your company's vision.* New York: AMACOM.

Blue Ocean Strategy: Management theories. 2008. VectorStudy.com. http://www.vectorstudy.com/management_theories/blue_ocean_strategy.htm (accessed February 10, 2010).

Börjesson, Martin. 2007. Scenario planning resources. Creative commons attributes. http://www.well.com/~mb/scenario_planning/#What_is_Scenario_Planning (accessed February 5, 2010).

Gordon, Lawrence A., and Vadake K. Narayanan. 1984. Management accounting systems, perceived environmental uncertainty and organizational structure: An empirical investigation. *Accounting, Organizations and Society*, 9: 144–159.

Heijeden, Kees Van Der. 2005. *Scenarios: The art of strategic conversation.* West Sussex, UK: John Wiley.

Hiemstra, Glen. 2010. Blog. Futurist.Com. http://www.futurist.com/blog/ (accessed February 10, 2010).

Hunt, Robert, Kathleen Khirallah, and Tom Brogan. 2008. 2009 top 10 business drivers, strategic responses and IT initiatives in retail banking. *Tower Group.* http://www.bankinfosecurity.com/external/TOWER _2009%20Top_10_Retail_Banking.pdf (accessed January 25, 2010).

Kiely, Laree, and Terry Benzel. 2006. Systemic security management: A new conceptual framework for understanding the issues, inviting dialogue and debate, and identifying future research needs. Institute for Critical Information Infrastructure Protection (ICIIP), USC Marshall School of Business. http://www.marshall.usc.edu/assets/004/5347.pdf (accessed December 16, 2009).

Kim, W. Chan, and Renée Mauborgne. 2005. *Blue Ocean Strategy: How to create uncontested market space and make the competition irrelevant.* Boston: Harvard Business School Press.

Longhurst, Tim. 2010. Timformation blog. Tim Longhurst.com. http://www.timlonghurst.com/blog/2008/ 05/22/define-futurist-what-is-a-futurist-futurist-definitions-quotes-from-futurists/ (accessed February 10, 2010).

McLaughlin, Ted. 2009. Enterprise architecture: Key to avoiding cloud computing. *WEB Security Journal: Security Blog Feed Post.* http://security.sys-con.com/node/1225694 (accessed January 25, 2010).

Olenick, Michael. 2008. Blue Ocean Strategy and technology business. *Value Innovation.Net.* http://www.valueinnovation.net (accessed February 10, 2010).

Porter, Michael. 1985. *Competitive advantage: Creating and sustaining superior performance.* New York: The Free Press.

Putt, Archibald. 2006. *Putt's Law and the successful technocrat: How to win in the Information Age.* New York: Wiley-IEEE Press.

Society of Competitive Intelligence Professionals (SCIP). 2010. About SCIP. http://www.scip.org/content.cfm? itemnumber=2214&navItemNumber=492 (accessed January 23, 2010).

Strategy-Scenario Planning. 2010. *Thermanger.org.* http://www.themanager.org/Knowledgebase/Strategy/ ScenarioPlanning.htm (accessed February 5, 2010).

Tomko, George M. 2009. Does business intelligence require intelligent business? CIORant. http://www.ciorant.net/2009/06/does-business-intelligence-require-intelligent-business (accessed June 18, 2010).

Chapter 5

Bradford, Robert W., and J. Peter Duncan with Brian Tarcy. 2000. *Simplified strategic planning: A no-nonsense guide for busy people who want results fast.* Worchester, MA: Chandler House.

Hutchins, David. 2008. *Hoshin Kanri: The strategic approach to continuous improvement.* Hampshire, UK: Gower.

Internet Center for Management and Business Administration. 2007. The strategic planning process. *NetMBA Business Knowledge Center.* http://www.netmba.com/strategy/process/ (accessed January 24, 2010).

Kaplan, Robert S., and David P. Norton. 1996. *The balanced scorecard: Translating strategy into action.* Boston: Harvard Business School Press.

Mintzberg, Henry. 1994. *The rise and fall of strategic planning.* New York: The Free Press.

Sherwood, John, Andrew Clark, and David Lynas. 2005. *Enterprise security architecture: A business-driven approach.* San Francisco: CMP Books.

Strong, Bart. 2005. Strategic planning: What's so strategic about it? *EQ Educause Quarterly*, 28, Issue 1. http://www.educause.edu/EDUCAUSE+Quarterly/EDUCAUSEQuarterlyMagazineVolum/Strategic PlanningWhatsSoStrate/157324 (accessed January 24, 2010).

Whalen, Judy. 2009. How to make strategic planning work for your organization. *Whalen: The Center for Strategic Change.* http://www.whalen.com/index.php?option=com_content&view=article&id=47%3A making-strategic-planning-work-for-your-organization&Itemid=59 (accessed January 24, 2010).

Chapter 6

The Alliance for Enterprise Security Risk Management. 2005. Security convergence: Current corporate practices and future trends. http://www.aesrm.org (accessed January 20, 2010).

The Alliance for Enterprise Security Risk Management. 2006. Convergent security risks in physical security systems and IT infrastructures. http://www.aesrm.org (accessed January 20, 2010).

The Alliance for Enterprise Security Risk Management. 2007. The convergence of physical and information security in the context of enterprise risk management. http://www.aesrm.org (accessed January 20, 2010).

The Alliance for Enterprise Security Risk Management. 2009. Security convergence and ERM: A case for the convergence of corporate physical and IT security management. http://www.aesrm.org (accessed January 20, 2010).

Bernard, Ray. 2008. The convergence of physical security and IT. *Security, Technology & Design Magazine*. http://www.go-rbcs.com.

Cisco Systems. 2008. *The convergence of physical safety and information technology on higher-education campuses* (White paper). http://www.cisco.com/web/strategy/docs/gov/federalbiz_011409_ConvergencePhysSec.pdf.

CSO Magazine. 2009, February. Physical and IT security convergence: The basics. http://www.csoonline.com/article/221736/Physical_and_IT_Security_Convergence_The_Basics.

Davis, Michael. 2009, February 20. IT and physical security systems evolve together. http://internet-security.suite101.com/article.cfm/convergence_in_information_technology_security.

Fennelly, Lawrence. 1997. *Effective physical security* (2nd ed.). Boston: Butterworth-Heinemann.

Forristal, Jeff. 2006, November 17. Analysis: Physical/logical security convergence. Information week analytics. http://analytics.informationweek.com/abstract/1/287/Application-Performance-Optimization/analysis-physical-logical-security-convergence.html (accessed June 6, 2010).

Howarth, Fran. 2006, September 11. The convergence of physical and IT security. Hurwitz & Associates. http://www.it-director.com/business/regulation/content.php?cid=8743.

Hurd, Scott, and Tim Williams. February 2006. The convergence of IT and physical security systems. *Nortel Technical Journal*, Issue 3.

Mehdizadeh, Yahya. 2004. Convergence of logical and physical security. SANS Institute InfoSec Reading Room. http://www.sans.org/reading_room/whitepapers/authentication/convergence_of_logical_and_physical_security_1308?show=1308.php.

Northcutt, Stephen. 2007, September 7. Security convergence and the uniform method of protection to achieve defense in depth. The SANS Technology Institute. http://www.sans.edu/resources/securitylab/convergence_did.php.

Open Security Exchange. 2007. Physical/IT security convergence: What it means, why it's needed, and how to get there. http://whitepapers.techrepublic.com.com/abstract.aspx?docid=966797.

RiskUK. 2006, May. The convergence of physical security and IT. *Risk UK magazine*. http://www.nice.com/bin/nice_in_the_media/docs/78_RiskUKOnline.pdf (accessed June 6, 2010).

Tyson, Dave. 2007. *Security convergence: Managing enterprise security risk*. Amsterdam: Elsevier/Butterworth-Heinemann.

Chapter 8

Gelles, Mike. 2010. Exploring the mind of the spy. http://www.hq.nasa.gov/office/ospp/securityguide/Treason/Mind.htm (accessed January 22, 2010).

Idaho National Laboratory. 2005, May. *Control systems cyber security: Defense in depth strategies*. http://csrp.inl.gov/Documents/Defense in Depth Strategies.pdf (accessed December 12, 2009).

Joint Staff. 2000, February. *Information assurance through defense in depth*. U.S. Department of Defense. Command, Control, Communications and Computer Systems Division of The Joint Staff.

Symantec Corporation. 2004. Worm propagation in protected networks. http://www.securityfocus.com/infocus/1752 (accessed January 22, 2010).

Chapter 9

Beebe, David. 2000. *Cheating Las Vegas*. Documentary video. Brentwood Communications International.

Johansson, Jesper, and Roger Grimes. 2008, June. The great debate: Security by obscurity. http://technet. microsoft.com/en-us/magazinebeta/2008.06.obscurity.aspx (accessed January 14, 2010).

Klein, Bruce David. 2004. *Breaking Vegas*. Documentary video. History Channel.

U.S. Department of Homeland Security. List of vulnerability notification services. The Common Vulnerabilities and Exposures (CVE). Mitre Corporation. cve.mitre.org.

Chapter 10

Golubev, Vladimir. 2002. Using of computer systems accountability technologies in the fight against cyber-crimes. Computer Crime Research Center. http://www.crime-research.org/library/Using.htm (accessed June 6, 2010).

Neumann, Peter G. 2007. Computer security and human values. University of Southern Connecticut. http://www.southernct.edu/organizations/rccs/resources/research/security/neumann/system_considerations.html (accessed February 5, 2010).

U.S. Government. 2001. Code of Federal Regulations Title 5 - C.F.R. Subpart B—Control and Accountability of Classified Information. http://law.justia.com/us/cfr/title05/5-3.0.2.3.7.2.html (accessed January 6, 2010).

Weitzner, Daniel J., Harold Abelson, Tim Berners-Lee, Joan Feigenbaum, James Hendler, and Gerald Jay Sussman. 2007, June. Information accountability. Massachussetts Institute of Technology, Computer Science and Artificial Intelligence Laboratory. http://dspace.mit.edu/bitstream/handle/1721.1/37600/MIT-CSAIL-TR-2007-034.pdf (accessed June 6, 2010).

Chapter 11

Bradner, Steven. 1997. Request for comments (RFC) 2119. Key words for use in RFCs to indicate requirement levels. Internet Engineering Task Force.

Gallagher, Tom, Bryan Jeffries, and Lawrence Landauer. 2006. *Hunting security bugs*. Redmond, WA: Microsoft Press.

Howard, Michael, and David LeBlanc. 2003. *Writing secure code* (2nd ed.). Redmond, WA: Microsoft Press.

Howard, Michael, and Steve Lipner. 2006. *The security development lifecycle: SDL, a process for developing demonstrably more secure software*. Redmond, WA: Microsoft Press.

Mead, Nancy R., Julia H. Allen, W. Arthur Conklin, Antonio Drommi, John Harrison, Jeff Ingalsbe, James Rainey, and Dan Shoemaker. 2009, April. Making the business case for software assurance (Special Report CMU/SEI-2009-SR-001). Carnegie Mellon Software Engineering Institute.

Microsoft Corporation, ISEC Partners, Inc. 2010, January 20. Microsoft SDL: Return on investment. http://www.microsoft.com/downloads/details.aspx?FamilyID=b2b59d79-3efb-4065-9c91-5910671dd30b&displaylang=en (accessed June 6, 2010).

Swiderski, Frank, and Window Snyder. 2004. *Threat modeling*. Redmond, WA: Microsoft Press.

Zajicek, Mark. 2003, April. *Handbook for computer security incident response teams (CSIRTs)* (2nd ed.). Carnegie Mellon Software Engineering Institute.

Chapter 12

Cappelli, Dawn, Andrew Moore, Randall Trzeciak, and Timothy J. Shimeall. 2009. *Common sense guide to prevention and detection of insider threats* (3rd ed.—Version 3.1). Software Engineering Institute, Carnegie Mellon University.

Forno, Richard, and Ronald Baklarz. 1999. *The art of information warfare: Insight into the knowledge warrior philosophy.* Parkland, FL: Universal.

Freedman, David, and Charles C. Mann. 1998. *At large: The strange case of the world's biggest Internet invasion.* New York: Simon & Schuster.

Maybury, Mark, Dick Brackney, Sara Matzner, Brad Wood, Tom Longstaff, Lance Spitzner, John Copeland, and Scott Lewandowski. 2005. Analysis and detection of malicious insiders (White paper). 2005 International Conference on Intelligence Analysis.

Mitnick, Kevin. 2003. *The art of deception.* New York: Wiley.

Noohan, Thomas, and Edmond Archuleta. 2008, April. *The insider threat to critical infrastructure.* National Infrastructure Advisory Council. http://www.dhs.gov/xlibrary/assets/niac/niac_insider_threat_to_critical_infrastructures_study.pdf (accessed December 20, 2009).

Raymond, Eric S. 1996. *The new hacker's dictionary.* Cambridge, MA: MIT Press.

Stoll, Glifford. 2000. *The cuckoo's egg: Tracking a spy through the maze* of *computer espionage.* New York: Pocket Books.

U.S. Army War College. 2010. *U.S. Army field manual (FM3-12-12).* Chapter 3: Intelligence, surveillance, and reconnaissance operations. http://www.globalsecurity.org/military/library/policy/army/fm/3-21-21/chap3.htm (accessed January 20, 2010).

Verizon Business Risk Team. 2008. 2008 data breach investigations report. http://www.verizonbusiness.com/resources/security/databreachreport.pdf (accessed December 15, 2009)

Verizon Business Risk Team. 2009. 2009 data breach investigations report. http://www.verizon.com/resources/security/reports/2009_databreach-rp.pdf (accessed December 15, 2009).

Winkler, Ira. 1999. *Corporate espionage: What it is, why it's happening in your company, what you must do about it.* Roseville, CA: Prima Lifestyles Publishing.

Chapter 13

Beaver, Kevin. 2005, February 23. Outsourcing IT services: Is it worth the security risk? SearchSecurity.com. http://searchsecurity.techtarget.com/tip/1,289483,sid14_gci1061490_mem1,00.html?ShortReg=1& mboxConv=searchSecurity_RegActivate_Submit (accessed December 12, 2009).

Kark, Khalid. 2007, October 2. Misconceptions about information security outsourcing. Forrester. http://searchsecurity.techtarget.com/tip/0,289483,sid14_gci1274374_mem1,00.html (accessed December 12, 2009).

Marlin, Steven. 2006, July 3. The basics: Outsourcing managed security. *Information Week.* http://www.informationweek.com/news/global-cio/showArticle.jhtml?articleID=189800154 (accessed December 12, 2009).

McCarttney, Laton. July 24, 2009. What CIOs need to know about outsourcing IT security. *CIO Zone.* http://www.ciozone.com/index.php/Security/What-CIOs-Need-to-Know-About-Outsourcing-IT-Security.html (accessed December 12, 2009).

Messmer, Ellen. 2008, March 20. Outsourcing security tasks brings controversy. *Network World.* http://www.networkworld.com/news/2008/032008-outsourcing-security.html. (accessed December 12, 2009).

Moscaritolo, Angela. September 29, 2009. Majority think outsourcing threatens network security. SC Magazine. http://www.scmagazineus.com/majority-think-outsourcing-threatens-network-security/article/150955 (accessed December 12, 2009).

SANS Internet Storm Centers. 2009, September. Top cyber security risks. http://www.sans.org/top-cyber-security-risks (accessed December 12, 2009).

Schneier, Bruce. 2002. The case for outsourcing security. *IEEE Computer Magazine Supplement.* http://www.schneier.com/essay-084.html (accessed December 12, 2009).

Swoyer, Stephen. October 13, 2009. Outsourcing's impact on network security debated. *Microsoft Certified Professional Magazine.* http://mcpmag.com/articles/2009/10/13/outsourcing-impact-on-network-security.aspx (accessed December 12, 2009).

Chapter 14

Balanced Scorecard Designer. 2000–2010. Employees training and development balanced scorecard (KPI) metrics template for Excel. http://www.strategy2act.com/solutions/training_metrics_scorecard_excel. htm.

Buckley, Rob. 2008. Employee education key to successful enterprise security. *SC Magazine for IT Security Professionals*. http://www.securecomputing.net.au/Feature/102774,employee-education-key-to-successful-enterprise-security.aspx (accessed January 13, 2010).

Chameleon Associates. 2009. Predictive profiling training: Profiling behaviors and situations is the foundation for every security procedure. http://www.chameleonassociates.com/predictiveprofiling.php. (accessed January 14, 2010).

Habber, Lynn. 2009. Security training 101: How to create an effective end-user security awareness program. *Network World: Security.* http://www.networkworld.com/news/2009/042709-user-security-training. html (accessed January 14, 2010).

Higgens, Stacey Mieyal. 2005. Staff training crucial to successful security program. *Hotel and Motel Management.* HotelMotel.com. http://www2.onity.com/images/media_elements/na_10.pdf (accessed January 13, 2010).

Nielson, Bryant. 2008. Training mojo: How to align training metrics with company metrics. Bryant Nielson's Blog on Training. http://www.bryantnielson.com/training-info/training-mojo-align-training-metrics-company-metrics (accessed January 13, 2010).

Radcliff, Deborah. 2004. Security simulations: This is only a test. *CSO: Data Protection.* http://www.csoonline. com/article/219719/Security_Simulations_This_Is_Only_A_Test (accessed January 13, 2010).

Rose, Joni. 2008. Staff training on computer security: Creating awareness of malware risks and infection prevention. Suite101®.com. http://designing-training-tools.suite101.com/article.cfm/staff_training_on_computer_security (accessed February 7, 2010).

Safe at Work Coalition. Success stories and educational materials: Liz Claiborne Inc. http://www.safeatwork-coalition.org/successstories/lizclaiborne.htm (accessed January 13, 2010).

Thompson, Barry. 2009. Successful training techniques. *BankersOnline.com: Compliance Gurus.* http://www. bankersonline.com/compliance/thompson_training.html (accessed February 7, 2010).

Appendix

Physical Security Checklists

This appendix contains checklists of physical security requirements that organizations should consider when evaluating or designing facilities. The requirements are in the form of check sheets governing campus considerations, exterior building characteristics, workspace characteristics, building security management practices, and electronic control systems. Each check sheet item should be evaluated based on these three primary physical security criteria:

1. **Observability** states that persons are less likely to commit a crime if they believe they will be observed. It is facilitated by field of view, lighting, and video surveillance.
2. **Access control** states that loss liability is reduced when access to valuable areas is limited. It is facilitated by locks, barriers, and electronic access control systems.
3. **Intrusion detection** states that loss liability is reduced when behaviors that are not permitted are reported and a response is initiated. It is facilitated by detectors, alarms, and traps.

By combining these criteria and the check sheets, organizations should be able to adequately evaluate the physical security characteristics of the facilities they are considering leasing or building.

	Campus Checklist
	Resistant to natural disaster (floods, lightning strikes, etc.)
	Away from manmade hazards (power lines, chemical plant, fireworks, etc.)
	Dual services available (power, telco, etc.)
	Clear field of view with no concealed approaches
	Good perimeter controls (fences, walls, guard patrols, lighting)
	Near fire, police, and emergency services
	In low-crime area

	Campus Checklist
	Water sources available for firefighting (hydrants, ponds, etc.)
	Limited entry points
	Entry points controlled w/EAC or guards

	Building Exterior Checklist
	Construction resistant to natural disaster (earthquakes, hurricanes, lightning)
	Roof construction resistant to leakage, snow load, etc.
	Low profile—building does not stand out as a target
	Attached devices (antennas, lightning rods, etc.) properly grounded
	Landscaping does not provide concealment
	Limited signage
	Building protected against vehicle bashing
	Building has no climbing points, ledges, or other staging areas
	Exterior equipment is protected against tampering (HVAC, power, telco)
	Trash bins are protected
	Exterior regularly patrolled by guard service
	Entrances
	Limited number of entrances
	Single entrance for visitors
	Entrances are constantly monitored (cameras, personnel)
	Entrances resist piggybacking
	Entrances are protected against vehicle bashing
	Entrances are proper illuminated
	Entrance doors and hardware are tamperproof
	Entrance locking devices are tamperproof
	Entrances have adequate access controls (card reader, guard, camera, etc.)
	Entrances are not concealed from view by bushes, alcoves, recesses, etc.

	Building Exterior Checklist
	Loading dock door and lock are tamperproof
	Crawl space and basement accesses are secure
	Other accesses secure (ventilation ducts, roof hatches, skylights, etc.)
	Windows
	Windows are placed high enough to resist bashing
	Windows are placed high enough to resist viewing of interior
	Window openings resist penetration (high off ground, small, narrow, etc.)
	Windows resist breakage, pop-out, and tampering
	Window hardware and locking device resist tampering
	Windows provide an unobstructed view of exterior
	Lighting
	Lighting is adequate to observe nighttime movement
	Lighting overlaps so outages do not leave blind spots
	Lighting is on redundant circuits and controls
	Lighting levels are consistent (bright spots do not obscure dimmer lighting)
	Lighting fixtures are tamperproof and breakage resistant
	CCTV
	Camera views cover entire exterior (no blind spots)
	Camera housing conceals configuration
	Camera resolution is adequate
	Camera sensitivity is matched to exterior lighting
	Cameras are not blinded by bright exterior lighting
	Camera housings resist wind and rain damage and resolution reduction

	Building Interior Checklist
	Entrances and reception areas are controlled (receptionist, guard)
	Reception has unobstructed view of visitor entrance

	Building Interior Checklist
	Guest access limited to reception area
	Access to public areas (bathrooms, elevators, conference rooms) is monitored
	Public area services (power, telco, LAN) are isolated
	Access to service closets (janitor, telco, power, elevator) is controlled
	Wall penetration accesses are protected against
	Under-floor access is protected against
	Drop ceiling or ducting access is protected against
	Interior corridors have good field of view
	Interior spaces have good field of view
	Interior lighting is adequate
	Nighttime lighting provides adequate interior viewing for patrols
	Interior spaces are regularly patrolled
	All doors, entryways, etc., locked and controlled
	Locking mechanisms are tamperproof
	Hinges and door hardware is tamperproof
	Windows provide an unobstructed view of exterior
	Interior configuration prevents exterior viewing of computer screens, etc.
	Zoned display for fire, flooding, etc., near main entrance
	Secure waste disposal available (shredder, locked container, etc.)
	Hardware and electronics key
	Unique for each access areas
	Securely stored in lockable container
	Access to key container is controlled
	Key distribution is controlled (especially master keys)
	Key turn-in required when employees leave
	Keys cannot be copied

	Building Interior Checklist
	Electronic keys resist tampering
	Electronic controls
	Interior accesses properly controlled (no loopholes, bypasses, etc.)
	Appropriate authentication required (single, dual, biometrics)
	Controls resist piggybacking (turnstiles, mantraps, etc.)
	Doors monitored with open/close switches
	Audio alarm on door open or close
	Devices (readers, etc.) resist tampering
	Failed and successful accesses logged
	Lockout on multiple failures
	Alarms on multiple failures
	Emergency exits have anti-tamper release bars
	Emergency exits sound alarm
	Emergency releases tamperproof
	Exit button placed properly
	Window breakage detected (tape or noise detection)
	Motion detection covers appropriate areas
	Detectors overlap so a failure does not create a blind spot
	Detectors deploy dual detection methods (limit false positives)
	Detectors cover under floor, ducts, and drop ceiling areas
	Detectors cover wall penetrations
	Detectors cover flooding and moisture
	Automatic notifications generated (phone, e-mail, etc.)
	Logs regularly reviewed
	CCTV
	Camera placement provides adequate coverage

	Building Interior Checklist
	Camera resolution is adequate
	Camera sensitivity matched to lighting
	Cameras are not blinded by bright lighting
	Camera housings conceals configuration
	CCTV is recorded
	CCTV monitored in real time or by periodic review
	Fire/Heat/Smoke
	Fire detector placement covers all areas
	Proper fire suppression deployed
	Automatic station notification
	Zone display near main entrance
	Dry system usage
	Scheduled checks and maintenance
	Guards
	Guard stations placed properly
	Guards have unobstructed views
	Properly equipped (radios, flashlights, etc.)
	Properly armed (mace, stick, firearm)
	Properly trained in use of equipment (register, etc.)
	Scheduled patrol of building and grounds
	Patrols validated by checkpoints
	Written procedures for alarm response
	Written procedures for escalation
	Secure containers for confidential information
	Log for guard activities

	Guest Handling Checklist
	Registration/Sign-in required
	Picture ID required
	Other validation required
	Visitor badge required
	Staff badges required
	Escort required
	Nonbadged personnel questioned
	Badge turn-in required
	Sign-out required
	Guests cannot exit unseen

	Data Center Checklist
	Power
	Redundant power sources—to building, to racks
	Power conditioning, brown-out, spike protected
	UPS and generator backup
	Access to power control room controlled and monitored
	Power feeds secured
	Power constantly monitored
	Alarms generated in real time for power failure
	Telco Network
	Redundant network feeds—to building, to racks (type)
	Conditioned against spikes, noise, etc.
	Operational status constantly monitored
	Monitored for attacks—DoS, etc.
	Alarms generated in real time
	Firewalled

	Data Center Checklist
	HVAC
	Vents protected against crawl access
	Condensation properly controlled (pipes wrapped, drip trays, etc.)
	Constantly monitored for operational status
	Humidity and temperature constantly monitored
	Alarms generated in real time
	Fire
	Fire suppression provides adequate coverage
	Nondestructive suppressant (FM200, Halon, etc.)
	Dual-zone triggering
	Bypass/hold switch
	Central alarm display panel by entrance
	Alarms generated in real time
	Under-floor areas covered
	Other criteria
	Access restricted by hardware or electronic access control
	Guest access restricted to specific entrances
	Accesses recorded in log and/or on video recording
	Raised floor access restricted
	Water detection under raised floor
	Raised floor access detectors
	Proper drainage under raised floor
	Raised power and cable trays
	Exterior walls resist penetration
	Layout provides good observation
	CCTV provides adequate coverage

	Data Center Checklist
	Visitor escort required
	Backup and media handling
	Procedures for performing backups
	Procedures for dealing with problems
	Procedures for cataloging and handling media
	Secure and fireproof local storage available
	Off-site storage available

Index